T. K. WHITAKER
Portrait of a Patriot

ANNE CHAMBERS

DOUBLEDAY IRELAND

TRANSWORLD IRELAND PUBLISHERS
28 Lower Leeson Street,
Dublin 2, Ireland
www.transworldireland.ie

Transworld is part of the Penguin Random House group of companies
whose addresses can be found at global.penguinrandomhouse.com

First published in 2014 by Doubleday Ireland
an imprint of Transworld Publishers
Doubleday Ireland paperback edition published 2015

A CIP catalogue record for this book
is available from the British Library.

ISBN
9781781620137

Typeset in Baskerville by Falcon Oast Graphic Art Ltd.
Printed and bound by CPI (UK) Ltd, Croydon, CR0 4YY.

Penguin Random House is committed to a sustainable
future for our business, our readers and our planet. This book is made from
Forest Stewardship Council® certified paper.

1 3 5 7 9 10 8 6 4 2

Contents

Contents

Foreword

Pressed many years ago to write an autobiography, I offered the excuse of some forgotten cynic that 'no man's reputation was ever enhanced by his autobiography'. I am also warned by Rilke: 'Glory is the sum of the misunderstandings which gather around a name.'

Since I was responsible for starting Anne on her writing career by publishing her article 'Land Prices in Ireland and the EEC' in a Central Bank *Bulletin* and launching her subsequent books, I thought it was right she should be encouraged to repay the compliment!

T. K. Whitaker
Dublin, 2014

Author's Note

In 2001, in a countrywide ballot, outpolling historical icons, politicians, celebrities, footballers and pop stars, an 85-year-old former civil servant was voted 'Irishman of the Twentieth Century' by Irish television viewers. Most of those who voted had rarely seen, much less ever been acquainted with, their choice. The public profile he had attained over the course of his life was associated mainly with matters not usually rated in popular perceptions – although, in the light of recent economic and financial scandals, perhaps they are now more relevant. His publications and public interviews seemed primarily of interest to economic and political analysts and commentators. His social profile, that *sine qua non* for any celebrity seeking popular appeal, was a publicist's nightmare, showing no trappings of wealth or opulent lifestyle, no celebrity friends, no presence in the pages of the glossies at glitzy parties or opening nights.

It says much for the intuitive judgement of the ordinary Irish citizen that so many saw through the subjectivity of historical and political iconology and the tinsel of celebrity status and conferred this accolade on someone whose work over the space of many decades in the service of the country had guided its fortunes and transformed and improved the lives of generations; someone who spoke with integrity on matters of public interest, who had neither sought nor acquired personal affluence in the process. As the so-called icons of Irish society, one by one, fell from their pedestals, as tribunals, trials and inquiries revealed the shortcomings of those entrusted with the care of the country and the welfare of its people, as greed and corruption became hall-marks of success in Irish society, as the two state institutions over which he once presided failed to prevent the loss of Ireland's economic independence, consigning generations to a future of chronic indebtedness, the Irish people's choice of T. K. Whitaker as 'Irishman of the Twentieth Century' seems now, more than ever, vindicated.

Some analytical and scholarly articles have been written about the work and achievements of Dr T. K. Whitaker in the economic and financial fields. His own books, *Interests* (1983), *Retrospect* (2006) and *Protection or Free Trade: The Final Battle* (2006), have, with characteristic modesty, reviewed some milestones on his epic journey. But his personal archive of files, reports, memoranda and correspondence, conserved over the course of his lifetime and which he has kindly made available to me, reveals, for the first time, the extraordinary extent and diversity of his under-takings, many on a voluntary basis, on behalf of the state and its citizens, while also providing a fresh and objective appraisal of the economic, financial and cultural events that have shaped modern Irish history.

His was the quiet presence, the rational and informed voice behind many of the most momentous episodes in recent history. For many decades he was principal negotiator on Ireland's behalf with international statesmen and institutions, adviser and con-fidant to every Irish political figurehead, including de Valera, Costello, Aiken, Sweetman, Lemass, O'Neill and Lynch – and, after his official 'retirement', to latter-day incumbents of political high office. Motivated by public service, his advice, honest and true, was more recently ignored, to the country's economic and political disadvantage.

In the past, public servants like Ken Whitaker preferred and were expected to remain in the background, anonymous and low-key, devoid of a public persona. This portrait endeavours to cut through the density of the economic and financial commentary that tends to shroud the name of the most influential of them, to seek the real man behind the public 'man of the century' and to unravel the reasons why the ordinary citizens of Ireland should choose Ken Whitaker as their ideal Irishman. It attempts to analyse and understand the motivation of someone who, having travelled from Dublin to tend his father's grave in Newry only to discover that another family member had already done so, set to instead on the nearby neglected grave of a complete stranger: an example of civic and Christian duty, perhaps, but also indicative of T. K. Whitaker's trademark practicality, as demonstrated in his public endeavours, in simply not allowing his time and travel go to waste.

This portrait of T. K. Whitaker is primarily based on his personal papers, some of which are deposited in the archives of University College Dublin but most of which are in his private possession. I have quoted extensively from this collection of papers, memoranda and correspondence, and also from a series of interviews I had the privilege and pleasure to conduct with Dr Whitaker and his family between 2012 and 2014.* I hope that this provides the reader with a sense of immediacy and direct connection with the subject of this biography. My initial intention to interview a number of other people in the political, financial and economic fields for their assessments of his work I deliberately abandoned on the realization that most of those who shared his commitment to public duty have sadly passed *ar slí na fírinne* – and that Dr Whitaker's work as a public servant needs no endorsement.

In order to bridge any distance between my subject and his legion of admirers, I have eschewed the formal 'Dr T. K. Whitaker' in the book in favour of the name 'Ken', by which he is known to his family and friends.

---

* Individually unreferenced quotations throughout the text are taken from these interviews.

Acknowledgements

To the 'Irishman of the Twentieth Century' for sharing his life story with me and for allowing me unrestricted access to his papers and correspondence. It has been a great privilege and his company along the way has made it a journey to remember.

To the extended Whitaker family, my appreciation for their help, trust and encouragement.

To Séamus Helferty and the staff of University College Dublin Archives for their assistance and for accommodating me over a lengthy period.

To Governor Patrick Honohan and the staff of the governor's office and archives department in the Central Bank of Ireland, for their 'welcome back' and for providing me with every assistance.

To the secretary-general and staff of the archives in the Department of Finance, the staff of Áislann Rann na Feirste, the Institute of Public Administration, National Archives, National Library of Ireland, my thanks.

To Dr Pádraig McGowan, Tomás Ó Cofaigh, Seán Cromien, John Nolan (NUI), Professor Frances Ruane (ESRI), Richard Boyle (IPA), Siobhán Fitzpatrick (RIA), Liam Cosgrave, David Madden and the Board of Management of St Joseph's Secondary School, Drogheda, Seán Collins, Drogheda, John Cosgrove, Bangor Erris, Noreen Duffy, Rannafast, my grateful appreciation, and also to Martina Chambers Farah and Thérèse Chambers for their translation assistance.

To my agent Jonathan Williams, to Eoin McHugh and Brian Langan at Doubleday Ireland, and to editor Gillian Somerscales, my sincere thanks.

To Tony, family and friends, thank you for your support.

Anne Chambers
Dublin, September 2014

1

Paradise Cottage
1916–34

One of my earliest memories of Drogheda is watching as a young boy of six from a downstairs window a wild-eyed, terrified man running into the street with a revolver in his hand pursued by Free State soldiers.

T. K. Whitaker

THE FIRST OBVIOUS aspect of the long life enjoyed by Ken Whitaker is how closely it parallels the history of the modern Irish state. From the Rising of 1916, the year of his birth, through the violent years of the War of Independence and the Civil War, and the faltering first steps as a nation-state; through the isolation of the Second World War and post-war protectionism; the abandonment of the British Commonwealth, the creation of the Republic, the insularity of the 1950s, with its mass emigration and despondency; through the unprecedented spell of optimism and economic growth that followed adoption of his innovative economic and social programme in 1958, almost totally derailed by the misguided economic policies of the 1970s; through the painful recovery of the late 1980s, the recklessness and greed of the Celtic Tiger years, the late 1990s and early years of the new millennium, and the shameful loss of financial sovereignty, to more recent economic rehabilitation, Ken Whitaker's life mirrors Ireland's momentous journey since achieving nationhood.

The second observation is how much his work as a public servant on the three national issues most associated with his name – economic and social development, Northern Ireland and the Irish language – emanated from and was nurtured by his personal experience and early upbringing. Born eight months after the Rising, he belongs to that minuscule portion of the Irish population who have lived in a united Ireland, albeit in his case for just the first five years of his life. A native of County Down, subsequently residing in County Louth, he can also claim dual nationality of both the Irish Republic and Northern Ireland, a fact that undoubtedly, both consciously and subconsciously, has influenced his lifelong commitment to and engagement with the evolving relationship between the two political entities on the island.

Thomas Kenneth Whitaker was born in Rostrevor, the son of Edward Whitaker, assistant manager of Forestbrook, a small linen mill. One of Ken's earliest childhood memories is of both the negative and positive sides of that once ubiquitous Irish industry. 'All the way to Greencastle – past Killowen – the ditches in August would stench of retting flax intended for Forestbrook. How lovely, on the other hand, the China blue of a field of flax in flower.' Edward Whitaker had been born in Killucan, County Westmeath, in 1865, where his father worked for the Midland Great Western Railway Company. On his father's transfer to Newry, Edward attended the local Christian Brothers school and later found employment in a local mill at Dromalane, owned by the Mitchell family, before moving to Rostrevor to work in Forestbrook, a mill exclusively engaged in the labour-intensive scutching, spinning and weaving of flax. Edward's sister Elizabeth, 'Auntie Lizzie', was the postmistress in the village. Formerly a governess to a titled English family, she had travelled widely in that capacity and brought an air of sophistication and urbanity to the small community in which she eventually settled.

The name Whitaker suggests an English background, and

2

there is some evidence that Ken's paternal line might well have originated in England. His father's brother lived there and served as a sergeant-major in the British army in the First World War. Ken recalls how, on arriving in Drogheda aged six, in response to schoolboy taunts about his 'English' name and Northern accent, 'I came to declare defiantly that we probably came over with Cromwell' – which in Drogheda, with its particular aversion to the name of the dreaded 'butcher', provoked either a schoolyard fight or a deferential silence and a wary determination not to meddle with the newcomer. Years later he was somewhat mollified to learn that the first recorded bearer of the name Whitaker in Ireland was Robert Whitaker, who in 1305, under Edward Bruce, was bailiff, coincidentally, of the town of Drogheda. But whatever his distant origins, he considers himself, as he says, 'Irish – *tout court*'. The choice of his name Kenneth, not being a family name, he attributes to the more prosaic consideration 'that my mother simply came across the name in a Walter Scott novel she was reading and liked it'. Little did he or his mother envisage that the name was destined to feature on more than one thousand million Irish banknotes to become one of the best known in the country.

His father's first marriage was to Kathleen Lowe, a Catholic schoolteacher from Killowen, a few miles from Rostrevor. They had a family of three girls. May settled in England; Teresa (Teesie) became a missionary nun, Sister Mary Attracta, in South Africa. Fifty years later Ken was reunited with Teesie, when, as governor of the Central Bank of Ireland, following a World Bank meeting in Nairobi he journeyed to Port Elizabeth and from there to the remote African village where she taught. Teesie was later permitted by her order to visit Ken and his family in Dublin, an event that created great excitement in the Whitaker household. On their introduction to their father's long-lost half-sister, one of Ken's sons was heard to exclaim: 'How do we know she's not an impostor!' His third half-sister, Kathleen, partially blind and

3

disabled from birth, continued to live with his parents and was looked after by his mother. 'To a young boy, my half-sister Kathleen seemed a fount of knowledge,' he recalls with affection. 'Because of her disability, she had a bed in part of the kitchen at downstairs level. She was always available for a chat, no matter what hour you came in. You could tell her about your good or bad fortune of the day and were always assured of a sympathetic ear.'

In 1914, following the death of his first wife, Edward Whitaker married 35-year-old Jane O'Connor, a native of Coolmeen (*Cúl Mín*), near Labasheeda in County Clare. Later, on childhood summer visits to her birthplace, Ken and his sister Peggie would tease their mother with the refrain 'Coolmeen – the nearer you get the *cooler* and *meaner* it gets.' Jane's father William, like his father before him, was a blacksmith, and as a youngster Ken remembers seeing 'ploughs inscribed with their names going back to the 1830s' in the old family home. Jane was born in what was then an Irish-speaking area, and her family epitomized the gradual fall-off in the spoken native language. 'In the 1911 census my mother's eldest siblings are recorded as Irish-speakers, while she and the younger members passed through a bilingual phase to becoming primarily English-speaking.' In the 1920s, Irish phrases and old words still abounded in his grandmother's home. He recalls as a young boy being asked to take a *dreas* (turn) at the butter churn or to go to the haggard for a *gabháil* (armful) of hay, and hearing the traditional Irish invocation 'the light of heaven to our souls' on the nightly lighting of the oil lamp, while throughout her life his mother continued to recite her prayers and nursery rhymes in Irish, experiences that nurtured her son's subsequent interest in the native language.

At a time when few options other than marriage were available to young rural women, the ability to converse and write in English opened up additional opportunities, albeit usually outside Ireland. Jane O'Connor's path was that taken by many young women from farming backgrounds in the early decades of the twentieth century. Education being then, as it became later for her son, 'virtually the only way to better yourself', having completed her basic primary schooling and an additional optional two years, Jane O'Connor, with her sister Minnie, left her home in Clare for Manchester to train as a 'Jubilee' nurse. This scheme had its origins in 1887, when 'the women of England' had marked Queen Victoria's Golden Jubilee by raising the sum of £70,000 and using it to establish the Queen Victoria Jubilee Institute for Nurses, with the aim of providing for 'the training, support, maintenance and supply of nurses for the sick poor'.[1] In 1897, to mark the Queen's Diamond Jubilee, the scheme was extended to Ireland, and by 1901 a network of Jubilee nurses was in operation throughout the country, providing care to patients in their homes. On completion of their training, Ken's mother and aunt returned to Ireland: Minnie became the Jubilee nurse in Lahinch, in west Clare, where the local doctor was the father of Paddy Hillery, later president of Ireland, while Jane secured an appointment as a Jubilee nurse in Rostrevor, County Down, where she met and married the widower Edward Whitaker.

Edward and Jane settled down to married life, with Edward's three daughters, in the family home in Rostrevor, a picturesque village on the banks of the Kilbroney river on the shores of Carlingford Lough. No. 1 Glenview was, as Ken recalls, 'a lovely red-bricked house in a nice little terrace facing towards the foothills of the Mourne Mountains, with the distinctive local landmark Cloughmore Stone, Cloch Mhór, a huge granite boulder on the mountain slope, which was clearly visible from the attic room of our house.' This relic of retreating glaciers and its associations with the legendary Fionn Mac Cumhail, the giant of the Irish sagas, fired Ken's boyhood imagination with images of Ireland's heroic past. Neighbours of the Whitakers in the terrace included the Larkin family, who lived there from 1914 to 1923 during the time when their father, the famous labour leader James (Jim)

Larkin, was in the United States. 'My half-sister Kathleen remembered playing with Denis Larkin in the back garden.'

Ken remembers his father as somewhat 'stern and remote'. Outside his work, his main interest was reading – especially *The Strand Magazine*, an English-published monthly containing a mixture of fiction, factual stories and 'brain-teasers' and famous for printing the first crossword puzzle. Edward's social life consisted of an occasional drink with friends, under the critical eye of his wife, whose only brush with 'the demon drink' was a recipe for 'Bees Wine' – a strongly alcoholic home-made concoction based on treacle and yeast – 'which my innocent teetotal mother dispensed liberally to us teenagers with Saturday lunch. It was quite a while before it was realized why we felt so muzzy.' While, as Ken reflects, his father 'had the disadvantage of appearing on the scene rather late', and was to remain distanced by both years and authority from the young son of his second marriage, it was his mother who became the greater influence on him. She was, as he emotionally recalls, 'a perfect example of what a mother should be': strong-minded, independent and committed. A tall, imposing woman, she was already treated with respect in Rostrevor, where she visited those in her care on her bicycle. Her advice and help were sought throughout the community, even after she left nursing on her marriage to become a full-time homemaker and mother not only to Ken and his sister Peggie, born in 1918, but also to her stepdaughters, who remembered her as 'a combination of kindness, love and patience and [someone] who always thought everyone else was the same'.[2]

Jane Whitaker was the typical Irish mother, devoted to her home and her family, for whom she cooked, baked and knitted. 'Her nursing training had brought out all the independence of spirit you might expect. She was always the decision-maker in the family,' Ken remembers, even to the extent of confining her husband's pipe-smoking to the back yard. His mother's role, both in the home and in the community, 'developed in me a sense of public service ... at any rate I never considered becoming a millionaire! I wanted something else, something that would give me personal satisfaction and be of some social benefit.' Many years later, in his capacity as a senior civil servant giving a talk to young students at a course on leadership in Clongowes College, he enunciated that sense of care and service instilled in him from childhood: 'To know, to understand, to be a civilised, independent, thinking, charitable member of society should be our aim; to be a constructive individual and citizen, not a negative, disgruntled cynic.'[3] These traits, inherited from his mother, together with the capacity not to take himself too seriously, to find the humorous in the most portentous, have almost subconsciously epitomized his own private and public life.

His mother's ability, her character and the impact she made in both her home and her public life also fashioned Ken's own belief in and support for female equality, long before it became either fashionable or a legal requirement. Under his governorship in the early 1970s, the Central Bank led the way in the implementation of equal pay and promotional opportunities for its female staff. On his recommendation, as this author can vouch, staff female authors of economic and financial studies were given their first opportunity to publish in the prestigious Central Bank *Bulletin*, previously an all-male preserve. Women were also to the fore in many of the organizations and committees he later chaired. 'One of the profound changes I have been glad to see is the improvement in the status of women. It is difficult to believe that it was not all that long since women were degraded and disadvantaged in so many ways ... They are [now] on a par with men in most professions and on their way in business.' His active support for female equality was later extended to the thorny issue of membership in his golf club, Elm Park, where he insisted that 'everyone who is accepted as a fee-paying participant in the facilities ... is entitled to the basic status of member and to a say in the running of the Club'.[4] His consistent support for female equality was rooted in his own background. 'I grew up in a patriarchal, male-dominated society but, happily, I have lived long enough to see it transformed into one in which the right to equality is recognised and discrimination on the basis of sex, race or otherwise, is unacceptable in principle.'[5]

His mother's prudent administration of the family's slender household budget may also have instilled in her son a similar prudence in respect of the finances of the country later entrusted to his care. '"A pound a day, three hundred and sixty a year, Sir!" was a song sung by the comedian Jimmy O'Dea and that was the sum of my father's wages.' The spending power of the ordinary 1920s family in Ireland was constrained both by means and by the availability of goods. Making do was the only way. 'We did not own a car but we did have bicycles.' Good housekeeping involved thrifty purchasing and expenditure and minimum waste, all enshrined within the credo of living within one's means. 'That was the environment and thinking in which I grew up. There was no extravagance, and money was always put aside for the rainy day, while indebtedness was considered a failing.' The profligate policies pursued by various governments, culminating in the gross excesses of the 'Celtic Tiger' debacle, continue to be anathema to one for whom good housekeeping was as essential to the national finances as it was to his mother's administration of the family resources. His 'moderately comfortable, solid upbringing' was conditioned by both the environment and his parents' standards which, as he admits, were 'stricter than we applied to our own children but without apparent disadvantage'. In later years Jane came to look after Ken's own children on their parents' occasional absences; one of her grandchildren recalls her as 'a strong, fit woman', for whom there were 'no back doors'. Jane O'Connor enjoyed a full and long life, taking in her stride the constant changes and innovations not even conceived of when she was born, an example her son is determined to follow. 'One should choose one's mother wisely!' he jokes, in the hope and expectation that he has inherited her longevity.

While both his parents were practising Catholics, 'I don't recall that piety was particularly oozing from them; they had a practical attitude to religion.' This was exemplified by his father's years of charitable service with the local St Vincent de Paul Society, an example later embraced by his son. During the course of his boyhood in Drogheda, Ken sang in the church choir, served as an altar boy – and, like countless others before and after him, occasionally succumbed to the temptation of altar wine. Throughout his life, adherence to the faith of his parents has been both natural and practical, as his regular attendance at and support of his local church in Donnybrook testifies. He never, however, inclined to the excessive devotions of what his eldest son calls a *grenouille de bénitier* (a frog of the holy water font). Informed by the works of Catholic theologians such as de Chardin, Augustine and Merton, Ken's faith remains deep and personal. 'I regard the ten commandments as a rational piece of work. A good civil service job! They are fairly comprehensive and don't leave much room for manoeuvre . . . You have a sort of a constitution or code for yourself and for your conduct and you try and abide by that in both your personal and public life. I don't think I've strayed too far from that but neither am I claiming to be a saint!' During his professional life he had contacts with churchmen of many denominations, becoming personal friends with Cardinal Conway, Bishop William Philbin, Bishop Donal Caird, Dean Victor Griffin and Australian-born Cardinal Edward Cassidy. But, as in every aspect of his life, in terms of religious belief he is his own man. 'Many of us today, myself included, live more comfortably in our own edited version of Catholicity than in the prescribed orthodoxy of *Humanae Vitae* and *Dominus Iesus*. We could never understand how natural law could be invoked against responsible exercise of our greatest natural endowment – intelligence. We are, one might say, closet heretics. A few centuries ago we would have been part of a major schism or have perished at the stake!'[6] Despite the recent scandals that have rocked the Catholic Church and alienated many of its congregation, Ken Whitaker is, as he readily admits, 'human enough to understand that there is a residual goodness that makes me continue to adhere to it, as well as to the fact that I haven't found anything else!'.

Life as a young boy growing up in Rostrevor seemed idyllic. Born before partition, when all Ireland was still governed by Britain, Ken spent his earliest years in a part of Ireland considered no different from the rest – where, as he recalls, he acquired 'quite a good Northern accent!'. His first taste of school was at Rostrevor National, to which he was often taken by his neighbour and fellow pupil Ben Dunne, founder of the department-store chain Dunnes Stores. 'He [Ben] was a few years older than me and would take me by the hand to school, passing his mother's little drapery shop on the way.' Ken's father was later inadvertently to play a role in the founding of the famous retail chain when he dissuaded its then jobless 18-year-old founder from emigrating to America and, through his friendship with the proprietor, 'got him a job with Anderson's, the biggest drapery shop in Drogheda . . . where he spent five or six years . . . Ben later regarded this as a turning point in his life, but it probably diverted him from achieving even greater success on a bigger stage!' What Ben Dunne might have achieved in America had he not been diverted by Ken's father is open to speculation; but being from childhood, as his schoolfriend recalls, 'a dynamic, proactive fellow, always wanting to be in the thick of things and later such a shrewd businessman, it seems likely it would have been something substantial'.

While their chosen paths in public life were destined to diverge, the boyhood friends kept in touch, Ben often visiting the Whitaker family home in Dublin. One of Ken's sons recalls as a child listening, fascinated, to the famous retailer's explanation that 'shrinkage in the stores' referred to shoplifting, for which the

Dunnes founder made a 10 per cent allowance in his calculations. 'Ben kept his management accounting system in his pocket,' Ken noted, 'a day-to-day comparative table of purchases, sales and stocks . . . He had the reputation of being tough in trade union negotiation but he had been a trade unionist himself and knew how the game was played.' Ben Dunne was also a generous and anonymous sponsor of various artistic and charitable under-takings at his friend's request – 'I had only to vouch for a good cause and he would almost let me write the cheque!' – but at the same time, as Ken is careful to point out, 'recognizing that by then we had quite different functions and interests'. Was Ken ever tempted to make his own fortune in the commercial world as the Dunnes Stores founder had done? 'No, my conscience I think would have started squawking about that. Anyway, the thought of making a fortune never had any appeal to me. What I was interested in was having a job that might stretch you "to the pin of your collar" (mixed metaphors!) and which might be of benefit to the wider community. No harm if it had *some* recompense but it was not the be-all and end-all.'

When Ken was six years old, the decline in the flax industry in the post-war slump necessitated his father's move south to the town of Drogheda, to a job in the sales department of the Greenmount and Boyne Mill, a cotton manufacturing plant. As a boy, Ken often went to meet his father there after school. 'I strayed into the steamy weaving shed to see the shuttles speed back and forth and sometimes pick up a bright steel cone for my spinning top. I watched the great bales of cotton sheeting being loaded for transport to India – a version of coals to Newcastle! I learned about spinning and weaving and how to recognize cotton, twill, canvas and damask, all of which made it easier to follow later at school the technical aspects of the Industrial Revolution!' It was in the middle of the Civil War that the family, including his invalided half-sister Kathleen, made the move, setting up their new home in Paradise Cottage – a modest corner house situated in a quiet cul-de-sac, 'the nearest', as Ken notes with a twinkle, 'I may ever get to heaven! We treated Paradise Cottage as a place that should live up to its name and we were happy there.'

It was in the far from paradisiacal environment of the new Free State, torn apart by the internecine atrocity of civil war, that Ken witnessed the fleeing IRA irregular from his bedroom window. This event, 'and its association with violence and fear', remained an evocative childhood memory throughout his lifetime, re-inforcing his adult aversion to violence as a means of achieving political ends. While neither parent was remotely 'militarist' and his father, especially, barely tolerant of anarchic Republicanism, they were not unaffected by the armed struggle happening around them. His mother's nephew, Sonny O'Connor from County Clare, was an active member of the Old IRA and 'came to seek refuge with us occasionally at Paradise Cottage'. Memories of the fierce riots between Blueshirts and Republicans Ken later witnessed as a youth in the streets of Drogheda were to remain vivid and further reinforce his antipathy to violence and public disorder.

As the new Irish Free State, cut adrift from empire, grappled with the stark reality of going it alone, life for a young boy in the 1920s carried on regardless. In comparison to Rostrevor, the large and busy market town of Drogheda, with a population of some twelve thousand, offered access to more varied pastimes and interests. Its location on the banks of the Boyne, 'the life blood of the town',[7] made Drogheda a centre of industrial and manu-facturing activity with its various mills and its leather, chemical and meat factories. Growing up there was, Ken recalls, 'an inter-esting, memorable, even at times magical experience'. Reminders of the town's eventful historic past were all around, from the twelfth-century tower of Millmount, built on an Anglo-Norman moat, the scene of Cromwell's massacre in 1649, which was partly razed during the Civil War, to St Laurence Gate, the

Magdalene Tower, Mary's Abbey, the ancient Tholsel, St Peter's Church with the preserved head of St Oliver Plunkett, salvaged from his execution at Tyburn, and the nearby site of the famous 1690 Battle of the Boyne. From the outskirts of the town stretched a hinterland of varied natural beauty: the famous Boyne valley, dominated by the hills of Tara and Slane and containing some of the most impressive prehistoric monuments in Europe, still then in their pre-restoration state, and two of the earliest Christian sites, Monasterboice and Mellifont. Here were opportunities aplenty to satisfy every boyhood desire for adventure and escapade.

Ken soon made friends and played boyhood games in William Street and Albany Terrace, from where he and his companions were invariably chased for playing ball against a neighbour's wall, or for taunting the unfortunate delivery man who, with donkey and cart, came to sell coal and coke to the neighbourhood's households. Pastimes were determined by the seasons: spinning tops in early spring, marbles played along the kerb in Fair Street in April, swimming in the invigorating waters of the Boyne from May; summer brought fishing in the canal and river, shooting rabbits near the antique ruins of Dowth, and searching for mushrooms and wild strawberries; autumn, conker fights and, 'if I may confess an early delinquency, the optimistic placing of half-pennies on the track of the Navan railway line to have them converted into pennies – unfortunately not a very profitable enterprise!' When other outlets lost their appeal, the boys would set up a fist-fight. 'Often the selected opponents were slow to get stuck into one another and the cry would go up, "Come on Joe, give him 'caijin' ",* exhorting the sometimes reluctant contestants. And the fellow so exhorted would kick the other or spit in his face, thus ending indecision.' As a former schoolmate recalled, the

* A corruption of the expression 'give him occasion', used in duels and bare-knuckle professional fights in the dim and distant past.

young Northerner was 'as handy with his fists as the next and many a scrap he was in, in Palace Street'.[8]

With pocket money scarce, 'one learned to be an "economic man"' at an early age. For a penny the best marginal value was a packet of Roche's Little Men – boiled sweets moulded in human form – or four NKM caramels or two long spirals of liquorice. Dates were a substantial, if sticky, buy in O'Hagan's shop, opposite St Peter's, when you got a kid's eye (3d) for choir practice or for good performance as an altar boy. Later, a present of his first bicycle, 'purchased for six pounds', provided access to the wider hinterland; to the golf course at Baltray, to sneak a few strokes on the famous links, to Mornington for a 'plunge in the unfortunately named Minister's Hole', to the farm of a friend of his parents to taunt the pedigree bull in the field before running headlong for safety. Films shown in the Whitworth Hall, the annual regatta 'held on the stretch of river between the Viaduct and Tom Roe's point', shooting cormorants to collect the bounty from the local board of salmon conservators – these were all schoolboy highlights. Club sport figured only sporadically, although, much to his own amazement, he is the proud owner of a Louth Minor Hurling Championship medal, 'of which I recall nothing, having possibly been only a sub'. With his school pals, he regularly walked the five-mile circuit 'up the ramparts, across the river at Oldbridge and back on the Louth side into Drogheda' – with the ulterior motive of a chance meeting with 'the Vision Splendid', a girl in a scarlet coat with long golden hair. 'My best pal, Tom Branigan, married the "vision" years later but in our early teens, a muffled red-faced "hello" was as much as either of us could muster.'

Both Ken and his sister Peggie looked forward to the annual summer holiday at their mother's home in Clare. 'We enjoyed all the new experiences – the ride by sidecar from Ennis station, watching the cows being milked, feeding the calves, taking a *dreas* at the churn, driving the donkey and cart to Coolmeen, fetching water from the pump, searching under the hedges for hens' eggs, eating cherries from the orchard in front of the house, even helping with the hay-making'; and for Ken there were also a daily swim with his father in the 'Puffin Hole' at Kilkee and fishing in the Cloon river with his Uncle Jacko. His grandmother, by now over forty years a widow, lived in 'a long, thatched pink cottage festooned with sweet briar in Kilmurraymacmahon, with a view to the right of the door of Clonderlaw Bay, which I remember before the ESB [Electricity Supply Board] chimneys went up at Tarbert'. Trips on the West Clare Railway, made famous by Percy French, 'the bustle and excitement at Moyasta Junction', were an exciting experience. 'We brought our own children on one of the last journeys on this renowned line,' Ken recalls. His grandmother had raised a family of eight virtually on her own, 'six of whom never married – a sad feature', as he notes, 'of the rural Ireland of the time'. The welcome, hospitality and generosity extended by neighbouring families to the two young visitors remained a vivid memory, 'and we came home to Drogheda with many a golden half-sovereign'.[9]

The foundations for two of his adult interests – salmon fishing and the Irish language – were also formed during his boyhood years in Drogheda. Watching the salmon leap the weirs and the Boyne fishermen in their ancient hide-covered willow coracles shoot their nets and haul their catch of fat salmon high onto the bank, 'wincing as the last rites were administered by a wooden truncheon known as "the priest"', fuelled his passion for angling. 'I can remember arming myself with a cane with a piece of twine and hook attached and throwing it out on the water near the weir in the vain hope of landing a salmon.' It would be many years before that first salmon was landed, far from the Boyne, but the passion remained evergreen. 'Everyone needs to have one irresistible temptation, preferably not an immoral one,' he insists, and for him it was to be salmon fishing, in which he has faithfully indulged throughout his lifetime, with not a little success. As a schoolboy he also helped a local Dominican friar, Brother Andrew Ryan, a breeder of prize-winning cocker spaniels, to exercise the dogs in the surrounding countryside. Later, on Ken's departure from Drogheda, Brother Ryan presented him with a dog called Dandy, 'a blue roan, dappled black and white, who had won many prizes at the RDS [Royal Dublin Society]'. The dog was subsequently handed over to the care of Ken's father, who, on his retirement, had more time than his son to ensure that Dandy got adequate exercise. 'I think I actually set my father up, by giving him Dandy. It prolonged his enjoyment of life.'

In common with many of his working colleagues and the political leaders with whom he would collaborate in adult life, Ken's formal education started with the local Irish Christian Brothers, at the national school at West Gate 'with its cold class-rooms and yard covered in clinkers'. Committed to providing the sons of Ireland's lower middle-class families with an academically solid education, grounded in Catholic belief and practice, imbued with a cultural nationalism, the Christian Brothers ran a strict, sometimes cruel, physical regime. 'Some of the brothers were agreeable types, some were the opposite. One of the more vindictive used the leather strap with such vigour and frequency that we boldly stole the strap and hid it in a hole in the floor, so at least he was left strapless for a while.' When the wielder of the strap subsequently abandoned his vocation in preference for a career with the Royal Canadian Mounted Police, to his young victims the relief smacked of divine intervention.

It was, however, in secondary school, at Sunday's Gate, just up the hill from his home, that the more 'agreeable types' entered Ken's life, encouraging the 'special' qualities they perceived in the young schoolboy which were later to mark him out (notwith-standing his disarming caution that 'after all these years one might be inclined to give an overly purple glow to one's reasons and ambitions!'). Despite the grim discipline, a resilience and strength of character, perhaps forged as a shield against the jibes and taunts of his schoolmates about his name and origin (and even his mother's tendency, as he ruefully recalls, to occasionally dress her only son like 'Little Lord Fauntleroy'), enabled him to absorb the school's more positive aspects. His contemporaries acknowledged him as one of the 'most brilliant – if not the most brilliant – pupils to pass through the portals of the CBS in Drogheda. He could trot up to the blackboard with the confidence of an Archimedes, and with a stub of chalk prove Pythagoras's Theorem as if it were just A, B, C, yet he was no book-worm and no swotter'.[10] The marks he attained in the Intermediate Certificate examination, which won him a national scholarship, indicated a pupil of exceptional potential.

Ken himself prefers to attribute the development of his early scholastic ability to enlightened teachers, who, as well as imparting their knowledge with enthusiasm and dedication over and above the call of duty, also gave him a consummate understanding and appreciation of their given subjects. Among them was Brother James Marcellus Burke, 'who combined clarity of exposition with a strong, personal sense (transmitted to many of his pupils) of beauty and order . . . In Mathematics too, in all its sections, he had the great gift of graceful and attractive presentation of new knowledge.'[11] From Brother Burke came not only an appreciation of English prose and poetry and an insatiable appetite for the 'classics' – the stories of Dante being an early favourite – mainly borrowed from the local Carnegie library, but also an interest in the intricacies and challenges of mathematics.

Newry-born Peadar McCann, revolutionary and scholar, whose love of the Irish language imbued a similar devotion in his young student and who, without any extra remuneration, also taught him extra-curricular French, was exceptional. 'To me Peadar was as much Drogheda as the St Laurence Gate.' This shy, intelligent teacher was to make a lasting impact. 'A man of principle, of independence of judgement and absolute integrity of character, he encouraged these traits in his pupils, never

17

imposing dogmatic interpretations but leading them, almost without their realising it, to make their own critical assessments, never to take anything for granted, never to take history as written or as being the last word.'[12] Peadar McCann was to follow the career of his most famous student with interest and pride. He lived long enough to see his own attributes develop in his star pupil, and to see him rise to the top of the civil service and become first chairman of Bord na Gaeilge, the Irish Language Board – but not long enough to know that he also became president of the Alliance Française of Dublin or that he conversed in French with the president of France. McCann found in the young Northerner an interested student prepared to go the extra distance, and responded by encouraging him to study outside the narrow confines of the school curriculum in the subjects he taught so well, history, Irish and French.

'In Irish, *An tOileánach*, *Fiche Blian ag Fás*, *Fearfeasa mac Feasa* and *Caisleán Óir* were favourites. By my late teens I had acquired enough French to be able, over the years ahead, to read authors such as Proust, Maurois, Mauriac, de Maupassant, and enjoy Molière, Racine and the whole oeuvre of Simenon and especially Marcel Pagnol,' the last of these being also the author of racy novels about the steamy side of life in Marseilles. His interest and proficiency in French were later augmented by family holidays in France and in 1961 by a course in French literature at the University of Rennes. This linguistic facility also stood him in good stead professionally in the many international conferences and meetings he was later to undertake in the course of his public work, and he readily acknowledges the role of Brother Burke and Peadar McCann in germinating it: 'I owe these two teachers an immense debt.' On leaving school in 1934, Ken presented McCann with a single-volume compendium of a Blackhall edition of the works of Shakespeare with the inscription: 'Comhartha beag buidheachais ó Kenneth W' (a small token of thanks from Kenneth W). Fifty-two years later, Ken's friend Seán de Fréine returned the volume to him, after finding it by chance in a second-hand bookshop. The 'Peadar McCann Award for Student Achievement', awarded annually at the CBS Drogheda today, is testimony to the dedication of this remarkable teacher to generations of Drogheda students. It was perhaps fitting that his 'most brilliant' student would become the first president of the school's past pupils' union.

'Ba é Peadar a mhúscail mo shuim sa Ghaeilge agus a chothaigh mo bhá léithe. Is saibhride go mór mo shaol dá bharr' ('It was Peadar who awoke my interest in Irish and who nourished my empathy for it. My life has been much enriched as a result'), Ken later wrote in tribute. It was Peadar who also encouraged him to seek out any residue of the old Irish in the immediate locality of Drogheda. 'We took down prayers in Irish from an old lady in Tullyallen,' Ken recalls. Sometimes the upshot was less pious, as 'when enquiring if he spoke Irish of the bent and bearded man who kept the key to the round tower at Monasterboice, to be told "yes, póg mo thóin!"' In their quest they visited the nearby small Gaeltacht or Irish-speaking region of Omeath, Ó Méidh Mara on Carlingford Lough, famous as the birthplace of Gaelic poets such as Séamas Dall Mac Cuarta (1647–1733). 'It was there I met the last survivors of that particular Gaeltacht at the pilgrimage of Lá Fhéile Muire Mór san Fhómhar [The Great Autumn Feast of Our Lady] on 15 August. I was about sixteen and this group, mostly women, as their forebears had done, came down from the surrounding hills to the traditional place of worship to do the Stations of the Cross in Irish. I went around the stations with them, talking to them in Irish.' Later, in adulthood, he returned with his friend Cardinal William Conway, also a fluent Irish-speaker, and this time met and spoke with the last surviving native Irish-speaker in the area, who told him that by then the only person she could converse with was her grandson, who happened to be learning Irish at school in Newry. The disappearance of this small Gaeltacht, in such a relatively short period of time, influenced Ken's later official policy in his capacity as chairman of Bord na Gaeilge towards the preservation of the remaining Gaeltacht areas as much as it did his personal commitment to the language.

His introduction to the Gaeltacht at Carlingford also directed his footsteps farther afield by way of a scholarship to Rannafast in the Donegal Gaeltacht. In 1912 Father Lorcan Murray, a diocesan inspector of schools, had organized an Irish summer school, St Brigid's, in Omeath, and in 1925 he established its successor at Rannafast – proclaimed by the 1931 college prospectus to be 'a 100% Irish-speaking district in the Rosses of Tír Chonaill' where 'the very children do not know English'. Over the following years the original small schoolhouse, still visible today, was extended, and summer students, mainly drawn from Northern counties, were boarded with local families, where, it was noted, 'the cleanliness and comfort ... have been a surprise to all visitors . . . the people of the district being noted for their kindness'.[13] This was an enticing prospect for the fifteen-year-old Ken Whitaker: 'I was in Ardee, at a feis and sports day, when I saw young people queuing to be interviewed. I asked what was happening and was told they were being interviewed for a scholarship for a month in an Irish college in Donegal. So I joined the queue, answered the questions in Irish and got away with it!' Going on his own to a place so far away from home was a new and liberating experience, and not just in cultural and linguistic terms. He set off by train, first across country from Dundalk to Letterkenny, where he then boarded 'a little train with wooden seats' on the narrow-gauge extension railway that serviced the Donegal coastline to Burtonport, stopping at many stations along the route. At Crolly, he and his fellow students were transferred by bus down the narrow, winding boreen to the college and were allocated to their host families. He was given accommodation in the cottage of Seán Mhicí Óig Ó Dochartaigh, *cois cladaigh* (by the shore). During the month-long term, classes in Irish were conducted at the schoolhouse each weekday from 11 a.m. to 3 p.m. with an interval of one hour for lunch. 'Céilís, *a mhair go maidin* [that lasted until daybreak], opened up a new world where you could ask a girl to dance without either chaperone or permission,' in contrast to home 'where everyone knew what girl you had met the previous day on the Rathmullen Road'. Socially it was a very different experience for a youngster from the Pale and he found there 'wonderful people who, despite the isolation of their environment, took so kindly to us "strange" children. There was a real difference in the mode of life, the culture. You were made to feel welcome and given hospitality even in the poorest houses . . . Bright in my memory still is the old *seanchaí* [storyteller] Gráinne Phroinsias, in the chimney corner, *tigh* [in the house of] Sheáin Mhicí Óig, the stories of Johnny Shéamuisín, and Seán Bán MacGrianna, the *céilidhe* and the songs, the early morning swims before breakfast in the *poll snáimh* [swimming hole], the wonderful sunsets creating *caisleáin óir* [golden castles] beyond the islands, the gleam of silver and amethyst in the gravel of the fuchsia-lined roads. *Tír na nÓg!*'

The music, songs, old stories told around the fireside, *caint na ndaoine*, the literature, *paidreacha agus mallachtaí – an chuid is buaine de theanga!* (prayers and curses – the core of a language!), the unique way of life and the environment lured the young student back to Rannafast in 1933 and 1935 (punctuated in 1934 by a month in Carraroe in the Connemara Gaeltacht) and to undertake a bicycle trip around Fanad, Ros Goill and Gleann Colm Cille in 1937. His experience as a student in the Gaeltacht encouraged him and some friends, in their final year at school in Drogheda, to establish an Irish-speaking club and organize a dance – Céilidhe and Oldtime – in the local Mayoralty Rooms. This was not Rannafast, however, and as he recalls, 'the girls' mothers came as chaperones, but this did not altogether spoil the fun!'

Like most Irish provincial county towns of the period, Drogheda had an established musical tradition. The MacGough sisters, one an organist at the Augustinian, the other at the Dominican church, taught violin and piano to generations of Drogheda children, including Ken and his sister Peggie. The sisters also staged the annual operetta, usually Gilbert and Sullivan, where young boys from the church choir sang in the chorus line. Miss Crilly and Miss E. C. Kenny at nearby Fair Street also had a hand in Ken's piano instruction; as the latter informed him in 1976, on his retirement as governor of the Central Bank, she was 'now free to admit, without you suffering from a swelled head, how I looked forward to your lessons and have followed your career over the years'.[14] His prowess as a pianist is still much in evidence today, as this author can testify, for the long hours spent researching his personal archive at his home were uplifted by his impromptu renditions of Chopin nocturnes, Handel's 'Silent Worship' and 'Danny Boy'.

The classical music to which he was introduced by learning violin and piano, and singing in the church choir and in the operettas, he considers 'a civilizing part of life that has been one of my joys'. He recalls in 1932 as a schoolboy of sixteen coming by train from Drogheda to Dublin for the final event of the Eucharistic Congress and that, 'standing by the Father Mathew statue in O'Connell Street, I heard John McCormack sing *Panis Angelicus* . . . an unforgettable experience'. In 2008 he unveiled a statue of the great tenor in Dublin's Iveagh Gardens. Chamber music, *Lieder*, opera and orchestral: he has developed a catholic interest in and appreciation of music, lending his practical support as a patron and donor to the National Concert Hall and the Irish Chamber Orchestra, and – endowed with a good baritone voice – participating for many years in the choir of his local church in Donnybrook. But for his desert island choice of composer, he is emphatic. 'It has to be Bach. I feel more influenced by him than by any other composer. I like his sense of orderliness. With Beethoven, for example, your heart is thumping, wondering what is coming next. Bach is more regulated but a great man for melody, in fact inventing melody. His range of competence is very large.' An analogy, perhaps, for the 'orderliness and inventiveness' he himself later sought to bring to the Irish economy? 'You are trying to draw a comparison between a symphony and a programme for economic expansion! But I suppose there is an element of congruity: both depend very much on inspiration and competence.'

As schooldays in Drogheda hurtled towards their inevitable close, the future ahead of the young Ken Whitaker looked somewhat uncertain. In 1930s Ireland, a career choice, even for talented students, was determined not by ability but by means. 'When I sat the Leaving Certificate in 1934, I was one of only six or seven CBS boys to do so.' Most of his schoolmates had been forced by economic circumstances to leave school earlier to earn a living, either locally in the town's manufacturing plants and factories, if they were lucky, or farther afield in Dublin or in Britain. Ken attained top marks in every Leaving Certificate subject; but at that time, when it came to third-level education, 'there were no points required, only cash', he recalls. A university education was then confined almost exclusively to the sons and daughters of Ireland's better-off middle classes. Ken's own ambition at this time was to be a medical doctor, influenced perhaps by his mother's nursing career and his own innate sense of caring and service that was to mark both his public and private life. However, at this time, his father was on the point of retiring from the Greenmount and Boyne Mill on a small pension, which could not stretch to encompass the expense of a university education. A possible way around the problem was to secure one of the few university scholarships available and for this, in the summer of 1934, the young Ken Whitaker settled down to study.

Fate, however, intervened to deny both Ireland's universities and the medical profession the undoubted talent of this aspiring student. At seventeen, as a matter of course, he sat the examination, 'as difficult as the Leaving Certificate', held at his school for

23

the clerical officer entry grade to the civil service. He was awarded first place in the country. This opened up a new avenue: a pensionable job in the public service was considered both respectable and secure, and was, moreover, one of the few career paths at the time operated on merit, as distinct from a job in a bank or in business where influence and contacts mattered. Thus the service attracted to its ranks, as Ken's future colleague the writer and satirist Brian Ó Nualláin wrote, 'people of intelligence whose parents have no money'.[15] Owing to the scarcity of jobs and the general lack of means of most of the population, competition for entry was fierce, with fifteen applications for every post advertised at Leaving Certificate level. After discussion with his parents, it was decided that 'a bird in the hand' was a more practical option than the hope of a university scholarship. It was a humble start to what would turn out to be a meteoric and record-making career in the Irish civil service, a promotion record that still stands to this day; as Ken humorously notes, 'nobody has apparently repeated that feat of jumping the hurdles since!'

During the course of his long and eventful life, Ken's affection for and gratitude to Drogheda, the town of his upbringing, never waned. He maintains contact with many friends and organizations there, is a member of the Old Drogheda Society and a former president of the CBS past pupils' union, and has penned many articles for the local press and for his alma mater. The town's pride in the achievements of its most famous citizen was exemplified in 1999 when he was made a Freeman of Drogheda, a rare and distinctive honour he shares with Pope John Paul II. The citation reads:

The Mayor, Aldermen and Burgesses of the Borough of Drogheda hereby resolve to confer the Freedom of the Borough on Dr Thomas K. Whitaker in recognition of his distinguished public service and to enter his name in the Register of Freemen. Dated the 12th day of December 1999.

The presentation casket made for the scroll on which the citation was inscribed was handcrafted from a fallen lime tree in the nearby Beaulieu estate which was planted in 1695, five years after the Battle of the Boyne.

More recently, Drogheda's sister town, Dundalk, named the new library in the Dundalk Institute of Technology in honour of the 'wee' county's famous native son.

2

Nostri Plena Laboris
1934–38

It is the duty of civil servants to think all round a subject and give Ministers
their unbiased opinions on matters referred to them when policy is being
considered and then, when policy has been decided on, to carry out that
policy to the best of their ability, regardless of their personal views.
T. K. Whitaker[1]

DUBLIN IN THE 1930S was still a post-colonial society, caught
between a latent but enduring sense of Britishness and a
Nationalist and Catholic triumphalism accentuated by the
election of the first Fianna Fáil government in 1932 and the
celebration in the same year of the Eucharistic Congress. The
transfer of power from the Free State government to its bitter
Civil War opponents and the virtually peaceful acceptance by the
Irish army, the Civic Guards – almost exclusively composed of
former Free State soldiers – and the civil service of their new
Republican masters was as astonishing as it was an important step
towards democracy. In the city, insularity and a narrow nationalism competed with a residual allegiance to the British Crown on
the part of its Anglo-Irish citizenry. Issues such as the playing of
'God Save the King', rather than 'The Soldier's Song', at social
functions, the reluctance of the Irish rugby authorities to fly
the tricolour at Lansdowne Road and, in the aftermath of the

Eucharistic Congress, the emergence of an increasingly strident and intolerant brand of Catholicism, which among other dictates decreed Trinity College Dublin to be out of bounds to Catholics, all marked the divided loyalties of the new Free State's capital city.

The remnants of Anglo-Irish landed society who remained after independence settled down to life in the new state, which, although cast adrift from the British mother ship, still retained its membership of the Commonwealth, and whose first government had made an attempt, by providing for their representation in the Senate, to accommodate their integration into Irish Ireland. The initial steps taken by Éamon de Valera's government, however, confirmed their worst fears when the oath of allegiance to the English monarch was formally removed in 1933 and the Senate became politicized. At the very time of Ken's arrival in the civil service, the first Constitution Review Committee, instituted by de Valera (many decades later Ken would chair its successor), challenged the 1922 Treaty with Britain, while de Valera's perceived closeness to a resurgent IRA led to another wave of departures by Ireland's old ascendancy. For the Protestant middle class, however, who controlled most of the professions, the banks and major businesses in the city, trade followed the flag. Despite the political changes that had occurred and those envisaged, they continued to work and live in the more salubrious southside suburbs of Kingstown, Dalkey, Dartry, Blackrock, Foxrock and Rathgar, sent their children to Protestant schools and socialized within their own class. Dublin society, meanwhile, was augmented by the arrival of job-seekers from the provinces, many of the brightest, like Ken Whitaker, finding in the meritocratic civil service one of the few opportunities available to pursue a 'respectable' career.

Today the daily commute to the city is a way of life for an army of workers based in outlying counties around the capital. In 1934 it was more of a rarity. People from the country lucky enough to obtain employment in Dublin usually moved in with relations or found lodgings in 'digs' or basement flats in the suburbs where, depending on their financial and other circumstances, they lived in various degrees of comfort, sometimes in deprivation and loneliness. A 1930s circular relating to the high incidence of sick leave among the lower clerical grades in the civil service blamed their meagre salaries, which made 'it hard to pay for proper lodgings, clothes, bus and train fares', and noted that 'most consequently resort to the expedient of paying merely for their rooms . . . and find themselves in the position of having to curtail expenditure on food . . . which over a considerable period must have a damaging effect on the health of young people'.[2] With the salary for the clerical officer entry grade in the civil service a lowly £150 a year (equivalent to some £4,000 a year today), Edward and Jane Whitaker thought it better that their seventeen-year-old son should continue to live at home and commute daily by train to his job in Dublin. As Ken observes: 'allowing for the cost of the weekly train ticket and five lunches, I had little left to compensate my mother for feeding me morning and evening and lodging me every night. Indeed, she was subsidizing the State!'

While an improvement in his salary was to occur earlier than he had perhaps expected, for four years he continued to commute between Drogheda and Dublin. Leaving Drogheda at 8.20 in the morning, he arrived in Dublin with just enough time to sprint down Talbot Street and be seated at his desk promptly at the 9.15 starting time. Punctuality, an essential obligation of a civil service job, was regularly thrown into jeopardy when the train made an unscheduled stop near Balbriggan 'for a cattle-dealer, who enjoyed a traditional right for the train to stop on his property, in the middle of nowhere, every Thursday to facilitate his travel to the Dublin cattle market'. The delay gave rise to anxious mutterings from Ken and his co-passengers 'to "hurry up" in case you got a late mark against you at work which (if you got many) could result in your annual increment being stopped'. From the evidence of his civil service personal records, however, despite the weekly delay to accommodate the Balbriggan cattle-dealer, lateness was not a feature of his attendance; nor was sick leave, despite its prevalence in the civil service. That sense of punctuality imbued in him from early life has remained a noticeable trait, to the apparent incredulity of his grandsons. 'The funniest thing about Granddad is his obsession with being early,' or, as Ken would see it, as simply 'being on time'.

When his sister Peggie acquired a job in the Land Commission as a writing assistant (a term Ken still finds amusing, 'as if holding the hand that held the pen!'), his time as a commuter ended when their parents decided to move from Drogheda to Dublin, purchasing a house, the first they ever owned, at Bangor Drive, in the expanding southern suburb of Crumlin. Entering the property market then involved little speculation or borrowing: 'There was no question of seeking a loan from a bank. They had saved the money to purchase it,' their son recalls.

Dublin city in the 1930s was compact and accessible, but large enough for a young man from a provincial town, as Ken recalls, to 'acquire, temporarily, a refreshing anonymity'. One of the more pleasurable novelties was the range of entertainment available: plays at the Abbey and Gate theatres, the latter run by the flamboyant couple Mícheál Mac Liammóir and Hilton Edwards, and cinema, which, with its glittering images and portrayal of a glamorous and seductive Hollywood life, offered an escape, notwithstanding the admonitions of religious conservatives, from mundane reality for all classes. Later, when he 'found his feet', old-time waltzes held in the Mansion House were an occasional diversion, as were day trips to the mountains and beaches of the city's attractive environs. By the standards of the time, Dublin offered most of its citizens a comfortable, if somewhat conservative and drab, lifestyle, with the exception of those less fortunate living in its notorious tenements – a problem beginning to be tackled by the construction of new housing developments in areas such as Fairview, Marino and Crumlin. On joining the ranks of the St Vincent de Paul Society, Ken came face to face with life in the infamous Dublin slums of the period, and it was, as he remembers, 'an eye-opener to see in what appalling circumstances people had to live'. On his many visitations on behalf of the Society, 'fleas were one of the minor irritants and you made sure that the ends of your trousers were secured by your bicycle clips'. Despite the misery, want and neglect he encountered in the tenements, however, he was also struck by the sense of stoicism and spirited independence of the families he came to know and who got to know him, greeting him with the familiar 'Hello, Brother' when their paths crossed. 'I had a quiet respect for how they managed their grim circumstances.'

Outside Ireland, the First World War had wrought great changes in the wider political and social order, as old empires and kingdoms toppled and new ideologies, not least communism and fascism, threatened the stability of what remained. When the world's richest and most 'free' economy collapsed with the Wall Street Crash of 1929, the reverberations sent the world economy into a downward spiral, with unemployment, budget deficits and taxation at record levels and production levels falling precipitously. In Germany it was reported that over 20 million of the population existed on state relief. For a newly independent country such as Ireland, whose economy was still inextricably bound to and dependent on its former colonial master, whose meagre resources had been expended to repair the ravages and repay the damages of a destructive civil war, whose new government had inherited a legacy of decades of economic neglect, and most of whose population existed on subsistence incomes mainly derived from agriculture (one person was employed in industry or services for every eleven working in agriculture), the very survival of the fledging state and its citizens was something of a miracle.

To ensure the new state's credibility as much as its viability, the protectionism and self-sufficiency promoted by Arthur Griffith and Sinn Féin were abandoned by the first Free State government in favour of free trade, the most generally accepted and widely practised economic philosophy of the day. In this context, and with priority being given to maintaining peace and restoring the infrastructural damage inflicted on the country during the Civil War, economic development was minimal – with the notable exceptions of the Shannon Scheme, which Ken records as being 'an amazingly bold venture',[3] providing native-sourced power for the economy, and also the establishment of the Irish Sugar Company. Internal and external difficulties alike baulked the hoped-for stimulation of home-based industries. In the grip of the Great Depression, America no longer offered a place of refuge and opportunity for Irish emigrants, while in 1931 Britain changed tack and embarked on an economic protectionist policy of its own that further threatened the fragile Irish industrial sector. The abandonment of the gold standard revived protectionism everywhere as each country strove desperately to limit the impact of the Depression on its own economy. Prices of basic products plummeted as demand fell, unemployment increased and uncertainty prevailed worldwide.

The election of a Fianna Fáil government in 1932 heralded a major change in economic policy, ushering in what Ken later referred to as 'a phase of lavish and indiscriminate industrial protection'.[4] This was to last until the mid-1950s, when the revolutionary strategy devised by the former clerical officer from Drogheda would finally offer the people of Ireland an alternative to almost four decades of despondency, isolation and poverty. In 1932, however, self-sufficiency was the goal of the government, pursued by means of a system of protective tariffs. One of the first acts of the new government was the introduction of the Control of Manufactures Act, which restricted foreign ownership of Irish manufacturing companies. The lack of private capital and the reluctance of the Irish banking system to invest in the new state led to the establishment of state-run monopolies, such as the Industrial Credit Corporation, Aer Lingus, Aer Rianta, the Irish Life Assurance Company and Ceimicí Teó (Irish Chemicals), all under the direction of the energetic minister for industry and commerce, Seán Lemass. In agriculture, a switch to self-sufficiency in wheat, beet and tillage, in preference to beef and milk production, was encouraged. A major building programme, which delivered thousands of new homes, was also initiated.

This change in national economic policy was further marked by the refusal of the Irish government to continue to pay the much-resented land annuities, constituting almost 18 per cent of the state's badly needed funding, to the British government, which reacted by imposing a 20 per cent duty on imports from the Free State. De Valera in turn retaliated with duties on British imports, and an 'economic war' of retaliatory tariffs and quotas between the two countries commenced. Britain's initial 20 per cent duty applied to all Irish agricultural produce, including the vital exports of live cattle, and the Irish Free State was also excluded from the preferential tariff rates offered to other Commonwealth countries at the Ottawa Conference in 1932. As Ken observed, it was political as much as economic factors that fuelled 'the heated atmosphere of retaliation, [and this] was not conducive to any careful adjustment of aid to need'.[5] The new government's policy of self-sufficiency was promoted, he felt, 'with more political zest than economic calculation', protection being granted 'rather freely and with little scientific measurement of need'.[6] It was a miscalculation he ensured would not be repeated when it came to the formulation of his alternative economic plan.

At the time, however, the drive towards economic protectionism in Ireland was approved by no less a person than the noted economist John Maynard Keynes, who took 'National Self-Sufficiency' as his theme in the first Finlay Lecture, delivered at University College Dublin (UCD) in 1933, and commented: 'If I were an Irishman I should find much to attract me in the economic outlook of your present government towards self-sufficiency.'[7] Keynes's advice, as Ken noted many years later in 2000, 'in my opinion was the worst advice an influential economist ever gave to Irish policy-makers. It confirmed the then government in persisting in a futile attempt, for a small and poor country, to reach full employment, at acceptable incomes, by protecting domestic production.'[8] The reversal of that policy in 1958 would become Ken Whitaker's outstanding national achievement.

While the economic and social legacy inherited from the British may have left much to be desired, the existence of an impartial and efficient Irish civil service, numbering some 21,000 staff, helped lay the administrative foundations for the new state. Between 1919 and 1920 the Irish branch of the civil service had undergone radical reform in its organization, coordination and staffing, and had emerged from the process a leaner and more efficient institution. In the transfer of power to the Irish provisional government in 1922, the British Treasury 'regarded it as part of their duty to hand over the Irish Civil Service in a good working order'.[9] One of the more significant results of the reform was the establishment of the authority of the Department of Finance and its close relationship with government. With the handover of the civil administration went an almost seamless transfer of senior civil servants, some of English birth, to head up the new service, many of whom were to have a major influence on the career and outlook of Ken Whitaker.

Cork-born, Cambridge-educated Joseph Brennan is remembered by Ken as being 'remote and somewhat cantankerous'. He had worked in the British civil service before becoming financial adviser to Michael Collins. Almost single-handedly Brennan organized the establishment of the financial institutions of the new Free State, before being appointed the first secretary of the Department of Finance and later chairman of the Currency

33

Commission and governor of the Central Bank. His successor as departmental secretary, Kerry-born J. J. McElligott, had won his revolutionary credentials in the General Post Office in 1916 and as a political prisoner in British jails, but, as Ken reflected, 'while he never made anything of his part in 1916, the politicians he dealt with could not claim to be any more nationalist than he and, as one of the "lads", he commanded both respect and authority. Being better educated in economics than most of his comrades, he managed to restrain individual ministers and keep government expenditure within reasonable bounds in the 1930s.' Arthur Dean Codling, a Yorkshireman by birth, served in the Irish civil service from 1900, and chose to remain after the establishment of the Irish Free State. A Methodist, gentle but meticulous and, as Ken remembers, 'a man of the utmost probity and of penetrating mind, he gave loyal service of the highest quality to his adopted country'. Another 'outstanding pre-1922 civil servant' was H. P. Boland, assistant secretary in the Establishment Division of the Finance Department, which oversaw the structural and personnel functions of the service: 'He laid down very good foundations for the civil service which has not departed fundamentally from them since.' The example of these backroom pioneers, who without fear or favour, or pursuit of personal gain or advancement, felt duty-bound to guide the young state through its difficult infancy, was to influence the work ethic of the next generation of public servants. To recall the atmosphere that prevailed across the intervening distance of time is, as Ken notes, like watching 'some play being acted out with these characters', stern and unbending, from whom, as a young civil servant, he received no quarter. 'Your proposals and theories were open to attack and criticism; every memo had to stand up to scrutiny. And if you were capable of defending your point of view there would be respect in the end, if you managed to sustain your argument rationally.' It was a tough but fair training ground.

While the civil service was often seen from outside as rigid and unimaginative, obsessed with control and power, most politicians found in it, as Dr Noel Browne attested during his tenure as minister for health, an 'immediacy and spontaneity of response . . . versatility, originality, and creativity'.[10] In 1934, Ken's first impressions 'were of its hierarchical structure and the respect given to rank. In this it resembled the Church . . . From the start, I never felt bored or contemplated seeking alternative employment.' Any lingering regrets about a medical career were subsumed by an almost instant rapport with and belief in the alternative career that had, it seemed, chosen him. While the public service, as he acknowledged, may have been 'an obvious but also a sitting target . . . a popular butt for criticism – by a very sound tradition we are not allowed to answer back'.[11] While to outsiders the image of the civil service may have been one of stagnation, repetition and boredom, of watching the hands of the clock move towards lunchtime, or eventual retirement, to many of those who worked within its myriad layers it could be a challenging, even crusading, career. For new recruits to the service, as Ken recalls, 'there was no systematic official programme of personal development . . . The newcomer was expected to learn how to perform by observation or intuition rather than by education or training. The ideal of the "gifted amateur" held sway.' It was an ethos that was to prove, in some instances, to the advantage of the public service – and never more so than in the case of Ken Whitaker.

The relationship between the civil service and its political masters was, perhaps surprisingly, generally cordial and mutually respectful. 'In my experience civil servants held their ministers in great respect; their personal relations might be warm or reserved but the office of minister was always treated with reverence.'[12] Contrary to the image promoted in the TV series *Yes Minister* there was no question, in Ken's mind, of government ministers being coerced or cajoled into policy decisions by their senior advisers. The civil service was, as he saw it, 'an integral part of a democratic constitutional system of Government ... but [one] which has no policy commitments of its own';[13] accordingly, its role in the promotion of national development 'must always be a subordinate one – the responsibility for economic policy rests with the Government ... but the Government rightly expects a significant contribution from the public service, if only because of its special qualifications, experience and access to information'.[14] Throughout his career as a public servant, while he enjoyed better personal relations with some ministers than others, he was careful to preserve that dividing line. 'I always thought it proper that senior civil servants should not only be independent but be seen to be independent of their ministers, and most ministers appreciated that. They did not want to be seen to be moulded by someone else. We respected each other's function.' The desired relationship, he considered, should be 'one of polite respect for person and office, and of helpful commitment, but devoid of subservience or political partisanship'. He still considered that detachment appropriate in retirement, 'a necessary obligation' that led him to decline invitations to speak at functions sponsored by various political parties. Never tempted to enter politics himself, he preferred the role of being 'a good adviser and to have my critical faculties unbiased'.

In more recent times he has observed, to his regret, a deterioration in the standards and practices, as well as in the calibre, of civil servants. The 'politicization' he observes in the more senior ranks of the civil service he views as compromising the traditional independence and integrity critical to the role of the civil servant as adviser to the government. To restore those standards, to ensure that senior civil servants concentrate on their original function of providing unbiased and critical opinion, and do not merely satisfy or rubber-stamp the aims or egos of their political masters, is, he feels, a more important national aim than even the restructuring of parliament or government itself.

When those early pioneering civil servants considered the

policies pursued by their political masters (while beneficial perhaps to the promotion of their political careers) detrimental to the national interest, they did not hold back from letting them know via the traditional departmental 'confidential memo'. 'It seems somewhat illogical in the same budget', J. J. McElligott informed his minister, Patrick McGilligan, in 1949, 'to be taking on heavy additional expenditure and at the same time remit taxation. It is like having your cake and eating it. It is a bad head-line for a Minister for Finance to set to a country untutored in economics.'[15] And McElligott's successor-in-waiting displayed no less forthrightness when government economic and monetary policies appeared misconceived. One of Ken's earliest criticisms was directed at the economic theorizing of Seán MacBride, minister for external affairs in the first interparty government, for supporting the use of national currency funds to promote forestry, land reclamation and deep-sea fishing. Then an assistant principal officer in the Department of Finance, Ken wrote of 'the curious spectacle of the Minister for External Affairs inviting the Minister for Finance to furnish proposals for expenditure' and hoped that 'it is not too late yet to subject the ideas that lie behind Mr MacBride's request to a critical examination' – ideas which, he adjudged, were 'completely out of touch with the reality of the present financial situation'.[16]

This ethos of forthright internal appraisal and criticism of government proposals, always with a view to the national interest, would become a constant thread running through Ken's future dealings with successive governments and ministers in his capacity both as secretary of the Department of Finance and later as governor of the Central Bank. Moreover, he was not averse, particularly in his latter role as governor, from making his criticisms public when his views were either ignored or dismissed by government, and his resolute interventions often made those in political power think again. His own assessment of that tenuous and, at times, uneasy relationship between politician and civil servant is modestly assessed in his article 'The Department of Finance': 'Misguided at times we undoubtedly were, but we obviously did not spare ourselves in striving for what we thought was right.'[17] The welfare of the country and its citizens was ever at the core of whatever comment and criticism he felt it necessary to make.

This expression of differences on matters of national policy was not confined to 'educating' politicians. It was also part of day-to-day interdepartmental exchanges, at times acerbic, between senior civil servants. In 1959, as secretary of the Department of Finance, an exchange of views with J. C. B. MacCarthy, secretary of the Department of Industry and Commerce, regarding the policy choice between protectionism and free trade, extended into a nine-week exchange of internal memos addressed to 'Dear Whitaker' and 'Dear MacCarthy' (at this time officials still tended to address each other by surname), in which both secretaries, with icy politeness, argued their respective cases, until they finally agreed to differ. 'Dear Whitaker . . . it grieves me to note that our exchange of correspondence seems to have done little to bring the discussion down to earth. The view expressed in your letter . . . is so far removed from our viewpoint that I agree there is no point in continuing the correspondence.' 'Dear MacCarthy, I suppose I am entitled to the last word in our correspondence . . . I am sorry it must be that I cannot accept . . . your letter . . . as being a fair or reasonable summary of the views expressed in my previous letters.'[18] The quality and cogency of these 'semi-official' interdepartmental letters and memos make them remarkable, even entertaining, reading. Despite their often technical, sometimes mundane, subject matter, the literary competence of their authors imbues them with an enduring freshness and immediacy. In Ken's case, his creative instincts found expression in a gifted writing style, embellished by a penchant for a humorous turn of phrase, making his comments on even the most complex and obtuse subjects compelling reading.

In 1934, however, his first step on the civil service ladder as a clerical officer lay in the more mundane work of a posting in the Civil Service Commission, located in Upper O'Connell Street. 'There,' he recalls, 'like Laocoon and the Serpents, we grappled with long strips of examination results, trying to paste them down in numerical order, a pre-computer ordeal.' Established by the Free State government in 1923, the Commission administered the recruitment of candidates to the civil service, from both outside and within the service, setting examinations and interviews for the various grades with efficiency and impartiality, in order, as one historian commented, 'to ensure that the new state would escape, at least in its central administration, the worst evils of the spoils system'.[19] Meritocracy was the order of the day; canvassing for support, the regulations warned, would 'not only render the applicant ineligible for appointment or promotion . . . but . . . in addition, render him liable to disciplinary action'.[20] Adherence to these principles contributed to Ken's spectacular rise through the ranks. It also instilled in him a respect for the concept of meritocracy as a means of advancement that characterized his administration of various public bodies, from the Department of Finance and the Central Bank to the National University of Ireland. In 1980, in a speech to the University Senate, he urged the adoption of the same criterion regarding all third-level educational institutions: 'that staff appointments will be on merit only, with no room for canvassing or favouritism'.[21] He meticulously applied the same criterion to himself when, on his retirement from the Central Bank in 1976, he declined Cardinal Conway's offer of the position of professor of economics at Maynooth College on the grounds that, in his view, 'I would not have been appointed on merit' – a sentiment most likely not shared by either his potential students or his would-be employer.

Eager and willing to work, he could not have been further from the caricature of the time-serving civil servant, perusing the newspaper, cigarette in hand, drinking endless cups of tea with one eye on the clock. 'It is, I think, important that every entrant to the civil service, no matter how junior, should be given plenty to do from the start. There is nothing more demoralising than any attempt, however well-intentioned, to "temper the wind to the shorn lamb". Once you have enjoyed an easy time for a while, you feel aggrieved at being expected to do a decent day's work.'[22] His application to duty, however, did not prevent him from seeing the humorous side to the red tape that abounded in the civil service. Among his papers, transcribed in his own hand, bearing the official stamp of *Saorstát Éireann* [Irish Free State], dated 1936, is the following piece of doggerel:

> The Official File
>
> A letter, an inquiry, a report –
> 'With reference to . . .' or something of the sort
> 'I am directed . . .' so, with words like these,
> It runs unto the end: 'Submitted, please.'
> Another step. A slightly higher mind
> Peruses it, to see what he can find.
> He reads it through, returns it with 'Please state . . .'
> Or, better still, perhaps: 'Elucidate.'
> Again it mounts, with slowly phrased reply.
> This time it pleases the superior's eye.
> Now all is well. The inferior has been twitted.
> The document is grudgingly 'transmitted'.
> Again a higher being reads it through
> And adds, as higher beings always do,
> A string of queries: 'Will you please explain
> (a), (b), (c), (d) . . . ?' and sends it back again.
> Once more it travels downwards to the source.
> It goes to him to whom it first had gone
> Again to be 'transmitted' further on.
> And so by easy stages up it goes

Until it reaches heaven only knows
What dizzy height of departmental power –
But all this does not happen in an hour.
The document is changing all the while:
It was a letter – now it is a File.
With every motion, with each fall and rise
It managed to acquire a greater size.
Its very thickness brings it to the Top.
It gets into a basket, there to stop
For many days, perhaps for many weeks,
Until the August One gives tongue and speaks.
The Great Decision waited for below –
The magic word 'agreed', or 'yes', or 'no'.
Then from its basket out is pulled the sheaf,
With codicils attached beyond belief.
And then – yes, in the end
It goes to Mr G. to see
And thence to Mr Stoat, to note
To the registry of Glues, to please peruse
Division L to smell
To Temporary Under-Sec, to check
To Typist, Clerk, S.O.
A dozen more, or so
And then – yes, in the end
Commences to descend.
Through all those many intermediate stops
No skipping is allowed – no sudden hops,
For all must add initials, pass it on,
With records that will last when they are gone.

The recruitment of young 'people of intelligence' to the civil service by competitive examination, at both school-leaving and university graduate level, produced a generally erudite and able workforce, led by an older, experienced brigade, most of whom had learned their craft in the British service. Given the lack of job opportunities in the private sector at this time, the civil service could count on attracting many of the most able school-leavers and university graduates; indeed, the contrast in educational level between the average career civil servant and the average politician was often marked, as many of the latter, through their involvement in the military struggles of the previous decades, had had little formal education.

Many of the young men who entered the civil service at the same time as Ken later became 'collaborators' in his 1950s economic crusade. Charles F. Murray, born in Dublin and educated at Synge Street CBS, was one whose career path paralleled Ken's own, as the latter recalls: 'Both our fathers lived for a time in County Down. We entered the civil service on the same day, in the lowest male grade, and were assigned to the same section. Both of us acquired a London University degree by private study. We became close colleagues. There was much in common in our upbringing, training and development.' Charlie Murray became Ken's principal 'collaborator' and his successor both as secretary of the Department of Finance and as governor of the Central Bank. While their relationship went through a somewhat confrontational period in the 1970s, during Ken's tenure at the Central Bank and Charlie Murray's at the Department of Finance, in relation to the monetary and fiscal policies being pursued by the government, even then they shared, as Ken acknowledged, the 'same anxieties and objectives' in respect of the management of the economy. Both received honorary doctorates from the National University of Ireland – and Ken 'had the pleasure as Chancellor' of conferring Murray's on him. Owen O'Neill also started out with him as one of the band of 'very junior civil servants' and became a lifelong friend. They shared a commendable youthful interest in charitable work: 'Freezing Sunday mornings in the early 1940s saw us both turning up on bicycles at Whitefriar Street Church to collect for the St Vincent de Paul Society at the early Masses from six a.m. onwards.'

Sports star, future Taoiseach and personal friend Jack Lynch, two years Ken's junior, joined the service in 1936, being appointed initially to the newly established Milk Board in Dublin. Much to the delight of his Cork hurling fans, however, he was subsequently transferred to the State Solicitor's office in Cork city, before embarking on a law degree at University College Cork. Lynch's brief experience of the civil service gave him, as a politician, an understanding of and an enduring respect for the organization. In his eyes, the high standards, conduct and dedication characteristic of the service were exemplified in the person of Ken Whitaker, on whom in 1990 the former Taoiseach bestowed the simple but ultimate accolade 'a good man and a real patriot'. Becoming his close confidant and adviser during the turbulent years of the 1960s and 1970s, Ken unobtrusively but determinedly, at times bluntly, advised and guided Jack Lynch, the safety and integrity of the state being his overriding aim. It is clear from the documentary record that their relationship transcended that of civil servant and politician, and their collaboration had a profound effect on the more recent economic and political history of Ireland. On a personal level, both men had an additional reason to be grateful to the civil service, in whose ranks they found their respective wives: Máirín O'Connor worked in the Department of Industry and Commerce, and Ken's future wife, Nora, in the Department of Education.

Some of Ken's colleagues were destined to attain fame outside the confines of a civil service career. From Anthony Trollope to the present day, the Irish civil service has provided opportunity and atmosphere conducive to the literary proclivities of its staff. In the 1930s one of the most controversial 'in-house' authors was undoubtedly the novelist, playwright and satirist Brian Ó Nualláin (O'Nolan). Born in Strabane, County Tyrone, and a graduate of University College Dublin, in 1935 he was appointed private secretary to the minister for local government. By any stretch of the imagination Ó Nualláin was hardly civil service material. The lack of a family fortune and the need to look after a large number of siblings saw him drafted, or drifting, into the service. The self-effacing ethos of the official environment rapidly came into conflict with Ó Nualláin's literary bent, much of which was of a satirical and political nature. No politician wished to be or indeed would tolerate being satirized in the national press – and especially not by a civil servant; thus his use of several famous pseudonyms – Flann O'Brien, Myles na gCopaleen, An Broc – to camouflage his identity as the author of biting, satirical, humorous, at times even manic articles and books which lampooned the country's every sacred cow from the government to the Irish language (in which he was fluent) to the 'plain people of Ireland'. But his identity was 'an open secret', Ken recalls. 'People in the civil service suspected him. I think there was a reaction of indulgent eyes to heaven, provided he didn't write something too outrageous. He did poke fun at the civil service but nobody took his satirical observations too seriously . . . He and I had some contact on a professional basis. I regarded him with a certain amount of caution . . . not wanting to feature in any of his entertaining satires' – and nor, he adds, with a twinkle, on reflection, would Ó Nualláin 'be the one I'd choose as a private secretary'.

The Civil Service Commission, in particular, perhaps because its duties were less demanding than those of more front-line departments, was a veritable nursery of literary talent. Among the writers who worked there at the time were Art Ó Riain ('Barra Ó Caochlaigh'), author of novels and short stories and pioneer of urban and science fiction in Irish; 'Fionn MacCumhaill', from the *fíor-Ghaeltacht* in Donegal, author of *Na Rosa Go Brách*, on the social life and customs of the Rosses; and the poet and translator Thomas Kinsella, who worked in the Department of Finance and to whom Ken later became mentor.

In 1981 Kinsella and his co-author, Seán Ó Túama, dedicated their landmark anthology *An Duanaire: Poems of the Dispossessed* to Ken, at whose instigation they undertook this momentous work. His support and encouragement of writers working in organizations under his leadership continued throughout his career, for which the present writer has reason to be grateful.

Ken's term as a clerical officer in the Civil Service Commission was destined to be short-lived. Barely six months into the job he was promoted to the grade of junior executive officer, the next rung on the male promotional ladder, and was sent 'on loan' away from the Commission – 'for fear I might get a glimpse of the examination papers in advance' – to the Department of Education on nearby Marlborough Street. It was to be a propitious move. He had been only a few months there when a further promotion, again as first candidate past the post, saw him assigned to the General Registry Section within the department, with a £30 increase in his annual salary. The Registry, where the post for the entire department was initially scrutinized, 'provided an overview of everything that was happening in all sections of the Department'. In Education he was to create another record, becoming at the age of twenty the youngest ever ministerial secretary, a step in his career he still recalls with bemusement. 'Writing official letters at that age . . . I still don't know how I got away with it!' Regardless of the subsequent records he created in his meteoric rise through the ranks of the civil service, it is this appointment that he considers the most unexpected and memorable.

The minister for education was Tomás Derrig, 'a placid easygoing man, a genuine father-figure' from Westport, County Mayo. Formerly headmaster of Ballina Technical College, he had impeccable Republican credentials, including participation in the occupation of the Four Courts in the Civil War; in the ensuing engagement he had lost an eye, and subsequently endured a forty-day hunger strike in Kilmainham Jail. The minister was perceptive enough to see the potential in the newest recruit to his department and, despite the latter's youth and inexperience, and in contravention of the seniority mentality that permeated promotional policy, had little hesitation in appointing Ken as his private secretary. It was 'an interesting but exacting job dealing with all the minister's correspondence, both in Irish and in English', and which also warranted a 'temporary and non-pensionable' addition of £50 per annum to his salary. Ken's proficiency in Irish stood him in good stead with his minister, Derrig being active in the drive to establish Irish as the principal language of the state. The futility of such a policy was not lost on the minister's young secretary.

While in Education, Ken experienced at first hand the effects of the byzantine array of internal regulations which permeated the working life of a civil servant. There were regulations on matters as disparate as timekeeping and economy in fuel and light; sick leave and smoking; civil servants and politics; use of the Irish language for official purposes; enlistment of civil servants in the Volunteer Reserve; civil servants and outside occupations; and procedures in relation to communication with the media. The allotment of an additional three days' annual leave to 'Mr T. K. Whitaker while serving as a Junior Executive Officer',[23] to compensate for his having been sent to superintend civil service examinations in County Monaghan, led to a flurry of 'semi-official' correspondence between the Departments of Finance and Education.

Ken was to spend almost two years in the Department of Education, a period with happy results in more ways than one, since it was there he met Nora Fogarty, a vivacious, practical young Dublin woman, who was a writing assistant in the teacher-training branch of the department. Educated in Loreto Convent on St Stephen's Green, Nora, almost three years Ken's senior, shared his interest in the Irish language, having spent summer holidays at Irish colleges in Connemara and Rannafast, although their paths did not cross at that time. Nora was born in Cornmarket in the old Liberties of Dublin. Her father, John Fogarty, had bought a public house at number 32 after taking early retirement from his job as a warder in St Ita's psychiatric hospital, Portrane, in north County Dublin. Ken and Nora's son, also named Ken, recalls as a child playing in the cellar of the old pub, known as Fogarty's, whose back wall 'was all that was left of the old Newgate prison'. Love blossomed in the Department of Education, or as Ken put it, tongue-in-cheek and somewhat less romantically, 'I found occasion to go to her office for files!' Principally because of financial necessity, their courtship was less than whirlwind. 'I remember bringing her to a céilidhe and old-time waltz on the bar of my bicycle as well as to the cinema.' It was not until 1941, when Ken's income allowed, that they eventually tied the knot; and under the 'marriage bar' then in operation, Nora was obliged to give up her job in the civil service.

While his initial period in the civil service resulted in two promotions in the space of two years and a record-making appointment as ministerial private secretary, Ken's interest in taking his education to the third level remained undimmed. 'I felt I was in danger of missing interest and reward if I ignored opportunities of advancing my education.' With no opportunity to pursue an external degree course in Ireland, London University offered the alternative of obtaining a degree by correspondence. 'The first time I entered a university was to deliver a lecture, not to hear one,' he muses. Choosing mathematics, Celtic studies and Latin, the last two more personal favourites than career-enhancing subjects, he renewed his studies; and in the summer of 1938 he travelled to London with his colleague Charlie Murray to sit the Bachelor of Arts examination. 'I remember that our pocket money was quickly exhausted, his through going to dances in Hammersmith and mine through frequenting the "gods" in theatres in Shaftesbury Avenue and Haymarket, so that we were both restricted in our second week to paying a few pence for seats at open-air concerts in London parks.' Their outlay was rewarded when both achieved honours degrees.

Ken's career continued on its upward trajectory. Emerging in first place from the competitive application for the post of assistant inspector of taxes, which involved a comprehensive written examination in Irish, English, history, mathematics and general knowledge, an interview, and an assessment of the candidate's 'judgement, zeal, accuracy, initiative, tact, conduct and personality', in October 1937 he transferred to the Dublin District Tax Office in O'Connell Street. It was preparation for this examination that introduced him, for the first time, to the subject that was to become his metier. 'I kind of came into economics sideways. Up to then I hadn't heard of it much before I found it was a subject for the Assistant Inspectors of Taxes examination. For six old pennies I could buy Penguin editions of Harold Laski, G. D. H. Cole and other Fabian socialist thinkers. They made very interesting reading for a young man,' he reflects, as did *General Theory of Employment, Interest and Money*, published in 1936 by the outstanding economist of the time, John Maynard Keynes.

From the start, economics appealed to Ken Whitaker as being 'more of an art than a science, something that deals with forces and tensions, rather than building blocks. It was more abstruse because you had to judge the force of certain elements that have an impact on society and see where you can most easily and with the least damage move things into a better place. I found it interesting because it related to everyday affairs and pressures.' Economics – especially for a civil servant – was, as the post-Keynesian economist George Shackle later wrote, 'a way of learning how to build and exhibit arguments on their own, to test and perhaps demolish those of others, to interpret and make sense of a complex mass of facts, to see through the casuistry of special pleaders and the verbiage of propagandists':[24] challenges that would preoccupy Ken Whitaker throughout his professional life.

His position as an assistant inspector of taxes was short-lived. Barely eight months in the office, and not yet 22 years old, in May 1938 Ken was promoted to the grade of junior administrative officer, having again come first in the examination. With a starting annual salary of £180, he was assigned to the Finance Division in the Department of Finance, a career move that was to be propitious not merely for himself, but for the country.

3

A Finance Man
1938–44

Whatever may be said of the part played by any of us as public servants, the good fellowship, the sense of shared duty and purpose, the willingness to work long hours, the team spirit which transcended hierarchical distinctions, created feelings of personal satisfaction and fulfilment which were more than adequate recompense for suffering, as Finance officials must, the slings and arrows of misunderstanding and criticism.

T. K. Whitaker[1]

HOW RELEVANT THE above sentiments are to the motivation of the modern-day Irish civil servant is open to speculation. To Ken Whitaker's generation, however, they reflect what was expected of anyone in the public service, especially 'a Finance Man' who viewed his role primarily as that of 'a trustee for the taxpayer'.[2] Such an ethos, to society's great disadvantage, may well be deemed somewhat anachronistic, even open to derision, in the all-pervasive, egotistical, entitled, 'I'm-worth-it', bonus-and-top-up-motivated mindset of modern-day Irish society.

The sense of belonging and responsibility experienced by the Department of Finance's new recruit on his arrival in the north block of Government Buildings on Merrion Street as a junior administrative officer on 1 June 1938 was to remain constant throughout his life. 'It warmed my heart as a new arrival to find that everyone was friendly and accessible, that an officers' mess atmosphere prevailed . . . Reaching the administrative grade in Finance, you felt you were on the golden route, at the heart of things.'[3] By reason of its controlling influence over other departments of state, the Department of Finance was regarded as the premier department, the Mecca for most aspiring career public servants. Divided into three divisions, Finance, Establishment and Supply, by 1938 it was still relatively small, with just some twenty-five officers occupying grades of assistant principal officer or above, all under the leadership of its legendary secretary, J. J. McElligott.

The principal functions of the department were laid down by the 1924 Ministers and Secretaries Act: 'The Department of Finance shall comprise the administration and business generally of the public finances of Saorstát Éireann and all powers, duties and functions connected with same.' This endowed it with a wide remit and authority. Ken later subscribed to this central controlling role of Finance and his belief that 'few great victories can be claimed in the long-drawn out fight for economic strength and stability but it is certain that more defeats are recorded where the Finance ministry is weak or subservient.'[4] At the time of his arrival in 1938, 'good housekeeping, living within your income', was, as he recalls, the essence of McElligott's economic policy and the annual 'balancing of the books' his prime objective. 'There was no consideration of the budget as an economic policy measure. It was all about balancing the public finance books. Government spending was regarded as a threatening influence. It would simply never have occurred to him [McElligott] that we should have run a deficit to, for example, improve employment or lift the economy. The idea of management via the budget would not have been an option to be considered. Like many at the time, to him the ideal situation was that the government played a minimum part, dealing with principles and guidelines.' Taken in the context of the time, that somewhat negative, pre-Keynesian outlook was understandable. It was not until the 1950s that what Ken describes as 'the McElligott–Brennan axis' in Finance was replaced by his more modern economic philosophy. 'The writings of Keynes had focused attention on demand management as a responsibility of good government. My assignment as an administrative officer to the Department of Finance meant studying how to manage total national spending so as to achieve full employment of available national resources of labour and capital, while avoiding excessive pressure on either' – an assignment that would eventually lead to a fundamental change of direction in Ireland's economic policy.

In the early and uncertain years of the first Free State government, the Department of Finance's staff of mainly British and British-trained Irish nationals fully employed the powers conferred on them and, in the process, often invoked accusations of being pro-British from nationalist quarters and ironically, of being anti-British from pro-British quarters. Unsurprisingly, given their training, the department's founders were, as historian Dr Ronan Fanning states in his authoritative history of the Department of Finance, 'wedded to the classic orthodoxies of British financial administration and to the full rigours of Treasury control'.[5] Their Republican background and credentials did not impinge on this attitude or on their professional work as civil servants. They did not subscribe to the more blinkered nationalistic assertion that everything British should be jettisoned by the new Irish state. On the contrary, in their pioneering determination to establish an independent, reputable and well-ordered administration, they embraced and promoted much of the ethos and procedures of their former British masters, which also conferred on the Department of Finance an ascendancy over other departments beyond its designated function. Mainly because of the ability and the revolutionary credentials of its senior officers and the confidence placed in them by their political brothers-in-arms, the control exercised by Finance over public economic policy in the early years of the new Free State was rarely challenged.

In 1932 Fianna Fáil came to power on an election manifesto that repudiated payment of land annuities (in effect a modern-day 'sovereign default', not uncommon during the period), espoused a protectionist policy geared towards economic self-sufficiency and a more interventionist role by the state, and proposed an inquiry into the rate of civil service pay. This policy platform was anathema to the likes of Brennan and McElligott, threatening as it did the established order of things. De Valera's subsequent 'economic war' with Britain further disrupted the relationship established with their British counterparts. But whatever government was in power and however far their policies might run counter to its ethos, the Department of Finance's control was sufficiently well established to withstand any undermining of its position as protector of financial orthodoxy. McElligott and his team were not for turning; as Dr Fanning records, the fact that 'the civil servants in the premier Government Department did not cut the coat of policy according to the political cloth of their new masters was a notable tribute to their integrity'.[6]

The minister for finance, Seán MacEntee, while more in tune than many of his colleagues with the approach of his departmental officials, did not enjoy a status at the cabinet table commensurate with his Finance portfolio. The main threat to the supremacy of Finance came from the Department of Industry and Commerce, under its dynamic and impatient minister Seán Lemass, an advocate not merely of protectionism, but of protectionism within a social context. Although senior to Lemass (both in years and in the formal cabinet hierarchy), MacEntee tended to be overshadowed and outmanoeuvred by his rival at the cabinet table. Nevertheless, many schemes and policies Lemass promoted were thwarted by the dispassionate, logical and, at times, scornful rebuttal of MacEntee's implacable departmental secretary, J. J. McElligott.

The struggle for supremacy between the two departments continued for many years, and was still being waged when Ken arrived in Finance in June 1938. At that point they were embroiled in a dispute over renewal of the Trade Loans Guarantee System, proposed by Industry and Commerce and objected to by Finance on the grounds that the system had failed to increase the volume of industrial activity in the previous five years. Such disputes between the two departments, as Ken later noted, were but a symptom of the divergence between 'the first Irish Government's desire to establish the standing of the State in the eyes of the world by observing a rather strict orthodoxy . . . in economic and financial matters when free trade was the accepted commercial philosophy of the day',[7] an ethos that appealed to MacEntee and McElligott, and 'the vigorous policy of protection and industrialisation' being promoted by Lemass in his desire to 'bring modernity to the nationalist idiom'.[8]

On the international front, the Department of Finance was engaged in talks with the Treasury in London on the land annuities question which, with war against Germany looming, was becoming an issue of some urgency to the British, anxious for a compromise in the long-standing dispute with their neighbour. McElligott's hard bargaining finally paid off when the British agreed to settle for a lump sum payment of £10 million – a substantial reduction on the £18.5 million owed. Deemed 'ransom money' by de Valera and a 'choice between two evils' by the British,[9] the sum was nevertheless paid in full by the Irish government in September 1938. While the annuity controversy did little to improve Anglo-Irish relations politically, it did not alter the mutual respect that existed between the principal officers in the Department of Finance and their counterparts in the Treasury. As Ken recalled, 'our relations were civilised, often friendly. Our mutual respect was deepened by competent and firm pursuit of our own interests, modified by a willingness in the end to see reason.'[10]

'Mr T. K. Whitaker, Junior Administrative Officer, assumed duty in the Department of Finance on 1/6/1938 and was assigned to the Finance division under Mr Bayne,'[11] his personal file in the Department of Finance notes. Assistant Principal A. W. Bayne, a Trinity graduate, Ken recalls as being 'eager and energetic'; his stoic attempts to pronounce Irish words in official correspondence evoked much mirth among his junior officers. His divisional boss was Assistant Secretary Arthur D. Codling, while at the top was the formidable figure of McElligott. Both these men were to play key roles in shaping Ken's life as a public servant. The veteran departmental secretary, who concealed his deep and genuine patriotism under a cover of sarcasm, was, as Ken recalls, 'a small, wiry man, remarkably tolerant of the cold and sharing only coffee and a bun with Brennan as a working lunch . . . this model of the austerity he preached . . . sat in his austere corner room in the Department of Finance, dressed in an alpaca coat, casting a cold eye on those who came to argue for more staff or bigger budgets.'[12] Later McElligott became more receptive to what must have appeared to him the radical, even revolutionary, economic policies propounded by his eventual successor. 'He might put on a mask of severity to say no . . . but if you pushed past his defences, you found he could be persuaded to yield to practical necessity.'[13] Codling, on the other hand, Ken found to be kindly and encouraging but meticulous. 'You could not chance your arm with Codling. He was rigorous, doctrinaire, a stickler for accuracy. When you lifted the phone and heard "Would you slip across please" in his Yorkshire accent, you wondered was it a wrong file number on the draft letter you had submitted for signature or something even worse.'[14] Codling was impressed by the division's most recent recruit, wondering 'if he [Ken] arrived at his conclusions by intuition or logic?'[15] The fearlessness and integrity McElligott exhibited in the administration of the country's finances, and Codling's requirement that any economic policy or recommendation emanating from the department be based on sound, meticulous and well-researched information, became touchstones for Ken's modus operandi during the course of his public service, as outlined in an internal memorandum from 1950.

> We must equip ourselves to pursue consistently a coherent and enlightened policy, based on reliable and well-sifted statistics and on a convincing analysis of the economic and financial situation . . . this must be followed up by a continuous review and we must be able to take the initiative in directing the Government's attention to the emergence of any undesirable consequences of its policy.[16]

The rigour of this approach is all the more remarkable in view of its apparent abandonment in more recent years. The older generation of Finance officers had, however, as Ken notes, little appreciation of the broader and long-term purpose and prospects of public expenditure. 'There was little sense of advancing the economic state of the country by anything you were doing in Finance. Your job was to cut down expense and put as little burden on state finances as possible.' It was this mentality in which he was to implement a radical change.

If Finance was rightly considered the premier department in the public service, the Finance Division within it, to which Ken was assigned, was undoubtedly its elite wing. The responsibilities and influence of the division were pervasive, not merely within the department itself, but throughout the public service. As well as preparing legislation and scrutinizing public expenditure, the Finance Division was also responsible for budgetary policy and taxation, matters that would assume even greater significance in the formulation of national economic and fiscal policy in the years to come. The definition of the function of an administrative officer in Finance, and one which Ken exemplified, was 'to think all round a subject and give Ministers their unbiased opinions on matters referred to them when policy is being considered and then, when policy has been decided on, to carry out that policy to the best of their ability, regardless of their personal views'.[17] One of the first tasks assigned to him was the preparation of an internal memorandum on the continuing controversy between the majority and the three minority reports emanating from the Commission of Inquiry into Banking, Currency and Credit, established by the government in 1934. Chaired by Joseph Brennan, chairman of the Currency Commission, and with J. J. McElligott among its members, the Commission's leisurely proceedings eventually concluded four years later. Without much enthusiasm, it recommended the eventual establishment of a central bank, the maintenance of the link between the Irish pound and sterling at the prevailing parity, restrictions on borrowing by the newly created semi-state bodies, such as the Agricultural and Industrial Credit Corporations, the ESB and the Irish Sugar Company, and closer financial scrutiny of government development proposals. In effect, the report's recommendations simply mirrored the current views and policy of the Department of Finance. These, however, were not shared by some members of the government, most notably Seán Lemass. Even Seán MacEntee was less than enthusiastic about the recommendations of the majority report.

Three minority reports, compiled by committee members who disagreed with the recommendations of the majority report, were issued at the same time, recommending more radical, socially oriented policies, invoking the admirable, albeit naive, sentiment that national economic policy should be made to fit human needs rather than being formulated according to the means available. One of the reports took Irish politicians to task for being 'hypnotised by British prestige and precedent and dominated by a British-trained Civil Service ... The Secretary of the Department of Finance was allowed to become the real ruler of Ireland and the urgent national need for reconstruction and expansion was cut down to fit his narrow vision.'[18] Recommendations from the Irish Trade Union Congress, advocating the nationalization of the state's banking system, rattled the orthodox bones of Brennan and McElligott. But such recommendations were garnering popular support, both inside and outside the Dáil.

In an attempt to kick the whole matter into touch, Seán MacEntee proposed that an analysis of the respective pros and cons of the majority and minority reports should be prepared for presentation to the government. The task was allocated to the Finance Division's most recent recruit. With a competence and understanding that belied both his youth and his lack of experience of such complex and controversial subjects, Ken eagerly set to and completed his summary of the majority report in record time. In relation to the minority report, which advocated the nationalization of the commercial banks, its proponents had failed to take into account, he noted, 'that Éire nationals ... might transfer their accounts to branches of banks outside Éire'; and he warned of an additional risk, one that has familiar reverberations, that 'it would also lead to an extension of the practice, understood to exist at present ... of keeping accounts outside Éire mainly for the purpose of Income Tax evasion'.[19] Marshalling arguments in support of the majority view of the commission's recommendations, showing a logic and sense of balance that were to become hallmarks of his future economic and financial analyses, he cautioned 'that the sponsors of such a revolutionary proposal must be able to prove that the existing system is defective in one or more essential respects and that such deficiencies would be cured by the proposed abolition of private ownership of banks ... From the standpoint of technical efficiency there is nothing in favour of making the banking system part of the civil service ... The vital objection to the proposal is, however, that it would create a monopoly of credit, placing the potential borrower completely at the mercy of a financial autocracy.'[20] Owing to his bosses' prevarication strategy, it was July 1939 before Ken's reports were brought before the government, which, in the event, decided that the more expedient course was to let the entire matter languish.

From a 22-year-old civil servant with less than five years' experience, such intuitive commentary was undoubtedly considered above par. His ability and work ethic in the Finance Division were already gaining him recognition. 'Mr Whitaker is shaping very well,' Arthur Codling attested in his first progress report. 'He is highly intelligent and shows promise of becoming an officer decidedly more than average.'[21] His work in the division was varied and interesting. 'My principal duty . . . was the critical examination of proposals for public expenditure and advising on budgetary policy.'[22] He was appointed to numerous interdepartmental committees, dealing with matters as diverse as the Irish-speaking Blasket Islands and the formulation of government white papers, and his expertise continued to expand.

The outbreak of the Second World War in September 1939 came as little surprise. 'We were perhaps better prepared for the war than the countries actually fighting in it,' Ken recalls, 'but it gave a physiological defence for all the difficult things the government had to do and it put the focus very firmly on the economy.' The resultant shortage of supplies caused a sharp rise in inflation, a rapid increase in the cost of living, the inevitable rationing and black marketeering and, later, a marked increase in infant mortality from tuberculosis. The worst effects of the tariff war with Britain had eased on the signing of an Anglo-Irish Agreement in April 1938, but de Valera's refusal of access to Irish ports by the British fleet, meanwhile, invoked additional retaliatory embargoes on essential imports.

To oversee the effective importation and distribution of supplies and services throughout the country during the 'Emergency', a new Department of Supplies was established, with Seán Lemass as minister. He and his departmental secretary

John Leydon proved a formidable team. The position endowed Lemass with an extraordinary degree of control over all aspects of the economy and over every department of state, including Finance. Seán MacEntee was moved from Finance to Industry and Commerce, to be replaced by Seán T. Ó Ceallaigh for the duration of the Emergency. Lemass's appointment to the cabinet Emergency Committee, headed by de Valera, with Ó Ceallaigh and Frank Aiken, further augmented his power and influence.

Ken's work in Finance brought him into contact with other departments seeking approval for their individual budgetary requirements. For a junior officer to have to make judgements on such requests was daunting, as he admits.

> I did not quite know how to deal with other Departments' proposals for expenditure. This ignorance I covered up by frequent use of high-sounding clichés about the critical position of the Exchequer and ominous references to the emotional state of the Minister who – as I represented and, perhaps, imagined him – never pleased nor satisfied, never convinced or even concerned, was always in a highly disturbed psychological condition![23]

During these initial years Ken Whitaker absorbed the salient lessons of what made a 'Finance Man': the checks and balances to prevent the unnecessary spending of public money; the inevitability and necessity of choice between competing demands – or, as he succinctly expressed it, the constant acknowledgement that

> nothing new can be undertaken except at the expense of some other possibility. Resources are not inexhaustible. There are, however, no limits to desires. There is no end to the number of things that can be said to be in the national interest. But there are definite and critical limits to the capacity and willingness of the

community to accept new burdens, as well as to the propriety of asking them to do so.[24]

One of Seán Lemass's less successful enterprises, to which Ken was assigned, exemplified these sentiments. Described by one historian as 'the most ineffective self-sufficiency and decentral-isation operation undertaken, an unsavoury example of Lemass's empire-building and a classic illustration of the problem of investment absolved from conventional economic criteria',[25] the establishment of a state company to extract industrial alcohol from potatoes was to prove an expensive failure. Ken was entrusted with the task of drafting the articles and memorandum of association for a company based on highly unreliable found-ations – relying for its viability on a constant supply of potatoes, at a time when open market prices were soaring far above the contract price. Ken saw the episode as a sharp lesson in the basic philosophy of supply and demand and the dictates of the market.

As the war continued, so his workload increased, with mem-bership of many interdepartmental committees established to regulate supply and price issues. In 1939 he was appointed to one such committee to investigate the price of sugar beet. Later in the same year, when the assistant principal of the division was tem-porarily seconded to another section, Ken took over most of his responsibilities as well his own, proving himself, as his superiors noted, 'equal to the anomalous situation . . . his work of consistently high standard . . . he has given complete satisfaction in its every aspect'.[26] In 1940, aged just twenty-four, he was appointed secretary of a committee to investigate the intro-duction of a children's allowances scheme, which gave rise to issues other than financial. First proposed by James Dillon in March 1939, the scheme was intended to supplement the income of agricultural labourers and small farmers whose interests were being neglected in the rush for industrialization. Ken had read the work of Eleanor F. Rathbone (wife of G. D. H. Cole and daughter of the British social reformer William Rathbone), an English MP and pioneer of a system of family allowances paid as a supplement to the income of the less well-off in Britain. The proposed Irish scheme was resisted by some members of the cabinet as being ethically and socially wrong, smacking of socialism, state intervention in the married life of Irish citizens and a disincentive to the poor to find work. Seán MacEntee, one of the main objectors, argued that it would also 'undermine parental authority, without which a peasant economy such as ours, based on the patriarchal principle, cannot exist'.[27] With both the minister and the secretary of the department hostile to the proposal, it required no little courage on the part of the two Finance officers, Ken and O. J. Redmond, to argue that, while employment with adequate wages might be the preferred objective, as matters stood 'we consider that family allowances should be adopted to mitigate the effect of one of the chief causes of poverty in the economic system'.[28] Despite their recommendation, which Seán Lemass endorsed, it was November 1943 before the scheme was eventually adopted and passed into law. An added recommendation, initiated by Ken, that a potentially embarrassing and cumbersome means-testing qualification could be avoided by cutting the income tax allowance for the better-off, was also adopted. The children's allowance episode served to exemplify the ideological gap that existed between the old nationalist rearguard in both government and the civil service, epitomized by de Valera, Ó Ceallaigh, MacEntee and McElligott, and the more modernizing practical nationalism espoused by the following generation of Fianna Fáil politicians and Finance officials, epitomized by Seán Lemass and Ken Whitaker.

Ken's work on the Family Allowance Committee did not go unnoticed. 'The members of the Committee, one and all, highly appreciate the industry and efficiency he displayed and the generous assistance he gave them at all times . . . and in reading voluminous published material.' In addition, Ken penned the first draft report, amended the many subsequent drafts and took the minutes at thirty-seven committee meetings, 'many of which extended well into the evening, involving more than 260 hours, all outside his ordinary office hours'.[29] In recognition of this devotion to duty, the committee recommended a gratuity of £70 as 'not being unreasonable'; it was reduced to £50 by his parsimonious boss, J. J. McElligott.

Notwithstanding his onerous workload at the department, combined with evening study, Ken's personal attention remained firmly fixed on the attractions of Nora Fogarty in the Department of Education. Ken and Nora were married on 6 August 1941 in the Church of St Audeon's High Street in the old Liberties, with one of Ken's boyhood friends from Drogheda and fellow civil servant, Patrick (Paddy) J. Doyle, as best man and Nora's sister, Mary-Jo, as bridesmaid. Because of wartime travel restrictions, the church ceremony and wedding breakfast at the nearby Clarence Hotel were held at an 'ungodly' hour in the morning, to enable the newlyweds to catch the 7.30 a.m. train to Galway. From there they were driven to Ashford Castle on the shores of Lough Corrib, one of Ireland's premier hotels, for which, as Ken recalls, 'I had scrimped and saved'. Ashford too had been affected by the war and, in the absence of its customary pre-war clientele of high-spending foreign visitors, was happy to open its doors to Irish customers 'for nine guineas per head per week'. In its fairy-tale surroundings the young couple celebrated their first week of married life, before moving on to Connemara to stay with the Benedictine nuns at Kylemore Abbey, in term time a renowned girls' boarding school that over the summer was open to paying guests. Ken had previously stayed there during a summer cycling break in Connemara. Hoping to spend a few days at nearby Renvyle House, they set out from Kylemore by pony and trap, Nora at the reins, owing to Ken's unease that the skittish pony was about to ditch its live cargo. On entering the avenue leading to Renvyle House, then owned by the writer and wit Oliver St John

Gogarty, they came upon a middle-aged, blond-haired woman whom they recognized as none other than the Irish prima donna Margaret Burke Sheridan, star of the stages of La Scala and Covent Garden, then enduring a less glamorous retirement in Ireland. 'We told her we were on our honeymoon and intended to spend a few days at Renvyle. Oh, she said, don't think of it. Find some excuses and go elsewhere. It's deadly dull here!' Following the famous soprano's advice, the young honeymooners duly returned to the nuns at Kylemore.

Back in Dublin, the couple initially rented a house on Whitehall Road in the southern suburb of Rathfarnham, before eventually purchasing their first house on Kimmage Road West, Terenure. Their first-born son, Kenneth Oliver (named after Drogheda's Oliver Plunkett), was born in 1943, to be followed by Gerald (1945), Raymond (1947), David (1948), Catherine (1950) and Brian (1952). As for most homes in Ireland during the war years, life in the Whitaker household followed a distinct and regular pattern. Wartime shortages resulted in the rationing of almost every commodity. Tea, the country's national beverage, was restricted to half an ounce per week per person, resulting in the recycling of tea leaves. Many everyday grocery items disappeared from shop shelves altogether. Petrol restrictions meant cycling or walking to and from work, while the 'glimmerman' became the *bête noire* of every gas-burning household. The cutting of turf from public plots in Glencree in the Wicklow Mountains and, as Ken recalls, 'carrying the knobbly bags full of turf the half mile over the bog to the roadside', was an energetic if economical task on summer weekends. 'While it was, up to then, something outside my experience, at least it put some realism into what I was thinking about at work regarding wartime economies!' The precious fuel, 'representing your blood sweat and tears', was used sparingly in the household.

By 1943 economics had become more than just an interest for Ken Whitaker; it was the means by which he would make his way by further advancement and promotion within the civil service. His interest in the subject was wholehearted, notwithstanding his view that 'many of the practitioners of the dismal science of economics love to wallow in misery. Like chameleons they take on the colour of their environment – they expect the sunshine to last or the bad weather to persist ... Some of course retain their natural frog-like condition and, when prodded, jump agilely in various directions.'[30] At the time of his marriage he had started further study towards a BSc (Economics) degree, again by correspondence as an external student of London University, for which, as he recalled, 'I remember writing essays at night while rocking our first-born to sleep'. Unable, because of the war, to travel to London in 1944, he sat the examination in Belfast, and duly attained an honours degree. 'It required staying overnight and I recall the sense of nervousness, wondering if there might be a blitz during the night.' While some bombs did hit the city, he escaped unscathed. He credited Frank Aiken, his future boss at the Department of Finance, as well as his colleague and friend Dr Brendan Menton, for 'keeping me at my studies' and encouraging him to continue to work as an external student towards an MSc (Economics), which he was duly awarded, again by London University, in 1952.

His belief that public servants, especially those in senior positions, should 'be as well-versed in economics and other relevant disciplines as university lecturers'[31] resulted in the establishment of a scholarship system for third-level education throughout the public service. Unhappy with the quality of courses available in Irish universities, he personally intervened to have the courses restructured to meet modern requirements. Noting firmly his concern that, as he later put it, 'the acute needs of the public service for people with top qualifications in economics with a mathematical approach are nowhere in sight of being satisfied,'[32] he urged the university authorities to introduce 'a fully integrated series of courses on mathematics, statistics and econometrics, with applications to practical problems', from which, he maintained, students would gain more value than those being taught 'in isolation and in a rather abstract fashion'. To expedite the formulation of such courses, he forwarded his own 'suggested syllabus',[33] much of which was subsequently adopted.

His influence and his belief that 'the variety and difficulty of administrative problems have so increased, and the tools and techniques for solving them have so developed, as to render administration more than ever a science', led eventually, in 1957, to the establishment of the Institute of Public Administration (IPA), catering exclusively for the educational, research, training and development needs of public servants. Over the decades the institute developed and adapted its services to cater for the professional requirements of the public sector. In 2001, much to Ken's delight, it received recognized college status within the National University of Ireland; and in 2004 the IPA honoured Ireland's 'most respected and inspirational public servant' by naming its new school in his honour. Today, the Whitaker School of Government and Management ensures the continued pursuit of his objective to 'provide a platform for the further professional development of the public service'.[34]

No one exemplifies better than himself Ken Whitaker's conviction that education should be a constant and unending journey. In the 1950s, in order 'to be better able to participate and contribute at international meetings', he attended conversation classes at the Alliance Française while also, as governor of the Central Bank, making time to take part in a series of seminars at Trinity College to keep abreast of the innovative mathematical topics being introduced in economic literature. From learning Scots Gaelic in his eighties to an immersion in the mysteries of modern scientific philosophy in his nineties, that quest continues.

Back in 1943, his work in the Department of Finance and his educational achievements did not go unrewarded. At the age of twenty-seven, he was promoted to principal officer (acting) with a starting salary of £550 per annum, more than doubling his previous basic pay of £260 per annum. One stipulation in the terms of his appointment, however, was later to prove problematic. Since his promotion was in an 'acting' capacity, future promotion, it was deemed, would be based on the level he had attained as a junior administrative officer, rather than on his new position, thereby placing him down the line in seniority. His immediate boss was G. P. S. Hogan, known, as Ken affectionately remembers, as 'Galloping Patrick Sarsfield Hogan ... you'd imagine him arriving on horseback like his famous historic namesakes.' An honours graduate and barrister, and a dedicated aficionado of Irish rugby, Gabriel Patrick Sarsfield Hogan was one of the first two graduates assigned to the Department of Finance in 1923, and was private secretary to the first minister for finance, Ernest Blythe. 'I held him in great respect and affection,' Ken recalls of his superior: 'respect for his outstanding ability, his clear mind and total dedication to public service and affection as a most likeable man of good humour, good sense and unfailing kindness.'

With the exception of random bombing incursions and the inconveniences caused by shortages, travel restrictions and rationing, the life of the average Irish citizen, isolated by the country's neutrality from the horrific effects of war, was little affected by the Emergency. The overriding priority of the public service during what Ken describes as the 'arid years' of the war was once more the economic survival of the Free State – an objective that chimed with the orthodoxy espoused by McElligott and his senior colleagues in Finance. Their preferred policy of frugality and stability was readily accepted by the government, underpinning as it did de Valera's own vision, as delivered in his famous 'Crossroads' speech of St Patrick's Day 1943. While Irish industry stagnated, the war brought other opportunities. Agricultural output showed a marked increase, fuelled by the official policy of compulsory tillage. Despite logistical problems and the risk of attacks on shipping, exports of live animals and meat to Britain grew. Fears of mass unemployment were not realized, owing mainly to emigration, as thousands of mostly rural-based men and women, attracted by the inflated wages available in manpower-strapped British factories, left the country. Emigration served a dual purpose: it benefited the Irish economy by decreasing the number of people dependent on it, while emigrants' remittances served to swell the coffers of the Irish exchequer.

As the war years continued, Ken's workload became ever more demanding. As well as his day-to-day work in Finance and his contributions to interdepartmental committees in policies as diverse as the future of the inland fisheries and the development of the Gaeltacht areas, he was also required to sit on interview panels for the Civil Service Commission and, in 1943, to serve for a period in the Department of Industry and Commerce to imple-ment the long-promised Family Allowance Scheme. All these demands contributed to his growing experience and expertise; but eventually he was forced to ask his minister to intervene, citing 'the official demands on my time, which are already heavy'. The minister took the point, stipulating that, in future, 'Mr Whitaker will not be available, owing to pressure of work, to act on the Board as desired by your Commissioners.'[35]

One task in Ken's Finance career during the war years, with more glamorous connotations than most civil service jobs, was in connection with the so-called 'Russian Crown Jewels Affair'. The jewels concerned, thought to have been appropriated from a Russian noble, had supposedly been given to de Valera's special envoy Harry Boland TD by a Russian government agent in New York in 1920 as security for a loan of $20,000 from the proceeds of Irish Republican bonds, issued in the United States by the first Dáil. The jewels were subsequently brought back from America by Boland and handed over to Michael Collins, then minister for finance, who deposited them in the department's safe, where they had lain ever since. After the Second World War John Dulanty, Ireland's high commissioner in London, was approached by a representative of the Russian government with an offer to redeem the jewels and repay the initial loan. Ken was summoned by J. J. McElligott to his office to witness the formal removal of the jewels from the safe. 'I expected to be blinded by the sparkle of diamonds on beautiful tiaras, but was disappointed to find a rather lack-lustre clump of objects which I recall as being mostly brooches, chains and crystal pendants, no gold, the silver blackened.'[36] On his recommendation, the cache was sent for valuation to Weir's jewellers in Grafton Street. 'We were not surprised to find that their intrinsic value was below the $20,000 owed: so the jewels were despatched to Dulanty; no claim was made for interest and the Russian cheque was lodged to the exchequer.'[37]

The war in Europe came to an end with the surrender of Germany in May 1945. Despite the industrial stagnation, shortages and rationing that marked the Emergency, as Ken later noted, 'Ireland came through the Second World War with an aggregate of £16 million in current budget deficits, a sum which would last barely a week at our recent rate of deficit financing!'[38] It was a remarkable achievement but one not destined to be repeated.

4

Public Servant
1945–56

*Expansionist ideas, however admirable, which involve adding to the public
debt and to future taxation, are completely out of touch with the reality of
the present financial situation.*

T. K. Whitaker[1]

WHILE ESCAPING THE devastation wrought in parts of Britain and
continental Europe, Ireland after the war languished in
stagnation, weariness and a yearning for an end to austerity.
Emigration continued unabated and the high wages earned by Irish
emigrants in Britain fuelled not merely the state coffers but similar
expectations among their compatriots at home. Irish neutrality
came at a price: supplies of the raw materials essential to sustain
agriculture and fuel economic growth, such as oil, coal and
fertilizers, were hard to come by. But there were some
positive aspects to the post-war scene. During the war the country's
external assets soared, and the future for agricultural exports looked
positive. Young minds, like Ken Whitaker and others such as Patrick
(Paddy) Lynch, who joined the Department of Finance in 1941,
were in tune with, indeed infused with, the spirit of change which
began to sweep away the debris and dust from war-torn Europe.
Quietly but determinedly they brought a new embryonic vision of
Ireland's future into public consciousness and debate.

Enthused by the 1944 British white paper on employment policy and the Beveridge Report of two years earlier (a seminal document which proposed widespread economic and social reforms to deal with what it identified as the five evils in society – squalor, ignorance, want, idleness and disease, and which eventually led to the foundation of the welfare state), Ken Whitaker and his colleagues set their thoughts on how best such policies might be applied in Ireland. The only 'suitably discreet forum', as Ken recalls, in which public servants of that time could air their views was the Statistical and Social Inquiry Society of Ireland. At a discussion on employment at the society's meeting on 27 April 1945, Ken and Paddy Lynch took the opportunity to expand their then revolutionary proposals. The long-term philosophy governing Department of Finance thinking, that of 'the Gladstonian ideal of a budget which was both balanced and as small as possible', had, Ken told his audience, 'gone by the board'.[2] It was now both acceptable and desirable to have unbalanced budgets to deal with periods of specific necessity. In the post-war world, he maintained, unemployment was now the greatest evil, greater than inflation, and coordinated government intervention was necessary to alleviate it, even if that entailed increased public expenditure. Demand was an unstable quantity, and government budgetary intervention was necessary to maintain and stabilize it. The time had come to shake off the rigid straitjacket of economic orthodoxy and embrace, albeit with due prudence, the new economic credo. But under a Fianna Fáil government, which had already been in power for fourteen years, led by an iconic figure who, as Ken somewhat generously notes, 'regarded economic matters as an inferior discipline . . . other things mattered more'; and a Department of Finance wedded to the status quo economic policy espoused by its cautious mandarin, change was destined to come 'dropping slow'.

This new post-war thinking was, however, beginning to percolate among individual holders of political office. In 1945, following the elevation of Seán T. Ó Ceallaigh to the presidency, Frank Aiken, former minister for coordination of defensive measures during the Emergency, was appointed minister for finance. He was the first departmental minister with whom Ken established a close working relationship. Aiken encouraged the talents of the young civil servant and, in the view of some of Ken's colleagues, was instrumental in his continuing and spectacular rise through the ranks. Representing Ken's 'home' county, Louth, Aiken was, as Ken attests, 'a most upright man, an innovator, untiring idealist, activist and reformer and was most likeable'. Well read in economics, Aiken was fascinated by social credit theories and the 'cheap money' regime being pursued by Britain's Labour chancellor of the exchequer, Hugh Dalton, to finance post-war reconstruction in Britain by forcing down bank interest rates. Dogged and inquisitive, he brought a new and determined attitude to his ministry. Alarmed at the appointment of such a proactive minister and, as Ken muses, 'no doubt in the hope of diverting him from the extremes of heterodoxy', McElligott assigned him as personal adviser to Aiken on the less contentious subject of monetary theory. Offering him un-restricted access to his minister, a rare privilege for a 28-year-old assistant principal officer, the assignment marked the beginning, as one of Ken's colleagues remarked, 'of the period when his [Ken's] influence within the Department became increasingly pronounced'.[3]

Aiken and his young assistant studied the methods employed by the western powers to finance their war effort. Of special interest was Dalton's low-interest policy and whether cheap bank credit could also be made available in Ireland. In a series of meet-ings with the Irish banks, Ken recalled how Aiken's demands 'were first met with incredulity: how could they lend for less than they paid their depositors, the bankers asked? Aiken would get annoyed with them and, at one particularly tedious meeting, I remember him pulling out a drawer in his desk and putting in his hand. I thought he was reaching for a gun!'[4] But some bank directors, like Lord Glenavy and Patrick Bourke, understood the minister's case (and its limitations), and an accommodation was eventually reached when they agreed to finance the exchequer's short-term requirements at a relatively low interest rate.

The minister and his assistant, as students of the new economic credo, assessed trends in imbalances in international payments. 'Aiken was prepared to listen but was not easily daunted or persuaded,' Ken recalls. 'It was best to acknowledge first the good points of any idea he put forward and introduce the caveats only tentatively and gradually. He pondered these in silence for extended periods, trying to neutralize them. There was a map of the world in his room, in one corner of which the heights of the highest peaks were recorded; in time I got to know these by heart. Keeping ahead of a ceaselessly inquisitive minister by attentive reading of economic and banking journals was, for me, excellent training' – and also led to a further promotion to the grade of principal officer.

Though the years 1947 to 1950 were plagued by commodity scarcities, a dollar shortage, sterling devaluation and the inflationary effects of the Korean War, 'the yeast of new thinking', as Ken notes, was also at work. In Frank Aiken's budget of 1946, a Transition Development Fund of £5 million as a 'voted service', financed by borrowing, to fund the new semi-state enterprises charged with development in the electricity, telephone, turf and tourism sectors, made the first major break with tradition and paved the way for the more comprehensive classification of 'voted capital services', introduced in 1950. In his advisory role to the minister, Ken's work included research on a diverse range of topics, from international interest rate policies, the 'unduly low' interest rates being offered through Irish savings certificates and the Post Office Savings Bank, the availability of goods and money in circulation in Ireland and its effect on the economy and unemployment, income tax rates, United States dollar expenditure, the European Recovery Programme (a US-sponsored financial scheme for the regeneration of the economy of post-war Europe) and the 1947 balance of payments to a report on 'prices and rations of certain foods in Ireland and England'.[5]

Ken's reputation was also beginning to win him an international audience. In September 1947 his first foray into print, *Financing by Credit Creation*, was published. 'Mr Whitaker has written that very rare thing in monetary debate – an account of what has actually happened,'[6] wrote the British Conservative MP Christopher Hollis, and press reviews were equally complimentary. The study examined the manner in which bank credit had been used by the British and American governments to finance wartime expenditure and its relevance in peacetime as an instrument of a policy of full employment, especially in the light of the 'cheap money' policy being pursued by the British government. In the clear and succinct style that became the hallmark of his official writing, Ken analysed both the advantages and the risks involved in credit creation, particularly in relation to inflation, seen as a negative by-product of this approach to financing under certain conditions. The book's final sentence reflected the sentiments that were to drive his later national economic policies and which, sadly, seem to have been forgotten by his successors in more recent times, to the detriment of the economic well-being of the country. 'Always in the background is the danger that the attractiveness of credit creation as a source of finance and the tendency to make concessions to public impatience with restrictions and controls may lead to such an expansion of expenditure as will upset rather than promote economic stability.'[7]

In 1949 Ken was invited to read his paper 'Ireland's External Assets' to the Statistical and Social Inquiry Society of Ireland. Addressing a subject of intense interest in Ireland at the time – an interest fuelled by calls from some politicians for the 'repatriation' of sterling assets in the light of post-war international economic and financial developments – it was hailed as 'a masterly paper' by the Society's president, Professor Roy Geary.

The Bretton Woods Agreement, signed in July 1944, set out to reshape the world's financial system in the wake of the war and led to the establishment of two international bodies: the International Monetary Fund (IMF), which sought to enforce a set of fixed exchange rates across the world, linked to the US dollar; and the International Bank for Reconstruction and Development (IBRD), later the World Bank, which made available long-term loans to facilitate the rebuilding of economies disrupted or destroyed by the war. The inaugural meetings of both bodies took place in Savannah, Georgia, in March 1946. Ireland did not initially seek membership of either organization. Anxious to dilute American international influence and to strengthen the sterling area's representation in the IMF, Britain urged the Irish government to rethink its position, particularly in relation to the IMF, and in June 1946 the Treasury sent the Irish-born Ernest Rowe-Dutton to Dublin to press the British case with the Department of Finance. That September, in a memorandum to the government entitled 'The Balancing of International Payments', Ken succinctly outlined the pros and cons facing Ireland. Given the realities of the current situation, he pointed out, with Ireland's trade almost exclusively with Britain, and its currency linked to sterling (97 per cent of Ireland's external assets were then in sterling), there appeared to be little advantage in joining either organization. The government accordingly remained, for the present, unresponsive to British pressure to change its stance.

Ken's international contacts were further extended through meeting the noted Canadian economist Louis Rasminsky, governor of the Bank of Canada and executive director of the IMF and World Bank, with whom he corresponded over a number of years on issues relating to Ireland and its future relationship with the IMF. It was perhaps fitting that ten years later, in his capacity as secretary of the Department of Finance, it was Ken who successfully negotiated Ireland's membership of the IMF – an institution which, fifty years on, would play a vital role in Ireland's economic and financial survival. On the question of membership of the IBRD, he maintained his opinion that he did not see any immediate necessity for this, unless 'it were proposed to use the Bank as a channel for the distribution of any United States assistance to Europe under the Marshall Plan',[8] until 1957, when he negotiated terms for Ireland's membership of the IBRD's successor, the World Bank. The reluctance of those in power in post-war Ireland to join international bodies such as the IMF and IBRD and, in 1949, the North Atlantic Treaty Organization (NATO), and their ambivalence towards securing a share of Marshall Aid funding to finance economic recovery, was in part symptomatic of the conservatism, isolationism and suspicion, as well as the culture of protectionism, that permeated Irish political and economic attitudes. It also stemmed from more practical realities, such as the Free State's continued dependence on the British market and its reluctance to look beyond the safety net of sterling.

Nevertheless, amid such entrenched establishment attitudes, sparks of more open thinking were beginning to glow. As well as Frank Aiken at Finance, it was perhaps not surprising, given his experience as minister of supply during the Emergency, that it should be Seán Lemass who would reassess the policy of indiscriminate industrial protection pursued in the pre-war years. As Ken acknowledged, 'he was too intelligent a man not to learn from experience and too patriotic to neglect any lessons relevant to the long-term development of the Irish economy'.[9] The 1947 Industrial Efficiency and Prices Bill represented, he believes, 'a watershed in Lemass's thinking', setting out to remedy the deficiencies and inefficiencies of Irish industry. Although its innovative mixture of 'carrot and stick, for those infant industries loath to grow up' was never implemented, owing to the change of government in 1948, it was, as Ken noted, 'a precursor of the more comprehensive measures of industrial survey, tripartite consultative and advisory machinery, grants for modernisation and adaptation, and even unilateral reduction of protection'[10] which eventually marked Ireland's full progression from protectionism to free trade, a journey led and directed by Ken Whitaker.

Even the Roman Catholic bishops, often considered protectors of the status quo, were by 1947 clamouring for change. They attacked the gross inadequacies of the health services, criticized state bureaucracy and also, in the process, demonized Irish civil servants as 'timorous, indecisive and procrastinating shirkers of responsibility, cowering behind a barrier of official anonymity'.[11] In these post-war years such demands and criticisms, whether from within or outside the government or public service, were random and individualistic. A prototype plan to encompass these tentative urges for change would have to wait for another decade.

On the political front, by 1947, like most parties too long in power, Fianna Fáil had become conservative and complacent. The economy of post-war Ireland was the weakest of all the countries not directly involved in the conflict. 'The results could be seen in slum, dole queue and emigrant ship.'[12] Fianna Fáil's much vaunted house-building programme had all but ceased. Unemployment was rising, wages were stagnant, and health services, especially in containing the scourge of tuberculosis, inadequate. At the top echelons of the Department of Finance, the government's complacency was reflected in pessimism and a dogged resistance to change. Such pervasive conservatism kept in check proponents of an alternative course of action. 'Seán Lemass and Ken Whitaker were both hobbled by the same political fetters: the need to hasten slowly to avoid the antagonism of more powerful peers.'[13] The constant quest for balanced books continued as the only plausible option. The 1947 Arctic freeze, gripping Ireland in blizzards and snowdrifts from January until

March, brought additional misery in the form of deaths, shortages and restrictions, followed by a severe supplementary budget, trade union unrest and the taint of political scandal surrounding the sale of Locke's distillery in County Westmeath, all of which heralded the death-knell for the Fianna Fáil government.

More radical and attractive policies were offered by a new party, Clann na Poblachta. Founded by the French-born lawyer and republican activist Seán MacBride, the son of Maud Gonne and Major John MacBride, whose nationalist credentials were as valid as those in power whom he sought to replace, the party caught the public imagination, as it did their votes in the February 1948 election. In what must surely have been one of the unlikeliest of coalitions, incorporating every available shade of political opinion, Republican Clann na Poblachta joined ranks with Fine Gael, Clann na Talmhan (a farmers' party), National Labour and an assortment of independents, the only apparent common denominator between these disparate participants being an intense antipathy to de Valera and Fianna Fáil. The ensuing interparty government divided the election spoils. Fine Gael's John A. Costello was appointed a somewhat reluctant Taoiseach in place of party leader Richard Mulcahy, whose controversial Civil War record was deemed to be a step too far for Clann na Poblachta. Ken recalled Costello as 'possessing a good lawyer's mind. He always struck me as being quick on the uptake and firm in his policy judgements.' William Norton of Labour became Tánaiste and minister for social welfare and Seán MacBride minister for external affairs, while Patrick McGilligan was appointed minister for finance. The appointment of Paddy Lynch, assistant principal officer in the Department of Finance, as economic adviser to the new Taoiseach signified for the first time in the brief history of the state the emergence of an alternative economic policy; and, as Ken acknowledges, Lynch was 'very helpful in getting Costello to appreciate in terms of economics what was possible', as was Alexis Fitzgerald, Costello's son-in-law.

Such an amalgam of political ideologies, interparty antagonisms and political and personal rivalries exacerbated the more mundane differences already existing between the Department of Finance and the spending departments, presenting a new challenge to the former's authority and control. Ever wary and tenacious, J. J. McElligott girded his loins for a battle royal with his new political masters. While the minister for agriculture in the interparty government, James Dillon, might well claim in the Dáil that 'no appeal to financial rectitude will induce this government to purchase a reputation untarnished in a financier's estimate by the expenditure of the life of a single child,'[14] to the old guard, both at Finance and at the Central Bank, which had replaced the Currency Commission in 1943, the stark economic realities remained unchanged. Well might McElligott and Joseph Brennan wonder from where the money was to come to underwrite such costly, albeit socially admirable, aspirations.

As diverse views on the economy were propounded by the various strands in the government, the sense of exasperation among those in command in the public service was palpable. 'The Central Bank', its governor Joseph Brennan stated, 'was anxious to understand what the monetary policy of the Government was – they were bewildered by reading the various speeches of Ministers.'[15] It is not hard to understand his sense of bewilderment. For in the new coalition there were not one but two de facto ministers for finance, between whose divergent policies and objectives the department was entrapped. While Seán MacBride may have been given the brief of external affairs, his penchant for intervening in economic and financial policy caused consternation and confusion in both government and civil service. Ambitious, acerbic and Anglophobic, MacBride was also suspicious and distrustful of civil servants in general, even attempting to have them excluded from regular cabinet meetings, and vented much of his spleen on the policies and advice forthcoming from officials in Finance. 'You never quite knew where you stood with MacBride,' recalls Ken, who on many occasions was called before the minister 'to answer, as best I could, his queries about various policy matters. He certainly had brains and willpower but I was always a bit wary of him. He was . . . stealthy. There was always a sort of veil . . . something hidden, and also a studied consciousness on his part of some sense of inherited patriotism.'

Even before Seán MacBride's appointment, however, the Department of External Affairs, under its energetic secretary F. H. Boland, the son of H. P. Boland (former head of the Establishment Division of Finance), had begun to nibble at functions and responsibilities considered the traditional preserve of Finance. International affairs, such as the Marshall Plan, Ireland's proposed membership of various international monetary bodies, and conferences on trade and sterling issues with Britain, were being encroached upon by External Affairs; and MacBride's arrival intensified that interference. 'The task ahead which faces this country now', he told an audience in University College Cork, 'is to reverse the disastrous economic policy which has been pursued since 1921 and to establish our economic independence as well as our political independence.'[16]

While such sentiments might well be privately espoused by up-and-coming policy-makers like Ken Whitaker, it was the methods by which MacBride wished to pursue them, as well as the timing of their expression, that posed the problem. Nor was MacBride the only one making such criticisms of the Department of Finance. An unsigned letter from a cabinet colleague in Patrick McGilligan's papers referred to the department as an 'intolerable octopus', whose control over other departments was such that they had to spend their time 'composing lies' in the hope of extracting money from it. The Central Bank, 'the wailing banshee of Foster Place', was similarly castigated by James Dillon, who accused it of reaching 'the nadir of its paradoxical gloom' and of having 'the wisdom which should test the capacity of the deepest saucer'.[17] Joseph Brennan and J. J. McElligott were hauled before the usually mild-mannered John A. Costello for promoting 'a tone and tendency contrary to Government policy'.[18] Neither the Department of Finance nor the Central Bank, however, succumbed easily to the slings and arrows hurled at them by the new political regime. McElligott and Brennan were too long in the tooth and too rooted in their role as 'watchdogs of public finance' to be unduly stirred or shaken.[19] Politicians would come and go, and their populist but often economically unsound policies with them; the Department of Finance and the Central Bank would continue to prevail long after their demise. 'I felt sorry for McElligott,' Ken reflected, 'confronted with all these different aspirations and how to pay for them.' And he notes, in one of his rare comments on the more recent financial debacle: 'Sadly, it is a question that can be asked again in more recent times.' The division of powers and functions between the Department of Finance and the Central Bank in determining economic and monetary policy was a grey area, dependent on the status and courage and, to a degree, on the personality of the individuals at the helm in the two institutions. In 1949 McElligott and Brennan, both men of stature and courage, were not for turning – any more than their successor Ken Whitaker would prove.

In the late 1940s, young public servants like Ken Whitaker and Paddy Lynch were on the cusp of the transition between the stern economic orthodoxy of their elders and the more expansionary doctrine being promoted by a new generation of economists. 'You could not deal brashly or contemptuously with the ethos propounded by McElligott,' Ken notes, 'but you did realize that it emanated from a much more controlled, strictly "ten commandments" type of thinking, while we took a more humanistic view which, I think, was one of the strengths of the new economic thinking. You had to get used to the idea that borrowing was not a sin, if it contributed to permanent national improvement. But on the other hand, it was quite easy to move from being pro-Keynesian to becoming pro-borrowing for everything ... it had to be qualified ... balanced.' Because of his training and background as a 'Finance Man', the skin of economic orthodoxy was not easily sloughed, and there was to be no Damascene conversion to expansionism for Ken Whitaker, but rather a steady and measured advance towards an alternative way. Paddy Lynch, on the other hand, emanating from the more rarefied and theoretical background of the university campus, Ken remembers as 'being more Keynesian than I was at that time ... My own position was that I was on the side of the Keynesians more than on the side of Adam Smith ... but neither was I a martyr for the cause! Because being a Finance Man places you in a more critical role. There was nothing miraculous about it, but simply that money was always scarce and every new scheme had to be paid for by the taxpayer. Money simply did not spring up like mushrooms!'

While imbued with that sense of public duty and responsibility, at the same time, as Ken acknowledged, public servants had also to operate within the prevailing political reality. 'We were always conscious that, after all, we were working under whatever particular political party was in government and I suppose you felt that it would make no sense to be opposed in your own recommendations to what the party's manifesto had promised. You had to pay attention to the political reality and recognize that, while you might be an economist, you were a particular type of economist, one involved in public policy, even though there were aspects of that which at times did not yield easily to economic measurement.'

There was much in the economic policies promoted by the interparty government that required such an approach. One of the first acts of the new administration was to abolish the taxes imposed by the previous government's supplementary budget. The new government viewed the net surplus of external assets, accumulated during the war years, as an opportunity to expand fiscal policy to include state financing of a capital programme. Such thinking rang the dual alarm bells in Finance of inflationary pressure and potential balance of payments trouble, prompting McElligott to commission an assessment for the government of the economic realities within which future financial policy should be framed. The task was entrusted to Ken, whose 39-page brief was detailed, meticulously researched, wide-ranging and hard-hitting. It covered an array of issues, from current and capital expenditure, realization of sterling assets and the use of American loan counterpart funds (for which he had been appointed one of the designated signatories) to taxation. While the Taoiseach praised it as 'a useful and informative document', with an eye perhaps to the stability of his multi-layered administration, and to the expectations of Clann na Poblachta in particular, Costello considered that it would 'not provide the kind of atmosphere in which I propose to have Cabinet deliberations take place'.[20]

Ken's new minister, Patrick McGilligan, was a native of Coleraine. 'He had a reputation for being a bit cantankerous but I never knew him to go beyond the bounds.' McGilligan came with some reputation. A lawyer and a professor of constitutional and international law, he had been minister for industry and commerce in the first Free State government. Between 1924 and 1932 he was engaged in the establishment of the innovative Shannon Scheme, then the largest hydroelectric project in the world, and was also responsible for setting up the ESB and the Agricultural Credit Corporation. Working closely with his new minister, Ken found McGilligan 'very able and also reasonable, even in his criticisms. He preferred oral argument to writing. I never recall him writing more than one paragraph! My help to him, I think, was in transforming his somewhat emotional thinking into something that could be put on paper and stand up to analysis.' That help was considerable, in quantity and in scope. The number of policy documents and memos on McGilligan's personal files compiled by his assistant principal officer (including his budget speeches), the minister's reluctance as a scribe, his reputation as a hypochondriac and his many well-documented absences from his official duties, which earned him Ken's nickname 'the Scarlet Pimpernel', were all testimony to the additional responsibility undertaken by Ken during McGilligan's time at Finance. This was especially evident in relation to two important issues that emerged early in the interparty administration: Marshall Aid and the link with sterling.

The dollar–sterling crisis of 1947 threatened a breakdown in trade between the sterling area, to which the Irish Free State belonged, and the dollar countries. While Britain may have emerged victorious from the war, its economy, wealth, prestige and status as a world power, especially following its withdrawal from India in 1947, were all weakened. Its economy was put under further pressure by the expansive programme of social reform embarked upon by the Labour government. On the world stage Britain was now overshadowed by two new superpowers, the United States of America and the Soviet Union, opposed in their divergent dogmas and in a power struggle for control in Europe. As well as helping to rebuild Europe physically and stimulate production, the United States Marshall Aid funding, distributed through the European Recovery Programme (ERP), had also the ulterior motive of helping to prevent the encroachment of Soviet control and, with it, the spread of communism.

As banker to other sterling economies, including Ireland, at the end of the war Britain owed over £3,000 million to its wartime creditors, mostly in the sterling area, as well as carrying a huge balance of payments deficit, and was heavily dependent on America to recapitalize its economy and provide essential equipment and consumer goods. The Irish Free State, with the substantial sterling assets accumulated during the war years at its disposal, also hoped to import vital commodities from the US. The dollar crisis of 1947, however, and the resultant inconvertibility of sterling into dollars, made the receipt of dollars through the Marshall Plan appear all the more desirable to some in the Irish government, especially the minister for external affairs. However, the Department of Finance had been sceptical about the likely benefits to the Irish economy since Marshall Aid had first been mooted in June 1947, given the country's link with sterling and its continuing dependence on the British market. It also feared that such funds would fuel non-productive development at home. The department's reluctance to claim Marshall Aid was, however, overruled by the Department of External Affairs under F. H. Boland, and in April 1948 Ireland signed the Convention for European Economic Cooperation in Paris, the mechanism by which it could gain access to American dollar aid.

Seán MacBride embraced Marshall Aid as a means of funding a programme of capital development through projects such as afforestation, land reclamation and drainage. His enthusiasm for dollars over sterling was not dampened when, despite his active courting of American officials in Dublin and Washington, it transpired that the actual amount of aid forthcoming to Ireland was to be $36 million and not the $120 million he expected. Furthermore, the aid was to be provided not as a non-repayable grant, as again he had expected, but as a repayable loan. The expansionary plans being promoted by the minister for external affairs and by other departments, all anxious, as Ken noted in a memo to McElligott, to get their hands on a share of the proposed funding 'for ambitious and costly schemes . . . before we have even a single ERP dollar', were merely piling up problems for the future. 'Borrowings from the United States Government will have to be repaid', Ken warned. 'None of the seven projects listed by Mr MacBride's memorandum can be said to pass the test of productivity in the sense of producing revenue for the Exchequer from which the interest and redemption instalments could be met as they fall due . . . Expansionist ideas, however admirable, which involve adding to the public debt and to future taxation are completely out of touch with the reality of the present financial position.'[21] His warning has an ominous resonance for more recent times. If the government was determined to accept Marshall Aid, Ken advised, then it should 'borrow as few dollars as possible and . . . use the counterpart funds in such a way as to facilitate repayment of the borrowings with interest'.[22]

Such advice found little favour with MacBride, whose expansionary vision was coloured by his antipathy to Ireland's economic dependence on Britain and the Irish currency's link with sterling. The minister's attitude to the sterling question Ken remembers as being 'emotional rather than theoretical'. On 23 June 1949, against a background of rumours regarding devaluation, MacBride advocated the repatriation of Irish assets invested in Britain to prevent their further devaluation and, as he saw it, to avert 'disastrous' consequences by using them instead to fund capital developments in Ireland. The Department of Finance saw things from a different perspective: in its view, as part of the sterling area, its industrial base underdeveloped and state-protected, the country had no justification for altering the connection with sterling, which functioned as a deterrent to inflation by curbing imports. McElligott set his assistant the task of presenting Finance's case to the government.

Addressing one by one the points raised by MacBride, Ken laid out the stark choice devaluation presented. The results for the country, 'though serious, could scarcely be described as "disastrous"', as the minister had predicted. In any event, he contended, 'it is not possible for a country whose foreign assets and current earnings from abroad are virtually confined to sterling, to insulate itself against the effects of sterling devaluation'.[23] There was no economic basis for a change in the existing relationship with sterling, because wages and prices were, in many cases, actually higher in Ireland than their counterparts in Britain – which, when 'taken in conjunction with the deficit in our Balance of Payments, would rather suggest that the Irish £ is overvalued in relation to sterling'. Regarding the minister's demand for the repatriation of sterling assets to fund development projects at home, Ken questioned whether he had given due regard to the fact that such sterling assets had been accumulated by Irish citizens and consequently were not at the disposal of the government to invest in capital schemes such as afforestation and drainage. Such schemes would simply 'use up the savings of the past' and were neither 'practicable nor economic . . . [nor would they] bring about any offsetting improvement in the standard of living'.[24]

Ken's less than enthusiastic reference to afforestation, in particular, invoked the ire of the ebullient leader of Clann na Talmhan, Joseph Blowick, who, perhaps with more of an eye to his Mayo constituency than to the national economy, insisted, as Ken recalls, 'that I was blocking a very important national investment programme and demanded that I appear before a cabinet meeting to be carpeted. It set a precedent and was quite daunting . . . confronted by all the ministers. I did my best to explain my position.' For an officer in the public service to be called to task before the cabinet was unprecedented. With an aversion to precedents per se, his boss subsequently ensured, as Ken recalls, 'that it was never done again' during McElligott's tenure at the helm in Finance.

On 17 September 1949, after months of speculation, the British prime minister, Clement Attlee, advised the Taoiseach of the imminent devaluation of sterling. At a hurriedly convened emergency cabinet meeting, which Ken attended with J. J. McElligott, G. P. S. Hogan and other senior Finance officials, the pros and cons of whether or not the Irish pound should follow suit were deliberated long into the night. Part of the cabinet meeting was held, significantly, in Iveagh House, the office of the Department of External Affairs, rather than at Finance in Merrion Street. Ken recalled 'MacBride sitting astraddle on a chair in the middle of the room (with other members of the government sitting around the sides) and relentlessly cross-examining his senior Finance colleagues'.[25] In the event, despite MacBride and the minister for health, Noel Browne, arguing against, with McGilligan and Dillon in favour and Norton rowing in behind his Fine Gael colleagues, the decision was taken to devalue the Irish pound from $4.03 to $2.80. 'The course of least disadvantage for us', the phrase coined by Ken in his drafting of the public announcement on this most sensitive national issue, received much praise in the media. The minister for finance acknowledged 'Mr Whitaker's skill in composition and knowledge of the matter [which] were such that even the patch-work later made of it by the amendments suggested or imposed on us, did not seriously weaken the original draft. *Palmam qui meruit.*'[26]

The differences of opinion between the Departments of Finance and External Affairs regarding devaluation and Marshall Aid continued to rumble on during the lifetime of the interparty government. There was no love lost between MacBride and the senior Finance officials, as the minister's (unsuccessful) objection to the reappointment of Joseph Brennan to a second term as governor of the Central Bank demonstrated. Ken's careful choice of words – 'the course of least disadvantage' – to describe the effects of devaluation on the Irish economy indicated his personal doubts about its potential negative effects. McElligott's contention that devaluation would not have an adverse effect on the economy was an opinion that, as Ken notes, 'would not have got one hundred per cent marks in a test in economics. It was quite obvious that there would be some negatives; indeed you would be quite mad to think otherwise.' As a junior Finance official, he was in a quandary at the time; but, as he attests, 'fortunately the dawn broke before anyone thought to ask my opinion'. In the event, the devaluation issue, the continuation of the Irish pound's parity with sterling and the ending of Marshall Aid in May 1951 were all victories of sorts for the policies McElligott and Brennan had promoted. Future dollar requirements for essential capital works would once more be sourced through the mechanism of the sterling dollar pool, while the government's planned spending spree on non-productive schemes, funded by Marshall Aid dollars, was contained.

While the sterling crisis, devaluation, dollar shortages and commodity scarcities were the dominant issues of the time, a significant milestone in the history of the modern Irish state also occurred during the term in office of the interparty government. On 7 September 1948 the decision to repeal the External Relations Act, abandon the Commonwealth and establish a republic was announced. Achievement of this long-cherished ideal, the motivation for almost every rebellion since its first enunciation by Wolfe Tone in the eighteenth century, was almost casually announced as a *fait accompli* by the Taoiseach, John A. Costello, during a visit to Canada. With almost unseemly haste, on 21 December 1948 he proclaimed the republic which was officially established the following April. Perhaps the removal of the statue of Queen Victoria from her habitual pedestal on the lawn of Leinster House – owing, as claimed at the time, to a shortage of car-parking spaces – provided some clue as to the Taoiseach's intent. The economic impact of Ireland's changed status *vis-à-vis* Britain and the Commonwealth was negligible. The Nationality Act, passed a few months previously, which granted British citizenship rights to Irish emigrants, continued in force and became vital in view of the increase in emigration from the new republic that ensued. The preferential trade arrangements existing between Éire and Britain were also, to the relief of

Irish farmers, maintained, while the Irish pound remained attached to sterling. The outcome politically was another matter. In 1949, at the behest of the Unionist government at Stormont, the imperial parliament at Westminster passed the Ireland Bill 1949, stipulating that Northern Ireland would not cease to be part of the United Kingdom 'without the consent of the parliament of Northern Ireland', thereby copper-fastening partition. Two decades later the results would return to haunt Ireland and Britain. In 1949, Ken Whitaker could not have foreseen how deeply engaged he was to become in the prolonged and bloody struggle that would ensue in the decades ahead.

His career in the public service continued its upward trajectory. During 1948, to 'cope with the increase in the volume and difficulty of the work' in Finance,[27] additional promotions were created, with his name once again to the fore. At this point, however, the anomaly that had arisen in 1943, pinning his future promotion to the lesser grade of administrative officer, surfaced. Pointing out that it was both 'unfair and illogical . . . that the date of my appointment as Administrative Officer is to determine my seniority *ad infinitum*', he sought to have his 'acting' principal grade changed to 'substantive'; and, after due deliberation, his appointment as principal officer (substantive) was eventually confirmed. With promotion came a yet more onerous workload. Pioneering the production of statistics for the first national income and expenditure publication, which involved much 'tedious slogging' in addition to his 'normal' work, he found himself, as he wrote, in 'the only period in a long stretch of public service when my health was threatened by overwork and stress'.[28] There was one welcome diversion from the 'slog': attendance with a colleague, James Meenan, in 1949 at the first meeting of the International Association for Research in Income and Wealth, at Cambridge University, with, as he recalled, 'dinners in King's College under the stern portrait of Milton, lazy punting in sunshine on the Cam and a pilgrimage to view Pigou's [the famous economist and mountaineer] climbing boots outside the door to his rooms.'[29]

By this point the Department of Finance, virtually unchanged in its organization and staffing since its foundation, was being stretched beyond its limits by both national and international developments. It was a mark, as Dr Ronan Fanning noted, of 'Ken Whitaker's remarkable and growing influence within the Department' that, despite its endemic resistance to change, he initiated a comprehensive review of functions and future development – 'arguably the most important change of direction of its kind since the Department's foundation'. Homing in on the inability of the present system to cope with 'the enormous development in capital expenditure', the result of 'boom conditions' funded by Marshall Aid dollars, with not, as he pointed out, 'a single officer concentrating whole-time on capital expenditure', he argued that Finance was vulnerable to 'having this important sector of public finance . . . removed from our immediate jurisdiction' and seeing it 'become a province of a cabinet sub-committee'[30] – the very thought of which would, he realized, serve to concentrate the mind of McElligott. Ken therefore proposed the establishment of a 'secretariat' or new section within the Finance Division, that would deal with issues such as economic, budgetary and monetary policy analysis, examination of capital expenditure, and the collation and study of economic and statistical information. 'I suggest – with some modest reluctance – that my experience and capacity could be used to greater all-round benefit . . . if . . . I were given charge of a general section . . . as compact and self-contained as possible . . . devoted to analysis of economic and monetary policies, preparation of ministerial budget speeches and to those quasi-personal duties which cling to me however much I try to shake them into someone else's tray.'[31]

These 'quasi-personal' duties included drafting articles and ministerial speeches on a range of economic and monetary topics and the composition of reports and articles. One such article, written anonymously (in keeping with civil service procedure), was published in the prestigious London financial journal *The Statist* in February 1951. In it Ken Whitaker forewarned of Ireland's inability to continue to fund anticipated deficits in the balance of payments, a warning that was later borne out with a vengeance. His recommendation regarding the establishment of a new section in the Department of Finance to oversee such developments was subsequently adopted. 'Mr T. K. Whitaker, whose experience in the Finance Division was believed to fit in peculiarly with this post',[32] was appointed its first head and with it promotion to the post of deputy assistant secretary. That this appointment too was intended to be in a temporary or 'acting' capacity bore the stamp of McElligott's reluctance to accede to any (as he saw it) unnecessary promotion or expense within the ranks, even of someone whom the long-serving mandarin respected, and perhaps even then viewed as a potential successor.

Ken lost no time in establishing his new section and putting it to work. His friend and colleague John O'Donovan and Dr Brendan Menton, assistant principal officer in the Central Statistical Office (CSO), both of whom possessed, as Ken testified, 'outstanding economic qualifications', were chosen to join his small team. 'I joined the Finance Division in 1952,' recalls Seán Cromien, another member and a future secretary of the Department of Finance. With a degree in economics and international constitutional law, Cromien was an ideal choice for this new, forward-looking unit. 'Ken's boss, Owen Redmond, had come up through the old orthodox economics and was rather out of touch. Ken was head and shoulders above him and others of the old school,' he remembers.[33] Another of Ken's recruits, Dónal Ó Loinsigh, recorded: 'It gives me pleasure and a little pride to be able to say . . . that I was on your team in those memorable years in the 1950s.'[34] The new section became Ken's laboratory for the exploration, analysis and formulation of innovative economic thinking. 'Whether one realized it at the time or not,' he says, 'it formed the nucleus for taking a more comprehensive look at policy and involving the talents of more progressive people, good people who had the urge to be creative and helpful to national economic progress.' It challenged from within what he later described as the Department of Finance's traditional 'inverted Micawberism, its slowness to see the merits of a case, its maddening questions, its dilatoriness, its blind devotion to precedent, the "dead hand" with which it stifles every initiative (if a dead hand can be so active!)'.[35] It also provided the means to search out new ideas to solve old problems. Ken was appointed to the boards of several other organizations, working parties and committees, including the Dollar Exports Organization on its establishment in 1951, the interdepartmental ERP committee and, in 1953, Córas Tráchtála (the Irish Export Board).

He considered 1950 to be not only a milestone in his personal career but also 'a distinct turning-point in financial policy when accounting convention, political advantage and practical economic justification joined hands',[36] and when Aiken's initiative on state capital investment became formal policy. The government's introduction of a capital budget he attributes to Paddy Lynch's influence on John A. Costello, but it was also, as he noted, 'recognised as an appropriate move by [at least some of] his Finance colleagues'.[37] Ken drafted the 1950 budget speech for the minister for finance, as he was to draft many more during his tenure in the Department of Finance. It was the largest budget in the short history of the state, at just over £106 million, some £31 million of which was earmarked for capital expenditure on projects such as housing, forestry, the expansion of medical services and land reclamation. The use of Marshall Aid borrowings to fund capital projects which, while aiding employment in the short term, were in the longer term non-productive was, as Ken noted, 'in the light of later developments an ominously liberal concession'.[38] The establishment in these years of Córas Tráchtála, Bord Fáilte (the Tourist Board) and the Industrial Development Authority, whose 'generous' budget and semi-independent status were frowned on by the 'old guard' in Finance, was also lambasted in the Dáil, including, somewhat surprisingly, by Seán Lemass.

By this time, serious cracks were appearing in the economy. Devaluation resulted in higher prices for imports, about 40 per cent of which came from non-sterling countries, as well as a decrease in the value of Irish sterling assets held in Britain. A sharp rise in commodity prices, caused by the Korean War, and static agricultural export prices contributed to a huge balance of payments deficit, accounting for almost 15 per cent of gross national product. The Marshall Aid expended on capital projects did not yield sufficient return to offset the corresponding interest charges and, as Ken had warned, was simply building up financial trouble for the future.

With the ending of Marshall Aid in May 1951, the wheels began to fall off the economic wagon, with rising costs, recurring shortages, growing industrial unrest (including strikes by railway workers and bank employees) and a stand-off between the minister for agriculture and the Irish Creamery Milk Suppliers. But it was a power struggle between the Catholic hierarchy and the minister for health over the introduction of what today would be looked on as an admirable and innocuous medical service that was to seal the coalition government's fate. As minister for health, Dr Noel Browne, with the support of his Clann na Poblachta leader Seán MacBride, had done tremendous work in providing enhanced medical facilities, especially towards the eradication of tuberculosis. In 1950 Browne attempted to implement a further public health programme known as the 'mother and child scheme'. Originally proposed by the Fianna Fáil government in 1947, the scheme aimed to provide free medical treatment for expectant mothers and for children up to the age of sixteen years.

In 1950 Browne was confronted by the massed opposition of the Catholic hierarchy, led by the formidable archbishop of Dublin, John Charles McQuaid, who considered the scheme to be contrary to Catholic social teaching, by the Irish Medical Association (IMA), which feared a loss in income, and by the combined conservatism and submissiveness of the body politic to the will of the majority church. Refusing to compromise with the church, the IMA or his coalition partners, the minister published his bill. But in 1950s Ireland, ecclesiastical power and professional vested interest were unbeatable opponents. The minister's resultant resignation led to the dissolution of the interparty government and to a general election in May 1951.

Returned to power with the assistance of a slew of independents, including Noel Browne, the new Fianna Fáil-led government was confronted with a stark economic outlook. Much to the relief of the old brigade in the department, Seán MacEntee was appointed as minister for finance, heralding restoration of the department to its position of pre-eminence and corrective action to redress the mushrooming economic imbalances. There was still, however, a growing unease in the department about the continued funding of capital projects from borrowing, especially once Marshall Aid had ceased. To bring the seriousness of the situation to the attention of the new government, Ken Whitaker compiled a memorandum on the worsening balance of payments situation, which, he asserted, 'for a country that was on a par with sterling was the proper scientific measure of whether or not we were living beyond our means'. The memo formed the basis of a government white paper published in October 1951. A renewed crisis in sterling early the following year resulted in the establishment of an interdepartmental committee, under his chairmanship, to investigate whether British policy was adversely affecting Ireland's economic interests. The committee found that, on balance, the Republic profited from its 'close economic and trading relations' with Britain in almost every aspect, from low-interest credit facilities and foreign exchange requirements to trade. The obvious outcome of such dependence, however, as Ken bluntly observed, was 'that practically every aspect of British economic and monetary policy impinges in some way or other on us'.[39] It was a sobering point. While the new republic might well bask in its political independence, its economic and financial fortunes remained fast bound to its former colonial master.

Talks on the sterling crisis with the chancellor of the exchequer and Treasury officials took place in London on 18 and 19 February 1952. Led by Lemass, minister for industry and commerce in the new government, and Seán MacEntee, the team also included the three main players in Finance: McElligott, G. P. S. Hogan and Ken Whitaker. As the sterling crisis deepened, Ken and Hogan remained in London to continue their talks with Treasury officials. Ken's relationships with his counterparts in London were in the main, as he noted, 'civilised, often friendly. Our mutual respect was deepened by a competent and firm pursuit of our own interests, modified by a willingness in the end to see reason.'[40] For their part, the Treasury mandarins considered him 'brilliantly able, with a quiet and unassuming but pleasant manner'.[41] Some of the Treasury gurus, too, possessed more than a professional interest in Irish affairs: Ken recalls 'one occasion in the Treasury ... [when] all four present – three Treasury knights, Rowe-Dutton, Rowan, Compton, and myself – suddenly recognized that we all came from Ireland.'

MacEntee's faith in the capabilities of his departmental officials eventually paid dividends. By July 1953, through their efforts, a remarkable reduction in the balance of payments deficit from £62 million in 1951 to just £9 million had been achieved. The balance of payments situation was undoubtedly eased by the introduction of a notoriously deflationary budget in April 1952 which, among other cutbacks, removed the expensive subsidies on food. Criticized variously but with equal force as 'cruel', 'savage', 'socially criminal' and 'nationally suicidal' by all shades of public opinion, including both unions and employers, it helped balance the books but did little to endear the government to an electorate already embittered and burdened by rising prices and falling standards of living. Public commentary was especially critical of MacEntee, who fell ill shortly after presenting the budget in the Dáil. 'Those who, with theoretical justification, are critical of the failure to expand demand at that period tend to forget the practical constraints,' Ken later pointed out.[42] As the principal architect of the budget, he stood four-square behind his reviled minister on that particular occasion. 'I could not let this opportunity pass without expressing my great admiration for the courage behind the 1952 budget and for your unsparing devotion to public duty when everyone would have had you executed,'[43] he wrote to MacEntee. Severe as it may have been, the budget did not go as far as the Department of Finance would have wished regarding the funding of capital expenditure, leaving it 'to a later stage in the rehabilitation of our finances'. As Ken prophetically noted,[44] 'this Augustinian procrastination' merely added to future balance of payments difficulties which, together with recurrent crises in sterling, continued to be a serious constraint on future economic development.

Still only thirty-six, Ken already enjoyed a well-established reputation as one of the country's most influential public servants. His public profile was growing both at home and abroad. Promotions had come at record speed and with them responsibility beyond his years, service or grade. Never far from the centre of the action, as his colleague Seán Cromien recalls, 'he gave the impression of a man who had ability and wanted to use his ability . . . a man on a mission'.[45] He had the ear, not merely of McElligott and other senior public servants, but of successive ministers for finance; incumbents from both wings of Irish politics held him in high regard and valued his opinion, which could at times be uncomfortable listening in its honesty but was never delivered in dictatorial fashion. To him, the role of public servants, especially in Finance, was simple: 'to state their views fully and fearlessly and then, if after due consideration these views were overruled, to do their best to carry out the policy decided upon by Government'.[46] Joining the civil service, as he once joked, was like 'joining a cloister. The minister was the abbot and the rest of us were bound by vows of obedience, silence and poverty!'[47]

While admitting to being 'a bit of a perfectionist' in his professional life, and an advocate of hard work – 'I like to see things well done and done quickly' – he also confesses, more surprisingly, that 'I also think a little element of laziness can improve your judgement. You need to sit down and think every so often.' His loyalty and regard for the Department of Finance was wholehearted, and he was unequivocal in his insistence that it was and must continue to be the department at the 'heart of the matter', a theme on which he expanded in an address to the Association of Higher Civil Servants in October 1953: 'I do not expect that we shall ever be popular as a department but I comfort myself by the thought expressed by an ex-Secretary of the Treasury, that "if at any moment it should become popular that fact itself would be conclusive proof that it was not properly fulfilling the purpose for which it exists".'[48]

To judge only from departmental and personal files, Ken Whitaker's day-to-day output in the Finance Section was truly staggering. His signature appears on a myriad of memos, letters, papers, reports, speeches and statistical analyses, further augmented by correspondence on a wide range of economic and monetary topics with colleagues in Ireland and abroad. This extraordinary output was all the more remarkable for being generated by the more ponderous communications technology of the day – pen, paper and the dictaphone – without the assistance of the technological advances of the modern-day information super-highway. His writing style, creative in execution, clear and cogent in exposition, imbued the most obscure and complex issues with clarity, often laced with a humorous or laconic under-tone. His appointment to various boards and committees, his work in an advisory capacity to successive ministers, including attendance at Dáil debates in the famous 'bull-pen' – an enclosure reserved for senior officials attending their ministers – and speech-writing, as well as the other 'quasi-official work' that con-tinued to 'fall into his tray' meant that as far as Ken Whitaker was concerned the nine-to-five, five-day working week normally associated with the public service was never an option. If the work was required to be done, then it had to be done, and done on your own time if necessary. It was his simply expressed opinion that 'there should be a social premium on excellence, on always doing one's best and performing what is promised. Non-material satisfaction will have to be cultivated and extended – satisfaction of aesthetic, cultural and environmental origin and the satisfaction to be derived from personal service to the community.'[49]

'I suppose a type of secular patriotism was at work then,' he reflects. 'It would not have occurred to us to seek extra pay. There were quite a number of us who wanted to be part of something that simply might bring about a better society.' Reluctant to dwell on his own role as a motivator of that mindset and attitude, he simply considers himself 'very fortunate to have like-minded people, just a rank below me, who wanted to do their job which gave them a sense of personal fulfilment and that what they had studied for was being given a national outlet. That was the stimulus.' It was a motivation that, as Maurice Hayes, former civil servant, ombudsman and mediator, maintains, appears far less in evidence among today's civil service elite, more noted for their

> unwillingness to share the common burden or to put the common
> good before personal privileges and protected pensions . . . It is
> not long ago since the archetype of the ideal public servant,

T. K. Whitaker, was elected in a popular poll as the Irishman of the century, epitomising the values of honesty and impartiality, respect for the law, respect for persons, diligence, responsiveness and accountability.[50]

These values, as Ken is at pains to acknowledge, were shared by many of his contemporaries working outside as well as within the public service, such as Paddy Lynch and professors Louden Ryan and Charles Carter, who on many occasions throughout his career voluntarily provided him with their advice and expertise. As Ken confesses, 'it never occurred to me to offer them payment. Looking back on it, I suppose they must have considered me a bloody miser!' The present-day bonus-and-top-up, incentive-oriented culture that pervades both the public and the private sector would have been anathema to Ken Whitaker's generation, just as the values they espoused are incomprehensible to many of the current generation of public sector workers, consultants and advisers, even, inexplicably, to the management of some national charitable-status organizations.

Despite his ever-increasing workload, Ken still made time for further private study. 'I am a believer in the "melting degree". I think the parchment it is written on starts to shrivel up as soon as you get it, so you've got to keep working at it all the time. You can never say, "I've arrived now."' In 1953, again through correspondence as an external student and after 'undergoing a lot of hard study to achieve the high standards demanded by London University', he was awarded a master's degree in economics. As 'an expatriate graduate', he needed to obtain a doctorate from the National University of Ireland to become 'naturalized'. In 1958, notwithstanding the number of significant economic publications to his credit, he was advised that, not being a graduate of the NUI, he was not eligible for a doctorate. While an NUI honorary doctorate was later to follow, in view of his achievements this seemed somewhat incongruous. To celebrate the sixtieth anniversary of his master's, in March 2013 London University, his alma mater (or 'foster-mother' as he humorously refers to it), chose to confer a DSc (Econ.) *honoris causa* on their star 1953 graduate. Since he was unable to attend the graduation ceremony in London, the university broke with tradition by conferring the degree on him *in absentia*, an award which, as he simply responded, 'I am pleased to accept.'

In 1953 Ken and his family moved from Kimmage Road West to a larger house on Stillorgan Road. Declining an opportunity to purchase a similarly priced house, albeit one needing modernization, in the more salubrious Ailesbury Road, as Ken ruefully admits, 'must surely have been one of the worst property decisions on record!'. The new family home was situated across from what became the campus of University College Dublin, but in the 1950s this was still farming land, on which Ken's eldest son recalls shooting rabbits and pheasants. Ken's spectacular rise in the civil service (with promotion in 1953 to assistant secretary) facilitated expenditure on the education of his own children which had not been available to himself. 'I set great store by education . . . It is the key to understanding, cooperation and progress.' His four elder children attended the best of Dublin's Jesuit schools, as well as an all-Irish school at Rinn, County Waterford. To escape the hurly-burly world of her all-male siblings, his only daughter, Catherine, boarded at Mount Sackville in Chapelizod, on the outskirts of Dublin. Brian, the youngest of the family, went to an all-German primary school near his home, his fluency in the language further enhanced by an annual student exchange with a family in Cologne who were to become lifelong family friends – to the extent that in 2011, in his ninety-third year, Ken travelled to Cologne with Brian to renew the acquaintanceship.

All the Whitaker children subsequently attended University College Dublin, with the exception of David, who studied dentistry at the Royal College of Surgeons. Above all, Ken wanted his children to have a good, rounded education; as David recalls, 'while he was ambitious for all of us, he was willing to let us do what we wanted in terms of a career and, if you wanted to do more in the educational sense, he was happy to support you' – even when it came to changing course mid-stream, as Brian remembers, having switched from commerce to law. Ken's daughter-in-law Teresa recalls his support and interest in her decision to enter third-level education as a mature student. 'He has that extraordinary capacity and willingness to encourage others. Coming in the academic back door, so to speak, I was initially hesitant and uncertain, but he made me go for it and was the first to congratulate me when I got my degrees.' Today, as programme director with Hibernian College, Teresa administers what could be regarded as the modern-day method of obtaining a degree by external study. As Ken notes, 'our children got a good upbringing and education. My father did not leave me any money, but gave me a sound education. It would not have done him or me any good if he had left me money. I was on my own when I became an adult and I show the same attitude to my own children.'

Family life was comfortable, without ostentation or over-indulgence. His sons remember an upbringing in the fifties and sixties 'of comfortable adequacy but with no great excess'. Their father's status as the country's principal civil servant was not, they recall, of any great relevance to family life. 'We were aware that he had an important job in the civil service,' David recalls; 'that he got invitations to certain functions and was in contact with many public figures, such as Jack Lynch, Garret FitzGerald, Cardinal Conway, Paddy Hillery . . . many of whom visited the house. De Valera used to ring him up on occasion, usually to discuss some mathematical theory or problem, and they always spoke in Irish.'

On the death of his wife Katherine, John Fogarty or 'Pa', as he was affectionately known in the family, sold his public house and came to live with Ken and Nora. 'A kindly, quiet man, full of interesting stories, it was fortunate for our children to have him around,' Ken recalls of his father-in-law, with whom he enjoyed a closer bond than perhaps with his own father. And, to his grandchildren, Pa was indeed special. 'Pa and I were best of buddies,' his grandson David recalls. 'He was always there when you came home from school and was great with us children,' bringing them on the tram to Howth, by bus to the zoo and on visits to his daughter, Mary-Jo, who lived in the northside suburb of Kilbarrack. It was Pa who also imbued some of his grandchildren with an interest in horse racing. His often-delivered line 'I'm going out to buy a bit of turf', they soon discovered, meant a visit to the nearest bookie's office in Donnybrook. While still youngsters, Raymond and David found their faith in the integrity of turf accountants severely tested. One summer, while studying at an Irish college in Spiddal, they cycled into Galway city armed with two 'dead certs', courtesy of Pa, and made for the nearest bookie's to place bets on both horses. To their delight, Pa's tips swept first and second past the post. But they then found it more difficult to prise their winnings from the reluctant bookie, who refused to pay out 'to young fellows like you'. Crestfallen but determined, in a loud voice Raymond demanded payment, to be told by the irate bookie that he was underage. His reasonable retort, 'I was underage when you took my bet!', struck a chord with the other punters who insisted that the bookie pay up or they would take their custom elsewhere. In high glee, their winnings secured, the two punters pedalled triumphantly back to Spiddal.

Pa did much more for the children than this. His prompt action in saving the life of his granddaughter Catherine, when her dress caught fire as she was standing too close to an electric heater at home, endeared him further to the whole family. There were also occasional disagreements, as when Pa took a pot shot from the upstairs window of the house on Stillorgan Road at pigeons feasting on his vegetable patch in the back garden below, provoking a memorable, if rare, contretemps between Ken and his father-in-law.

Nora was at the centre of the household, both as a homemaker and as an imperturbable, shrewd and loyal companion to her husband throughout their fifty-three years of married life together. 'Mother was in charge; she was a fixer, organizer, the decision-maker in the home,' her eldest son Ken notes. 'She played a central role in both worlds . . . from baking in the kitchen to attending international gatherings with Ken . . . you couldn't panic her.' Like his own mother, Ken's wife was endowed with an inner strength, energy and resolve. Over the years of their marriage they came to share many interests and pastimes, from travel to music to fishing: like her husband, Nora had an interest in Irish and French, and took to angling, successfully netting an occasional salmon.

Pa's constant presence and the affectionate relationship he enjoyed with his grandchildren allowed Ken and Nora greater freedom to pursue their interests and commitments outside the home. In 1953 both joined the nearby Elm Park Golf Club, where Nora enjoyed a more than respectable golf handicap of nine: 'far better than mine', Ken notes, though he is proud of being a finalist in a 'highly competitive' match play singles at the club before pulling a muscle in his back and being forced to concede. Nora became lady captain of Rush Golf Club and in 1972 of Elm Park. She passed on her love of golf to Raymond, David and Brian, the last of whom developed a particular talent, playing off a handicap of two. Like many mothers, however, there was method in her encouragement, knowing that 'the little white ball will keep them out of trouble'. More interested in social than competitive golf, from the sidelines Ken supported his sons' endeavours at the sport and, despite his onerous workload, made time to watch them play competitively. In 2011, when Brian and his son Gavin reached the final of the father-and-son competition in the Castle Golf Club in Dublin,

Ken drove around the course in a buggy to observe their play.

An avid follower of sport on TV, Nora was particularly keen on snooker, soccer and rugby. Her son David recalls, to his acute mortification, his mother rushing onto the pitch during a rugby match in which he was taking part, umbrella raised to strike a player who had tackled him to the ground with what she perceived to be undue determination. At a time when few women drove cars, Nora was first in the family to take to the wheel, then teaching her husband to drive and later each of her children. She ran the household 'in an efficient and highly organized manner', ensuring that her sons did their share of household chores and 'odd-jobbing'. 'Nora brought up her sons with a lot more household skills than their father possessed,' her daughter-in-law Maeve notes. 'I married a husband who could cook, sew, knit and do DIY!' Unusually for mothers of the period, Nora had, as her daughter-in-law Teresa recalls, 'tremendous confidence in her children and gave them a lot of freedom . . . She was not a "fussy" mother'. While Mrs Duggan, the family housekeeper, gave her time to indulge her interests outside the home, Nora was a dedicated homemaker, an excellent cook and an accomplished hostess. 'They were a sociable couple, had many friends and were forever entertaining at home, with dinner parties being subject to the same planning as the economy,' Teresa recalls. Her husband's work gave Nora an independence not usually associated with mothers of Irish families in the 1950s and 1960s, as well as the opportunity to travel outside Ireland, and not just as the consort of her husband. In the 1960s, with David, Catherine and Brian in tow, she embarked on a driving trip through Italy and France. Piling everyone into her small Morris, sharing the driving with David, staying in camping sites and modest hotels, it was some adventure. An inheritance from her father enabled her to purchase a property in Dublin's Belgrave Square which she rented out in apartments. 'We had to cut the grass, do general maintenance, collect rents for her in our spare time,' Brian remembers.

Home life was orderly and regulated, 'like being in a religious order!' Ken muses. The weekdays were devoted to school and office routine, while weekends centred on family life and the occasional game of golf with Nora or friends. While his mother's teetotalism did not transfer to her son, Ken never became a regular pub-goer and, on the rare occasion he did imbibe with work colleagues, 'I was always', as he says, 'able to get the bus home!' Being, as he readily admits, 'not a great man of the house', he was more than happy to leave the home front and family matters in his wife's capable hands. His honorary fellow-ship of the Institute of Engineers of Ireland, awarded in 1976, was thought 'hilarious' by his family, conferred on 'someone who thought you should hammer a screw into the wall!' However, as another of his sons recalls, Ken redeemed himself by being, like most fathers of the time, 'good on a picnic for lighting the fire or primus stove'. While there were unbreakable house rules and their mother often resorted to the familiar verbal threat 'wait till your father comes home', his children were 'never suitably terrified' since Ken's 'punishment' was usually restricted to a verbal 'telling off' for any childhood misdemeanour. His sense of parental duty was demonstrated in such matters as school home-work. 'If you had a problem, he would help but not do it for you,' David says; but because his father's advice usually extended to a demonstration of more examples than required, 'it was easier in the end just to phone a friend!'

As in his approach to his work as a public servant, so at home Ken could, as Brian notes, 'be a tough enough taskmaster if work was not done right'. He could also make his disapproval felt in other spheres. Brian's dalliance with the pop music, long hair and psychedelic dress of the 1960s and early 1970s was not appreci-ated by his father and led to an occasional contretemps. 'I recall how playing my latest Rolling Stones acquisition on Dad's gramo-phone with its special quality needles for his classical collection did not go down too well.' Television was a late addition to the

Whitaker household in the mid-sixties. Ken is remembered for being especially addicted to the American Western series *The Virginian*. Weekends meant trips to visit historic sites, many associated with Ken's childhood, such as Dowth and Knowth, Mellifont and Glendalough, or to his old homes in Drogheda and Rostrevor. Despite childish protests, there was also a compulsory family walk after Sunday Mass. Aside from fishing and an occasional round of golf and being 'very good at playing rings', Ken had few other recreational interests. Once, on being asked: 'What do you do for exercise?' he replied: 'I exercise my mind.' Surprisingly, perhaps, given the sheer scale and scope of his public work, other than occasionally seeing some 'old-type Civil Service files, with green treasury tags attached,' on the dining-room table, his family have little memory of their father working from home.

Each summer, at the end of the school term, for a few weeks the family moved to the seaside town of Rush, in north County Dublin, for a traditional bucket-and-spade holiday. Their first holiday home was a chalet converted from an old railway carriage, owned by a colleague in the Department of Industry and Commerce; later they rented a house on the main street in Rush, where their holiday friends included the deJongs and Amerkynks, children of Dutch-born immigrants, with whom, as Raymond remembers, 'we had a great time cycling around, fishing and visiting their greenhouses'. 'We played outdoors with another gang of kids, the Malones, on the beach and in the sand dunes,' David recalls. Evenings were spent playing cards and board games until it got dark, when 'the fragile mantle gas lights were lit'.

From Rush, Ken commuted daily to work in Upper Merrion Street before joining his family full-time for his own annual holiday. While both he and Nora enjoyed a round of golf on the adjacent nine-hole golf course, the opportunity their absence afforded their children was not wasted. They became experts at jump-starting the car, and would 'drive it up and down the little track leading to the chalets', David remembers. 'You had a good hour and a half before the parents got to the seventh green, where the course crossed over the track; then you'd have to sit tight until they were out of sight again. We were always amazed that neither of them seemed ever to notice why the car was turned in a different way or parked in a different place from where they had left it!' Other summer holidays were spent in west Cork, Donegal and Connemara, and one in a rented wing of Myrtle Allen's Ballymaloe House, now an internationally famous restaurant and cookery school. Ken knew the Allen family from when they had a linen mill in Drogheda, and the farm holiday provided the Whitaker children with new outlets, such as feeding animals and 'driving' tractors.

France became the family's foreign destination of choice. In 1946 Ken and Nora had travelled by car to Brittany where, as he notes, 'we were so struck by its resemblance to Connemara'. In 1950, in the family Morris Oxford, they drove across France and Germany to Oberammergau to see the famous Passion Play and from there across the Brenner Pass into Austria and northern Italy, where they left the car, as Ken recalls, in the care of a German-speaking resident of the former Austrian Tyrol, travelling on by train to Rome. As the family grew, holidays in France continued. Travelling from Ireland by car in the 1950s, before the advent of direct car ferries, was, as Ken's eldest son remembers, quite an operation. 'It started at the B&I docks at the North Wall when the car was put into a net, hoisted by ropes and swung above the deck before being lowered into the hold. On reaching Liverpool the same procedure applied.' The long drive through England to Dover then ensued, followed by the Channel crossing to Calais and then the drive onwards to their destination, often punctuated by overnight stays in camp sites, a new and exciting holiday development of the period.

While Ken's star was in the ascendancy in Finance, another,

which had guided the faltering first steps of the new Irish state for over a quarter of a century, was on the wane. In March 1953 the reign of J. J. McElligott as secretary of the Department of Finance came to an end. 'Tenacity of purpose and fearlessness in expressing his views were amongst his great qualities,' wrote Ken in tribute: 'He had a penetrating mind and a most enviable capacity to present his thoughts in perfect order and with classical precision.'[51] Few ministers for finance, regardless of party, were spared McElligott's often caustic criticism when he felt their plans threatened to jeopardize the integrity of the economy. But his brand of economics, like himself, was past its sell-by date. The state which McElligott had spent his years defending, from 1916 to 1953, needed new weapons in its economic arsenal if it was to survive. And inwardly at least, McElligott, despite his perceived conservatism, recognized that fact. 'He was very well qualified for an earlier age but became more and more bewildered,' Ken recalls. 'I don't think he had any great belief ever in a state's obligation to manage the whole economy . . . to look at things in the round . . . see how the economy needed to be sustained. He did not have the broad Keynesian outlook. He became more reliant on younger people, like myself, who could use a more modern sort of critical analysis to implement policy.' But the old soldier did not disappear from the economic battlefield entirely, succeeding his colleague Joseph Brennan as governor of the Central Bank. Ken's immediate superior, Owen Redmond, was on the verge of retirement but, following established seniority rules, succeeded McElligott as secretary of the department.

Shortly after McElligott's departure Ken found himself on the opposite side of the economic fence from his former boss. With the difficulty in the balance of payments momentarily rectified and inflationary pressure eased, in his view the time was right to adopt more expansionary methods to tackle the two most compelling national issues – low economic activity and high (and increasing) levels of unemployment. And to this end he targeted the Irish commercial banks, pointing out that they, unlike their counterparts in many other countries, were almost totally exempt from providing finance for government capital expenditure. Noting the healthy increase of £12 million in the banks' net sterling assets between 1952 and 1953, he threw down a challenge. 'They must realise', he argued, 'that no government could cut down capital expenditure while the external balance is satisfactory but unemployment and emigration are relatively high.'[52] But the former secretary of Finance's economic conservatism had journeyed with him from Merrion Street to Foster Place, and McElligott held firm against the proposals of his former protégé, considering it inappropriate for the Central Bank to permit any expansion, productive or otherwise, in the money supply.

Throughout the final months of the second Fianna Fáil government, unemployment, emigration and lack of investment to finance capital works continued to be at the forefront of national debate. The key point on which Ken focused in his departmental memos and reports was the *type* of capital works envisaged by some members of the government, including Lemass, and the crucial distinction, in his view, between productive public works and those of a solely amenity nature: the latter, he considered, were a waste of public money, merely providing artificially generated work with little prospect of a sustainable increase in production. A proposal by Frank Aiken (acting minister for finance during MacEntee's illness) to establish a National Development Fund, financed by the banks, and recommendations from Lemass, regarding tax-free allowances and grants for industry, led to the establishment of a committee of inquiry and, in January 1954, to a review of the sacred policy of protectionism. These steps, while disjointed and tentative, pointed in the general direction of a fresh and eventually more integrated approach to economic thinking.

The general election of June 1954 produced a second

interparty government, led by John A. Costello, composed of Fine Gael and Labour, and supported by Seán MacBride's Clann na Poblachta. The 45-year-old Gerard Sweetman was appointed minister for finance. Dapper, determined and independently minded, a solicitor by profession, Sweetman came from an established and well-to-do background, having been educated at Downside public school in England and at Trinity College Dublin. From the start, the minister and his assistant secretary hit it off. 'We spoke the same language, even if not always agreeing,' Ken recalls. 'Sweetman was devoted to public service, not from any interest in personal promotion but out of a sense of genuine nationalism . . . He was a man of honesty, directness and great analytical ability, animated by a sense of concern for the national well-being, of great acuteness of mind, of boundless energy, taking the steps three at a time with a boyish ebullience and with a liking for mischief. Yet he was something of an outsider among his party colleagues, perhaps because of his "county" associations and the accent he had acquired at public school in England.' The two men spoke often about policy matters. Inheriting a nightmare economic scenario, aggravated by a deep recession in Britain, as Ken recalls, 'Sweetman wanted to do a good job on the basis of good advice, even if what he had to do was unpopular.'

In November 1954, on Ken's recommendation, Sweetman obtained government approval for the establishment of an interdepartmental committee to review the state capital programme. Chaired by Ken, the committee completed its in-depth report and presented it to the government in December 1955, together with an additional memo, personally written by Ken, entitled 'Applicability of Keynesian Theory to Irish Circumstances', as a further encouragement to the 'yeast of new economic thought' gradually permeating the political outlook of both government and opposition. In October 1955 Seán Lemass had promoted plans for full employment (albeit with somewhat vague costings) in his '100,000 Jobs' speech; Costello followed up in October

1956 with his 'Policy for Production' document (partly written by Ken) while, not to be outdone, Seán MacBride produced a lengthy memorandum on his ideas for a ten-year development plan. Within the public service, too, Ken, together with colleagues like Charlie Murray, assistant secretary in the Department of the Taoiseach, were beginning to question the appropriateness of the straitjacket of protectionism. It was, however, as Ken realized, not only an economic crisis that held the country in a vice, but a crisis in national self-confidence, brought sharply into focus by the latest census returns, which confirmed that emigration was running at record levels.

On 25 May 1956 Ken delivered his second paper to the Statistical and Social Inquiry Society at the Royal Irish Academy in Dublin. Ten thousand words in length, excluding statistical analyses, and bearing the somewhat prosaic title 'Capital Formation, Saving and Economic Progress', the paper came to be recognized as the match that was 'to blaze a trail for the radical new departures in policy which characterised the years ahead'.[53] Speaking in a plain and straightforward style, significantly in a public forum and aiming his words at the ordinary Irish citizen as much as at those in power, Ken sought, as he simply noted, 'to assemble some facts and considerations regarding the relation of capital formation and saving to the raising of real incomes in Ireland. In other words, my concern is with national development and with some of the means necessary to attain it, in our par-ticular circumstances.'[54] Calmly but boldly, he listed the unpalatable but indisputable facts covering every aspect of the economy: low living standards (half those in Britain), high emigration, low production output, low output from land, savings not being put to best use, inflated wage levels out of line with the cost of production, state funding being expended on non-productive schemes – all were analysed and set out plainly. It made for dismal listening. Savings, he told his audience, should be increased to finance more *productive* capital investment if the country and its people were to have any hope of achieving an economic upswing. But there could be no magic remedy that did not involve a sacrifice in current welfare and consumption; this was something 'which everyone would need to understand and accept as an inevitable condition of a higher rate of permanent improvement in living standards'.[55] In addressing the ordinary citizen as much as his professional audience, Ken Whitaker was giving expression to the social and populist dimension that would characterize his brand of economics.

On Gerard Sweetman's recommendation, the paper was later published in *Administration*, the newly launched quarterly journal of the Institute of Public Administration. It also received wide coverage in the media, ensuring that, as Ken intended, its message reached a bigger audience outside politics and academia. 'Mr Whitaker has made the most useful and objective approach to our problems,' one newspaper review remarked. 'And his words must have effect . . . He has done a big service to the country by putting them down, he being a person of special knowledge with no axe to grind and only serving the public weal.'[56] The *Irish Times* praised the 'ground-breaking' nature of the paper, not merely for its content but for penetrating the cordon which traditionally surrounded public servants and which denied the public an insight into 'the quality of Civil Service thought', resulting in the fact that the 'concept of an unthinking, precedent-bound bureaucracy has been allowed to become an accepted legend. Mr Whitaker's paper', it concluded, 'should go a long way towards disturbing that legend.'[57] Ken's old teacher in Drogheda, Peadar McCann, also sent his congratulations. 'It will, I am confident, add greatly to your prestige both within and without the Civil Service. But I am sure that you will feel that your labour has been in vain, if it does not effect some change in the outlook of our legislators and our public men in general.'[58] It was a hope shared by his star pupil.

Also in response to Ken's paper, Gerard Sweetman set up an

external Capital Advisory Committee. Under the chairmanship of John Leydon, former secretary of the Department of Industry and Commerce, it was charged with the task of examining the desirable volume and composition of public investment, how such investment might be financed in the immediate future, and how best the level of real incomes might be raised. The committee brought together representatives from agriculture, industry and trade unions, together with three economics professors from outside the public service – Louden Ryan of Trinity College Dublin, Paddy Lynch of University College Dublin and Charles Carter of Queen's University Belfast – and the redoubtable managing director of the Irish Sugar Company, Lieutenant-General Michael J. Costello.

By the middle of 1957 the crisis in the public finances had worsened and criticism was again being directed at the Irish banking system for its reluctance to play its part in relieving the financial impasse. The June edition of *The Statist* claimed that a controlled inflationary policy was necessary 'to put Ireland back on her feet' but was being prevented by the fact that most of the country's banking assets were held outside the state, thus depriving the country 'of a great deal of the capital which she so desperately needs'.[59] The article recommended increasing the power and control of the Central Bank over the Irish commercial banking system. Taking the editor of *The Statist* to task for recommending such an inflationary policy to resolve the economic crisis, Ken Whitaker reiterated his view that, while 'there is a case for repatriating at least some of these assets for good purposes at home', in view of the crisis in the balance of payments any changes in credit policy would have to be gradual and deftly handled. On the issue of investigating other methods of credit financing, as proposed by Professors Ryan, Carter and Lynch, Ken was equally unequivocal: 'I see no reason for facilitating . . . the waste of reserves for unproductive purposes, whether the reserves are under the control of the banking system or some other authority. I would repeat that the difficulty is not lack of finance but rather lack of specific plans for productive development.'[60] In a further reply to Professor Carter, Ken pulled no punches. 'Anyone contending that economic expansion can be promoted by pump-priming or by further enlargement of the infrastructure of homes, hospitals, public utilities etc. would have some difficulty in explaining why the tremendous effort in this direction since the war, resulting in an aggregate balance of payments deficit of £200 million, has failed so conspicuously.'[61] In his plan for the economy there was to be no easy option, especially not one that did not pay productive and long-term benefits. After further consultation with the minister, it was decided that, for the time being, the most that could be achieved was 'to secure the participation of banks and insurance companies in the future financing of the Industrial Credit Corporation',[62] and to encourage increased industrial production.

While the banks had been persuaded to finance the balance of payments deficit in 1955, they had now, as Ken advised Sweetman, 'come virtually to the end of their willingness and capacity to create credit'.[63] Sent by Sweetman to persuade the Central Bank's governor to increase the £1.3 million on offer to meet the current borrowing needs of the government, reckoned at £3.5 million, Ken found his former boss unresponsive. While critical of the banks' reluctance in the past to increase their lending to the government, in the present situation Ken found himself in agreement with McElligott. Without a national plan for productive development, to provide the requested funds would simply be to squander good money after bad. By mid-September, in a situation that has a more recent echo, the Department of Finance was struggling to meet its day-to-day public expenditure. 'Very few appreciate the difficulties that we have had to overcome to maintain up to this month the smooth flow of finance for public expenditure. You are the only Minister who fully understands how narrowly we have avoided failure in recent months,' Ken confided to Sweetman. 'If some day in the near future we have to say "sorry, we have no money", there will be a reaction, first of incomprehension and then of alarm.'[64]

In a more hard-hitting secret memorandum to the minister, in language at times bordering on insubordination, and with an ominous resonance in the light of more recent events, Ken unequivocally set out the nightmare scenario of potential national bankruptcy. All pools of likely revenue were exhausted, he told Sweetman. Since the liquid reserves of the commercial banks had already been 'drained away by the continuing deficit in our balance of payments, they would be failing in their responsibility if they were deliberately to expand domestic credit further . . . The Central Bank's capacity to help by substituting Irish securities for sterling in its Central Fund is virtually exhausted.' The depletion of government liquid reserves, especially those of small investors in state savings banks and holders of saving certificates, had, Ken maintained, 'already gone too far. It would not be consistent with our duty to the small savers who have entrusted their money to us on the guarantee of repayment on demand, that we should deplete our liquid reserves any further. I feel, therefore,' he warned, 'I must take the position that I will not order any further sales of the sterling securities of the Departmental Funds . . . unless I am expressly directed to do so.' The country was spending more than it currently earned, and Ken Whitaker's purpose was to highlight 'where present trends were leading, so that the Government may not be taken unawares, but rather, while there is yet time, may decide on adequate corrective measures . . . *I see no prospect of obtaining what we need, if the balance of payments drain continues and I am anxious that this should be known to you and the Government.*'[65] The message was simple, courageous and unambiguous.

Matters did not improve. International events such as the invasion of Hungary and the Suez crisis further exacerbated the worsening economic situation, while the fallout from a renewed IRA border campaign threatened political stability. When Seán MacBride withdrew his support for the second inter-party government, a new Fianna Fáil government, enjoying its first overall majority since 1944, was elected in March 1957.

Gerard Sweetman, often considered to be the right person in the right place at the wrong time, had not been minister for finance long; but his many innovative and formative policies, as Ken attested, 'laid the foundations . . . for the industrial expansion of the nineteen sixties'.[66] Sweetman was, however, destined to be most remembered as the minister responsible for breaking with traditional civil service procedure by effecting the promotion of Ken Whitaker as secretary of the Department of Finance. Then a junior administrative officer in the department, Seán Cromien recorded the excitement of the occasion:

Tuesday May 29 [1956]. Mr Redmond's last day as Secretary . . . Speculation about his successor during the day. Then about 4.30 news leaked around: the unbelievable had happened – Mr Whitaker had been appointed. Great excitement and a very popular choice . . . he has been promoted out of his place in seniority, purely on merit, at every turn. It's like the beginning of a new reign. We all wonder what it will mean. We feel it will bring changes. Home, feeling very excited about the news.[67]

At the age of thirty-nine, Ken Whitaker became one of the youngest holders of the office. But there was nothing fortuitous about his promotion. He was, as Sweetman simply acknowledged, the most qualified man for the position. G. P. S. Hogan, the assistant secretary, accepted what must have been a substantial reversal of his own expectations in the promotion of his younger colleague, as Ken remembers, 'with gentlemanly generosity'.

Other than a starting salary of £2,625, the perks of Ken's new appointment were few. The private secretary allocated to him, Miss Maureen Stuart, he remembers as being 'competent, cool, calm and collected' under pressure. Preferring his present office, he declined to move 'across the corridor' to the office usually designated for the departmental secretary. His elevation to the most senior post in the public service, for which, as he humorously notes, 'I thought I'd have to wait until Sarsfield Hogan had his day!', came as little surprise to those who had recognized his potential from the start of his career. But, as was only to be expected, such a break with traditional procedures, one of his colleagues noted, 'raised some eyebrows over his leap-frogging of Sarsfield Hogan who was very well liked and respected'.[68] Ken personally remembers Owen Redmond, given the task of informing him of his promotion, telling him rather ominously that 'it was not my doing'. But he also recalls 'being touched by the kindness of Frank Aiken in calling to my home to congratulate me'. With the country on the verge of bankruptcy, it was in everyone's interest to have someone as qualified, as experienced and as obviously dedicated to public service as Ken Whitaker, and there was no opposition to his elevation from any part of the political spectrum. Sarsfield Hogan was part of the old brigade and represented the more traditional economic thinking, which by then was out of kilter with 'a situation that needed', as Ken recalls, 'a deeper knowledge of economics that would contest ingrained thinking and see another way'.

From his wife and family there was little fuss or excitement at his elevation. 'I don't think they comprehended it at all,' he laughs. 'Nora, I suppose, was delighted for me but I don't recall that she overdid the adulation! I think my mother was chuffed enough but did not have much sense of what it entailed.' To his children, meanwhile, life went on as before and 'Daddy' just continued to go to work as usual. In the less regulated and security-conscious years of the 1950s and 1960s, they remember waiting on occasions in the family car parked outside Government Buildings for Ken to finish his working day or, on entering his office, finding him with Lemass or some other government minister.

For the country at large, however, the appointment of Ken Whitaker as Ireland's premier public servant was of huge significance. It changed the direction of economic policy, spearheaded the move from protectionism to free trade, and guided the country on its momentous journey towards European integration.

5

Fortune Teller
1957–58

It had become clear by the 1950s that the economic policies pursued up to then were ineffective and inappropriate. The reversal of these policies – the decision to abandon protectionism in favour of competitive participation in a free trade world and to welcome foreign investment instead of virtually prohibiting it – was the greatest change of my time as a public servant.
T. K. Whitaker[1]

By 1957, NOWHERE in the public arena was the difference between the worn-out policy of protectionism and the energizing policy of free trade better exemplified than in the age profile and economic insensibility of the country's newly re-elected 75-year-old Taoiseach, Éamon de Valera.

Though by then almost sightless and increasingly remote, 'The Chief' retained his legendary aura and still clung to the levers of power, ruling his cabinet through ties of loyalty and awe. Unseeing and indifferent to the practical realities of a collapsing economy and a despondent people, de Valera 'lacked the capacity to act on the economic challenge but he cloaked this with the lofty pretence that his vision was set on higher things than the mundane matter of the economy', as one of his biographers, Tim Pat Coogan, noted.[2] This seems all the more surprising given de Valera's much-lauded mathematical faculty. By 1957 'Dev' appeared to many as an ancient warrior whose energies had been drained by the achievement of his country's political independence, albeit an independence compromised by the country's continuing economic dependence on its former colonial master. He had become, as Ken succinctly puts it, 'a symbol of Éire passé'. Dev's incapacity or reluctance to acknowledge the economic maelstrom that had enveloped the country is exemplified by his assertion at a political meeting in County Cavan in 1955 that, despite the perilous state of Ireland's economy, mass emigration and the despair of its citizens, 'I would put the restoration of the Irish language as Fianna Fáil's greatest national objective.'[3] While the restoration of the Irish language was an aspiration also shared by the new secretary of the Department of Finance, in 1957 there were more critical and urgent matters demanding attention.

Behind de Valera's formal reserve, however, lurked a sense of humour that occasionally sparked to life. During one Dáil budget debate he sent Paddy Lynch to enquire if Ken knew what constituted an 'epicycloid circle'. Ken replied that he thought it might be a circle enclosing a smaller circle which it touched tangentially. 'Paddy Lynch came back later to say that Dev wished him to tell me that it was reassuring to know that there was someone in Finance who understood mathematics and that the tangential nature of the two circles touching contained about the same contact with truth as did the opposition's attack on the budget!' But Dev's mathematical prowess did not enlighten his myopic view of Irish economic development. Escorting a delegation from the IMF and World Bank on a courtesy call on the ageing Taoiseach in 1958, Ken recalls that 'they were treated to a version of Dev's 1943 St Patrick's Day speech. I tried without success to introduce a more developmental note. After we left, Charles Merwin, the United States member of the IMF group, noted: "He's a strange man, your prime minister."' On their meetings in the Dáil or in Government Buildings, Dev invariably referred to Ken's job as secretary of Finance as 'minding the purse' which was, perhaps, as far into the complexities of the national finances as he cared to venture.

More than an unsighted political leader, however, stood between the economic survival of the Republic and the doomsday scenario with which it was faced. Between June 1951 and March 1957 there were three changes of government, with no fewer than four different ministers at the helm in Finance. There was little opportunity to develop an alternative economic policy that didn't involve merely clinging to protectionism. With an overall majority, however, the new Fianna Fáil government that took office in March 1957 looked set to run the distance and, despite the physical and philosophical impediments of its leader, it had the political freedom to tackle the economic impasse. Already there were signs of more positive intent. De Valera was being persuaded that his idealistic views for Ireland and the Irish people would no longer be tolerated by an electorate grown more demanding through want and emigration. Ever the consummate politician, he listened to the advice of his trusted lieutenant and confidant, Seán Lemass, and realized that the time had come to set out on a different economic path. Adherents of old-school Gladstonian economic policy, such as Seán MacEntee, were adroitly sidelined in the new government. James Ryan, a close ally of Lemass, was appointed minister for finance instead. A medical doctor and founder member of Fianna Fáil, Ryan had seen military action at the GPO and the Four Courts. Tomás Ó Cofaigh, then part of Ken's team in Finance, remembers him as 'one of the best finance ministers, a great actor in the Dáil, with an ability to bamboozle people into doing what he wanted'. In comparison with the 'boundless energy' he associates with Gerard Sweetman, the new minister appeared to Ken to be more pedestrian and more inclined 'to ruminate over things'. On their first introduction, Ryan told him: 'You look after the administration. I'll look after the politics.'[4]

In a departure from the protectionism of which he was principal architect, minister for industry and commerce, Lemass promised a state-financed capital programme, amendments to the Control of Manufactures Act, abolition of import tariffs, provision of capital investment and the modernization of agricultural practices. While more aspirational than analytical, Lemass's new plans for the economy were nevertheless an encouraging sign of a politician who 'had the courage and readiness to depart from the sacred path of orthodoxy'.[5] Up to then, according to Ken, 'policy seemed to be on the side of hoping that things would get better but not taking the right actions to achieve it. But it was difficult to dismantle that protectionist–self-sufficiency thinking at the time. It had become a sort of patriotic ideal and any change contemplated could be viewed as undermining nationalism, as letting Britain in, so to speak.'

In his maiden speech, one of Fianna Fáil's newly elected deputies, Lemass's son-in-law Charles Haughey, accused the civil service of holding itself aloof and remote from the problems that beset the economy: 'If we are to achieve national recovery, it will involve a tremendous national crusade. It must be made clear to our civil servants that they also must take part in that crusade,'[6] words which must have stung, as well as motivated, public servants like Ken Whitaker. A national fusion of personalities and ideas was beginning to occur. His new position made Ken, as one observer noted, 'less of a civil servant ... Whitaker plays the system and then transcends it.'[7] His elevation encouraged him in his belief that the time was right to embark on his own particular economic mission. Informal talks with J. J. McElligott at the Central Bank, J. P. Beddy, chairman of the Industrial Development Authority, and Charlie Murray in the Department of the Taoiseach helped inform his thinking.

The appalling economic prospect alone, however, would have served as sufficient motivation for change. For, over three decades since independence, in the late 1950s the Irish state was, in effect, struggling to survive. Even in the desperate famine years of the previous century the population had hovered around nine million; now, a century later, despite achieving statehood, the country seemed incapable of providing a living for a population of under three million. In 1957 alone almost 60,000 people left the country, mainly for the UK, in search of employment and a better lifestyle. Despite this human drain, unemployment in Ireland remained among the highest in western Europe. Agriculture, which 'employed' 40 per cent of the population and which was traditionally acknowledged by all shades of political opinion and none as the mainstay of the Irish economy, was in a 'prehistoric' state, rife with outmoded practices, under-funded and badly managed, its resources under-utilized, farmers demoralized, under-educated and lacking any real motivation for change. Agricultural output was less than half that obtaining in other countries. Between 1949 and 1955 GNP increased by a mere 10.5 per cent, compared to 36.5 per cent in the rest of Europe, with industrial production at 35 per cent (and falling) compared to 55 per cent elsewhere. As Ken observed,

> the perception we all had in the mid-50s was of a country whose economic and social development had dismally failed to live up to expectations engendered by the struggle for, and achievement of, political independence. Emigration, unemployment and painfully slow growth were the marks of our failure. Our dependency was hugely pronounced – dependent for industrial employment on a limited and highly protected home market and dependent for sale of our surplus agricultural production on a British market where prices were deliberately held low in the interest of consumers and to which even access was insecure.[8]

Major societal as well as economic difficulties abounded, from a consuming national despondency to lack of ambition, a low level of education, absence of entrepreneurial skills, and a pervasive lack of civic patriotism. As Ken realized only too well, it was not merely government policy that had to change, but people's attitudes and expectations. 'Unless the individual members of the community have sufficient patriotism and realism to accept the standard of living produced by their own exertions here – even if it should continue for some time to be lower than the standard available abroad – the basis for economic progress simply does not exist.'[9] For any plan to work, he warned, 'aspirations must be accommodated within the total availability of resources . . . or else the plan will merely express wishful thinking and irreconcilable desires'.[10]

It is significant that the now famous 1958 plan, which was to become synonymous with Ken Whitaker's name and which perhaps did more than anything else to win him the accolade 'Irishman of the Twentieth Century', did not suddenly emerge as a blinding light illuminating the darkness. Typically for the work of so thoughtful and methodical an intellect, it emerged from a gestation period of observation and analysis and with the intention, as he puts it with characteristic understatement, 'having myself experienced for some time past a sense of anxiety and urgency about Ireland's economic and political future . . . to make some positive contribution towards the betterment of the country'. His plan could not have been more ambitious: for, while he certainly planned to use his ability, experience and position to try to correct the practical issues that beset the economy, something both more enigmatic and more animate, was, as he noted, at the heart of his cause. 'It is vital to sustain an atmosphere of confidence in which enterprise is favoured, difficulties do not overawe and temporary reverses do not cause despondency. The creation of such an atmosphere was the primary aim in preparing the First Programme for Economic Expansion.'[11]

From early 1957, in what Ken refers to as 'this dark night of the soul', what would become *Economic Development* began to take shape. In February, before the general election, he went on an exploratory mission to Washington to assess Ireland's prospects of joining the IMF and World Bank. There was a bigger world out there that 'Ireland Inc.' could no longer ignore. The country needed not merely the technical advice and training which institutions like the World Bank and IMF offered, but also sources of finance for the capital investment necessary for the plan he contemplated. If this was to be forthcoming, a five- or ten-year national development programme would have to be constructed; lurching short-term from one budget to the next was no longer an option. In Washington Ken made valuable contacts with Benjamin King, a senior economist at the World Bank, and Charles Merwin at the IMF, both of whom he invited to Dublin.

On his return, he let fly the first salvo in the battle for economic independence. On 21 March, his first day in office as minister for finance, James Ryan was confronted with a document entitled 'The Irish Economy', written by the new secretary of his department on the state of the economy and its implications for the survival of the Republic as a political entity. Ken's words were blunt:

> In the *political* field the primary national objective is the re-unification of the country. Until that is achieved, however, and no doubt after it has been achieved, the principal *economic* problem of the Irish Government will continue to be the safeguarding of political independence by ensuring economic viability. Without a sound and progressive economy, political independence would be a crumbling façade. The European Free Trade Area proposals have held a mirror up to the Irish economy. The picture revealed has been most disquieting.[12]

In language that could be interpreted as breaching the traditional boundary between public servant and politics, but which he deemed necessary in view of the desperate circumstances, he continued: 'We have come to a critical and decisive point in our economic affairs. It is only too clear that the policies we have hitherto followed have not resulted in a viable economy.' He urged the government to stop sheltering 'behind a protectionist blockade' which not only condemned the people to a lower standard of living than the rest of Europe but also, in turn, encouraged emigration and thereby threatened to make 'it impossible to preserve the 26 counties as an economic entity'. He urged ministers to accept instead 'the challenge of free trade'. Resorting to rhetoric that he knew would more than ruffle Republican feathers in the government, he continued: 'If we do not expand our production on a competitive basis . . . it would be better to make an immediate move towards re-incorporation in the United Kingdom rather than wait until our economic decadence became even more apparent.'[13]

He outlined the essential, albeit potentially tough and unpopular, steps that had to be taken: educating the public that higher employment rates and better living standards could be achieved only by their own efficiency and by drawing on what the country actually earned to fund capital development; maximizing savings, both voluntary and compulsory, to finance productive projects in industry and agriculture; conserving and expanding capital resources for productive purposes by curbing consumption for non-productive purposes; and joining the IMF and the World Bank to gain access to development loans and technical expertise. It could no longer be left to politicians alone to put the national economic house in order; as he told the minister, 'in a small country like this where not only information but talent is locked up in the Civil Service, it is desirable that there should be free communication between the service and the public. Even the Border has its "approved" roads'.[14]

Whatever reprimand he might have expected for such outspoken criticism of government failure, which in times past could well have cost a 'keeper of the purse' his head, did not materialize. The government's immediate response was to accept his recommendation that it seek membership of the IMF and the World Bank, and the Articles of Agreement were formally signed that August. Most in Ireland, even in the government, as Ken ruefully recalls, had 'hardly even heard of the IMF . . . not to be too mealy-mouthed about it!' For Ken, however, membership was vital; and it was only a first step. For, while the flame may have been lit, he knew it would have to be fanned to prevent its being snuffed out by political inactivity. To keep the mind of the body politic focused, he used James Ryan's first budget speech, which he personally drafted, to urge the need 'for a comprehensive review of our economic policy'.[15] Little did the minister realize that, behind the scenes, with the help of some willing colleagues, Ken Whitaker had the 'review' already in hand.

The planning that produced *Economic Development* did not start with any great fanfare or indeed with any one single action. During 1957 Ken was already quietly at work putting various aspects of the plan into place. In a memo dated 24 May 1957 he outlined his objectives to the principal officers in his department. 'One of the biggest problems is how to reshape and redirect the public capital programme so that, in association with develop-ments in agriculture, industry etc., it will provide *productive* and *self-sustaining* employment.'[16] This aspect of the programme he considered of particular urgency because of the projected decline in more socially focused but non-productive public projects. He established a departmental committee to pursue 'energetically' a 'thorough study' of productive projects that could be wholly or partly financed by the state. 'I have in mind that the results of this study will be placed before the Minister and, as far as may be thought proper, be communicated to the Capital Advisory Committee.'[17]

For Ken Whitaker, 'planning' represented 'the approach of reason and order as opposed to drift and social unrest'.[18] It was only from the mid-1950s, following the introduction of the Monnet Plan in France and the Vanoni Plan in Italy, that the idea of a comprehensive national plan was considered 'respectable' by democratically elected governments, the concept previously being associated with the communist system and thereby suspect. What Ken Whitaker envisaged for Ireland was, however, not a plan in any rigid or overly ambitious sense:

> I am convinced of the psychological value of setting up targets of national endeavour, provided they are reasonable and mutually consistent. There is probably a particular need in this country to harness the enthusiasm of the young and buttress the faith of the active members of the community in this way. But there is nothing to be gained by setting up fanciful targets. Failure to reach such targets would quickly produce disillusionment and renew the feeling of national despondency.[19]

That, indeed, was something he was determined to avoid. Like every plan, *Economic Development* had, as he knew, its own time. 'Everything has to grow, even ideas come in waves. Idealism must be fitted into the framework of realism.'

By July 1957 the most vital element of the plan, the one he consistently promoted – the replacement of non-productive by productive capital expenditure – was, on his instructions, being implemented in the Department of Finance, as a test for future applications by other departments of state. International developments, such as the establishment of a united Europe by the creation of a common market and the progressive harmonization of social policies, and the prospect of Ireland's membership of the Organisation for European Economic Co-operation (later the Organisation for European Economic Development, the OECD), added an additional dimension and urgency to the need to combat protectionism.

Another piece of the jigsaw was put in place when, together with James Ryan and J. J. McElligott, Ken travelled to Washington to attend the annual meetings of the IMF and the

World Bank, the first at which Ireland was officially represented. At the meeting he presented a memorandum outlining Ireland's economic development needs and its willingness to embrace foreign investment. The World Bank subsequently agreed to send an official delegation to Ireland. The first of many journeys Ken was to undertake to both the IMF and the World Bank, the long transatlantic voyage from Cobh to New York also afforded him the opportunity of forging relationships with economic and financial representatives from other European countries. On his return from Washington, he continued to correspond with contacts made in the IMF and the World Bank on aspects of the proposals he contemplated for *Economic Development*, and also with J. F. Cahan, deputy secretary-general of the OEEC in Paris. During subsequent visits to America, when staying in New York he often visited his former mentor Frank Aiken, minister for external affairs from 1957 to 1969, 'in his modest room in the San Carlos Hotel' – 'our relationship no longer as formal as that of our Finance days' – and also enjoyed the 'friendly company' of F. H. (Freddie) Boland, who from 1956 to 1963 was Ireland's representative at the United Nations.

As Ken set off on that first trip to Washington, his embryonic plan for the revival of the economic fortunes of the country received a further stimulus from a most unlikely source. *Dublin Opinion*, a popular monthly magazine, satirized the topical issues of the day through cartoons and caricatures, both humorous and sombre. The cover cartoon of the September 1957 issue, a copy of which Ken bought as light reading for his trip to America, showed a crone-like, irate fortune teller admonishing an attractive but dejected Kathleen Ní Houlihan figure to 'get to work', to which Kathleen replies: 'Get to work! They're saying I have no future.'[20] Encapsulating the essence of the country's economic difficulties, the cartoon was an added motivation for Ken Whitaker to try to give 'Kathleen' a future.

It struck me then, having been put in the top Civil Service job at a fairly early age, I ought to get some thinking going to dispel the cloud of despondency. Also I had the feeling that perhaps a new psychological stimulus to national effort might, strangely enough, come most effectively from the most improbable and least revolutionary of places, the Department of Finance.[21]

The first working folder he opened on his journey towards the compilation of *Economic Development* bore the title 'Has Ireland a Future?'

Aside from the existential threat facing Ireland, it pained Ken as a patriotic Irishman that his country had fallen so far behind almost every other economy in western Europe. 'Even the most phlegmatic could scarcely be unaffected by this general air of pessimism. It would be unnatural for anyone to enjoy the prospect of the progressive decay of the Irish economy and the undermining of political independence which must accompany it.'[22] The reports of the Commission on Emigration (1948–54) and the unremitting human drain from the land confirmed by the 1956 census highlighted the demoralizing side-effects that unemployment and emigration wrought on the community, especially in rural Ireland. From an economic point of view, the haemorrhage of young people in particular was robbing the country of an active and able potential workforce, leaving behind villages and towns denuded of youth and vigour.

The common talk amongst parents in the towns, as in rural Ireland, is of their children having to emigrate as soon as their education is completed in order to be sure of a reasonable livelihood ... setting up a vicious circle – of increasing emigration, resulting in a smaller domestic market depleted of initiative and skill and a reduced incentive ... to undertake and organise the productive enterprises which alone can provide increased employment opportunities and higher living standards.[23]

In an assessment that reverberates today, J. F. Cahan of the OEEC noted that a lack of available risk capital 'discouraged . . . bright young men in Ireland . . . from setting up new enterprises in the country . . . and that they tend therefore to seek their fortunes elsewhere and to return to Ireland, if at all, only in their old age'.[24] Emigration also fuelled unrealistic expectations among those who remained, since the higher standards of living enjoyed by emigrants encouraged those at home to demand commensurately higher incomes for themselves.

The 'intricate problem' of emigration and its devastating propensity to undermine the confidence and morale of those left behind continued to challenge and animate Ken Whitaker throughout his public career. During a family summer holiday to west Cork in 1960 he experienced the practical implications at first hand. Owing to a decline in traditional occupations such as fish-curing and quarrying, the area was experiencing a major decline in its population, especially of its youth. In a memo to J. C. Nagle, his counterpart in the Department of Agriculture, Ken outlined his concerns.

> They need help to acquire the land available to them and, as hired labour has never been available in this area, they also need machinery. It would be best if this could be provided on a cooperative basis. It struck me that there was a great field here for a well-trained organiser who could rally all the help needed – psychological, social and economic . . . If something worthwhile could be organised in a particular area like West Cork, it could, I think, do a lot to rebuild confidence and influence the attitude generally . . . towards emigration . . . Is there anything in this?[25]

Subsequently the West Cork Development Association was formed and grant-aided, helped by Ken's intervention with the then Taoiseach, Seán Lemass.

During the course of 1957 work on what Ken called his

'manual of recommended change' continued apace. One of his most valuable traits is his capacity not only to lead by example but to motivate and encourage others. 'I found it desirable,' he recalls, 'as soon as I was appointed secretary, to draw the various divisions of the department together to develop a broader consciousness and consistency of policy by holding a Monday morning meeting with the assistant secretaries to go through a tabular survey of the major matters under consideration and the decisions in contemplation . . . I favoured it as promoting awareness of problems, despatch, good sense and consistency in dealing with them and a stronger *esprit de corps*.' While the idea for *Economic Development* originated with Ken Whitaker, many others, as he is ever at pains to acknowledge, collaborated in its compilation. Charlie Murray, then strategically placed as assistant secretary in the office of the Taoiseach, became his principal collaborator. From within his own department he gathered together a band of willing young acolytes – Maurice Doyle, Séamus Ó Ciosáin, Maurice Horgan, Dónal Ó Loinsigh, Jim Dolan, Tomás Ó Cofaigh and Dr Brendan Menton – with others more junior, like Seán Cromien, working in the background. Further advice and comment was willingly offered by the three university professors Ryan, Lynch and Carter, and by the director of the Central Statistics Office, M. D. McCarthy. Encouragement and advice was also forthcoming from Ken's contacts in the IMF and World Bank, who 'applied some stimuli and made me feel that I was going on the right path'.

The enthusiasm of the project's instigator spread to his colleagues. 'We were chuffed to be asked,' recalls Tomás Ó Cofaigh, whose brief was the examination of every aspect of the tourism industry:

> We were encouraged to seek out new ideas for development, re-think all current expenditure, advise how to spend money, rather than not to spend anything at all, but to get better value for our

expenditure. Every detail of every department was examined for new ideas that might contribute to national development. I recall, for example, regarding the tourist industry, deliberations over how the tourist season might be extended and, at one stage, we even considered abolishing summer time![26]

Without any notion or expectation of monetary or promotional recompense or even if, in the end, the result of their travails would be accepted, much less acted upon by the government, Ken's team absorbed his drive and motivation. 'It was a challenge for us,' Ó Cofaigh acknowledges. 'We felt we were doing something new, something worthwhile. The other departments got used to us asking questions and they too became involved, offering opinions and ideas. Everyone worked after hours on their particular submissions, which were read by others in the team and commented upon, before being submitted.'[27] A sense of innovation, enthusiasm and purpose penetrated the stale air of the Upper Merrion Street corridors as through the autumn and into the winter of 1957 the minutiae of state, semi-state and private enterprise were analysed and the numerous and varied strands that would eventually constitute *Economic Development* were drawn together. 'We worked late into the night,' Ken remembers, 'and were early to work with real enthusiasm the next morning. We were refreshed by our release from a purely negative role and the feeling that we were doing something constructive and worthwhile.' For him, two lines of William Wordsworth's sum up the atmosphere:

> Bliss was it in that dawn to be alive,
> But to be young was very heaven!

The fact that, with the exception of Charlie Murray, Ken's team was composed of Finance staff, and was conducted in a low-key and semi-unofficial way, thus bypassing interdepartmental bureaucracy and rivalry, undoubtedly contributed to the relative speed with which *Economic Development* was completed. He assigned sections of the plan to individual members of the team who gathered and assessed relevant statistics and information on their designated fields, meeting on a weekly basis to discuss progress and problems arising. As well as editing the document, Ken personally wrote the introduction, the first four chapters on the economic position, financial policy, monetary policy, and development resources and needs, chapter 12, 'State Aid to Agriculture', and the final chapter, 'Conclusions and Recommendations'. 'When Ken got his hands on our individual submissions, of course, a terrible beauty was born, being greatly improved by his clearer and more lucid presentation,' Tomás Ó Cofaigh recalls.

In early December Ken informed his minister of what he and his colleagues had, by then, all but completed, and of 'the desirability of attempting to work out an integrated programme of national development', which he believed was critical 'for the country's survival as an economic entity'.[28] 'To do him justice,' Ken says, 'Dr Ryan took it in his stride and saw the virtue of a stimulus of this kind.' Ryan became Ken's buffer as well as a conduit to the government and agreed immediately to present the idea to cabinet, an indication of the extent of his trust and belief in his chief civil servant. In a follow-up summary of their initial conversation, which the minister circulated to members of the government, conscious of how closely he was skirting, if not actually transgressing, the traditional boundary between public servant and politician, Ken chose his words with diplomatic care. Anxious to avoid cabinet ministers baulking at any suggestion that they were being presented with a *fait accompli*, after a brief summary of the economic situation, he outlined the heads of the proposed scheme on which his team had been working. Anxious, too, that the other public service departments would not feel left out in the cold, to complete the project he proposed that his team should have free access to the advice and assistance of other departments and semi-state organizations. Knowing from experience that old habits and territorial jealousies were entrenched in some departmental thinking, he was insistent that the study should continue under his direction and under the auspices of the Department of Finance, whose 'central position . . . gives us a special responsibility for studying how economic progress can be promoted . . . I would willingly, and as quickly as possible, complete the work in hand . . . if it is felt that it serves a need and would be of assistance to the Government.'[29] In his capacity as secretary of the Department of Finance, and as a 'Finance Man' through and through, there was, perhaps, another more pragmatic motivation: to reinforce the department's predominant position and rid it of its image of 'inverted Micawberism' – of being always 'waiting for something to turn down'.

On 17 December the cabinet considered his request to continue the study to completion, and in doing so to have access to other government departments. Although he had secured his own minister's approval, Ken's proposal had yet to run the gauntlet of other ministers, including the 'chief architect of protectionism', the Tánaiste, Lemass, and the Taoiseach, de Valera. Where Lemass was concerned, Ken found he was pushing at an open door. 'You could not ask for a better minister if you wanted to put new ideas forward. After all, he was the apostle of protectionism, so if you could convince him that it was time to move away from it, there was nobody else in the cabinet who would defend it.' De Valera 'withdrew from the whole thing and left it to Lemass', but not before later claiming, as Ken good-humouredly recalls, 'that free trade had been his policy from the beginning . . . He sort of claimed it retrospectively!' With full cabinet endorsement secured, Ken lost no time in writing personally to the secretaries of the other departments, requesting their cooperation and support. 'I look upon this work as an effort by the public service to make a contribution to national development.'[30] The response was positive and wholehearted.

The sense of excitement the programme evoked within Finance now spread throughout the other public service departments, as those involved in collating the information and statistics became aware that something innovative and worthwhile was in the making and wanted to be part of it. Setting a deadline for the rest of the team, Ken completed his own draft of the first two chapters by 3 January 1958, running the chapter on financial and monetary policy before his former boss, J. J. McElligott. 'Nobody else has seen the draft – or will see it, until I hear from you.'[31] Others, including the trio of academics, Professors Ryan, Carter and Lynch, also contributed their views and comments. Paddy Lynch advocated the use of more forthright language than Ken had employed in his introduction: 'I would have expected you to begin with a recognition that our present plight is particularly serious, not because successive Governments have been remiss, but because they have done their best and their best has not been good enough.'[32] Ken, however, in his capacity as secretary of the department and coming face-to-face on a daily basis with government ministers whom he sought to win over, considered more diplomatic language the wiser option. Some opposition emanated from the Department of Industry and Commerce, under its intractable secretary J. C. B. McCarthy, who felt both his status and the traditional protectionist stance promoted by his department to be compromised by some of the study's recommendations. To placate him, Ken agreed to some minor changes, but the battle of wills between the two departments was to run for some time longer.

By May 1958 the first draft of the 249-page document *Economic Development* was completed. On 29 May a proof copy was presented to the government, whose rapidity of response must surely have set a record. The day following its presentation, the cabinet recommended 'as a matter of urgency' that the document be examined by all state and semi-state bodies, with observations to be forwarded to the minister for finance no later than 20 June, and stated that the minister for finance 'in the light of these observations will have a submission ready for the cabinet meeting on 1 July'.[33] In a strategic move, on his own initiative, Ken also forwarded the document to his contacts in the IMF, World Bank and OEEC. 'They had the money, the clout and were at the heart of international economic analysis and development. If you got them on your side, you were well on your way. And I did get them on our side.' With such international endorsement, he could expect less opposition from the government.

Detailed, meticulous and comprehensive, *Economic Development* surveyed and analysed the principal constituent parts of the Irish economy, from agriculture to tourism, examining their deficiencies as well as their potential, and offering proposals for future remedial action. It assembled and laid bare before the political and public gaze the inadequacies endemic in the economic structure of the country: the backward and unproductive state of agriculture; the meagreness of industry, hiding behind tariffs and quotas, producing products for which there was little export demand; the decline in population and the scourge of emigration; the scarcity and timidity of private capital and the tendency for public capital to be expended on projects that, however socially desirable, were economically unproductive. But, above all else, *Economic Development* offered hope and a way out of the economic quagmire in which Ireland and its people were fast bound. 'Possibilities of improvement are there, if we wish to realise them. It would be well to shut the door on the past and to move forward, energetically, intelligently and with the will to succeed but without expecting miracles of progress in a short time.'[34] *Economic Development* was a first step towards the framing of a programme of national development, a journey on which Ken urged the government to embark without delay.

The reaction was immediate and mainly positive, both inside and outside Ireland. 'Noble in concept, brilliant in execution and generous in feeling' was the verdict of the chairman of the

Agricultural Credit Corporation. The Irish ambassador to the United States acknowledged the text of the document to be 'manifestly the work not only of a masterly hand, but, as well, a ministering hand'.[35] From international bodies came similar praise. Louis Rasminsky, executive director of the IMF and the World Bank, offered Ken his personal congratulations on the completeness and objectivity of the study, while Charles Merwin of the IMF wrote that 'Ben King [World Bank]. . . seems to feel you have pretty well done his job for him.' From Paris, J. F. Cahan, the Canadian deputy secretary of the OEEC, enthused: 'It fills me with admiration . . . I should like to make the first four chapters required reading for anyone who is charged with examining the problems of economic development in any country.'[36] In June a fact-finding mission to Dublin by the World Bank urged the publication of *Economic Development* and the adoption of an economic plan based on its recommendations, which the Bank considered a prerequisite for any future assistance to Ireland. At his attendance in October at the annual meeting of the World Bank and the IMF in New Delhi, Ken presented a preliminary draft of a proposed development programme based on *Economic Development* and received a positive reaction from delegates.

His stay in New Delhi also gave rise to an unusual mission outside his Finance brief. William O'Brien, a director of the Central Bank and former general secretary of the Irish Transport and Workers Union, asked J. J. McElligott to present to the Indian prime minister, Pandit Nehru, a package of letters written by the 1916 Rising leader, James Connolly, describing his experiences in India as a British soldier in the 1880s. Through his friendship with Sir William (Bill) Iliff, president of the World Bank, Ken succeeded in getting an audience with the Indian premier. Ushered into the office by, as Ken recalls, 'an angelic lady swathed in a colourful sari', they found Nehru 'listless and abstracted; he had just come back from a visit to either Kashmir or Nepal . . . I had the impression that his mind was far away.'[37]

McElligott duly handed over the letters to Nehru. In 1999 copies of the letters were returned by the authorities in India for inclusion in a new published collection of Connolly's correspondence.

Negative reaction to *Economic Development* was confined to some left-wing commentators, who dubbed it a sell-out to foreign capital. One noticeable omission was any reference to investment in education (with the exception of agricultural colleges), an indication, perhaps, of the control wielded by the Catholic Church at the time in this sector, which was therefore deemed to be outside the domain of the Department of Finance. Ken's departmental colleagues offered their congratulations and support for the implementation of the recommendations. When their amendments and comments were submitted, the final draft of *Economic Development* was quickly prepared and circulated. It became known as *The Grey Book* because of the colour of the cover, although to Ken's eyes 'it looked to be green'. On 22 July his recommendation that a programme for economic development become government policy was accepted and a committee created, chaired by Seán Lemass, to draft a white paper based on *Economic Development*. The committee's members included ministers James Ryan, Erskine Childers and Patrick Smith, together with a group of departmental secretaries, headed by Ken. Charlie Murray was appointed committee secretary. The white paper officially endorsing *Economic Development* was entitled the *Programme for Economic Expansion*; just fifty pages long, it was presented to both Houses of the Oireachtas on 11 November 1958 and was published the following day. Covering the years 1959–63, it heralded a fundamental and historic change in traditional national economic policy. As Ken testifies:

Both these documents bade farewell to the old outmoded ideas for economic and social progress. Self-sufficiency was abandoned and, to oversimplify a little, the new Programme put grass before grain and, on the industrial side, put export-orientated expansion, even under foreign ownership, before dependence on protected domestic industry, lacking adequate enterprise and skill.[38]

The fate of the more comprehensive original document remained to be decided. Given its influential international backing, its greater detail and the fact that it formed the basis of the government's white paper, it seemed logical that *Economic Development* should also be published, despite being at variance with the white paper on a few points. Unlike the governmental document, for example, it did not predict any precise level of growth in national income, merely noting that the annual rate of growth between 1949 and 1956 was a mere 1 per cent and that, if the new proposals for the economy were adopted, the rate of increase might be expected to double – in time. This 'was a deliberate strategy on my part', Ken explains, 'in the hope it would be exceeded and give the necessary psychological boost', whereas if higher targets were set and not attained, this failure would merely exacerbate the prevailing air of despondency. In the event, the programme achieved a remarkable average annual growth rate of 4 per cent over its five-year span.

The main dilemma regarding the publication of *Economic Development*, however, related more to the question of its authorship than to its recommendations. Publication of a work attributed to one or more identifiable public servants was unprecedented. Civil servants were expected to remain anonymous, preserving the traditional boundaries that existed between them, the government and the public. In relation to *Economic Development*, Ken's former ministerial boss, Seán MacEntee, was adamant that any transgression of this principle would undermine ministerial prerogative and responsibility. James Ryan, on the other hand, was equally insistent that the study be published under his secretary's name. The issue was finally put beyond doubt when Seán Lemass rowed in behind Ryan. There were ulterior reasons for this break with tradition, other than the wish of the government to give credit where it was due. Ken had been appointed secretary of Finance by the previous government and therefore it was presumed that the opposition could hardly question or contravene the advice of its own appointee. 'Publication as an anonymous government publication would give it political aspects which we did not want . . . the association with the name of a non-political civil servant would help to get its acceptance over political boundaries . . . It was a deliberate decision, part of our effort to get economic development away from party political tags,' Seán Lemass later confirmed.[39] But other less altruistic reasons were also in play. After decades of disappointment and economic stagnation, the Irish voting public had become disillusioned with politicians and had little faith in their pronouncements or predictions. If the latest recovery plan was to have any credibility, it had to be seen to be 'above politics'. Moreover, the recommendations in *Economic Development* embodied a reversal of the protectionist central pillar of policy upheld for decades by Fianna Fáil and, as Ken recorded, 'they saw the advantage of attributing a total reversal of policy to acceptance of the advice of independent civil servants'.[40] Lemass, in particular, Ken recalls, 'recognized that there was an inherent honesty about what was being advised . . . that we were not seeking controversy but that we could be trusted. But, of course, it also gave the politicians an out. If it drew down terrible condemnation, they could say it was not the work of the government but a group of characters in the civil service who were never asked to do it in the first place, perhaps wasting their own and the Department's time in the process!' After almost sixty years since the publication of his most acclaimed opus, 'the courage of the government in being prepared to publish, under their own auspices, critical comments on their own policy' still amazes Ken, as does the fact that such a major reversal of policy – the abandonment of industrial protection and agricultural self-sufficiency – took place without even a debate in Dáil Éireann, possibly because the opposition saw it as urgently desirable, the government could ascribe it to the objective advice of civil servants, and, above all because it shone a light of hope in what was 'a dark night of the soul'. The psychological boost was all the greater coming from the arch-pessimists of Finance!

On 22 November, ten days after the publication of the white paper, *Economic Development* was finally published, bearing an acknowledgement written by Ken Whitaker: 'This study of national development problems and opportunities was prepared by the Secretary of the Department of Finance, with the co-operation of others in, or connected with, the public service.' Described by the eminent historian F. S. L. Lyons as 'a watershed in the modern economic history of the country',[41] like a kind of Magna Carta in the context of Irish official documents, over the decades following its publication *Economic Development* acquired an iconic status, both for itself and for its principal scribe. Ken Whitaker, one report later claimed, 'had lit a fire under our stagnant economy, brushed sentiment and history aside and set a calculated target for a future that was to prove so beneficial not only to the present generation but perhaps for generations to come'.[42] At the time of its publication, an *Irish Times* editorial claimed the study as 'almost revolutionary' and lauded its author as 'a singularly independent, far-sighted and progressive civil servant',[43] while the *Financial Times* proclaimed 'a major contribution to economic thought and planning'.[44] Meanwhile, throughout the country the pages of this 'revolutionary' document were perused by ordinary citizens frustrated and demoralized by decades of economic stagnation.

Like every programme of radical change, especially when taken out of the context of prevailing economic thought and circumstances, *Economic Development* did attract some (mainly ret-rospective) criticism. Its modest projections and expectation that the agricultural industry, when suitably modernized, would offer the greatest basis for economic growth and export, which in the event did not fully materialize, have in the assessments of some later economic commentators overshadowed the document's obvious and intended achievement as a revolutionary blueprint for the Irish economy. It should be recalled that in 1957/8 the data available to Ken and his team on which to construct plans and projections were limited, while widespread access to European markets for Irish agricultural produce was still a pipe-dream. The policy assumption that social needs, such as housing, would con-tinue to decline was not borne out by events, owing to the very success of the *Programme for Economic Expansion*, which generated an expansion of the economy and a subsequent decline in emi-gration, with a consequent increase in demand for houses and schools. Above all, with his trademark insight into both the public mood and the mindset of the body politic, Ken Whitaker judged acutely what was feasible and what was not in the climate in which he had to operate. 'How quickly forgotten', he wrote to one critic in 1982, 'can be the perception so prevalent in the mid-50s of a country whose economic and social development had dis-mally failed to live up to expectations.'[45]

Some criticism bordered on the bizarre. In his book *Ireland in Crisis*, published later, in 1986, the maverick economist Raymond Crotty made the claim 'that foreign borrowing played the part in the 1960s and 1970s that the potato did in the economic growth of late-Georgian Ireland, possibly threatening similar long-term results', and that T. K. Whitaker 'was more responsible than any other person for Ireland's unique public indebtedness'.[46] Given that, owing to Ken's consistent aversion to, and control of, credit during the period, Ireland's foreign borrowing rose from £40 mil-lion at the start of the 1960s to a mere £78 million at the close of the decade (of which £31 million represented a short-term

recourse to IMF grant aid), the statement was ridiculous as well
as libellous. The intervention of Professor Louden Ryan, who
challenged Crotty that his statements did 'not accord with the
facts', brought a counter-challenge from the latter to debate the
points 'in an open public forum'.[47] Given that by then the economist was campaigning as a candidate for election to the European
Parliament and refused 'to be deflected from his prejudices by the
truth', Ken considered it pointless to engage in a public debate,
since his critic 'would probably relish a free opportunity to boost
his candidature'.[48]

While Crotty sought to portray him, as Ken recalls with amusement, as 'a profligate borrower and expansionist', two other
authors, Paul Bew and Henry Patterson, in their 1982 biography
of Seán Lemass, whose policies they claimed were 'undoubtedly
in the political interests of the dominant class', accused Ken, with
no more justification, of pursuing a policy 'of deflation and
reliance on private capital' to promote industrial development.[49]
While he dismissed such claims as revisionist 'nonsense', Ken well
realized that such 'nonsense' tends to gain legs with repetition, as
evidenced in the first edition of the historian Roy Foster's *Modern
Ireland 1600–1972*, in which the assertions of Crotty, Bew and
Patterson were reiterated. On Ken's personal intervention with
the author, however, these were later amended. More recently,
criticisms resurfaced in 2011 when the industrial policy promoted
in *Economic Development* became the subject of critical debate in the
Economic and Social Review. Such retrospective criticisms, as Ken
notes with resignation, are merely testament to the veracity of the
old Gaelic proverb, 'the in-between man is never safe!'.

In 1958, however, supporters of *Economic Development* far out-
numbered its critics. The practicality and simplicity of its
message, assessments and recommendations, and its honest,
unambiguous and non-partisan tone, struck a chord, not merely
among politicians, businessmen and academics, but among the
ordinary people of Ireland, both rural and urban. 'It brings a ray

of enlightened hope to a situation seemingly irredeemable ...
There must be thousands like myself who see in it a proof that
amid the eddying forces of politics which bedevil the administration of this country, there is a wise hand at the helm. Long
may it remain there,' a County Cork farmer wrote to Ken. 'It
should be made compulsory reading for all politicians – a chapter
a day in the Dáil,' another recommended. 'I don't suppose you'll
get a medal for it but you are entitled at least to the thanks of us
all.'[50]

Economic Development lowered the barriers that Ireland had
erected around itself and allowed the Irish people to look at their
country and themselves, not from some mystic, historically
idealized vantage point, but from eye level. What they saw may
not have been attractive or inspiring, but Ken Whitaker and his
team offered them a way out of the morass and the realization
that the remedies, some painful, lay within their own grasp. As
Ken more modestly puts it:

> It was my good fortune to be able to advance a simple policy idea:
> the way to higher incomes and employment in industry and
> services was not through protectionism but through competitive
> participation in world trade and the welcoming of foreign invest-
> ment to supplement increased productive domestic investment.
> For agriculture, then still the main source of exports, the best
> course was to concentrate on realising the natural advantage of
> grasslands as a source of quality meat and dairy produce.[51]

As Tomás Ó Cofaigh notes, Ken's 'outstanding characteristics
were (and are) his intellectual clarity and honesty. These led him,
fruitfully, to cry halt to the economic and social drift of the
nation, to take a clear view of appropriate corrective action, to
convince decision-makers and provide them with a blue-print for
action.'[52]

For historians such as Dr Ronan Fanning, '*Economic Development* ultimately succeeded because so many wanted it to succeed. People craved the beat of a different drum and if the tunes to which they now began marching were still patriotic – albeit from a new hymnal of economic patriotism – then so much the better.'[53] For politicians such as the late John Kelly, the study's 'jargon-free assessments, devoid of political trumpeting, its statement of priorities, not all of them popular, its setting of simple, modest, credible targets',[54] still served to inspire twenty-five years later. The 'plain people of Ireland', for whose betterment *Economic Development* was initiated, would not forget the dedication, integrity and inspiration of its main proponent and author.

6

The Promised Land
1959–62

*It would be well to shut the door on the past and to move forward
energetically, intelligently and with the will to succeed, but without expecting
miracles of progress in a short time.*

T. K. Whitaker[1]

THE COMPILATION OF *Economic Development* and its derivative
Programme for Economic Expansion was the easier .part of the
enormous task of transforming the Irish economy. While Ken
Whitaker had produced the blueprint, it was the government of
the day that had to make it, as he wrote, its 'supreme policy . . .
and the degree to which the plan's objectives are achieved should
be the foremost measure of the success or failure of a
Government's economic and social policy'.[2] He envisaged it as
conducive to good government as well as to good economic
management, shifting government policy away from the
hyperbole of election promises and what he terms 'the Santa
Claus syndrome' that often afflicted annual budgets and, for the
duration of a five-year period, towards the setting of realistic
aims and the promotion of policies that were soundly based and
flexible enough to accommodate unforeseen changes. But, as Ken
admitted, 'no unique set of prescriptions, handed down from
Mount Sinai by the Government', could, in themselves, become

'the guide to the Promised Land'.[3] For a plan to be successful, it must, as demonstrated by the French planning experience, have wide community support. 'As many people as possible must feel that it is *their* plan, that they are committed to its success,' and become involved in the constructive shaping of their own future. But participants in the plan had also to be aware of the inevitability and significance of the choices that would have to be made; to accept that aspirations would have to be restricted and confined to the reality of the situation and to available resources. Otherwise, as he conceded, 'the plan will merely express wishful thinking and irreconcilable desires'.[4]

While a certain serendipity, not least in the form of an international economic upswing, may have played a part in the success of *Economic Development* and the *Programme for Economic Expansion*, domestic developments and attitudes also played their part. One significant event occurred on 15 January 1959 when, at the age of seventy-seven, de Valera announced his intention to stand down as Taoiseach and as president of Fianna Fáil – a decision precipitated, perhaps, more by revelations regarding his financial interest in the *Irish Press* newspaper group than by choice. The vacancy in the office of president created by the retirement of Seán T. Ó Ceallaigh provided an appropriate exit route from politics for 'the Chief'. Despite giving his assent to the dramatic change in economic policy being promoted by the secretary of the Department of Finance, de Valera's later comment to Ken, 'Ach tá rudaí eile níos tábhachtaí' ('But other things are more important'), indicated how out of touch he continued to be.

Despite opposition from some of his parliamentary colleagues, on 23 June 1959 de Valera's preferred successor, Seán Lemass, stepped into the breach at the age of fifty-nine. At the same time, the old guard in Fianna Fáil were gradually being replaced by up-and-coming 'soldiers of destiny'. Some, like Charles Haughey, Neil Blaney and Kevin Boland, would come to national and international prominence for reasons other than their respective cabinet briefs. Among those drafted into the new cabinet were Paddy Hillery and Jack Lynch; the latter, who replaced Lemass as minister for industry and commerce, was later to collaborate with Ken on issues of national importance. De Valera's retirement was quickly followed by the exit of other members of the political establishment: Richard Mulcahy, leader of Fine Gael, was replaced by James Dillon, and Brendan Corish succeeded William Norton in Labour. New hands at the helm of the three major political parties further epitomized the country's mood for change.

For Ken, the most important political change was undoubtedly the election of Seán Lemass as Taoiseach. 'A pragmatic nationalist, able, forthright and effective,' Lemass, he recalls, was simply the right man in the right place at the right time. Lemass's vision of Ireland reached beyond the bitter confines of Civil War politics, while 'like St Augustine', as Ken notes, he had become a late convert to the new credo of free trade. And it was Ken who, inadvertently, had played a part in setting Lemass on the road to economic conversion. Shortly after Fianna Fáil returned to government, Lemass fell ill and was confined to bed for a short period. 'I got an urgent message from him that he would like some textbooks to read on economics and banking. The explanation, I gathered, was that Mr de Valera was pressing him to use that golden opportunity to learn Irish!' Whether as a result of the reading matter chosen for him by the secretary of the Department of Finance, which included subjects such as international banking and development economics, or whether of his own volition, by 1958 Lemass's conversion was complete. 'He was the best person to lead the new policy. Nobody could have got rid of protectionism except the chief architect himself.' It was Lemass who steered the *Programme for Economic Expansion* past the potential obstacles, both at the cabinet table and, not least, in the form of diehard supporters of protectionism, subsidies and tariffs within his own department, standing four-square behind the programme's free trade philosophy. Like Ken, Lemass also considered the psychological dimension of the programme to be essential in providing a much-needed fillip to public confidence and encouraging a sense of a more practical patriotism. An acknowledged organizer, cool under pressure, intelligent and an indefatigable worker, Lemass was also a noted poker-player, a skill that would stand him in good stead in the coming years. 'He was always willing to take decisions', Ken noted; 'indeed, he loved taking decisions. He was forever seeking to anticipate events and problems and to influence developments in good time.' This made him the ideal political ally to support and implement radical changes to take the Irish economy out of the doldrums.

As well as the political transformation, legislative changes to pave the way for future industrial policy signalled a key change in economic direction. With symbolic irony, the Control of Manufactures Acts, instituted by Lemass in 1932 and 1934 to protect Irish industry from foreign takeover, were replaced by the Industrial Development (Encouragement of External Investment) Act 1958, inviting foreign investment in Irish industry. Other measures, including the removal of price and profit controls, tax relief to encourage exports, tourism, new factory buildings, plant, machinery and shipping, assistance to exporters, and – heralding a further incentive to foreign invest-ment – freedom for foreign investment companies to repatriate their profits, all came into being. Shannon Free Airport Development Company (SFADCO), a state-sponsored develop-ment agency, was established to oversee a customs-free area created at Shannon Airport. The Irish Congress of Trade Unions was formally inaugurated in February 1959, providing workers with strength in unity which, in the immediate future at least, would contribute to the implementation of a national wages policy. Immediately before the publication of *Economic Development*, Ken had himself participated in a Workers' Union of Ireland seminar in Wicklow. The Federation of Irish Industries and the National Farmers Association (NFA) were also established to promote the interests of the industrial and farming sectors respectively.

Internationally, a more progressive profile of the country was being presented. The national airline prepared to fly the Atlantic, the Irish army embarked on United Nations peacekeeping duties in the Congo, and Ireland's representative to the United Nations, Freddie Boland, was elected president of the General Assembly. Representation by Irish business at international trade fairs increased, while a trade delegation to Bonn resulted in improved arrangements for Irish exports. On the home front, as the Republic's national TV station RTÉ prepared to go on air, and the social and cultural revolution epitomized by the 'swinging sixties' exploded, Irish society emerged into the world's glare to expose itself to critical comparison and self-analysis.

On the publication of the *Programme for Economic Expansion* and its adoption by the government, Ken sought to maintain the momentum within the public service. The programme, as he envisaged it, was not to be a static set of rules but a flexible mechanism, open to change, which, if it was to succeed, must involve all sections of the public service as well as the population at large. A committee of secretaries of the departments of Finance, Agriculture, Industry and Commerce, and Lands was established to consider, at quarterly intervals, the progress achieved, recommend modifications or extensions to the programme, 'to ensure maximum speed and co-ordination in carrying them through',[5] and to inform the general public of the initiatives being taken. Anxious that the invigorating influence, coordinating role and cooperative effort generated within his own department during the compilation of *Economic Development* be maintained, Ken established an Economic Development Branch, with responsibility 'to seek out ways and means of advancing economic growth and to develop ideas and projects to the point at which they can be placed with the appropriate department or agency'.[6] Headed by Charlie Murray, the branch liaised with all public service departments and semi-state bodies, which were urged to submit ideas about productive investment projects, whether in the public or the private sector. To link the new branch with the work of the committee of secretaries, Ken gave it the added task of compiling the committee's quarterly reports.

The drive for public interest and involvement in the new programme was further extended when, despite the opposition's claim that it was nothing more than 'a big bluff', the government invited proposals for schemes of economic merit from the wider public. From corporations, county councils, industrialists, chambers of commerce, farmers' groups, trade unions, community groups and individuals, over seven hundred proposals were received. Many, however, advocating socially desirable projects such as the construction of municipal swimming pools, as Ken wryly notes, 'did not get a lot of attention', failing to make a case for economic benefit.

Prepared by Ken Whitaker and driven by Seán Lemass, the first *Programme for Economic Expansion* proved enormously successful in transforming the Irish economy. As the message and opportunities it embodied sank home, it released a reservoir of suppressed energy and optimism in the country, helped by the buoyancy of international trade. Targets set in the programme were surpassed. The modest annual growth rate of just 1 per cent in GNP achieved between 1949 and 1957 rose to almost 4.5 per cent and, significantly, without any negative impact on the balance of payments. Employment and investment increased, and emigration, the country's most persistent affliction, was finally arrested in 1966 with a population rise of sixty-six thousand. Ken encouraged the establishment of the Committee of Industrial Organization (CIO), an innovative partnership between the government, industry and trade unions, which conducted a major review of Irish industries. Special grants, loans and tax incentives were provided to help firms to modernize and adapt to international trading standards. Protective tariffs were dismantled and, on the strength of attractive grants and tax concessions, international companies established bases in Ireland. Native private enterprise, on the other hand, long indulged and protected, proved disappointing in developing Ireland's economic potential, demonstrating a lack of entrepreneurship and ideas and a reluctance to make use of the investment capital made available by Irish banks.

Semi-state bodies, such as the Irish Sugar Company, Bord na Móna, Aer Lingus, Ceimicí Teo, the Industrial Credit Corporation and the Industrial Development Authority, on the other hand, demonstrated, as Ken acknowledges, 'that we had a second string to our bow and did not entirely depend on private enterprise. Those appointed to manage them were genuine entrepreneurs who regarded what they were asked to do as a privilege and never betrayed that trust.' With a mixture of affection and admiration, tempered with exasperation, Ken recalls one of this band of public-service entrepreneurs, the redoubtable Lieutenant-General Michael J. Costello, managing director of the Irish Sugar Company. An unusual mix of military man and business pioneer, an intelligent man and a natural-born soldier, he brought, as Ken recalls, 'some of the best features of the army into commercial business, including doing the best with the resources available'. He often tended, however, to 'think on the large scale' and had on occasions to be 'gently reined in'. The gradual demise of the Sugar Company over succeeding years and the eventual dismantling of its infrastructure represented a shameful decline from, and contrast to, the pioneering and public-spirited work undertaken by its first managing director.

Expressing the wry contention that 'the evolving Department of Finance made no pretence to a monopoly of economic wisdom',[7] Ken was also instrumental in establishing a range of independent economic research bodies away from the coalface, which would play an essential role in maintaining the momentum. In the course of compiling *Economic Development*, he had become aware of the shortcomings in both quantity and quality of the economic research and analysis available to the public service. In 1959, while attending World Bank and IMF meetings in Washington, he travelled to New York to make contact with the secretary of the Ford Foundation, Joseph MacDaniel, and his Irish American associate, Peter Shanley. 'Knowing that Mr Shanley regularly served eight o'clock Mass in St Patrick's Cathedral, and breakfasted afterwards with Mr MacDaniel in a nearby café, I also became a devout attender at this Mass, joining the two afterwards for breakfast and developing the case for a Ford Foundation grant to establish an independent economic research body in Dublin!'[8] The result was a $280,000 grant and the establishment, in June 1960, of the Economic Research Institute (ERI) with, on Ken's recommendation, Dr Roy Geary, then a renowned statistician at the United Nations, as its first director. On Ken's further intervention in 1963, the institute's functions were extended to cover social as well as economic research and analysis, and it was subsequently renamed the Economic and Social Research Institute (ESRI). When the funding received from the Ford Foundation expired in the mid-1960s, Ken organized replacement financing for the institute through the Department of Finance. Today the ESRI continues to fulfil its role in the development of the Irish economy, its reports and commentary making a valuable contribution to the formulation of national policy. In 2010 the institute celebrated its fiftieth anniversary, at which Ken was guest of honour in its new headquarters, located appropriately in Whitaker Square.

In 1962 Ken helped establish, and served as the first chair of, the Institute for Advanced Studies; and in 1963 the National Industrial Economic Council (subsequently renamed the National Economic and Social Council, NESC) was founded. Freddie Boland was initially proposed as its first chairman but, because of a number of directorships in private industry he had accepted on retirement from the public service, he was deemed unacceptable by the trade unions. Ken was appointed chairman in his place. Given his position as principal civil servant, the posting might well have proved fraught but, with his customary tact and integrity, Ken made it work. Under his chairmanship, the NIEC did not baulk at issuing constructive criticism whenever it was merited. 'The best work of the Council was done in studying the conditions on which full employment might, in time, be attained . . . and in outlining the principles of a prices and incomes policy.'[9] Over subsequent decades, and to the present day, he has continued to give these independent research bodies his support. 'I have no doubt that this intermeshing of co-operative study and action played a significant part in preparing Ireland, psychologically and technically, for the approach of free trade.'[10]

As Ireland set about translating the blueprint for its economic future into reality, however, developments on the international stage threatened the project's success. Both Lemass and Ken had their sights set on joining the new Europe emerging from the destruction and divisiveness of the Second World War; but Ireland's admittance to European markets was not to be achieved quickly or easily. Both *Economic Development* and the *Programme for Economic Expansion* were drafted on the assumption of the establishment of a European free trade area. As Ken maintained, 'it would be unrealistic, in the light of the probable emergence of a Free Trade Area, to rely on a policy of protection similar to that applied over the past 25 years or so'.[11] The future of native industry lay in the export market; but the rules governing European free trade would mean a systematic, albeit gradual, reduction in Irish subsidies and tariffs, leaving weaker and inefficient home-grown industries exposed and having to adapt or die. In the event, negotiations regarding a free trade area broke down, and on 1 January 1958 the European Economic Community (EEC) came into being as a common market of just six countries: West Germany, France, Italy, Belgium, the Netherlands and Luxembourg. Two years later, in 1960, the nations left outside – Britain, Sweden, Denmark, Finland, Norway, Austria and Portugal, known as the 'Outer Seven' – formed the European Free Trade Association (EFTA); but the EFTA, unlike the EEC, had no support mechanism for agriculture, and so had less attraction for Ireland. With Europe split into two groups, Ireland subsequently found itself isolated and, as Ken noted, its new 'faith in free trade was in danger of being lost'.[12] Ireland consequently drifted into a period of suspended animation in which, despite all his work and everything he had planned, a relapse into protectionism became a nightmare possibility.

This, as he wrote, was 'the crunch period in the move to free trade',[13] a juncture at which steady nerves and strong convictions were needed to negotiate the obstacles that presented themselves. In 1959 the options for Ireland's industrial and agricultural interests were stark. The country's main trading partner, Britain, was on the verge of aligning itself with countries to which it would be expected to give preferential concessions. EFTA was primarily concerned with industrial free trade, and the dismantling of British tariffs against its EFTA partners would consequently have implications for Irish industry. British concessions granted to allied countries, such as Denmark and Norway, especially in agriculture and fisheries, would have even more serious consequences for the Irish economy. Whether Ireland joined EFTA or not, or sought further trade concessions from Britain, in Ken's opinion the status quo was simply not an option. What was required was an international outlet that, in return for the dismantling of industrial protection, which in his opinion was in the long-term interest of the country, would also provide worthwhile benefits for the country's all-important agricultural exports.

The committee of departmental secretaries, under Ken's chairmanship, prepared a comprehensive review of Ireland's economic relationship with Britain. In the light of the evolving European trade situation, the review urged a substantial widening of previous trade agreements with Britain and the encouragement of additional British investment in Ireland which, in turn, required further dismantling of protective tariffs in favour of British goods. The suggestions were guaranteed to raise hackles, economic and nationalistic. In an unusual break with precedent and an affirmation of his standing with the cabinet, and with Lemass in particular, Ken wrote directly to the Taoiseach recommending the gradual dismantling of Irish protective tariffs, a move which would, he maintained, be conducive to industrial expansion and enable the country to avoid 'condemning ourselves to a static situation'.[14] Talks at ministerial level on future trading relations with Britain took place in London in July 1959 and were followed, over the succeeding months, by a series of official meetings with British officials to investigate the possibility of establishing a 'free trade area' with Britain in return for the lowering of tariffs. While Britain ultimately refused to go down the road of free trade, a more modest trade agreement was eventually signed on 13 April 1960. In return for a review by the Irish government of protective duties imposed on British goods, the British government agreed to give formal contractual status to some Irish agricultural exports.

Despite the setbacks, free trade continued to be widely accepted as the reality of the future. Nevertheless, the debate regarding the ability of Irish industry to survive the associated lowering of protective tariffs and subsidies reverberated within the corridors of the civil service and developed into a war of words between Ken, J. C. B. McCarthy and J. C. Nagle, his counterparts in the departments of Industry and Commerce and Agriculture respectively. From October 1959 to January 1960 their differences gave rise to an intriguing exchange of 'semi-official' letters on the pros and cons of protection and free trade, which Ken subsequently published in 2006 under the title

Protection or Free Trade: The Final Battle. Originally all three were 'Finance Men' and, as Ken recalls, 'there was something almost fated about the current Finance Man going in a different direction to them, as advocates of protectionism, so that when that policy was attacked it was as if it was an attack on them personally'. There was also a more territorial aspect to their stance, especially in the case of McCarthy, who, as secretary of a department that traditionally did not see eye-to-eye with Finance, viewed Ken's vigorous promotion of free trade as impinging on his preserve, and even undermining his authority.

While Ken remembers McCarthy as 'an engaging sort of a fellow', others recall him as a more authoritarian figure, conscious of his status. After months of polite skirmishing over their divergent views regarding the advantages and disadvantages of free trade, and its effects on Irish industry, employment and emigration, an element of strain became apparent. Referring to Ken's detailed and considered memorandum on the reasons for reducing protection, McCarthy dismissed it as 'an idealistic approach', backed merely by 'faith in the operation of the economic laws', instead of 'tempering economic theory to the facts of our industrial life'.[15] In response, Ken reminded McCarthy that even the Federation of Irish Industries recognized free trade as inevitable. 'We both know people who are more Catholic than the Pope. Should Industry and Commerce not guard against being more protectionist than the Federation of Irish Industries?'[16] Having failed in his attempts to persuade his counterpart 'that a progressive lowering of tariffs is necessary for our economic progress regardless of what is happening in the outside world', and that 'the indisputable principle that the future expansion of industry here is almost entirely dependent on attracting external demand', Ken and his antagonist eventually agreed to a truce, leaving Ken, as the senior secretary, 'entitled', as he wrote, 'to the last word in our correspondence'.[17] Such exchanges between departmental heads within the public service were significant not just as expressions of conflicting views between two senior civil servants; they provided the government with a choice of viewpoints on which to base decisions on the direction of future economic policy, especially against the rapidly changing economic background in Europe.

The question of the future of tariffs and subsidies, in the light of free trade, also prompted an exchange of views between Ken and J. J. McElligott. Highlighting what he considered to be the excessive range of duties imposed on the Irish consumer on such items as refrigerators, motor cars, cameras and other non-essential items, McElligott remarked that 'instead of dismantling our tariff wall we seem to be constantly adding to it'.[18] This elicited a firm response from Ken. 'So far as the consumer is concerned, I find it hard to reconcile a strong sympathy for purchasers of refrigerators, motor cars and cameras with the general philosophy that consumer spending in this country tends to be excessive . . . With very few exceptions the items mentioned are eminently suitable for taxing.'[19] By 1964 substantial tariff reductions had come into effect and Ireland had become firmly focused on gaining membership of the EEC.

In 1960, however, the prevailing uncertainty and isolation turned the government's attention to the possibility of joining a wider international trade group – the General Agreement on Tariffs and Trade (GATT). Founded in 1948, by 1960 it had thirty-seven contracting parties, accounting for 80 per cent of world trade. From Ireland's perspective, attaining full membership would enable it to share in the trade and tariff liberalization measures promoted by GATT. That Britain was already a member added to the attraction of this option. On the other hand, as a contracting member, Ireland would be forced to make changes in its current tariff and protection regime, as Ken had advocated both in *Economic Development* and in the *Programme for Economic Expansion*. In a detailed report he advised the government that, subject to acquiring a waiver in relation to the tariff preferences already in place with Britain, Ireland should seek admission to GATT.

There was much at stake for the country and further private discussions between Ken and Lemass followed, one of which, as the former recalls, took place during a family holiday in Durrus, County Cork. Before the advent of private, not to mention mobile, phones, he was summoned to the local village shop to take an urgent call from the Taoiseach.

> It was about GATT, which we were about to join, and I had to take the call in the local all-purpose grocery and hardware shop, with a bar in the back and an old-fashioned phone in a corner, beside flitches of bacon and spools of binder-twine. The men in the pub had their drinks and argued away, indifferent to the complicated issues under discussion.

This whimsical picture was a potent reminder of the social realities of Irish rural life of the period. In the event, it was decided to leave membership of GATT in abeyance because, by then, a more tantalizing goal beckoned as Ireland started out on what has been described as the 'tortuous path' towards membership of the EEC.

In 1960, interest in Europe did not extend far beyond a small pro-European group of people in public life, such as Garret FitzGerald, chairman of the Irish Council of the European Movement. The European Common Market did not rate as a subject of discussion among the Irish public. Debate about the introduction of an international dimension into Irish economic affairs had tended to centre on membership of other bodies such as the OECD, EFTA and GATT. Garret FitzGerald recalls in his autobiography a visit to Ireland in 1959 by Dr Hallstein, the Community's first president, during which he was asked by an Irish journalist if Ireland was a member of the Common Market! Even among those who were interested in Ireland's journey towards EEC membership, few had bothered to read President de Gaulle's *Mémoires de guerre* and his statement of his post-war political motivation: 'regrouper les pays qui touchent aux Alpes, au Rhin et aux Pyrénées' to create a continental bloc as a global power – a vision of Europe that ominously did not include either Britain or Ireland. Having read the general's words, Ken realized that the road towards the 'promised land' of the EEC was likely to be a long and rocky one.

While progress in Irish industrial production and exports on the basis of the *Programme for Economic Expansion* had been spectacular, a similar turnaround had not materialized in the agricultural sector. Consequently, for farming organizations the proposed Common Agricultural Policy (CAP) contemplated by the EEC offered the prospect of enhanced markets and prices for Irish agricultural exports, and farming organizations pressed the government to apply for membership of the EEC. But here Ireland's 'special relationship' with its main trading partner posed a problem. While some form of associated EEC membership had been contemplated during trade discussions, the British had made it clear that any move by Ireland towards full EEC membership would have serious implications for the preferential trade arrangements they had granted to their neighbour. Such was the importance of the British market that even Lemass was cautious, and spoke only in terms of 'a link' or of 'associate' EEC membership. For Ken, on the other hand, who, as he says, 'never believed in half-measures', full EEC membership was the goal, as a route not only to economic independence but to political independence as well. For him, economic independence, rather than militaristic nationalism, was the true measure of political freedom and the only rational way to achieve it.

During April and May 1961 speculation mounted that Britain was contemplating EEC membership. This led to a flurry of activity by the Irish government. On 5 July a white paper containing basic information about the EEC and the Treaty of

Rome, as well as the options available to the government, was introduced in the Dáil by the Taoiseach, who also outlined the necessary adjustments that Irish industry and agriculture, and Irish workers, would have to make in advance of membership being granted. On 31 July 1961 Britain formally announced its decision to open negotiations for entry to the EEC. Pre-empting the British application, on the same day, in a letter to President Ludwig Erhard, a framed copy of which hangs on the wall of Ken's study, Seán Lemass formally submitted Ireland's application for full membership of the EEC.

Considering it 'an economic disaster' should Britain gain entry and Ireland be left out in the cold, in April Ken asked Garret FitzGerald, then an economic journalist, to sound out reaction to the possibility of Ireland's membership during the latter's impending trip to Brussels. Following Ireland's formal application in July 1961, the government sent Ken and Con Cremin, former ambassador to France and then secretary of the Department of External Affairs, 'fluent in French and a very agreeable Kerry man', to visit the capitals of the six member states to allay doubts about Ireland's economic capacity and political suitability (in light of her neutrality) as a prospective applicant. Over a period of eight days they held discussions with ministers of the Six in European capitals and were left with an uneasy feeling that the issues might well prove a stumbling block. This was duly confirmed when Britain and Denmark were allowed to proceed to the negotiation stage while the EEC Council requested further consideration and discussion on 'the special problems' raised by the Irish application.

Despite the outcome, their excursion had its share of lighter moments. At the Quai d'Orsay, as both men strongly argued Ireland's case, in both French and English, to a sceptical French minister, Olivier Wormser, 'suddenly', as Ken recalls, 'to our consternation dogs started to bark – Wormser had pet poodles under his table'. In Rome they attended an audience with Pope John

XXIII, who had baptized Con Cremin's daughter when he was papal nuncio in Paris. On being reminded of this and meeting Ken as Cremin's Finance counterpart, with a roguish smile the Pope intoned: 'La foi chrétienne peut purifier même les affaires economiques' (Christian faith can purify even economic matters). In Luxembourg they were greeted by the prime minister, Pierre Werner, with whom Ken had become acquainted during transatlantic voyages to IMF conferences, as being the 'first Irishmen to have presented themselves since the time of Saint Willibrord!', a seventh-century Irish-educated missionary who had resided in the duchy. Although they were received with courtesy and friendliness, it was apparent to the two latter-day 'missionaries' that Europe was not to be easily converted this time and that Ireland's admittance to Europe would be no instant miracle.

While domestic support for membership of the EEC on economic grounds was quite strong, the political implications for Ireland's neutrality, especially in relation to NATO and how it might affect partition, the long-running sore in relations with Britain, as well as the longer-term objective of European political union, gradually became a national issue. Having heard at first hand the doubts expressed by member states about Ireland's economic readiness for membership, Ken advised Lemass not to let the political controversy at home detract from the economic necessity of membership, especially if the application of Ireland's major trading partner, Britain, was successful.

> Nobody has yet told us that this [NATO] is a condition of membership of the EEC. On the other hand, nobody so loves us as to want us in the EEC on our own terms. The Community have difficulties enough without adding those introduced by a 'contrary' new member who will bring the Community no particular benefits but will inflict on it additional problems, including (as they might well view it) this tiresome 40-year-old squabble with Britain.[20]

In 1992, when neutrality once again became a subject of national debate during the Maastricht Treaty referendum campaign, in a thoughtful contribution Ken Whitaker sought to offer a way out of the dilemma. If Ireland was duty-bound to defend itself, albeit with limited capability, against external aggression, given its interest and dependence, economically and socially, on Europe, he argued, 'so we should be prepared to participate in some reasonable fashion in safeguarding the security of the European Community'.[21] While Ireland would not be obliged to join any military alliance for the defence of the Community, it could accept the responsibility of defending against any anti-Community aggression, as well as cooperating with the Community by preventing the country from becoming a base for attack on other member states. Such a policy, he felt, could reconcile Ireland's opposition to military commitment with a degree of participation in an EC common defence policy. It would also enhance the Community's political flexibility and extend its international influence, in that a smaller member state that had decided to remain militarily neutral could be regarded as a more acceptable participant in sensitive international peacekeeping undertakings.

During 1961, however, Ken advised a wait-and-see approach to NATO and a declaration by the government that Ireland was not 'ideologically' neutral. The fact that most of the diplomatic and political wrangling at this time, as one commentator noted, 'went through Whitaker is significant in that it shows the crucial role of Finance with regard to membership of the EEC'.[22] It also demonstrated the integral role he played in the formation of government policy and the extent to which Seán Lemass valued his opinion.

On 18 January 1962 Ken accompanied the Taoiseach and the minister for industry and commerce, Jack Lynch, to a council of EEC ministers meeting in Brussels, presided over by the French foreign minister, Maurice Couve de Murville. Before leaving

Dublin Airport, Lynch expressed the somewhat optimistic hope that 'the negotiations will be completed by the end of the year and membership would then become effective from January 1 next'.[23]

Lemass presented Ireland's case to the Council, stressing Irish acceptance of the ideal of European unity and, following Ken's advice, his view that the 'special circumstances' which prevented Ireland from joining NATO did not deter it from supporting the aims of that organization. His assertions were met with diplomatic coolness, especially by the French, who had taken over the council presidency on 1 January 1962. When Ireland's application was not placed with those of other applicant states, including Britain, before the Council of Ministers, alarm bells began to ring loudly in Dublin. Ken urged a 'dignified calm' and 'a tactful and moderately worded approach' through diplomatic channels. In relation to the political 'elephant in the room' – membership of NATO – which had become the cause of much rancorous debate in Ireland, he urged the government to clarify the political implications of membership in an objective and logical public statement. His advice appeared to bear fruit and during the summer months more positive signals emanated through diplomatic channels. The Taoiseach's further visit to European capitals in October, culminating in an official state visit to the Federal Republic of Germany, added to the air of optimism. On 22 October the EEC Council finally agreed to open negotiations on Ireland's application. The government responded with an immediate unilateral 10 per cent cut in protective tariffs and prepared applications for membership of the other European agencies: the European Coal and Steel Community and European Atomic Energy Community (EURATOM). Plans were also put in place for a second programme of economic expansion in the expectation that Ireland would attain full membership of the EEC by 1964.

While Ireland's application appeared to have gathered

momentum, British negotiations, though proceeding slowly, were expected, following a cordial meeting in December between the British prime minister and French president, to be successfully concluded. Then, on 14 January 1963, within three days of a reception at the British Embassy in Paris planned by British foreign secretary Edward Heath in honour of the French foreign minister, de Gaulle dropped his bombshell. Speaking at a public press conference, later described by Heath as 'a terse and splendid event',[24] the French president vetoed the entry of Britain and the other applicant countries, unwilling – despite recent appearances to the contrary – to depart from his long-held belief that the new European power bloc should be confined to mainland Europe. Britain's participation in EFTA, its obligations to the Commonwealth and its close ties with the United States were cited as reasons against granting the country membership. International nuclear politics also muddied the waters, following an accord reached by Britain and the United States in December 1962 over the use of Polaris missiles.

For Ireland there were undoubtedly pluses and minuses to the unexpected outcome. On the one hand, it was both a rebuff and a reminder of how little Ireland mattered in the course of European politics at the time; on the other hand, and of greater practical benefit, it provided space and a motivation for Irish industry to adjust, modernize and eliminate problems that would not have been offset by the benefits of membership. In retrospect, as Ken recalls, 'perhaps Ireland owes de Gaulle a vote of thanks for delaying enlargement. It certainly was to our benefit to delay, because we saw the writing on the wall and did something about it.' Membership of the EEC was to remain Ken Whitaker's touchstone for the future, and a goal towards which he would continue to shape national economic policy.

7

The Golden Age
1963–68

*Among the salient features of the 1960s are an arrest of the population
decline, an increase in employment and a growth of over 4 per cent per
annum in Gross National Product . . . The Republic, indeed, for most of
this decade enjoyed what has been described as 'a virtuous cycle of growth'.*
T. K. Whitaker[1]

UNDETERRED BY THE INITIAL repulse from Europe, at home the
development and streamlining of the Irish economy continued
apace under the *Programme for Economic Expansion*. That disappointing outcome to the country's first foray into Europe was
offset by the historic state visit of US President John F. Kennedy
in 1963. For a few days the international spotlight focused on
Ireland and lifted the spirits of the nation. For Ken Whitaker,
however, it was back to the drawing board. With the bridge to
Europe once more raised, the immediate future lay in continuing
the positive results being achieved at home, prising open further
the door to the now even more vital British market.

The *Second Programme for Economic Expansion* was drawn up by
the newly established economic development division in his
department, under the direction of Charlie Murray. The com-
pilers of the new programme had access to developments in
statistical analysis and correlation not available to, although

initiated by, the first programme and in consequence the document they produced was far more complex and technical in nature than its predecessor. Covering the period 1964–70, the second programme, part one of which was published in August 1963, aimed for an annual aggregate growth rate of 4 per cent. Based on the expectation of entry into the EEC before 1970, and on consultations with national organizations representing industry and agriculture, employers and trade unions, the programme set out detailed and specific projections for individual sectors. Despite, or perhaps because of, its greater detail and precision, as well as the re-emergence of balance of payments difficulties for a short period midway, not all its ambitious economic targets were fulfilled. This may be attributable in part to this second programme's lacking what Ken Whitaker deemed an essential ingredient in planning – flexibility, being open to review and adaptation in the light of unforeseen internal and external developments.

The 1965 general election saw Fianna Fáil, under Lemass, returned to government, the promotion of younger TDs, such as Donogh O'Malley, to ministerial positions, and the elevation of others, such as George Colley and Patrick Hillery, to more senior ministries. Neil Blaney was appointed to Local Government and Kevin Boland to Social Welfare, while Charles Haughey, after a successful and innovative tenure as minister for justice, was given the agriculture portfolio. After comfortably heading the poll in Cork City, Jack Lynch was promoted to the senior post of Finance. 'I am sorry that my first submission to you as Minister for Finance makes rather cheerless reading,' Ken wrote to his new minister. 'The fact is, however, that there are serious difficulties looming up from which we have happily been free since 1958.'[2] A continuing drain on reserves resulting from an increase in bank credit, much of it for non-productive purposes, and a marked tendency towards wage increases that exceeded productivity, necessitated immediate action to restrict the capital programme in the forthcoming budget for 1965/6 to £100 million, in line with the projections of the second programme. To achieve that figure it was essential, Ken advised Lynch, to initiate cutbacks in the budgets of every department. It was a difficult initial task for the new finance minister. As a hint of what was to come, his subsequent direction to effect departmental cost savings was rebuffed notably by Charles Haughey, by Neil Blaney, who embarked on a public housing spree, and by Donogh O'Malley in Health. Despite a tough budget and reassuring comments, as the months went by the deterioration in the public finances continued, with a deficit looming large and menacing on the horizon.

Unfazed by the obstinacy being shown by some government ministers, Ken intervened directly with Lemass. At a private meeting with the Taoiseach and the minister for finance, he bluntly outlined the main cause of the problem. In words that hinted at Lemass's loss of control over his ministers, there was no point in imposing limits, he wrote, only to have them sidestepped by individual ministers. It sent out the wrong message at home and abroad. It had, he informed the Taoiseach, been brought to his attention by one of his contacts in the Bank of England that the minister for local government, Neil Blaney, was 'shopping around' for funds in London finance houses to fund his building programme. His words had their effect. On Lemass's intervention, the corrective measures Ken advocated to reduce the public capital programme and restore equilibrium in the balance of payments were, though politically difficult at the time, carried into effect; and, for a period, stability was once more restored to the public finances.

The setback experienced regarding accession to the EEC was offset by the negotiation of a new trade agreement with Britain in 1965. The previous year, on the accession of a new Labour government under Harold Wilson, Britain imposed a temporary surcharge of 15 per cent on the value of imports of manufactured goods, in an attempt to correct a deterioration in its balance of payments. As well as being in violation of earlier trade agreements with Ireland, this was also a body-blow to the newly vitalized Irish industrial sector, rendering some 21 per cent of Ireland's total exports liable to the surcharge. In view of the failure to gain EEC membership, access for Irish industrial and agricultural exports to the British market on realistic terms was vital. The stakes were high and the battle ahead to break through the impasse with Britain was a tough one. While the difficulties were eased by the good working relationship established between the two prime ministers, Lemass's illness, his participation in a general election, and his role in overseeing the re-election of de Valera for a second term as president left much of the preparation and conduct of negotiations in the hands of his principal civil servant.

Over the summer months of 1965 Ken became immersed in the hard bargaining and horse-trading relating to the dismantling of tariffs and duties between Britain and Ireland. Fears expressed by the Northern Ireland government regarding the province's agricultural exports to Britain further complicated the discussions. Ironically, Ken found himself in the unlikely situation of having to introduce the Northern Ireland negotiators to their British counterparts on their arrival in London, having become acquainted with the former through talks he had previously conducted regarding existing trade tariffs between the Republic and Northern Ireland. The lengthy deliberations with the British finally culminated in a ten-day period of intense negotiations in London in December 1965. Endowed with plenipotentiary powers, Ken and his team finally reached agreement with their British counterparts.

The Anglo-Irish Free Trade Agreement, signed on 14 December, was broadly welcomed by all sectors of the economy. In the main, it provided for the elimination of British protective import duties on Irish goods with effect from 1 July 1966, and for a corresponding elimination, over a period of ten years, of duties on British goods into Ireland, with some minor exceptions. Agricultural exports – of critical significance to Ireland – were granted unrestricted and equal access to the British market for most categories. While Lemass expressed his unease at the time about the likely effects of the removal of the lowest 10 per cent of Ireland's 'protective shield' of tariffs, as Ken recalls: 'I remember assuring him that the pound sterling was almost certain to be devalued again in advance of Britain's entry into the EEC and that this, whatever its disadvantages, would at least afford both countries some "residual" protection against the stronger Continental members',[3] a prediction that proved true.

While neither Lemass nor Lynch sought to capitalize on the success of the Anglo-Irish trade talks, Lemass's son-in-law Charles Haughey, the minister for agriculture, showed no such reticence, grabbing national headlines regarding the improvements won for Irish agriculture. Lemass and Lynch, on the other hand, recognized that whatever accolades were forthcoming did not belong to the politicians. In a personal letter to Ken Whitaker, as the principal negotiator, Lemass was generous in his gratitude; indeed, even today the recipient finds the sentiments expressed somewhat surprising, being out of character, as he wryly observes, with Lemass's more usual terse, distant and businesslike approach.

Dear Mr Whitaker,
On my own behalf, and on behalf of the Government, I wish to commend and thank you most sincerely for the valuable personal contribution you made to the successful conclusion of the Free Trade Agreement with Britain. During those last few days in London, I saw at close quarters, with the greatest admiration, the almost super-human application of yourself and your colleagues to a task of outstanding complexity and importance. I know that I saw only the culmination of ten days of undivided attention to the business of the nation. What you and your colleagues did in

London went far beyond the normal call of duty and has enhanced the already high reputation of the Irish civil service for devotion to the public interest.

May I take this opportunity to wish you and your family a very happy Christmas.[4]

The 1965 Anglo-Irish Free Trade Agreement, as one of Lemass's biographers has recorded, 'not only undid the worst effects of the protectionist policies adopted by the Wilson government late in 1964 but, in a formal way, marked the end of the protectionist economic philosophy that had guided Lemass and Fianna Fáil since the 1930s and had been progressively whittled away since the late fifties';[5] and it was achieved mainly through the efforts of Ken Whitaker.

Lemass's regard for his senior civil servant was reciprocated. In his address to the first Seán Lemass Memorial Lecture at the University of Exeter in 1974, Ken stated: 'We can salute Seán Lemass for having so effectively pursued policies which have taken Ireland from the embattled and impoverished protectionism of the nineteen thirties into the more exposed but also better-off nineteen seventies.'[6] They were the ideal partners in bringing about Ireland's economic revolution. To Ken, Lemass 'represented a restless, frustrated potential which, in the agonies of the country's gravest hour, symbolised Ireland's determination to survive, recover and grow'.[7] He had profound respect for Lemass's determination, his leadership qualities, his readiness to 'grasp the nettle' of unpopular decisions, often when on a political knife-edge, his ability to familiarize himself with complex economic briefs and, not least, his understanding of and rapport with the functions of the civil service, enabling him to 'out-civil-service' the civil servants themselves. While critics of Lemass saw him as an urban-orientated mover and shaker, a facilitator of foreign and native speculators, the 'Taoiseach of the new money',[8] such views seem ungenerous when one takes into account his relatively unpretentious lifestyle, as well as his undoubted political and economic achievements. Lemass's ethos and conduct, like Ken Whitaker's, in both personal and public capacities, hardly bears out such a characterization. Both men exercised a certain fastidiousness and restraint in their personal conduct and lifestyle that extended into their public lives at a time when such restraint was gradually becoming somewhat obsolete with the emergence of a new breed of ambitious and self-promoting Fianna Fáil politicians waiting in the wings, epitomized by the Taoiseach's own son-in-law, Charles Haughey. 'Lemass seemed uncomfortable with his son-in-law,' Ken recalls. 'Their relationship never became warm or genial. I suspect that Mrs Haughey had a lot to do to keep things right between them.'

Like Seán Lemass, Ken viewed his office not as a right or as a means to personal endowment, but as a duty of service to the state and people. The myriad of extra-curricular and subsidiary tasks he undertook beyond the formal duties of his office he considered merely part of his job as a public servant. For the countless lectures, papers and reports written over the course of his lifetime, in both his public and private capacities, no fee was ever requested; likewise for his service on numerous state and charitable organizations, groups and committees.* 'The question of payment never appeared on the horizon. It was simply a part of one's public duty as a civil servant.' Even when most of these extra-curricular undertakings occurred after his retirement from public office? 'But I was still on a public service pension,' he contends. The personal lives of political and public servants like Lemass and Whitaker, while they may not have conformed to the exigencies of de Valera's 'frugal living', were low-key and modest, displaying no signs of ostentation. By the mid-1960s, however, this ethos was beginning to be replaced by a more self-seeking approach on the part of both sectional groups and individuals,

* For details, see the appendices to this book.

who viewed public office more as a means of personal advancement than as a duty of public service.

Lemass presided over a period which Ken later alluded to as 'a kind of golden age'. Real growth averaged 4 per cent a year, with virtually no increase in prices and no balance of payments problem. Perhaps, as he conceded, it was inevitable that this economic 'nirvana' would not last. As he had previously warned, an economic plan 'indicates objectives, it specifies an agenda but it does not guarantee fulfilment . . . unless there is a controlled and orderly development of money incomes and public expenditure within the framework of the plan, the plan will be pulled apart'.[9] And after 1966 the cracks began to appear. The achievements of 'the golden age' also had their downside, arousing higher expectations in the general public, manifested in the latter half of the 1960s by industrial unrest, excessive income demands and public expenditure increases. The time for making the necessary adjustment had come, as Ken informed his minister: 'The economic situation is more serious than we have been admitting officially. We now have to increase the corrective measures. We should also, without being alarmist, be more forthright about the nature and extent of our problems. We would be deluding ourselves if we continued to make reassuring comments about their temporary nature.'[10] In a pre-echo of 2010, the 'corrective measures' Ken recommended necessitated an emergency $22.5 million loan from the IMF.

The new brand of Fianna Fáil politicians emerging in this period were self-motivated, acquisitive and flamboyant. Known as the 'mohair suit, Groome's Hotel' brigade, they projected a more modern and liberal image than their predecessors; they also, as Ken diplomatically noted, were 'young and ambitious . . . eager to make their name by introducing new and inevitably expensive schemes'.[11] One of the most flamboyant was Donogh O'Malley, appointed minister for education in the last Lemass government. Education in Ireland at the time was complicated by the traditional vested interests of the religious orders which owned most of the country's educational infrastructure. Although a long-stated political aspiration, in 1966 state plans to improve the educational system remained largely unfulfilled, and education lagged behind the level of development achieved in the wider economy. Secondary education was fee-paying and thereby restricted to parents with means, to those able to win scholarships or to the recipients of the vagaries of clerical benevolence. While indicating his intention to improve the educational system in 1961, Lemass did not aim beyond ensuring that children remained in school until the age of fifteen. As ministers for education in the 1960s Jack Lynch and Paddy Hillery laid the foundations for new thinking and reform. A commission composed entirely of lay participants to investigate education policy was established and its report, *Investment in Education*, published in 1965, did for education what *Economic Development* had done for the economy: it highlighted the inequality and deficiencies in the system and recommended gradual changes and improvements.

In July 1966 the mercurial, charismatic and hard-living Donogh O'Malley was appointed minister for education. In his previous tenure at the ministry for health, not only had his caustic and critical comments alienated almost every branch of the medical profession, he had also left his department, as Ken noted, 'gravely insolvent'. Shortly after his appointment to Education, at a seminar hosted by the National Union of Journalists, O'Malley 'startled and thrilled the nation',[12] and guaranteed himself instant national media coverage, by publicly announcing the introduction of free secondary education and a free transport system for students. 'My impression', Ken recalls, 'was that it was a deliberate decision on his part to announce it in such a way and in such a public forum, while also knowing that he would be reprimanded from both above and below!' Founded on both his own personal experience and his passionate belief in education, Ken Whitaker's support for the development and improvement of the Irish educational system was beyond question. As 'keeper of the national public purse', however, he had overriding priorities: and the facts that O'Malley's proposal had been neither discussed at cabinet nor costed by his department, that no provision had been made for it in the financial estimates, and that it had been sprung on the public while the minister for finance was out of the country, startled him enough to reach for his pen. 'It is astonishing,' he informed the Taoiseach,

> that a major change in educational policy should be made by the Minister for Education at a weekend seminar of the National Union of Journalists . . . If substantial commitments are to be announced by individual Ministers without the consent of the Department of Finance or the approval of the Government, we shall have a situation which is the negation of planning. It will become increasingly futile to be drawing up 5- or 7-year programmes, and even the financial and economic policy of the Government in the short-term will be seen to bear no relation to what the country can afford.[13]

While accepting that education should be given priority, as far as the ability of the exchequer to pay extended, this should be done, Ken further noted, 'in the light of a proper assessment of the trend in these resources and of the cost of educational and other desirable improvements'.[14]

O'Malley claimed that he had cleared the full text of his pronouncement with Lemass, but, from the tone of his subsequent reprimand, this appears unlikely, although, as evidence also indicates, Lemass himself was not averse to 'flying political kites'. As for Jack Lynch, whom O'Malley had somewhat disdainfully wrong-footed, on his return he warned his cabinet colleague that any further proposals would have to be framed with strict regard to financial possibilities and in such a way as to avoid a considerable addition to the total estimates in any one year, words that bore the hallmark of Lynch's departmental secretary.

While O'Malley's announcement may have brought him the public attention he craved, ambitious plans, however socially appealing, had to be paid for by the very same taxpayers, as Ken, with his customary logic, pointed out: 'To describe this scheme as "free" is misleading. The scheme really means that many parents at present paying moderate school fees voluntarily will have to pay an equal or greater amount compulsorily in the form of additional taxation.'[15] It was a moot point. Non-boarding fees at secondary schools in the 1960s ranged from as little as £10 to £100 pounds per annum. Most parents, even those with slender resources, as Ken knew from personal experience, usually made the necessary sacrifices to find the means to pay. In the event, O'Malley's 'free' education scheme pressed ahead with notable public acceptance and a spectacular increase in the number of pupils attending secondary school, from 104,000 in 1966 to 144,000 in 1969. Ken's intervention was, as he saw it, simply a case 'of doing my duty. Our relationship never became one of antagonism. It was a good idea but it was the way he went about introducing a not unsubstantial-costing scheme.'

Donogh O'Malley's audacious stroke was the harbinger of more solo initiatives emanating from a band of strong-willed, independently minded ministers pursuing indulgent, populist policies that frequently ran counter to budgetary and financial constraints and were pursued often with a view to the enhancement of their own public profiles, sometimes their own purses. The building boom and potential profits arising from the transformation of agricultural land adjacent to Dublin and other centres of population into land with development potential were also beginning to smudge the dividing line between public duty and personal gain. In 1965 the Department of Finance sought to introduce a tax on profits derived from land speculation, but a subsequent court ruling ensured that enough loopholes remained for developers and builders to evade its control. With the

Left: Edward and Jane Whitaker on their marriage in 1914.

Above: 'Little Lord Fauntleroy' and Peggy in the early 1920s.

Paradise Cottage, Drogheda – 'The nearest I may ever get to heaven!'

Above: Ken and Nora on honeymoon in Connemara, 1941 . . .

Below: . . . and stepping it out in Dublin.

Above: The Whitaker family, Christmas 1964 (*standing, left to right*: Gerald, Catherine, Ken, Nora, Brian; *sitting, left to right*: Raymond, Ken (junior), David).

Below: Proud parents with Catherine on graduation day at University College Dublin.

'The beginning of a new reign' – at the helm of the Department of Finance, 1956.

Above: On a mission to the EEC capitals, July 1967 (*left to right*: Michael J. Dargan, Aer Lingus; Paolo Canali, Italian ambassador; Taoiseach Jack Lynch; Charles Haughey, minister for finance; T. K. Whitaker, secretary, Department of Finance).

Below: Holy medals from Pope Paul VI for Jack Lynch, Charles Haughey and Ken at the Vatican.

Jack Lynch, Terence O'Neill, Frank Aiken, Seán Lemass and Ken Whitaker, Iveagh House, Dublin, 9 February 1965.

Jack Lynch, Ken Whitaker and Terence O'Neill, Stormont, 11 December 1967.

Above: An O'Neill in the Áras: Ken with Baron O'Neill of the Maine, President Éamon de Valera and aide-de-camp Colonel Sean Brennan during the private meeting at Áras an Uachtaráin, 21 April 1972 . . .

Below: . . . and in the library of Áras an Uachtaráin.

Above: 'Baptism of fire': the controversial Central Bank building under construction in Dame Street in the 1970s.

Below: The Governor.

establishment of the notorious TACA, Fianna Fáil's fund-raising agency, some five hundred 'businessmen' were given personal access to individual ministers, and to government contracts, in exchange for 'pouring cash into party coffers and the hands of individual politicians'.[16] Greed and corruption now threatened to replace the idealism that had motivated the founding generation of Fianna Fáil.

In November 1966, the year of the fiftieth anniversary of the Easter Rising, Seán Lemass, the last of the old guard with the gravitas and ability to curb such self-seeking attitudes among the younger guns in the government, resigned because of ill-health. The hard-won economic development and fiscal equilibrium that he and his principal civil servant had diligently achieved appeared threatened. Much to the chagrin of the party elders, Lemass had identified no clear successor, and his unexpected resignation initiated a tussle for power between George Colley, representing more traditional party values, Charles Haughey, embodiment of the brash, acquisitive, urban-based coterie and, initially, Neil Blaney, embodying the party's more strident Republican ethos. With repercussions that would haunt Irish politics for many years to come, Jack Lynch emerged as a reluctant compromise successor, albeit Lemass's preferred choice. Surrounded by a cabinet of ambitious colleagues, some of whom regarded him with ill-concealed disdain, Lynch embarked on a period as Taoiseach unprecedented in political and economic turbulence. Over the succeeding years, ill-served by many of his cabinet colleagues, he would need all the independent support and advice he could muster to keep his nerve and maintain his grip on the country. He was to find them in Ken Whitaker.

Whitaker and Lynch had much in common, and their working relationship broadened into a lasting personal friendship. 'Jack's whole nature induced loyalty and affection,' recalls Ken. 'Softness of speech and manner, readiness to listen, absence of pomp, a sense of humour were elements of a most attractive personality which combined modesty and unpretentiousness with good judgement and a deep sense of responsibility and firmness of purpose.' The last traits, in particular, made this a leader, albeit one less self-assured than Lemass and lacking the same Republican pedigree, to whom Ken Whitaker could relate. Of similar age, background and outlook, neither of them burdened by the weight of ideological Republicanism, both were motivated by a sense of duty and the desire to advance the country's economic and social future. They had established a positive working relationship during Lynch's tenure as minister for finance and had travelled together on official business to Britain, Europe and the United States. Indeed, it was while attending a meeting of the IMF in Washington that Lynch confided to Ken that Lemass had approached him about becoming his successor, but that he had decided to discuss the prospect with his beloved wife, Máirín, before making up his mind.

On Lynch's elevation as Taoiseach, Charles J. Haughey became minister for finance. With a record as an innovative minister for justice, he took up his new office with a reputation for being able and ambitious, but also for a tendency to ostentation hardly commensurate with either the demeanour or the salary of a minister for finance. As a controversial minister for agriculture, he had become embroiled in bitter disputes with the principal farming organizations, resulting in illegal picketing and the imprisonment of farmers' leaders. Also while minister for agriculture, Haughey had already crossed swords with Ken, refusing in 1965 to revise the estimates for his department in line with other departments. 'He would have been regarded by most of us', Ken recalls, 'as thrusting, ambitious, ruthless and able but not really true-blooded in the sense of an Irish republican ... someone more interested in using the vacant slot to promote himself.' Ken found his new boss 'not overly inspiring ... tending to be over-confident and to favour the spectacular. Yet,' he admits, 'you had to admire his tenacity and ruthlessness ... but that did not mean you supported it. He had great ambition and worked very hard.' Given their divergent personalities, outlook, substance and style, it is to the credit of the professionalism of both men that their relationship as minister and secretary survived any length of time. Haughey's penchant for publicity and self-promotion, which saw him take personal credit for the introduction of popular policies, such as subsidized electricity, free travel for senior citizens, and tax exemption for artists and writers, was at odds with the more traditional Finance ethos of anonymity and reserve, as well as budgetary control. 'He was all for being on his own, the sole author and promoter of any popular reform or policy, and thereby eliciting the ensuing praise and publicity,' Ken recalls. Accustomed as he was to working in close collaboration with previous holders of the office, such as Ryan, Sweetman, Lemass and Lynch, Ken found in formulating and directing policy with Haughey that 'what was clearly lacking was any real cordiality or camaraderie of spirit'.

Haughey's background in accountancy might have been expected to give him a better understanding of his ministerial brief, and his confident assumption of authority to enable him to push through policies, however unpopular, to alleviate the emerging problems in the national finances. His first budget, however, gave little indication of either understanding or will, the opportunity to gain popularity proving too strong a temptation. His approach cut little ice with his departmental secretary. Ken's comment – 'The new Minister for Finance considered it justifiable to raise the total public capital expenditure to £108.6 million for 1967/68 as a stimulus to the economy which had grown only slightly in the previous two years'[17] – is a clear criticism, albeit couched in careful civil service terms, of the new minister's approach. However, as a public servant, his function was to provide the minister with advice based on best practice and on the information at his disposal. It was the minister who must legislate; as a good public servant, Ken knew that he 'had to work within the atmosphere created by individual ministers', and to use his expertise and influence, as best he could, to lessen the damage to the economy of what in his view were inappropriate policies.

Despite Haughey's intimidating reputation, especially in relation to his treatment of civil servants, Ken affirms that 'I was well able to defend myself', secure in the knowledge, as he candidly puts it, that 'I think he would have known that, if it came to any sort of public disagreement, the people would respect my views more than his'. From the tone of their correspondence it seems apparent that Haughey concurred with that opinion, recognizing that the secretary of his new department would not readily 'roll over' – a fact that also made him wary. But Haughey had also a long and vengeful memory, which he would bring to bear in the future. For his part, Ken was prepared to put his personal feelings aside and give the minister the best advice at his disposal, even though it was not the advice Haughey always wanted to hear. In January 1969, describing the prospects for the year as 'truly worrying', he apologized for being the bearer of bad tidings but nevertheless told Haughey that 'at a time when "pie in the sky" is seasonable, I have to serve cold porridge but *magna est veritas*'.[18] Policies 'for sound and responsible management of the economy' were therefore being prepared by his department, significantly, as he told the minister, 'for submission to the Government'.

During the course of Charles Haughey's tenure in Finance from 1967 to 1970, the annual increases in public expenditure, both capital and current, resulted in increased levels of borrowing, adding to inflation and bringing about a further deterioration in the balance of payments. Haughey's expansionary policies were adopted in response to those presented in the 'Just Society' programme promoted by Declan Costello and Garret FitzGerald, representing the more liberal wing of Fine Gael. However imaginative and justifiable in principle tax cuts and free schemes might be, as Ken knew, they could be funded only by additional taxation or by foreign borrowing. During 1967 and 1968 there was a flurry of correspondence between Ken and the governor of the Central Bank, Dr Maurice Moynihan, the latter demanding urgent corrective action in relation to bank credit being sought to fund the government's additional spending. While personally in agreement with the governor's concerns, Ken sought to find a compromise strategy. From Carna in the Connemara Gaeltacht, on his annual family holiday in August 1968, he urged the governor to wait for the publication of the September bank returns before making a judgement. 'While caution and watchfulness are necessary, we should not be premature in putting a brake on economic activity when we need to keep it high on employment grounds.'[19] At the same time, he informed his minister that, while he had taken 'a no fuss' line with the governor, 'the inflationary pace is hotting up too much and I would not be against a little braking now . . . else both income and public expenditure increases may get out of hand. A stitch in time . . .'[20] The stitch, however, was not to be sewn.

Thirty years later, Ken was to become Charles Haughey's somewhat unlikely defender during the Moriarty Tribunal's investigation into the former Taoiseach's financial affairs. In November 1967 the British Labour government of Harold Wilson took the momentous decision to devalue sterling which, together with the US dollar, was then one of the world's major reserve currencies. The 14.3 per cent devaluation had serious implications for the Irish pound. To deter currency speculation, strict secrecy and protocols were enforced by the British government, with the official announcement scheduled for Saturday, 18 November at precisely 9.30 p.m. News of the imminent devaluation was first divulged by the British ambassador to Ken on that Saturday morning, with a request that the news be withheld until the formal announcement was made in London later that day. 'I could not find Charles Haughey . . .' Ken later recalled, 'but I knew Jack Lynch was unveiling a statue of Wolfe Tone in St

Stephen's Green, so I went around and drew him aside to tell him.'[21] Ken caught up with Haughey later that evening as he was delivering a speech to a bankers' conference at the Intercontinental Hotel in Ballsbridge. Ken informed him of the impending devaluation and warned him against mentioning it in his speech until after the agreed time. By way of a transistor radio, which Ken brought to the conference, they were able to ensure that Haughey delivered the news during his speech only when the formal announcement had been made on the BBC.

In 1998, when the financial affairs of the former Taoiseach were laid bare before the Moriarty Tribunal, the question of the origins of Haughey's accumulated fortune hovered momentarily over the 1967 devaluation episode. Accusations that as minister for finance he had had insider information regarding the devaluation, and that, together with some business friends, he had gained financially by speculating on currency movements before the official announcement, were widely reported in the media. Haughey's denial was defended publicly by Ken Whitaker, who noted that while 'the possibility of a sterling devaluation was in our minds since 1965',[22] no formal notice of devaluation was given to the Irish government by the British until the Saturday morning of the announcement. 'I don't think devaluation would have come as an enormous surprise to any astute businessman',[23] he concluded.

By 1967, the prospect of EEC membership had surfaced once again. On the day of Seán Lemass's resignation, Harold Wilson had announced Britain's intention to reapply for membership, and on 11 May 1967 Britain, Ireland, Denmark and Norway all formally submitted applications. Since Ireland's initial application, much had been achieved to prepare the country for eventual admission. Detailed surveys and studies had been undertaken, resulting in the reorganization and streamlining of the Irish industrial and agricultural sectors, including improvements in skills and training for both management and employees.

Ireland had become a member of GATT, and diplomatic relations had been established with other European institutions. Meetings between Irish ministers of Finance, External Affairs, Industry and Commerce, and Agriculture, and their departmental secretaries, with relevant officials in the European Commission were held on a regular basis.

In July 1967 Jack Lynch led a delegation, which included Charles Haughey, Ken and Hugh McCann, secretary of the Department of External Affairs, on a round of discussions with the heads of member states, pointedly leaving the crucial meeting with President de Gaulle in Paris to last. As before, the Irish delegation was received with courtesy and friendliness by the governments of the Six. In Brussels they held meetings with individual members of the European Commission, including Jean Rey, Dr Sicco Mansholt and Raymond Barre. At the Mauritshuis Palace in The Hague, discussions with the Dutch prime minister, as Ken recalls, were momentarily interrupted when the Taoiseach unwittingly set off alarms by tapping the surface of a still-life wine glass! There was a good deal of support for Ireland's accession. The German chancellor, Dr Kurt Kiesinger, received the delegation warmly in Bonn, while in Italy they found the prime minister, Aldo Moro, and his foreign minister, Amintore Fanfani, particularly receptive to Irish membership, although at the same time adamant that any enlargement of the EEC could not be at the expense of the Six. As a memento of their meeting, Aldo Moro presented the Taoiseach with a personal gift of a magnificent reproduction of the famous *Dante Urbinate*. Later, in 1998, when Jack Lynch indicated that he wished to donate the gift to the nation, Ken recommended the Royal Irish Academy, where the manuscript is now housed. The meeting with the Italian prime minister was followed by a private audience and the presentation of 'holy' medals by Pope Paul VI to the Taoiseach and his party.

The critical meeting of the tour took place in the Elysée Palace on 3 November. The Irish delegation was under no illusions about the difficulty of persuading President de Gaulle of Ireland's suitability and readiness for accession to the EEC. Before the formal luncheon, the Taoiseach and the president, with an interpreter, met *tête-à-tête*. The stumbling block to Irish admission, de Gaulle informed Lynch, as previously, was Ireland's close economic and financial ties with Britain, which with its reserve currency, its close association with the United States and its current economic problems, was not, to his mind, suitable EEC material. The Taoiseach emerged 'rather crestfallen', as Ken remembers, 'telling us that de Gaulle favoured association rather than full membership for Britain (and consequently for Ireland). The message was: we couldn't let our ears back over lunch, however excellent the cuisine!' Ireland's case was further pressed over the meal. Endeavouring to enliven the sombre atmosphere, or perhaps to elicit by Irish humour what was obviously not forthcoming from Gallic pragmatism, Charles Haughey enquired of the president how he could successfully rule a country that produced three hundred varieties of cheese. While understanding English perfectly well, de Gaulle still waited for the obligatory translation before contradicting him. 'Non,' he then retorted: 'trois cents quatre-vingt dix' (no, three hundred and ninety), thus abruptly ending the exchange.

Placed beside the French prime minister, Georges Pompidou, who appeared intent on discussing the differences between Gaelic football and rugby, Ken found himself at a loss, 'as some of the finer points were obscured by the inadequacy of my French and I did not know much about either game!' In proposing a toast to Ireland, de Gaulle reiterated that the primary aim of the Six was to reinforce and develop the Community as it presently stood and to extend 'association' status to those countries outside. 'Everything indicates that Ireland can and should be closely associated with the accomplishment of this great work', he told his guests.[24] It was later reported in the press that some confusion existed among the Irish delegation as to what exactly de Gaulle meant by 'association'. As Ken stated, however, 'the nuances and implication of the [president's] toast were quite clearly understood by the Irish delegation. I can say that there was no "puzzlement" over the meaning of "association" as used by the General.'[25] While Jack Lynch later stated that he had 'discussed the possibility of arriving at some "interim arrangement" for Ireland, pending the solution of Britain's problems',[26] Ireland's continued dependence on the British market prevented the Irish government embarking on any such arrangement.

After lunch, President de Gaulle indicated 'that he wished to speak with the non-ministerial members of the delegation individually, starting with me,' Ken remembers. It was an unexpected move, a departure from both protocol and procedure. 'It is still a puzzlement to me. Perhaps the General had been briefed that, as public servants, we carried some clout with the politicians.' Modesty perhaps prohibits him from saying that it is more likely that Ken's singular efforts in transforming Ireland's economy had been noted in European political circles.

I was wobbly at the knees knowing so much depended on this as I followed the General into another room. Asked by the official interpreter whether I required his services, I declined. The situation being desperate, I thought that our interests required that I should try and converse in French, to distance ourselves from the English language. The President took me aside and very courteously outlined the various points he had already made to the Taoiseach. Then he turned to me for my response. I began by saying that we Irish, 'depuis des centaines d'années, nous essayons . . .' I could not think of the obvious word 'détacher' and instead used the stronger word 'arracher à l'Angleterre' (*tear* ourselves apart from England), a word which the General seemed to approve of, replying 'bon, bon' and listening with attention to the rest of my argument.

In the event, the devaluation of the pound sterling some two weeks later, followed immediately by that of the Irish pound, confirmed the general's suspicions. In yet another celebrated press conference, he insisted that Britain must first make fundamental changes 'to establish its own equilibrium and modify its character before it can join the Community'.[27] This latest French rebuff sent the British press into overdrive in its condemnation of the French in general and de Gaulle in particular. By contrast, there was little if any expression of anti-French feeling in Ireland, but neither was there any effort to seek further clarification of what de Gaulle had meant by 'an interim arrangement' between Ireland and the EEC. It was still a question of Britain in – Ireland in; Britain out – Ireland out, as much for the Irish government as for the French president.

In retrospect, Ken regarded de Gaulle's long-sustained veto of EEC enlargement 'as a blessing in disguise'. In his view, it 'gave Ireland breathing space to conduct analysis to assess the implications . . . of the dismantling of protectionism, with a view to preparing ourselves for our participation in economic integration and to adjust to the obligations of membership . . . It also meant that when Ireland ultimately joined in 1973, the economy was better prepared than it would otherwise have been.'[28]

In 1969 Ken met General de Gaulle again, this time on home soil. After his shock retirement, the general came to Ireland to spend a six-week holiday to be, as he wrote, 'face to face with myself' in the land of his maternal ancestors, the McCartans. 'It was a sort of instinct that led me towards Ireland . . . One always goes back to one's source.'[29] The famous black-and-white photo of President de Valera and President de Gaulle, Europe's two elder statesmen, standing tall under the portico of Áras an Uachtaráin, records a memorable moment of that visit. 'I had a second conversation with General de Gaulle in French, at Áras an Uachtaráin, during his visit to President de Valera,' Ken recalls. 'This time, I was trying to modify the general's fascination with the gold standard.' While staying in Connemara, de Gaulle attended Mass in a local church. Ken, who happened to be there on holiday at the time, gave a lift to a local youth returning from attending the same Mass, asking him in Irish what he thought of the famous French president. The youth shrugged, telling Ken that there were so many visitors in the church he did not recognize him.

Ireland's 'tortuous path' towards EEC membership finally ended on 1 January 1973 when, together with its main trading partner Britain, and with Denmark, it was admitted to the Community, with the support of the vast majority of the Irish electorate. By that time Charles de Gaulle had passed away, while Ken had opened a new chapter in his career. Was he disappointed not to have been involved in the final push for membership of the European Community? 'I have no regrets on that score. The important thing was to carry through the decision to join.' By 1969, however, he felt that the original ideals, as enshrined in the Treaty of Rome, had become somewhat 'clouded by developments in recent years'. These 'developments' he saw as a preoccupation with national, as distinct from Community, interests 'and a reluctance to surrender anything to community institutions',[30] a comment that has new resonance in the light of more recent events. Despite the dismantling of trade barriers, 'a lively sense of political idealism', he insists, must also apply 'to animate the evolution of the Community or it will peter out', a prediction that has relevant and indeed ominous undertones for the future of the European Union today. Nevertheless, in the years immediately after accession, despite the failure of some EEC mechanisms, such as the subsidies and interventions that replaced more direct marketing initiatives, and the problems encountered with surplus production, in Ken's judgement the outcome had been positive. 'On an overview,' he wrote in 1983 on the tenth anniversary of Ireland's accession, 'membership of the EEC has been of significant economic benefit to Ireland, has greatly increased Ireland's international role and enhanced its political independence vis-à-vis the UK and other countries.'[31]

The role played by Ken Whitaker in securing Ireland's membership of the EEC, the single most important step, both economically and psychologically, the country had taken since independence, was pivotal. The consequences of that step were of immense significance for the country. Access to a wider market and higher prices for Ireland's vital agricultural industry reduced dependence on the consumer-driven British market, while the Common Agricultural Policy and the infrastructural-building funds helped lift Irish incomes to equal and eventually, for a dizzy time, to exceed European standards. 'As one who remembers the hopelessness of the '40s and '50s,' Ken wrote, 'I am happy and privileged to have lived to see an almost unbelievable improvement in economic and social conditions, much due to EEC membership'[32] – itself much due, as he omitted to record, to his own efforts. But there were setbacks too, and he feels that over the years the combination of idealism and realism that had motivated the founding fathers, Monnet, Schuman and de Gasperi, had evaporated. As a member of the EEC Committee of Central Bank Governors in the 1970s, he noted: 'It seems to me the EEC has lost much of its dynamism and sense of purpose . . . the *élan vital* has been sadly missing.' And he warned in 1983 that, 'without positive and sustained moves towards greater political union, even the economic and social gains already made will be increasingly threatened or frustrated by preoccupation with self-interest and internal bickering and obstruction'.[33] While strong in his support for European membership and integration, he was less supportive of what he described as Ireland's 'quixotic gesture' in abandoning sterling in 1979 to join the European Monetary System.

Why Ken Whitaker left the Department of Finance in 1969, at the relatively young age of fifty-two, remains a matter of speculation, given his reticence on the matter and the absence of material evidence. Diplomatically, he sought to assuage public disquiet or controversy regarding his departure. 'As far as leaving the Department of Finance is concerned,' he told a reporter in February 1969, 'many of the things I played a part in are now well established and the department is well equipped technically and administratively to carry on without me'.[34] Nevertheless, it is obvious, both from the available personal record and from the opinions expressed to this author, that the Department of Finance represented for him, not merely 'the best years of my life' but also, as he candidly admits, the pinnacle of his public service: 'I never thought the Central Bank, a more remote although respectable institution, was as important an institution as the Department of Finance.' For him, Finance represented the heart of the public service, controlling and bringing into line the (at times) divergent impulses of its sister departments – and, more especially, those of its incumbent minister – with informed, constructive advice and criticism, which occasionally, as he had demonstrated, could be quite revolutionary in content. He had led the department away from its more negative, restrictive preoccupation with 'the saving of candle ends' and transformed it into a constructive and dynamic institution, capable of exercising pervasive and positive effect nationally and ushering in a 'golden age' of economic growth.

Despite media comments at the time, which hinted at a contretemps with Charles Haughey as a reason for his retirement, Ken is emphatic that he 'was not pushed' but left having accomplished all he could at Finance. Even so, he readily admits that it was a difficult decision to walk away from so crucial and fulfilling a position. With the economy experiencing a dangerous dip, a third *Programme for Economic Expansion*, to cover the years 1969–72, announced just three weeks before his departure, and membership of the EEC once again on the frontline, the need for his experienced and steady hand on the tiller in Finance seemed greater than ever. Asked on his departure for his thoughts about his 'unfinished business' in the Department of Finance, his reply, was, as ever, diplomatic: 'There is always unfinished business and there is plenty in the Central Bank too!'[35] Yet the 'very high and lonely responsibility', as he described it, of the governorship seemed an odd choice for someone with a proven preference for being a 'team player'. His departure perhaps points to more personal reasons.

Ken Whitaker's respect, even affection, for the finance ministers with whom he had previously worked – Frank Aiken, Seán MacEntee, Gerard Sweetman, James Ryan, Jack Lynch – appears to have been noticeably absent from his relationship with Charles Haughey. More used to dealing with those who viewed their office, as Ken viewed his, as a public duty, Ken could not but see Haughey's ill-concealed ambition, let alone the rumours which by 1969 were circulating regarding his wealth and nefarious business contacts, as blatantly at variance with ministerial duty, especially that of a minister for finance. These reservations prevented the development of the cordial and intimate working relationship he had enjoyed with previous holders of the office across the political spectrum. But it was to be Haughey's involvement in the emerging crisis in Northern Ireland that, more than anything else, polarized the differences between the two men.

As a public servant, Ken had no say in the choice of minister and, with his customary optimism, tact, patience and good humour, made the best of the hand he was dealt, and endeavoured to direct the minister along the road of fiscal propriety while serving out his remaining time in office. By early 1969, however, the economic woes that *Economic Development* had highlighted in 1958, and the first *Programme for Economic Expansion* had rectified, were resurfacing. Excessive public expenditure and public service income increases were, as he told Haughey in January 1969, 'raging uncontrolled',[36] raising the prospect of a £50 million balance of payments deficit and a sizeable drop in the country's external reserves.

Ken's final undertaking as secretary of the Department of Finance was to lead a delegation on new trade talks to London. In November 1968 renewed balance of payments problems forced Britain to introduce a series of measures to reduce imports. A scheme which required British importers to deposit 50 per cent of the value of each import consignment had major repercussions for Irish exports and was also deemed to contravene the Anglo-Irish Free Trade Agreement which Ken had negotiated in 1965. His final two days as secretary of the Department of Finance were spent in the British Treasury trying to find a way out of the impasse. 'We needed a make-weight to balance the trade bargain we were trying to conclude,' Ken remembers. Eventually he recalled an obsolete and long-forgotten undertaking, the Damage to Property Annuity, a £250,000 yearly fine payable to the British under the 1925 Anglo-Irish Financial Agreement, which J. J. McElligott had tried in vain to have wrapped up in the 1938 settlement and which by 1969 was worth an annual saving of £4 million to the Irish exchequer. The cancellation of this provision was accepted by the 'very reasonable' British secretary to the Treasury, Harold Lever, thus concluding the vital trade negotiations to the satisfaction of both sides.

It is difficult to dispute Dr Garret FitzGerald's assessment that Ken Whitaker's tenure in Finance entitles him

to the accolade of the most outstanding public servant of independent Ireland in the twentieth century. He shared all the great qualities of the first generation of civil servants – but with the crucial addition of imagination – and a recognition that the Department of Finance must not be content to rest on oars of fiscal rectitude but must also offer positive leadership in economic development.[37]

During the 1950s and 1960s, few outside a small group of public figures such as FitzGerald, Gerard Sweetman and Seán

Lemass had much comprehension or appreciation of the economic and fiscal issues facing the country. Few politicians, and even fewer of the general public, were *au fait* with the complexities of national, let alone international, economic and monetary policy. This placed the responsibility for national economic policy on the shoulders of non-political public servants, and especially Ken Whitaker. His ability, knowledge and trustworthiness in his capacity as secretary of the Department of Finance were accepted across the spectrum of political opinion and beyond and what he accomplished during his term of office helped transform a nation, as the political journalist John Healy testified:

> We came out of that recession [1958] in a wondrous burst of creative politics and leadership that moved and changed a whole society. It was not done by batteries of computers, digital technology, teams of national handlers, press agents or the rest; just a handful of men who wanted to change things and, thank God, got their hands on the levers of power and used the levers to maximum effect, for the welfare of the nation.[38]

Quoting from the memoirs of Saint-Simon, chronicler to the French court of Louis XIV, Ken more elegantly sums up his tenure as secretary of the Department of Finance:

> Ses joies sont visibles mais fausses;
> Ses chagrins sont cachés mais réels.
> (His joys are visible but false:
> His vexations hidden but real.)[39]

8

The Ivory Tower
1969–76

One has to bear in mind that the role assigned to a Central Bank is to be cautious, to be the warning light. I feel that the Central Bank may have to say unpalatable things in the future.
T. K. Whitaker[1]

THE RELEVANCE OF Ken Whitaker's perception of the role of the Central Bank, as expressed above in an interview on his appointment as governor in 1969, would reverberate loudly forty years later, when that vital Central Bank warning light failed to flash during the reckless credit-creating early years of the twenty-first century. That malfunction, and the muted 'unpalatable words' emanating from 'the ivory tower' in Dame Street, left him, as he admits, perplexed and appalled. His choice of words in 2011 to Governor Dr Patrick Honahan – 'I'm counting on you to save the country from national humiliation' – expressed perhaps – as Dr Honahan ruefully acknowledges – the depth of his disappointment at the Bank's failure to discharge its obligation to prevent it and an additional imperative on the present governor to repair the damage! Although consistent in his refusal to comment publicly on the recent financial debacle, on which, he says, 'he no longer understands or feels equipped to comment', it would be fair to assume that on Ken Whitaker's watch the warning lights would have been flashing in Dame Street long before the banking collapse occurred. His words on taking office as governor in 1969 put the government of the day on notice that, under his leadership, the warning light would be fully functioning. His appointment was widely welcomed and seen, as one press report noted, 'as an expansion of the authority and responsibility of the Bank'.[2]

His remuneration as governor, set by the board of the Central Bank, was a relatively modest £8,500 per annum, with a car and an annual allowance of £750 towards official expenses. Expressing his thanks, but considering the payment over-generous in relation to current public sector standards, he agreed to a starting salary of £7,500; accepting the allowance of £750 for personal expenses related to his office, he declined the proffered new bank car and opted for an allowance towards his family saloon, which he considered adequate for his needs. Future salary increases, he requested, should be kept in line with those pertaining in the public service, a position he adhered to throughout the course of his governorship, despite the board's attempts, as he acknowledged, 'to be more generous than I felt I could accept'.[3] Such a gesture, rare in today's money-motivated culture, was to Ken Whitaker merely fair and proper at a time of 'rapidly rising prices' and depreciation of money values, which could be construed, as he humorously reminded his board, as representing 'a failure to safeguard the integrity of the currency'. On the other side of the coin he was equally scrupulous in seeking a fair and proper settlement of his pension rights in the event of his resignation after his seven-year period in office when, nine months short of retirement age, he would not be eligible for superannuation benefit. Following the publication in 1972 of the Devlin Report on the remuneration of higher public servants, 'an embarrassing and misleading inference' (later retracted by the financial magazine in question) was made about the remuneration of the governor of the Central Bank. The irony of his salary, which at his own insistence had been kept in line with public service pay guidelines, being publicly touted as an example of 'one high flier whom the Review Body wants to cut down by as much as £6,000'[4] was not lost on Ken.

Before taking up his new post, he undertook a preliminary task unique to it: providing a specimen of his signature that would appear on every note of legal tender issued during his term of office. His friend and colleague in the civil service, Owen O'Neill, recalled witnessing the 'ceremony' in Ken's office in the Department of Finance and his abiding memory being of 'how boyish' his friend at fifty-two appeared for such a 'venerable' posting. For his family, his signature on the country's banknotes was the most visible sign of their father's new job, which, as Ken recalls, other than 'hoping that I would have more banknotes to distribute among them, they otherwise took in their stride. It certainly did not bowl them over in any way!' On 18 December 1968, accompanied by the Taoiseach, Jack Lynch, he was driven to Áras an Uachtaráin, where his appointment as governor, effective from 1 March 1969, on the formal retirement of Dr Maurice Moynihan, was confirmed by President de Valera.

The Central Bank occupies a unique position between an independent and a state institution. It is distinguishable from other banks in that it is 'a *national* bank in the sense that its responsibility is for the public interest rather than for the interests of stockholders ... A modern central bank is concerned solely with banking from the point of view of the public interest and does no commercial business with private persons or firms.'[5] The Irish Central Bank was something of a late arrival, replacing the earlier Currency Commission in 1943. Its principal duty was to take whatever steps it deemed appropriate to safeguard the integrity of the Irish currency and also to ensure, as Ken pointedly indicated shortly after his appointment, 'that, in what pertains to the control of credit, the constant and predominant aim should be the welfare of the people as a whole',[6] a duty he sought to discharge throughout the course of his tenure as governor.

Because of the Bank's unique position, differences with the government of the day, especially in relation to monetary policy, were bound to arise, and had even led to the resignation of one governor, Joseph Brennan. As Ken realized, these difficulties were part of the job: 'The position of Central Banks and governments always poses this potential conflict . . . This is why', he noted on his appointment, 'there should be an active exchange of information and argument between the Central Bank and Government Departments.'[7] Indeed, in this regard he set the wheels in motion before his departure from Finance. Any sigh of relief Charles Haughey may have breathed at the departure of his independently minded and highly respected departmental secretary was no doubt stifled by Ken's public statement indicating that he had no intention of disappearing into some 'ivory tower' or underground vault in Foster Place. One of his final memos to Haughey might well have induced the minister to invoke the words of King Henry II about Thomas à Becket: 'Who will rid me of this meddlesome priest?'

> As the time of my departure approaches I have been thinking of what my role as Governor of the Central Bank should be. That it should not be one of glum isolation in an ivory tower, relieved only by the hurling of belated thunderbolts against erring Governments, I feel quite strongly; and I think that both you and the Taoiseach would favour my adopting a less frustrating and wasteful role, one involving a more active and useful exercise of the knowledge and experience I have acquired in the Civil Service. This does mean, however, that there will have to be a far more active interchange of information and ideas.[8]

While careful to acknowledge that, in the last resort, the Central Bank was 'an instrument of government', he none the less reminded the minister that, since the functions of the Bank were so closely bound up with national economic objectives, a proper delineation of fiscal and monetary policy, as well as an incomes strategy, were essential if these objectives were to be attained. He pointed out that the lack of communication that habitually existed between the minister for finance and the governor needed to be redressed, especially in relation to budgetary policy, where the latter was rarely if ever consulted, and yet, as he reasonably pointed out, 'the budget proposals – current *and* capital – create an economic environment in which the Central Bank has to try and operate a credit policy consistent with the major objectives'.[9] Outwardly, at least, the minister appeared to agree, adding a comment on Ken's memo: 'All this goes to prove how fortunate it is that we are about to have a wise, skilled, progressive Governor take over in the Central Bank.'[10] It was an auspicious start, but the positive tone was not to last long. However, his friendship and the sense of public duty he shared with his departmental successor, Charlie Murray, ensured that, while successive ministers for finance may not have taken up his offer of consultation, he ensured that he was kept briefed, albeit sometimes belatedly, on the budgetary and economic policies being contemplated by the government.

By 1969 the Central Bank of Ireland had assumed some of the characteristic functions more usually associated with a central bank. In addition to managing the issue and redemption of legal tender notes, it was further empowered to act as 'lender of last resort', to operate interbank clearances, to safeguard the integrity of the currency and to control credit. It had not, however, acquired full custody of the external cash reserves of the commercial banks, nor did it act as banker to the banking sector or to the government (this last role continued to be filled by the Bank of Ireland). Also, the licensing and supervision of the commercial banks had yet to come within its orbit. In 1969 a bizarre situation existed whereby a licence to establish a bank was available on application to the Department of Industry and Commerce, with few strings attached, on payment of the sum of one pound (the same fee as a dog licence!). The degree to which the Central Bank could use its power and carry out its functions on behalf of the people of Ireland depends to a large extent on the influence, ability and status of its incumbent governor. In March 1969, the appointment of Ken Whitaker heralded not merely an expansion in the functions of the Bank, but a firm commitment to its duty on behalf of the people of Ireland. The governor was designated as being:

> The chief executive officer of the Bank and shall on behalf of the Board have the direction and control of the administration of the assets and general funds of the Bank with authority to act and to give decisions in all matters which are not by the Currency and Central Bank Acts, 1927 to 1942 or any amendments thereof . . . specifically reserved for the Board.[11]

In 1969 the Central Bank board consisted of representatives of commercial banking, business and farming, as well as Ken's former boss in Finance, the redoubtable J. J. McElligott, and his successor, Charlie Murray. The governor's relationship with his board could be both complex and sensitive. The presence of members from the commercial banks required deft and diplomatic handling by the governor of matters such as exchange rate and interest rate policy. The relationship between Ken and his board of directors, he recalls, was generally 'harmonious. They were never inhibiting or negative.' His own ability, status and personality undoubtedly contributed to the respect and confidence with which they regarded him, giving him an independence and authority that at times extended beyond the (ill-defined) functions of his office – and which would later come under scrutiny in the glare of a controversial legal case in the High Court.

The work of the Central Bank was familiar territory to Ken well before his appointment as governor. His first assignment in the Department of Finance in 1938 had been to prepare a sub-mission to the government on the recommendations of the Banking Commission which led to the conversion of the old Currency Commission into the Central Bank in 1943. 'I had therefore seen at close quarters, and with an insider's view of rela-tionships, the beginnings of the Central Bank and the gradual coming into play of its powers and functions.'[12] As secretary of the Department of Finance, he was also a Central Bank director, and as such had contributed to the development of a number of the bank's functions under the governorships of his predecessors, Joseph Brennan, J.J. McElligott and Dr Maurice Moynihan. These included the legislative changes of 1943 and the additions of US and Canadian dollars to the two main Central Bank accounts: the General Fund and the Legal Tender Note Fund (a capital fund initiated to maintain cover for the redemption of the country's outstanding legal tender notes), in order to offset the depreciation in sterling. Further securities were introduced on Ireland's joining the IMF and World Bank, and in 1959 Irish government securities were added. In 1955 Gerard Sweetman agreed to Ken's proposal (with the concurrence of the Central Bank) that the Irish commercial banks should not raise their lending rates in tandem with the Bank of England. Hailed as the 'first occasion on which the Irish banks had not automatically changed their rate following a change in the bank rate in Britain', this development was regarded by the government at the time 'as an occasion for legitimate pride',[13] and represented a brave but short-term step towards modifying the traditional inter-dependence of Irish and British interest rates.

Traditionally, the Irish commercial banks looked to London for their liquidity. In 1956, on Ken's recommendation, the Bank commenced rediscounting both commercial bills of exchange and exchequer bills for the Irish banks. In 1958, through its settlement of interbank clearances, it assumed, for the first time, the role of 'lender of last resort'. After the devaluation of sterling in November 1967, when the Bank set about diversifying its sterling reserves into other less vulnerable assets, Ken promised his counterparts in the Treasury that, 'to avoid any undue repercussions on sterling, we would proceed quietly and by stages from March 1968 onwards towards our objective ... with deliberate modesty and sensitivity.'[14]

At the start of his governorship he initiated the transfer of sterling assets from the Associated Banks to the Central Bank, making it the depository for almost all the country's external reserves. In his capacity as governor, he also represented the Bank at meetings of international bodies, such as the IMF, the Bank for International Settlements (BIS) and the World Bank. Following Ireland's accession to the EEC in 1973, he became a member of the Committee of Governors of EEC Central Banks, which dealt with monetary policy and with foreign exchange arrangements within the Community. These monthly meetings of Central Bank governors, held in Basle under the aegis of the BIS, were, as Ken humorously remembers, 'useful, informal gatherings which inevitably and wrongly prompted conspiracy suspicions. We dined rather well, relished Swiss cheese and white wine, and came to be distinguished from the Gnomes of Zurich as the Gastronomes of Basle!'[15] However, as he also notes participation in such international gatherings in the 1970s helped in 'elevating Ireland's status. You might sit down beside someone like Georges Pompidou or Reginald Maudling. It also provided an opportunity for the country's representatives to demonstrate that we comprehended technically what was going on.'

Back home, it was not just the relationship with the minister for finance that required careful handling. That between the governor and the secretary of the Department of Finance could at times become fraught, given the potential for divergence of opinion and policy between the two institutions.

As I found from experience, there are seeds of difficulty in the relationship between a Secretary of the Department of Finance and the Central Bank, of which he is also a member, and particularly between him and the Governor, as full-time Chairman of that Board. But, with understanding, these difficulties can be minimised, the more so when the parties recognise that they have more in common than divides them and, in particular, that fundamentally they share the same anxieties and objectives.[16]

His predecessor at the Central Bank, Maurice Moynihan, for example, had expressed reservations regarding a recommendation in *Economic Development* that the Legal Tender Note Fund could provide £3.5 million annually for domestic investment. He also questioned Ken's suggestion that funds be transferred from the commercial banks to the Central Bank. And during his own governorship, in a tension with resonance in more recent times, the Bank's reluctance to provide additional credit to fund government expenditure, especially current expenditure, and its efforts to curb excessive credit expansion in the private sector, gave rise to particular differences. However, in Ken's own tenure as secretary of the Department of Finance, while he may have differed in extent and interpretation with his predecessors, J. J. McElligott and Maurice Moynihan, on the question of credit expansion in the economy he was more often in accord with them. As he explained in a private letter to Declan Costello TD in 1956: 'It is a form of escapism to think that expansion of credit by a "fully-fledged" central bank would solve our problems. It would in fact accentuate them.'[17] As successive governments ran up a series of ever-increasing budget deficits in the 1970s and looked to the Central Bank under his governorship to ease residual financing problems, he remained unmoved, noting that 'to yield even a legitimate inch in financial matters may be to give an inordinate mile. The appetite grows by what it is fed on.'[18] This belief would bring him into conflict with the government on many occasions during his term of office.

To the general public in 1969, the Central Bank was a vague entity. Other than its name printed on the country's banknotes, little was known about its functions or place in the economy. Its very location, secreted in a quiet, leafy cul-de-sac off Dublin's College Green, in the shadow of the impressive former Irish parliament buildings, whose armoury and guardrooms the Bank occupied, added to the air of mystery surrounding the rather demure and relatively 'Young Lady of Foster Place'. Only a small brass plate on the door bearing its name in Irish and English announced its presence. Few of the thousands of citizens who daily passed by on College Green were aware that the smoke that issued forth from its chimney twice-weekly bore the costly whiff of millions of discounted banknotes being incinerated in its furnace, or that beneath the cobblestones, in a warren of underground vaults, the liquid assets of the state rested in the form of foreign currencies and gold bullion.

Ken's first impressions of his new 'headquarters' in Foster Place were 'of a Dickensian atmosphere . . . an odd sort of place . . . everything had an ancient look about it . . . an afterthought . . . and an unsuitable image for a central bank.' Past a compact and ornate banking hall, with its rococo plasterwork ceilings and mahogany counters, a labyrinth of narrow, winding, windowless corridors led to the Bank's counting rooms, where the contents of the country's coffers were daily received, checked and consigned to oblivion. In their place their equivalents were reissued, the new notes crisp and pungent, the coin bright and shiny, by a small army of female or, as they were called with the courtesy of the time, 'lady' clerks. A smaller number of exclusively male clerical staff managed the Bank's accounts, while an even smaller number of economic staff composed prudent, if rather dull, articles and commentary for the Bank's quarterly bulletins and annual reports. The dearth of career opportunities, especially for the female staff, was anathema to the new governor in an age when the struggle for gender equality in the workplace was beginning to become a hot issue. Ken's working relationship with such pioneering women as Thekla Beere, the first secretary of a public service department in the Irish civil service, as well as his inherent respect for female capability, was to make him a willing proponent of equality in the new institution under his care. His private secretary, Maura Mullane, managed the administration of his office with quiet and efficient authority, earning his gratitude with the words 'no man can be a hero to his private secretary who sees so much of his imperfections!'[19]

Shortly after his arrival as governor, the Bank assumed responsibility for the issue of exchequer bills, at monthly rather than, as previously, quarterly intervals; then, in December 1969, the Bank became for the first time registrar of a National Loan. These additional functions, along with others envisaged in legislation then in train, all led to a substantial increase in staff numbers. The new functions and responsibilities eventually came into play under the Central Bank Act 1971 (effective from 1 September that year), by which the Bank finally assumed the range of powers commensurate with the role of a modern central bank. The act provided for the transfer of the exchequer account, which covered all government income and expenditure, from the Bank of Ireland to the Central Bank. It also underpinned the Central Bank's role in the supervision of the Irish banking system, empowering it, at its own discretion, to grant, refuse or revoke a banking licence; to carry out inspections of banks, both clearing (Associated) and non-clearing (non-Associated); and to supervise and regulate the activities of banks, including bank mergers which, in the 1970s, were a marked feature of the Irish banking sector. While there was some initial resistance by the commercial banks, especially by those represented on the board of the Central Bank, to such 'intrusive' inspections and spot-checks, under Ken Whitaker's governorship the Central Bank's control over the Irish banking system strengthened and evolved.

The primary responsibility of a central bank is the formulation and implementation of credit policy, today known as monetary policy. Under his governorship, Ken extended the scope of that policy and applied it more rigorously. The Bank's annual credit policy statement became more explicit and was directed not merely at the Associated Banks but also at the non-Associated banks (which included subsidiaries of the clearing banks, as well as more recently established branches of international banks). Specific targets were set for total domestic credit or lending by each bank. Unwarranted increases in excess of these targets were penalized by requiring the offending bank(s) to place non-interest-earning deposits with the Central Bank. A limit was placed on each bank's annual net inflow of funds from abroad to finance credit expansion within the country; excessive inflows were also discouraged by the required placement by the banks of non-interest-bearing deposits with the Central Bank, thus reducing the amount of credit available for lending to the public. The new legislation of 1971 further empowered the Central Bank to apply what were known as 'liquidity ratios' to the banking system, to help it manage variations in the liquid assets of the banks and, in turn, the rate of increase in credit offered to their customers. The banks were required to place a minimum proportion of their Irish monetary savings, in the form of their customers' balances in current and deposit accounts, in Irish government bonds and in cash balances with the Central Bank. In essence, these liquidity ratios channelled a proportion (initially around 20 per cent) of the national monetary savings lodged with the banks into the public sector (both the exchequer and the Central Bank), rather than into the provision of credit to the private sector. The liquidity ratios helped to underpin the management of the Irish banking system and to restrain the indebtedness of the private sector, especially during times of inflationary pressure. These arrangements also helped establish a domestic liquidity base for the Irish banking system in Ireland, rather than, as previously, in London.

Before the extension of the regulatory and supervisory powers conferred on it by the 1971 act, however, the system over which the Central Bank presided included a number of smaller or 'fringe' banks, many of them operated, in effect, to fund the personal investments of their owners. The additional powers conferred on the Central Bank came too late to prevent the much-publicized failure of two of their number, the Irish Trust Bank (ITB), founded by the British-born speculator Ken Bates, and Merchant Banking, founded by the Irish builder and developer Matt Gallagher. Both had taken advantage of the ease with which a bank licence could be acquired in Ireland before 1971. In 1972 Bates challenged in the High Court the validity of the conditions subsequently imposed on ITB by the Central Bank. In his evidence Ken contended that, at the time ITB was granted a licence, Bates had failed to reveal 'particulars of his career and early activities'. Information Ken had subsequently received from the Bank of England and other sources had put him on notice 'that I should proceed very cautiously because very grave doubts had been raised as to the suitability of Mr Bates to be a director of an Irish licensed bank'.[20] In his ruling, however, while mindful of the governor's right to entertain such concerns, the judge nevertheless considered the conditions imposed by the Central Bank on ITB to be unlawful, because of the Central Bank's failure to provide the plaintiff with sufficient time to make representations. He also questioned the validity of the governor's acting *ultra vires* in imposing such conditions on ITB on the basis of his own opinion rather than through the board of the Central Bank. Judgment and costs were consequently awarded against the Central Bank.

The case received widespread publicity and the ruling was embarrassing both for the governor and for the Central Bank. Nevertheless, while the case challenged its new supervisory powers, the Bank continued to enforce additional restraints on ITB in relation to its share capital structure and liquidity ratios, as well as prohibiting it from opening additional branches in

Ireland. Such vigilance was well justified. Following further investigation in 1975, ITB was deemed to be insolvent, and in February 1976 a liquidator was appointed. The fate of the ITB's depositors, small, individual savers, mostly located in the UK who, despite the publicity of the court case and the Central Bank's public prohibitions, had continued to deposit savings with the ITB, then became a public and political issue. The 1971 Central Bank Act, as Ken reasonably pointed out at a public press conference, explicitly stated that the Bank was not empowered to guarantee deposits in licensed banks. At the behest of the minister for finance, however, a compromise was eventually reached. The Bank agreed to provide the necessary funds through the office of the liquidator for the repayment in full of those depositors 'who had no connection with its [ITB's] directors or shareholders',[21] while ensuring that it was fully reimbursed by the Department of Finance.

The case of Merchant Banking also became an issue for the Central Bank. Founded in 1961 by the builder Matt Gallagher, a TACA supporter and associate of Charles Haughey, and controlled by a trust based in the Cayman Islands, when Gallagher died in 1972 it was taken over by his flamboyant and equally ambitious son Patrick. The relationship between the bank and the Gallagher Group, which consisted mainly of building companies, was complex and irregular. Following the 1971 act, the Central Bank attached conditions to Merchant Banking's licence, but the bank attempted to evade control through obfuscation and even physical obstruction, barring access by Central Bank inspectors to its premises. In this way it continued to operate for a time before being declared insolvent in 1982. The fall of Patrick Gallagher's subsidiary bank in Belfast followed, and in 1989, on the collapse of his building empire, he was convicted of fraud in a Belfast court.

Compared to the failure of many banks both in Britain and on the Continent, the Irish Central Bank performed its newly acquired supervisory functions effectively during the course of Ken's governorship, and the Irish banking system emerged from the 1970s recession in a strong and stable position. Nevertheless, the increasing number of small non-Associated banks (merchant, industrial and North American) established in Ireland during the period was a cause of personal concern for Ken, who recalls, 'I was always wary of them. They were on the fringe of immorality as far as I was concerned,' and he ensured that they were kept firmly in line. Reserving its right to alter the powers conferred on it by the 1971 act, the Central Bank further strengthened and extended both its licensing and supervisory controls. In 1974 it introduced revised non-statutory requirements and standards, initiated bank inspections of the commercial banks' books by its own auditors, required detailed information on a monthly and quarterly basis on the assets, liabilities and credit advances of the Associated and non-Associated banks, and initiated regular meetings with the banks under its supervision.

Of particular concern was the failure of the 1971 legislation to extend the Central Bank's supervisory control over the provident building societies, even then considered 'the rogues in the deposit-taking business'.[22] This was a sector that over future decades of property boom was to undergo spectacular growth. 'We have made representations,' Ken stated at a press conference in 1975, 'and we are hopeful something will be done about it.' These representations, however, took time to have effect. Much of the reluctance was politically motivated, given the Fianna Fáil government's determination to expand the housing market, even to the extent of insisting that the commercial banks advance the necessary credit to building societies. At the time, the regulation of the building societies came within the remit of the Department of Industry and Commerce – a situation Ken considered at variance with sound banking practice. After his resignation as governor in 1976, he continued to advocate that the societies be brought under the supervisory control of the

Central Bank. Given the huge expansion of resources in the sector – from £100 million to £1,000 million between 1971 and 1980 – as he pointed out in a Senate debate in December 1980, 'Building Societies should be brought under the control of the Central Bank so that all interest rates and charges would be under specialised supervision by reference, not only to the protection of depositors and borrowers, but also to the broader needs of monetary and economic policy.'[23]

In the event, it was not until 1985 that the government finally agreed to review the sector. In a letter to the minister for industry and commerce, John Bruton, at the time, Ken noted that 'it is the Central Bank and not the registrar or departmental officials who should be monitoring critical questions such as prudent liquidity ratios [of the building societies] and the balance to be held between short-term liabilities and longer-term loans.'[24] He also expressed concern regarding the upsurge in unexplained 'management expenses', which in one society, he noted, had more than doubled in four years, while total income had risen by only one-third, and the conflict of interest which allowed the building societies to appoint non-independent auditors to produce their accounts – all of which suggested a blatant abdication of duty by the boards of management. In 1990, on the enactment of the Building Societies Act 1989, the sector was finally brought within the scope of Central Bank regulation.

For many years during and after Ken Whitaker's tenure the Central Bank's supervision and regulation of the Irish banking system proved effective. In more recent decades, however, as Ireland embraced the European Monetary System in 1979 and the euro in 1999, the banking sector evolved into a global industry (as manifested in Ireland from 1987 onwards with the establishment of the Irish Financial Services Centre or IFSC) and international banking standards underwent unprecedented change. The introduction of 'light-touch' regulation, originating in the American sub-prime mortgage sector in the 1990s, and spreading to Europe, resulted in the removal or watering down of the prudential banking rules and supervisory standards previously in place, especially in relation to credit and bank borrowing. Embraced by the free-wheeling environment of the Celtic Tiger years, this had a particularly negative impact on Irish banks and building societies, allowing them to borrow without restriction from overseas banks and to advance a greater proportion of their assets to the overheating building industry at home. The political decision taken in 2003 to shift the regulation and supervision of the Irish banking system from the Central Bank to a new quasi-independent regulatory authority, answerable to the Department of Finance, further undermined the cohesion and independence that had formerly existed, eventually contributing to the virtual collapse and bankruptcy of the Irish banking system.

While the hands of the Irish Central Bank may well have become tied by such politically motivated developments, the introduction of 'light-touch' regulation, the dilution of its regulatory authority over the Irish banking system, the phenomenal growth in bank credit, and the over-exposure of Irish banks to housing and construction-related activities would all undoubtedly have been opposed by Ken Whitaker. Given his status, reputation and experience, it seems likely that he would have been an outspoken critic of such developments, regardless of government policy or preference, or that, as a board member of the European Central Bank, he would have registered his aversion to such watering-down of international banking regulations. But whatever he may or may not have been able to achieve on the European stage, it is certain that on the domestic front, he would have acted firmly and decisively to prevent bank lending to the construction industry rising from 25 per cent to an incredible 60 per cent, the provision of 100 per cent (even 110 per cent) house loans by institutions under Central Bank supervision, and the development of a situation in which over half of Irish bank lending came from funds sourced abroad.

In 1969, further developments in Irish central banking were heralded by the publication of a report by Professor Louden Ryan, with a foreword written by Ken Whitaker, on the desirability of establishing money and bond markets in Dublin for exchequer bills and short-term government securities, which up to then had been traded on the London money market. During 1970, despite a lengthy bank strike, the Bank developed internal money market facilities to provide a more extensive and competitive market for short-term deposits. Also in 1970, it began dealing in foreign currencies. Following the rapid rise in the number of non-Associated banks, an interbank market, dealing in short-term funds under the supervision of the Central Bank, also came into being at this time. This was followed in November 1972 by the establishment of a Central Exchange in the Central Bank, where every day at noon the Associated Banks, some of the non-Associated banks, the Paymaster General and the Department of Defence presented cheques, payable orders and other payment instruments drawn on each other for clearing, with settlement being effected through accounts held by each participant with the Central Bank.

The establishment of a more extensive staff and a more professional approach in economic and financial research was another feature and personal interest of Ken Whitaker's governorship. This led to an expansion, in both extent and variety, of career opportunities for the Bank's existing staff, including its female officers, as well as an intake of specialist staff from outside. The research structures he established in the Bank in the 1970s have remained, more or less, to the present day. With the new Bank headquarters then presumed to be just a few years from completion, the already limited space in Foster Place was augmented by the rental of additional premises to accommodate increased staff numbers. The governor, senior management, economic and banking departments were located at Fitzwilton House on the banks of the Grand Canal, while the accounts and government loans departments, the latter having undergone a sizeable expansion as a result of the transfer of the exchequer accounts from the Bank of Ireland, were located in Apollo House on Tara Street. The Bank's note and coin issue and redemption function remained at Foster Place for a time, before moving in 1974 to a new custom-built facility in Sandyford, County Dublin. The decimalization of the Irish currency and the issue of the new coin and note denominations were completed by February 1970. As well as introducing a new internal audit system, Ken also established an innovative internal management committee, through which contact was maintained with developments in each department, to facilitate the formulation of policy for presentation to the board.

The reputation and status of the new governor influenced both the image of the Bank and its staff, as he made his presence felt in ways of which he may not even have been aware. It was noted that he drove a modest car, which looked incongruous beside the chauffeur-driven limousines of the emerging 'captains of industry' who frequented Fitzwilton House. He carried a well-worn briefcase, and wore an anorak long before it became a certain Taoiseach's accessory. He smiled a lot, for a governor, chatted with staff, with whom he shared the communal lift to his office on the fourth floor, and put in an appearance at the staff Christmas party. He handed out prizes at the Bank's annual sports day, remarking on one such occasion to this author, as he presented the trophy for tennis, how her game had benefited by virtue of the vantage point her office enjoyed overlooking the original Fitzwilliam Lawn Tennis Club! The appointment of such an energetic, independently minded and high-profile governor enhanced the status of the Bank as well as the morale of the staff. Gradually, the Bank shed the musty image of the old Currency Commission and emerged as a confident custodian of the country's finances and regulator of the banking system. What the Bank had to say on the economy, as much as on monetary policy, became hot news. Standing room only was the order of the day in the packed boardroom in Fitzwilton House on the publication of the Bank's annual report, as television cameras and photographers vied for room with reporters and commentators eager to elicit comments on the state of the country from a governor from whom they knew they would receive an honest, informed and forthright assessment. The Bank's publications, its main artery for public commentary, underwent a transformation in the range of topics covered, including the introduction of a section of signed articles, many written by the governor, more in-depth monetary and economic analyses, and a modern presentation and design.

For Ken Whitaker however, this new posting represented a certain loss of influence and involvement. The camaraderie and *esprit de corps* he had enjoyed during his lengthy tenure in the Department of Finance were difficult to replicate; the position of governor was a lofty and lone one by contrast. He came with quite a reputation, which made senior bank staff wary of both his undoubted ability and his uncanny memory. He expected high standards and could be critical if these were not met. His personal and public aversion to immoderate pay increases in the public and private sectors extended not merely to himself, but also to Bank staff. In his view, the Central Bank should lead by example, practising the pay restraint it preached. This eventually led to the unionization of the Bank's staff, who hitherto had made their representations regarding pay and conditions via direct and less confrontational negotiations with management. As governor, he seemed to have little affinity with the markets, his interest being centred on the supervision of the banking system and on the state of the economy. His aversion to the introduction of credit cards by the commercial banks might well, in the light of more recent developments, be interpreted more positively today than it was then, while he did not favour the proposal by the commercial banks to introduce term loans as a substitute for overdrafts. But it was the field of monetary and incomes policy, and specifically curtailing foreign borrowing and controlling the rampant inflation that threatened to envelop the country, that became his main interest and challenge as governor.

In this regard the first issue confronting him was the annual budget for 1969/70 (the financial year running 1 April to 31 March). While the minister for finance could, with some justification, claim that '1968 was the best year in our economic history',[25] his statement, as Ken noted, hid a number of disturbing features. Increases in public capital and current expenditure were beginning to form a pattern. In early 1969, what Ken regarded as 'an ominously steep increase in pay' (over 20 per cent) was awarded to maintenance craftsmen which, as he predicted, set the standard for future pay increases throughout the economy. With current public expenditure rising at an annual average rate of 12 per cent, in contrast to an annual average 4 per cent growth in GNP, there were ominous implications for the balance of payments. The devaluation of sterling in November 1967 was also beginning to have an impact on the Irish economy. Writing initially to the minister for finance, Charles Haughey, and then to the Taoiseach, Jack Lynch, Ken urged a budget that would slow down the rate of increase in prices and incomes, make Irish goods and services more competitive, and ensure a more manageable balance of payments. 'The issue which we are facing has been stated before in terms of this simple but inescapable piece of arithmetic,' he informed them. 'If our rate of real growth is four per cent and prices abroad are rising by say two per cent, we cannot have money incomes rising by more than six per cent without risk to the competitiveness of our products.'[26] Credit resources in the commercial banks were so low that, if they were to meet only the government's credit needs, let alone those of the private sector, a considerable amount of money would have to come from the Central Bank, with a resultant diminution of the country's external reserves. But 1969 was a general election year and a policy of soft options prevailed, with, as Ken noted, the 'failure of this first attempt by way of income tax relief and social welfare improvements, to prevent the exorbitant maintenance men's pay increase from being extended to workers in general'.[27]

June saw the election of another Fianna Fáil government. Despite enduring a bruising election campaign, sparked by controversy surrounding the sale of his house in Raheny for a substantial profit to the developer Matt Gallagher, a transaction from which, it was alleged, he had benefited financially through an amendment in the 1965 Finance Act which he had introduced, Charles Haughey was reappointed minister for finance. His political rival, George Colley, retained his post at Industry and Commerce, while Ken's former mentor Frank Aiken retired to the back benches, to be replaced by Paddy Hillery at External Affairs. In his capacity as governor, while not allowing the allegations surrounding the minister for finance to impinge on their professional relationship, such apparent abuse of public office served to put Ken on guard and, as he recalls, to be 'very careful' in his dealings with Haughey. It also made him wary of attempts by the minister to circumvent the Central Bank's statutory obligations, especially in relation to credit expansion in the economy. As in his dealings with all government ministers, he preserved a due detachment in his relationship with Haughey. However, subsequent revelations about the minister's implication in covert operations relating to Northern Ireland would finally, in Ken's estimation, place Charles Haughey 'beyond the pale'.

August 1969 Ken was ever to remember as 'a wicked month'. It marked a serious eruption of violence in Northern Ireland, the harbinger of almost thirty years of bloodshed, as the North made its pain-filled way, over countless killings, bombings, hunger strikes, marches and demonstrations, towards a democratic solution in which Ken Whitaker was to play an integral part. That August, as the situation teetered on the brink of civil war and the Whitaker family were on holiday in Carna, in the

Connemara Gaeltacht, as he recalls: 'A plane brought to Castlebar and a car to Connemara, the governor of the Bank of Ireland, Dr Don Carroll, whom I was meeting to make arrangements for the transfer to the Central Bank of all the remaining net sterling assets of the Associated Banks.' And in the same month planning problems emerged over the building of the proposed Bank headquarters in Dame Street. Even at Sunday Mass in Carna, it seemed there was no escaping the responsibilities of his new job: as from the altar, the local priest fulminated against his congregation's habit of putting old predecimal halfpenny pieces into the collection box. 'Níl maith ar bith ag iarraidh iad a thabhairt dona sagairt – ni fiú tada níos mó iad', he thundered. ('There is no point giving them to the priest – they are no longer worth anything!)' 'I was glad to be in the crowd at the back for fear he might turn to me for confirmation!' Ken remembers.

August 1969 also brought his first disagreement as governor with the minister for finance, recently recovered from the effects of a car accident in County Wicklow. In the light of the preparation of the new Central Bank Bill, the issue of the ultimate responsibility for credit control was brought into sharp focus when 'a packet arrived from Dublin [to Carna] which suggested that the Department of Finance was seeking statutory control over the exercise of credit policy by the Central Bank'.[28] In relation to the regulation of credit in the economy, the Central Bank indicated that the new legislation should include a provision whereby it could, by the prescription of liquidity ratios, supplement the guidelines it regularly issued to the commercial banks, which were in practice ineffective in controlling credit levels in the economy. The issue, however, heightened a wider and more sensitive one – the relationship between the minister for finance and the Central Bank. In his usual clear and cogent style, Ken reasonably pointed out to the minister that, while the government exercised ultimate responsibility for economic policy (of which credit policy is an integral part), the Central Bank Act 1942 ordained that 'in what pertains to credit, the constant and predominant aim shall be the welfare of the people as a whole', and taking that, as well as the long-term interest of the Bank and the public into consideration, decisions regarding the effective application of credit control in the economy should remain with the Central Bank, 'subject to broad conformity with national economic policy.'[29] Such conformity could be enhanced, he maintained, by greater consultation between the minister and the governor, as he had requested on his departure from the Department of Finance.

The issue continued to be a source of disagreement during the autumn, as the new Central Bank Bill was being prepared for a reading in the Dáil. At a meeting on 14 January 1970 the minister again pressed his case, but the governor was not for turning. Even if the minister had power to issue such a directive to the board of the Central Bank, this would not, Ken informed him, absolve the board of its statutory or, indeed, its conscientious obligations; and, if the differences of views could not be reconciled, then the governor and board would have no option but to resign. 'I told the minister', Ken recalled, 'that, like a good Catholic, I recognized the supreme authority of the Pope, but like a good bishop, I claimed jurisdiction in my own diocese'; and, for reasons 'both of principle and expediency', he advised the minister to abandon the idea. No doubt realizing that to proceed against someone of status and proven record, who was not prepared to carry out 'a monetary policy which in good conscience he could not regard as being in the national interest',[30] could have serious political repercussions, Haughey let the matter drop. Ken's first attempt to maintain the autonomy and integrity of the Central Bank had proved successful, but had done little to endear him to a minister unaccustomed to being so thwarted.

Regardless of the coolness that marked their relationship, Ken continued to fulfil what he perceived to be his duty as governor.

During the lead-up to the publication of the government's public capital programme for 1970/1, Ken advised the minister, through his departmental secretary, that his proposals did not, as the minister had publicly claimed, represent the reconciliation of the needs for prudent financial management and for economic and social development.

> I do not accept that the former need is being served, while the latter, in my view, does not require any volume of increase just now in capital outlay . . . I am sorry to have to write in this strain but I can see great economic difficulties ahead and a tragic upset to the growth of the economy, unless the Minister takes stronger action to curb the growth of public expenditure . . . and succeeds in bringing the trade unions to some sense of proportion regarding money incomes from now on.[31]

In a subsequent meeting with Jack Lynch, 'to discuss a number of matters . . . I impressed on the Taoiseach the need for corrective action . . . the primacy of curbing the growth of Government current expenditure and the great importance of the Government being seen to be in control of the situation and determined to restore order'.[32] The Taoiseach promised to address Ken's concerns in the Dáil before the Christmas adjournment and asked him to prepare a note with that end in view. Conscious that their private discussions might drive the wedge further between himself and the minister for finance, Ken diplomatically advised Jack Lynch that 'it might be more politic to have the note looked over in the Department of Finance, without, of course, stating its provenance'.[33]

The following spring, against a rising tide of inflation largely propelled by domestic factors, Ken urged the minister for finance to break this 'vicious spiral', motivated, as he saw it, by 'sectional greed', and to avail himself of the advice of the newly published NIEC report on incomes and prices to advocate a 'breathing space'[34] in the alarming rise in incomes. The minister did not reply to his letter. Subsequently, in his capacity as NIEC president, on the formal presentation of the Council's annual report Ken took the opportunity to urge the Taoiseach to implement what he had advocated to the minister. The following day he sought a meeting with Charles Haughey to discuss the forthcoming budgetary proposals which, as he discovered from Charlie Murray, contained a proposal to double turnover tax to 5 per cent. The minister, however, declined to meet him, sending him a message that 'suggested annoyance at my having been in direct communication with the Taoiseach'.[35] Haughey's suspicions about Ken's 'extra-curricular' work at this time, as adviser to Jack Lynch on Northern Ireland, may also have been symptomatic of his antagonism.

In Ken's capacity as a public servant, however, duty prevailed, and he was not afraid to incur Haughey's displeasure – or, indeed, that of any other politician – or inclined to take personal umbrage when, as he saw it, the public good was at stake. Writing again to the minister, he explained the circumstances that had prompted him to make his concerns known directly to the Taoiseach. 'I am genuinely worried about our economic prospects, the more so as I have the impression that you are tired of hearing from me. I am not by nature pessimistic and I am certainly not putting on some "Central Bank act".'[36] The minister finally relented and agreed to a meeting. To ensure that there would be no misunderstanding, 'I expressed my views to him both orally and in the form of manuscript notes which I handed over to him',[37] Ken subsequently recorded.

The notes contained a detailed analysis of Haughey's budgetary proposals and the levels of increased public expenditure, both capital and current, they entailed, with resultant heavy borrowing and unsustainable price increases. The budget would not, as the minister claimed, have any deflationary impact either on the rise in incomes and prices or on the threatened £90 million deficit. Ken further drew his attention to the over-estimation of tax revenue contained in the budget proposals and the effects the proposed doubling of turnover tax would have on incomes. On 'economic and social equity grounds', he urged him to 'recast' the budget to take these pitfalls into consideration. At the time, few would have had the courage to confront Charles Haughey, much less point out to him the error of his ways. It took a brave man not only to beard the lion in his own den, but to try to divert him from his path. Having done his duty, and leaving the minister in possession of a copy of a note he had prepared in advance, bearing the title 'Some Reasons for Avoiding a Devaluation' – a further sobering reminder of the likely effects of the minister's budgetary proposals – Ken departed from his presence in the realization, as he admitted, that he had 'no reason to hope that his [Haughey's] proposals would be changed'.[38]

In the event, Charles Haughey did not present the controversial budget. On budget day the news that the minister had been seriously injured in a riding accident resulted in the budget speech being delivered in the Dáil by Jack Lynch. 'The thought occurred to me,' Ken recorded, 'to press the Taoiseach to use the Minister's personal mishap as a ground for postponement and reconsideration of the budgetary proposals!'[39] Budgetary proposals, however pressing, soon paled into insignificance when subsequently the conspiratorial plots of the 'parallel government', composed of cabinet ministers such as Blaney, Haughey and Boland, which had stalked Jack Lynch since the outbreak of 'the Troubles' in Northern Ireland began to emerge. A series of revelations and accusations culminated in the arms trial, centring on Haughey and Blaney's alleged complicity in a plot to import illegal arms into the country for the IRA, their subsequent removal from office and their later acquittal. At the end of Charles Haughey's three-year period as minister for finance, the annual balance of payments deficit had risen to £70 million, total public expenditure, which had been 25 per cent of GNP, started an inexorable rise that would see it reach 40 per cent by 1972, and the exchequer's borrowing requirement had almost doubled. Despite this alarming downturn in the public finances, as Ken recorded, 'one bulwark had, however, held – no one had yet undermined the disciplinary safeguard of not deliberately incurring deficits in the current budget'.[40]

Despite the traumatic political events that engulfed the country during the summer and autumn of 1970, the nation's financial and economic life continued. A bank strike, resulting in the closure, from May until November, of all branches of the Associated Banks countrywide, caused major disruption to banking services which the Central Bank tried to ease by providing cash facilities through the non-Associated banks and building societies. The lengthy strike also made the Central Bank's monetary policy, especially in relation to credit advice, difficult to apply or monitor. On Ken's recommendation, the government accepted, in principle, the NIEC's report on incomes policy, and a new organization bringing employers and workers together was established in May. On Charles Haughey's dismissal, his rival George Colley was given the finance portfolio.

If Ken had expected any substantial change in the direction of the country's economic policy on Colley's appointment, he was to be disappointed. Against a background of pay-related strikes, work stoppages and the worsening situation in Northern Ireland, on his first meeting with the new minister on 2 June he again pressed for the establishment of closer liaison and communication between the Department of Finance and the Central Bank. Stressing the urgent need for the government to demonstrate 'the confidence factor' by being seen to take the situation in hand and allay 'the feeling abroad that, by reason of other preoccupations, the state of the economy had not received sufficient attention in the course of the past year,' and pointing out that 'a failure of confidence, either at home or abroad, could quickly make serious inroads into reserves',[41] he further reminded the minister that the continued inflow of foreign capital, as well as the country's ability to access foreign sources of credit, depended on the maintenance of confidence in the government to manage the economy efficiently and defend the exchange rate. Colley's subsequent public assessment of the economic situation and the state of government finances made Ken baulk at his claim that recent action taken by him in relation to incomes and fiscal policy had dampened down demand: 'I don't think there has been any such action,' Ken bluntly informed Charlie Murray in the Department of Finance, 'and I hope the Government won't lay any balm to their bosoms on this score.'[42] In an effort to set the minister on the road to redemption, as the annual holiday season approached Ken sent him a detailed assessment of the difficulties facing the economy and how they might be best overcome. While his memo may not have been the minister's preferred choice of holiday reading, Ken's advice that the government should show leadership on incomes policy bore fruit. When the Employer–Labour Conference failed to produce a pay agreement by the autumn, the government threatened to impose statutory control on all forms of income. The threat was quickly followed by further discussions, and a voluntary pay agreement between employers and employees was subsequently hammered out.

Other proposals introduced by the government in 1971, as Ken recalls, 'drew fire from the Central Bank'. As an inducement to the trade unions to accept a degree of wage restraint, the government proposed to introduce a wealth tax 'some time in the future'. Regardless of the principle of introducing such a tax, as he informed the Department of Finance, 'public notice that such a tax, of unspecified scope and form, would apply from a future date would, in my view, risk setting in train a massive outflow of funds . . . It would be folly to add deliberately to the grave risks we already face.'[43] Convinced that such a tax would contribute little to the economy in proportion to the damage its announcement in advance was likely to inflict, he decided to risk ministerial

223

wrath by alerting the Taoiseach directly to the danger. 'Don't bring unnecessary trouble on your head,' he advised Jack Lynch – advice that was, to his relief, subsequently adopted. Another bone of contention emerged in October when the minister for finance attempted to extend government price control to bank interest rates. Following Ken's robust assertion that the control of bank interest rates was the responsibility of the Central Bank, the proposed legislation was duly withdrawn.

The year 1972 is remembered by Ken as a major, albeit adverse, turning point in the country's financial history. The economic portents were darkened by Bloody Sunday (30 January) and the subsequent burning of the British Embassy in Dublin. Despite these disturbing developments and their negative consequences for an already troubled Irish economy, the government saw fit to dismantle the final bulwark of financial propriety, as Ken judged it, by departing from the tradition of balancing the current budget. As Ken prophesied, 'once a large deficit had been allowed to appear the Government would find it extremely hard on political grounds ever to close the gap again'.[44] For the first time in the history of the state, the budget provided for a £28 million current account deficit which, as Ken predicted, opened the door to an unstoppable annual increase in the deficit: by 1977 it would stand at an extraordinary £777 million, fuelling the twin fires of inflation and increased foreign borrowing. 'I regard the opening up of current deficits as a most regrettable decision. I cannot but think that it was taken without full advertence to its longer-term economic and political implications.'[45]

Another 'regrettable legacy' of the economic landscape in 1972 was the government's failure to obtain, as a precondition of a budget that contained no tax increases and generous social welfare provisions, a quid pro quo commitment from unions and employers to moderate pay increases. Instead, even leaving aside the budgetary concessions awarded, a further inflationary pay agreement granted a record 21 per cent increase over an eighteen-month period. For some years wages and salaries in Ireland had been rising much faster than output and prices and also much faster than wages in other countries, especially Britain, thus adversely affecting the competitiveness of Irish exports. The alternative Ken advocated was to lower the rate of increase in money incomes, which would bring down the rate of price increases and thereby lead to a rise in *real* incomes. This would in turn improve competitiveness, safeguard existing jobs and help create new outlets for employment through increased sales of Irish products and services abroad. His advice fell on deaf ears, and the spiral of wage increases continued throughout the rest of the decade; as Ken noted, 'the remissness of 1972 was the first of a series of failures to make sure in advance that budgetary risk would be at least partly recompensed by incomes restraint'.[46]

In July 1972 his summer vacation, this time in Iceland, was again destined to be disturbed. At the invitation of Johannes Nordal, the governor of the Icelandic Central Bank, he was invited to Reykjavik to give a talk on Ireland's economic development. Ken had made friends with the Icelandic governor in the course of their participation at various meetings in Europe, and also through Nordal's friendship with the eminent Ulster-born folklorist Seamus H. Delargy, who was acquainted with Nordal's father, a collector of Icelandic folklore. After the lecture Ken and his wife Nora stayed on to enjoy a few days' fishing, living in a small hut on a river in a remote corner in the north-west of the island. On 31 July a Land Rover arrived from Reykjavik bringing an urgent telex message from Bernard Breen, general manager of the Central Bank. Following the floating of the pound sterling in June, Irish rates had become seriously out of kilter with established differentials between the two countries. To forestall the danger of an outflow of funds to Britain, the Irish Banks Standing Committee requested an immediate increase in their rates of 1 per cent. 'Press the Department of Finance to accept 1 per cent all round' was Ken's instruction. But, anxious to preserve the advantage to Irish industrial exports, the minister for finance sought to retain the lower rate for as long as possible. On his return from Iceland, Ken advised George Colley that he was 'playing a dangerous game which we could not win in the long-term and which was likely to be unprofitable from the national economic standpoint', and urged him to 'trust the judgement of the Central Bank'.[47] An appropriate increase in bank interest rates duly followed within days. As well as avoiding a potential outflow of capital from the country, Ken's intervention further consolidated the Central Bank's authority in the matter of credit management.

On 1 January 1973 Ireland's long journey towards EEC membership finally reached its destination. In a confidential note at this time, Ken emphasized to George Colley that the need to tackle incomes and prices was now even more urgent. 'A policy of supporting growth by fiscal and monetary means against the background of a relatively high inflation rate is doomed: our manufactures would become un-saleable and our hotels and guesthouses too dear for foreigners,' he argued, while the Irish pound would come under strain, even from a weak pound ster-ling.[48] In the event, a general election put his advice on the back burner. For once Ken's natural optimism seemed to dim. The response from the minister to his advice, given publicly in Central Bank reports and in speeches and articles, as well as in private, as he noted, 'so far has been merely to thank me for my interesting views'.[49] In a letter to Professor Louden Ryan, Ken bemoaned the absence of any commitment to economic planning to cover the years of transition to full EEC conditions and 'bring about a degree of consensus on economic and social developments which might make possible a *rational* solution of our major economic problems'.[50] But, mindful of the setbacks encountered in the two previous plans, he cautioned that simply 'to hand down a Fourth Programme from Mount Sinai without extensive prior consul-tation with the major economic interests would be to make planning even less acceptable and effective than it has been in recent years'.[51] His suggestion that an independent non-government body, such as the ESRI, be given the task of formulating optimal suggestions for economic growth, which 'could then be studied by all interested parties', did not, however, find favour with the Department of Finance, while the idea of planning per se in the immediate future found even less favour with the incumbent government. A further four years would pass before medium-term economic planning was resumed.

The general election in February 1973 saw the coming to power of a coalition government of Fine Gael, led by Liam Cosgrave, and the Labour Party, led by Brendan Corish. The cabinet comprised an eclectic mix of right- and left-wing politicians. As well as representing divergent political ideologies, both parties had their share of dissidents within their ranks. It was a tribute to the pragmatic leadership of Cosgrave that the government ran its course but, given the socialist leanings of some of its members, it also made for greater difficulty in keeping a rein on the national finances. The hyperbole of election promises from all political quarters heralded little change in economic policy. The pre-election commitments of the coalition government were expected to create a current account deficit of over £60 million, but Ken lived in hope that the new government might resist the temptation to load those commitments onto the country's borrowing requirements and further exacerbate the already large deficit. Despite the continuing upward spiral in wages and prices, initially an air of optimism prevailed, propelled by a growing economy, increased levels of employment and a fall-off in emigration. However, the new inflow of financial resources from the EEC budget, especially through the CAP, was allocated to improvements in social welfare, rather than, as Ken had recommended, to more productive purposes. The first budget presented by the new minister for finance, Richie Ryan, continued in the vein of his predecessor so that, by the end of the year, familiar difficulties in financing the public capital programme were once again evident.

The problems in the domestic economy were further aggravated in October by the worldwide economic crisis following the quadrupling of oil prices by Middle East producers. As energy costs rocketed, wage inflation and prices accelerated even further. In October, while attending the IMF annual meeting in Nairobi, Ken contracted a serious virus, at first thought to be glandular fever. On his return home, he was confined for a number of weeks to Cherry Orchard Fever Hospital. 'Condemned to a few weeks' convalescence', he was impatient, as he told the minister, 'to return to stability!'[52] But as the economic situation worsened, the minister's *cri de coeur* about the difficulties in financing public expenditure for 1973/4 brought a sharp retort from Cherry Orchard. 'As you well realise', Ken confided to Charlie Murray, 'the Minister is unlikely to get much sympathy from his colleagues at this stage. Indeed, in so far as the gap is due to increases in the capital allocations beyond the budgetary figures, he cannot very well cry over spilt milk; he has licked most of it up himself . . . As you know, I think he extended himself too far regarding both capital and current expenditure.'[53] As the grim economic scenario, exacerbated by increased oil prices and shortages, unfolded over December, difficulties in financing the exchequer grew even more alarming when, as Ken noted, 'the budget-makers were confronted with a formidable current deficit and with the dilemma of cutting expenditure or raising taxes to narrow the current account gap. The dilemma was dodged by resort to borrowing.'[54]

Frantically, the minister for finance looked for assistance to 'the lender of last resort'. As far as Ken was concerned, government borrowing from the coffers of the Central Bank would indeed be a last resort and his duty as governor, as he saw it, was to ward off such attempts by government to ease its residual financing problems. Despite large-scale external borrowing, by December the minister found himself in need of additional funding to the tune of £25 million (later scaled down to £20 million). While accepting that, in view of the constrictive impact of the oil crisis on economic growth, *some* intervention was justifiable, Ken was at pains to clarify the Central Bank's position. Reminding the minister that the Central Bank considered funding of the exchequer, except for very short-term advances repayable within one year, 'as altogether abnormal', he insisted that 'future reliance on the Central Bank as a major and continuing source of finance for the Exchequer would be at variance with the responsibility which the Bank must retain in regulating the total money supply, so that it accorded with national economic objectives'.[55]

Constrained, however, by the cabinet's reluctance to curb its public capital programme, the minister reopened the possibility of acquiring additional borrowing from the Bank. In a lengthy and considered reply, Ken pointed out the effects of recent government policy, noting that the resultant state of affairs was not, in his opinion, 'a situation that can be remedied by pumping more money into circulation'. The problem, as he viewed it, was not the financing of public expenditure (difficult though that was) 'but the excessive rate of increase in such expenditure'. Pointing to the fact that a sum of £67 million in foreign borrowing was being mentioned by the minister for finance to fund the capital programme alone, in addition to £55 million being sought by semi-state bodies and £19 million to be borrowed from the World Bank and the European Investment Bank (EIB), attempts to raise such funds abroad in a twelve-month period, he felt, 'would be treated with growing reserve in world capital markets and would bring into question the soundness of this country's financial management'.[56]

These views received endorsement from many financial and business interests. 'The irony is that the Central Bank's assessment of the economy is probably sounder than that of the Government',[57] one commentator noted. But there were few signs of public recognition of the state of the public finances in the pay demands being made and met in the public service. 'I have always regretted the Government's failure to treat the end-1973 situation as the emergency it really was,' Ken later recorded. 'An opportunity was lost to gear ourselves to get through the critical years that followed with less unemployment and less foreign borrowing.'[58] It is a statement that has a familiar echo today. But, as he also observed with a sense of realism, as well as resignation, borrowing to fund tax relief and social welfare improvements was a more popular option for a government than borrowing 'to accelerate the provision of capital assets and the remedying of infrastructural deficiencies'.[59] The resort to deficit financing of current expenditure was destined to continue until 1976, with the exchequer borrowing requirement rising from £206 million in 1973/4 to a record £601 million in 1975.

While the seemingly unrelenting deterioration in the country's finances may have been the most critical and frustrating issue of Ken's term as governor, another even more contentious obstacle in the shape of the new bank headquarters emerged to become, as Ken recalls, 'my baptism of fire at the Central Bank'. The saga, or nightmare, that surrounded the building of this now signature Dublin landmark reeks of alleged political cronyism, breaches of planning laws, public hearings and public outcry, appeals, objections and numerous delays incurring enormous public expense. 'It took three years to build the Eiffel Tower,' one newspaper report noted at the time. 'It has taken eleven years to build this eight-layered granite sandwich, and I doubt in years to come busloads of the American blue-rinse brigade will include it in their itinerary.'[60]

The saga of what turned out to be one of the most controversial building projects in modern Irish history had commenced long before Ken's appointment as governor. As far back as 1961 a suitable site for 'new offices and vaults' for the Central Bank had been mooted. In 1963 the share capital of Commercial Buildings (Dublin) Ltd was acquired by the Bank. The acquisition of this Georgian edifice, built in 1796 and part of the classical façade of Dame Street, with the intention of razing it to the ground, was met with objections, especially from An Taisce and the Dublin Civic Group, a conservation lobby chaired by Professor Kevin Nowlan. It was the first in a long list of many ill-fated decisions in relation to the building. A second was made in December 1967 when, on being presented by Ken's predecessor, Maurice Moynihan, with a choice between 'a building on older traditional lines, similar in appearance and height to existing buildings in Dame Street', and a high-rise modern block, the minister for finance, Charles Haughey, as the governor recorded, expressed 'a definite preference' for the latter.[61] Another was the appointment of the architect Sam Stephenson, 'a bosom buddy' of Charles Haughey,[62] and a construction team that included many Fianna Fáil supporters, one of whom was chairman of TACA, the fund-raising arm of the party.

The original plan incorporated a mint and printing facility, and in 1965 the Bank acquired additional properties on Dame Street, Fownes Street and Cope Street. The method of construction envisaged, considered revolutionary for the time, was a suspension or 'hanging' structure, with successive storeys built from the roof downwards, supported by two central towers or cones. Planning permission for a fifteen-storey office block over a two-storey basement was refused in 1968 on the grounds of unsatisfactory design and excessive height, considered out of scale with the surrounding buildings. On appeal, the Bank offered to forgo provision for a printing and minting facility, to reduce the building to thirteen floors in order to retain the classical façade of Commercial Buildings, and to set the new building back from the street line. This submission was approved by Dublin Corporation in November 1968. Significantly, the approved plan gave no indication of the actual height of the proposed building. A separate mint, printing and distribution facility was subsequently constructed at Sandyford, County Dublin, on a 124-acre site purchased from the Irish Sisters of Charity. This project also had its problems, arousing the ire of local residents as a result of blasting work in the development of underground vaults.

By the time of Ken's appointment as governor, it seemed that the new Bank headquarters in Dame Street was set to proceed without further difficulty. On appeal by An Taisce in November 1969, however, the minister for local government, Kevin Boland, reversed the planning permission. Following further discussions with Dublin Corporation, a revised application for a seven-storey building, incorporating the façade of Commercial Buildings, was granted on 30 September 1970, again without any specific reference to height. At the end of 1971 the Bank purchased the former Chase and Bank of Ireland offices at the east end of the site, for which supplementary planning permission was obtained in 1972. Demolition of the old buildings was completed in 1971 and excavation of the site and the construction of the two towers began in 1972.

As the twin reinforced concrete cones rose, dramatically incongruous, on the Dublin skyline, the project became embroiled in the wider 'war' being waged, both in the national press and on the streets of Dublin, between conservationists and developers in relation to other signature developments at Wood Quay, Hume Street and Fitzwilliam Street. On the election of the coalition government in 1973, the project also became the butt of political innuendo, speculation and point-scoring relating to alleged political favouritism and cronyism surrounding the awarding of the initial architectural and engineering contracts. One report accused the main architects, Stephenson & Gibney, 'this big well-connected firm', of having most of the key developments in the city 'handed to them on a plate'.[63] Rumours abounded that the day the Fianna Fáil government fell, 'the planning authority reached for the CB file and the ebullient Sam Stephenson's problems began.'[64] For Ken Whitaker, the entire project became a nightmare of delays, escalating costs – building, legal and remedial, all exacerbated by the rampant inflation of the time –

and unwelcome and largely negative publicity.

In November 1973 the Central Bank was notified that the building, then constructed to roof level, was in breach of planning permission; this resulted in an immediate cessation of work on the site. The development became an instant news story. 'Illegal Shock Skyscraper' one newspaper headline screamed; another accused the Bank of showing arrogance in defying the planning laws. The Dublin Civic Group demanded to know 'if the authorities of the Central Bank were aware of the extra work carried out in defiance of the planning regulations and if they sanctioned such a breach of the planning code?'[65] In a sharply worded letter to the Bank's architect, Ken Whitaker expressed his 'grave concern' that 'the Bank has not authorised any departure from the Corporation's requirements ... The Central Bank must retain its right to explain its position in this matter to Dublin Corporation and to the public generally. The Bank must also hold you and your firm responsible for any expense, loss or delay arising out of non-compliance with planning permission conditions.'[66] In reply, Sam Stephenson maintained that when the original design had been reduced from thirteen to seven floors no specific height limit had been stipulated by the planning authority and that the additional height was required for essential structural reasons and not to provide additional office space. A subsequent submission for retention was refused. An appeal to the minister for local government, following a public hearing in February, was also refused.

As the stalemate continued, the debate gathered momentum, becoming the subject of scores of letters in the national press. 'Here we have the Central Bank breaking the law and "regretfully" shedding crocodile tears over it,' the *Irish Times* recorded. The saga caught the eye of the international press, too. 'An Irish Tall Story', *The Times* headlined. And some were turning the debacle into a more personal issue. 'How did "Canny Ken" miss this?' a headline in the *Sunday Independent* asked.[67] But there was also support and sympathy for the governor in the intractable situation in which he found himself. 'The problem has landed in the lap of Dr Whitaker who, after all the years of service to the nation, does not deserve such a fate', one editorial noted.[68] But, as he well realized, regardless of the origins of the problem, he was the incumbent governor and so the proverbial buck stopped with him.

The alarming costs accruing to the public purse were Ken's prime concern. Demolition or abandonment of the project, at an estimated cost of £1.3 million, in addition to the £2.75 million already expended, was rapidly becoming a nightmare possibility. Because of the unusual suspension method involved in the building, as he advised the minister for finance, any substantial restructuring would be 'so disproportionate as to be unthinkable'.[69] In addition, the loss of earnings and disruption to the hundred-plus subcontractors, many of whom had invested large sums of money in labour, materials and equipment, at a time of scarce employment, was a further consideration. Enlisting the help of independent consulting engineers, as well as the services of the Office of Public Works, Ken sought a compromise solution. Meanwhile, an interview given by Sam Stephenson in *The Irish Times* hardly helped his case in mollifying public antagonism. In an unapologetic defence of his creation, the architect argued 'that it is required of an important building that it should stand out among lesser structures in the neighbourhood. Apologetic self-effacement should perhaps be left to public lavatories, VD clinics and other necessary minutiae of society.'[70]

Ken's publicly voiced concern regarding the waste of public money that would be entailed in demolishing the structure gradually began to sink home. Behind the scenes the Dublin city manager proposed that the Bank might 'purge its sin' if it agreed to make a substantial contribution to a worthy community purpose, mentioning a sum of half a million pounds. This, however, was not the way Ken Whitaker did business, and he dismissed the proposition as being one that might appeal to politicians or businessmen but one to which the reaction of ordinary people would naturally be suspicious and unfavourable. Insisting on a more open approach, he chose to reapply for planning permission, with the aim of ensuring 'that all relevant facts about waste of time, money and materials would be made public and the feasible alternatives and independent consultants' views would become generally known'.[71] At a subsequent press conference, he announced the Bank's decision to seek planning permission for a compromise plan, at a cost of £100,000, which would reduce the building height by over 15 feet, judging that this was 'as much as the Bank could do without departing from the suspension-building principle and needlessly spending money'.[72]

In September the revised plan was rejected by the planning committee, but again without specifying exactly what height would be acceptable. Following another public hearing in November, revised plans were once again rejected by the planning committee. On appeal, however, perhaps daunted by the prospect of the enormous cost involved in dismantling the partially completed building, or by the Bank's intimation to seek an alternative site, or perhaps merely worn out by the whole sorry saga, the minister finally granted permission in February 1975. As one city counsellor subsequently pointed out, he had, in effect, acted illegally by giving permission 'for a design for which permission had not been sought.'[73] The altered design involved minimum changes to that for which planning had been initially granted, with the exception that the steel ribs at the top of the structure, which were intended to be encased in a pitched copper roof, were allowed to protrude uncovered, thus taking a mere two feet off the overall height. The unsightly compromise was destined to remain a blot on the Dublin skyline for many years until 1990 when, ironically under the government of Charles Haughey, they were finally hidden from view under a copper canopy, as had initially been intended, thus bringing to an end one of the longest and most acrimonious, costly and, as it turned out, needless planning disputes in recent history. Work on the Dame Street site recommenced in February 1975 and was completed in January 1979, twelve years after the first planning application was submitted. With additional architectural, engineering and legal fees, building costs, security charges and rental fees for alternative accommodation, the outlay came to over two and a half times the original estimate. The Central Bank sought compensation from the architects and a modest fine, in the region of £200,000, was subsequently secured.

Today the Central Bank building has, perhaps, fulfilled the prediction of its architect, Sam Stephenson, who at the height of the controversy in 1974 defiantly asserted that 'virtually all buildings, even those born in riot and commotion, progress via acceptability to respectability'.[74]

That the Central Bank building has become a Dublin landmark is beyond question; whether it is a landmark out of place and incompatible with its Georgian neighbours remains open to debate. Still, Ken Whitaker, inheritor of both its design and the controversy that engulfed it, has, like many others, 'got to like the building'. Like many of his fellow citizens, he is amazed and dismayed that the Central Bank headquarters is now set to move from Dame Street to what was to be the new headquarters of the disgraced Anglo Irish Bank, a move he considers, in the light of recent events, 'symbolically very bad'. That the unfinished high-rise skeleton of what was to be the headquarters of the most notorious institution in Irish banking history should remain a monument to and a reminder of a period of national excess, greed and corruption is perhaps more appropriate than that it should serve as the new headquarters of the Central Bank. Despite the trials and tribulations he was forced to endure in its development, Ken was not destined to move into the new Dame Street headquarters, having retired before the building was completed.

*

On 1 January 1974, Ireland assumed the presidency of the EEC for the first time. While it may have been an exciting and significant event in the modern history of the country, it did little to relieve, indeed perhaps even exacerbated, the prevailing difficult economic situation. As preparations were made for the 1974 budget which, to bring Ireland into line with the rest of Europe, covered just nine months from April to December, it became obvious that there was to be no let-up in what even the Department of Finance referred to as 'the extravagance of the estimates for both current and capital expenditure'.[75] The enormous increase in capital expenditure could only intensify inflationary pressure, as Ken confided to Charlie Murray.

> Surely some good sense should be intruded to prevent decisions being reached which seem certain to be the opposite of what is appropriate ... The ballooning of the *uncovered* Exchequer borrowing requirement to the figure of over £100 million, at present in prospect, leaves me with a most uncomfortable feeling that effective management of our financial affairs is slipping out of our hands. I have not had this feeling so strongly ever before.[76]

In view of his experiences in the 1950s, this was a startling observation. As the situation worsened over the coming months, the Department of Finance was forced to seek policy directives from the government on how best to tackle the deteriorating economic and budgetary situation.

The Central Bank, meanwhile, continued to enforce its credit guidelines by flexing its muscle power over the commercial banks. Credit was to be restricted to productive purposes, penalties were to be inflicted for any increase in gross lending in the financial and personal categories and, except 'where the national interest was clearly involved',[77] external financing through the banking system was controlled by the threat of severe penalties. 'No net increase should be allowed to occur between May and November in bank lending to the personal sector or to property companies,'[78] the Bank explicitly instructed the chairman of the Irish Banks Standing Committee. The minister for finance, Richie Ryan, made belated attempts to stall the galloping advance of capital and current expenditure, but he was running just to keep pace with the ever-growing deficit. In September, on hearing from Charlie Murray that the government was contemplating an additional increase in the proposed non-pay allocations to the tune of £90 million, Ken did not hold back. 'I find it hard to credit that the Government could be seriously contemplating budgetary dispositions involving such enormous (and even impossible) increases,' he informed the minister for finance. 'As a public servant who has had reason to believe in the predominant influence on our economic development of a general public confidence founded on evidence of good management of the national economy, I am most disheartened by the prospect ahead.'[79] Already pay and pensions, as he pointed out, accounted for half of current public expenditure. The rate of income increases had to be contained, and he urged the minister to consider income indexation, a policy he had previously recommended in private to the Department of Finance and in public in the Central Bank *Annual Report*, as the only remaining option. The minister circulated Ken's letter among his cabinet colleagues.

On 24 September, Ken received a phone call at his home from the minister for finance asking him to attend a cabinet meeting that afternoon in Leinster House, to discuss the economic situation. Ken had much sympathy for Richie Ryan, whom he recalls as having put his heart into what was effectively an impossible job. Like most ministers for finance, especially in a government professing such conflicting views, he needed all the help he could muster. 'I had on a few occasions in my Finance career been called to government or cabinet committee meetings

but never before as governor of the Central Bank.'[80] Taoiseach
Liam Cosgrave asked Ken for his views on the economic situation. Reminding the cabinet 'that I was giving sincere, personal
views based on my experience and training, not just voicing some
partisan "Central Bank" viewpoint',[81] Ken outlined the problems
and how best, in his opinion, they might be redressed. The issue
at stake was not one of whether or how to *meet* public expenditure
requirements, but rather of how much expenditure there *ought to
be*. The present rate of inflation, fuelled by rising incomes and
prices, was the single greatest threat to employment and could
not be solved by spending more, which would result only in an
unsustainable external deficit, leading inevitably to a sudden
sharp reduction in consumption, investment and employment.
The critical policy, he reiterated, was to control the upward spiral
in wages and salaries, which bore little relevance to the economic
situation pertaining either at home or abroad. Industrial relations
had to be set in a much wider context than before, to take into
account the connections between pay increases, prices, and social
and fiscal reforms, if a socially just and fair income strategy for
all, not just for sectional interests, was to be realized. He again
recommended the immediate introduction of a pay indexing
system, linking remuneration to the consumer price index, to
relieve the burden on the public finances. Pay, he pointed out,
amounted to an exceptional 50 per cent of current public expenditure. As for the generous tax relief and social welfare increases
granted by the government over the previous eighteen months,
these were, he told the cabinet, simply not affordable. It would
be far better if the government were to maintain existing *real*
standards in social welfare and in health. The possibility of further borrowing abroad would, in his opinion, place the
sovereignty of the state at risk. On the question raised by the cabinet of the possibility of separating the Irish pound from sterling
and aligning it with some other currency, the situation, he told
them, was under constant review by the Central Bank and there

would be no delay in reporting, 'if *par miracle*, a move towards alignment with US $ or European "snake" [an arrangement by which participating countries maintained the exchange rates of their currencies within fluctuation margins of plus or minus 2.24 per cent] seemed nationally advantageous.'[82]

Accepting Ken's recommendations on pay restraint, the government subsequently issued a white paper on 'national partnership' and announced its intention of commencing talks with the Trade Union Congress to initiate new pay negotiations. But its approach to this task found little favour with the governor, who questioned its 'over-cautious stance' in allowing the unions to set the tone of the negotiations. Instead, he argued, it should be for the government to take the initiative in securing, either by agreement or, failing that, by statutory enforcement, a limit on income increases, and not merely on employee wages but also on profit margins, rents and fees, as well as on social benefits, by reference to the previous quarter's rise in the consumer price index. The trade unions should agree to this course of action in advance of any tax or price concessions granted in the budget; 'budgetary secrecy' was now, he told the cabinet, 'an irrelevance in this context.'[83]

When the minister for finance subsequently stated that the idea of income indexing 'was killed because it had been advocated by the Central Bank', Ken protested that 'the Government had had ample time to make it their own, having in mind that I wrote privately to Finance about it in December 1973 and in January 1974, long before it appeared in our Annual Report in July 1974.'[84] Ken's incomes strategy was based not merely on strict fiscal or indeed economic grounds, but on a sense of social justice and fair play, a philosophy that is again so relevant today in the aftermath of the greed-driven debacle of more recent years. 'I fear, particularly,' he wrote, 'for the effect on our young people who are nowadays given little example of devotion to duty or of concern for the common good but see all around them a work-to-rule mentality, a preoccupation with selfishness, envy and greed and an irresponsible disregard for the progress and welfare of the nation.'[85] And, as he later explained, he considered the promotion of sectional interests reprehensible:

> The rule of law is an essential guarantee of personal freedom and social order. Lobbies have legitimate functions in protecting and advancing particular interests but society as a whole cannot be expected to tolerate abuse of their power, particularly by intimidation in any form, or defiance of the current law of the land. It may be unpopular now to praise Mrs Thatcher but her most creditable and enduring achievement was to re-establish the supremacy of Government and Parliament over sectional interests. Governments and Parliaments, democratically elected, should never surrender their independence of judgement to group or media pressure.[86]

While a national understanding on pay was reached in 1979, it was to take almost another decade for a more realistic, orderly and equitable incomes policy, of the kind Ken had long advocated, to be achieved. The coordinated, wise and balanced use of all three principal instruments of financial policy – fiscal, incomes and monetary – he considered vital if 'even limited success is to be attained in this almost unmanageable world'.[87]

During 1975, however, in an effort to stimulate the economy, the government continued to resort to a current account deficit to fuel additional budgetary concessions in tax relief and social welfare. 'It was no surprise', Ken noted, 'that the Central Bank should again be seen as a possible source of much-needed Government finance in 1975',[88] this time to the tune of £72 million. While conscious of the precedent being set for, in effect, the provision of an overdraft facility for the exchequer, because of the 'extreme circumstances' facing the economy, he reluctantly agreed to the government's request – provided, as he informed the secretary of the Department of Finance, 'that there are no substantial departures from the already budgeted levels of public expenditure and revenue'.[89] To ensure the overdraft did not become a permanent source of exchequer finance, he further stipulated that the government account must be in credit with the Central Bank for at least thirty days in every year. In a further letter to the Department of Finance, he made it clear that 'should . . . a departure [from this arrangement] occur, the Bank would feel discharged from its obligation to continue the arrangement and would be unwilling to advance sums in excess of those that had already been provided . . . To do otherwise', he stated, 'would be incompatible with the discharge of the Bank's responsibility in regard to monetary policy.'[90]

With the exception of allowing a temporary emergency increase in the exchequer overdraft, which he considered justifiable to ease the effects of the oil crisis, he resisted the government's attempts to extract additional funding from the coffers of the Central Bank. In February 1976 he refused to commit, in advance of the budget, any additional funding. 'We would have to see the entire picture – fiscal and incomes – before we could assess our role, if any, in the financing of the Exchequer.' Any premature concession, he maintained, would 'compromise the Bank's discretion in exercising its responsibility to try and manage the money supply so as to safeguard the integrity of the currency'.[91] The government eventually applied the brakes on foreign borrowing for current purposes, but not before the total exchequer borrowing requirement had trebled between 1973 and 1975.

Ken Whitaker's discomfort with the constraints of his office as governor of the Central Bank was evident even before he intimated to the government, in March 1975, that he did not wish to consider a second term. However important its role in the licensing and supervision of the banking system, for him the main function of the Central Bank was to 'try to influence

Government policy in favour of protecting, to the utmost, the value of the monetary unit'.

> Our principal obligation was to give appropriate and forceful advice on economic and financial policy before it was decided; to criticise policy decisions, both in private to the Minister of Finance and in our publications, if we thought them unwise . . . If our advice was constantly set aside or ignored, and our disagreement with policy became acute, the only course, in my view, was to resign.[92]

As for how far the government either listened to or acted upon his advice, the evidence, on the surface at least, would lead one to take a pessimistic view, as Ken admitted. 'There was hardly ever more than a polite acknowledgement of the Bank's written submissions, and views expressed orally were usually heard in silence.'[93] Nevertheless, his refusal to toe the government line, his fearlessness in speaking publicly when, in his view, the integrity of the public finances was compromised by the government, and his personal reputation all made his advice hard to ignore and ensured, as he noted, that it 'did not fall entirely on deaf ears but had at least some corrective or restraining influence'.[94]

The absence of such fearlessness in Dame Street in more recent times makes Ken Whitaker's stance in the 1970s appear all the more admirable. Even in a period when, as he described, 'temptations to stray from financial orthodoxy were stronger and not always resisted',[95] his forthright advice was a safeguard against even worse excesses. Dictatorial enforcement was not his way; he preferred persuasion and consensus management by society of its own affairs. As he had advocated back in the 1950s in *Economic Development*, in his view improvements in the national economy could be achieved only through the participation, cooperation and contribution of all sectors of the community in the cause of the common weal. 'I continue to believe', he wrote at the end of his term as governor, 'that democracy can be made to work, not through reliance on automatic regulation or enforced discipline, but through informed discussion of options and objectives, leading to a wide measure of acquiescence and co-operation.'[96] At the same time, he understood the dilemma facing policy-makers, whose chances of political survival were not enhanced by the implementation of policies that were neither popular nor understood; consequently, as he realistically admitted, even to have 'an approximation of your advice implemented was all you could ever hope for'.

Ken Whitaker's decision in 1975 not to seek a second term as governor was received with shock within the government and with regret among the wider community. The resignation or pre-mature retirement of such a respected figure was a sensitive issue, especially if it was perceived that his departure was the consequence of disagreement with government policy. Ken's private notes of his meeting with the minister for finance on the subject confirm that perception: 'I thought it well to say that the real reason I wished to relinquish the office was that I felt that if I were to accept reappointment this would in some way com-promise my critical independence and could be interpreted as a condonation of policies I considered to be wrong.'[97]

The minister asked him to reconsider his decision but, while reassuring him that 'there was no personal, special or new cause of disagreement', other than those he had already voiced publicly and in private, Ken declined. He agreed that public notice of his intention to resign should be withheld until after his attendance at an IMF meeting in September. Consistent to the last, he also informed the minister 'that I thought there had been a significant weakening of economic management by the Government over the past decade' and urged him 'to use more muscle on his colleagues in Government with a view to better management of the public finances'.[98] During the remaining months of his governorship, his contacts with the minister for finance tapered off and there was no consultation about the terms of the 1976 budget, of which he noted that 'the same mistake was again made of making budgetary dispositions before the course of money incomes was settled'.[99] Despite his sense of isolation, he saw his duty out to the last, submitting a summary of his advice and criticism on government proposals to the minister as his *envoi* as governor.

When news of his intended departure became public, it was the subject of much discussion and speculation. With his penchant for a humorous turn of phrase, he made light of his decision. 'Forty-one years in public service is a reasonable stint,' he told one reporter. 'I find it difficult having to explain about getting out of a good job when so many people are trying to get into one.'[100] But he also used the publicity his resignation provided to hammer home his concerns about the state of the national finances and to make public his call to the government to reactivate economic planning. 'Clearly policies to curb the rate of growth in government current expenditure and to diminish the massive deficit must be in the forefront of any medium-term programme aiming at economic recovery and greater stability of prices; and such a programme needs to become operative soon.'[101] In a personal letter, giving voice to sentiments he may have felt unable to express in his official capacity, Richie Ryan thanked him 'for looking after Ireland's economic and financial health so well and for protecting your charge from the worst effects of her own excesses'.[102]

For the management and staff of the Central Bank, the departure of such a respected and independently minded governor marked a milestone and an end to an innovative and fulfilling chapter in the development and status of the Bank. At his final, packed press conference on 29 January 1976, Ken took the opportunity to make a last summation of the advice which, under his governorship, the Central Bank had proffered. 'His pupil has been for the most part the Government,' one editorial stated, 'and for the most part a dull, cowardly and unheeding one.'[103] He left to the dismay and regret of the country's business and financial community, as well as the general public, from whom he received many messages of appreciation and good wishes. The governor of the Bank of Ireland acknowledged his role 'as an adviser "of last resort" in difficult times', and thanked him 'for his forbearance without which few of the major changes in banking would have been started and certainly none finished'.[104] Commenting on his stewardship of the country's finances, the editor of *Business and Finance* testified: 'When necessary he was a fearless critic of Government's fiscal policy and that is as it should be; what good is a Central Bank that meekly rubber stamps the schemes of the politicians? Ken Whitaker was nobody's rubber stamp.'[105]

His departure was also regretted by the international bodies in which he had served – the World Bank, the BIS, the EEC and the IMF. As one director of the Fund testified: 'We can desperately ill-afford to lose someone so mature and reflective from our counsels.'[106] In response, Ken reassured his correspondent: 'I shall remain a strong supporter of the IMF and its efforts to maintain equity and order in an unruly world.'[107] From his counterparts in central banks from all over the world came messages of good wishes and regret.

As he had commenced his tenure as governor, so he ended it by declining an offer made by the board to incorporate the few allowances commensurate with his post into his salary to provide a more generous pension base. 'The allowances being intended to cover expenses,' he simply noted, 'it would seem inappropriate now to transform them into income.'[108] His pension as it stood he considered ample to his future requirements, a sentiment in stark contrast to that prevailing today.

The Central Bank Whitaker Lecture series, inaugurated in his honour in 2004, is a fitting tribute to his national and international status as a Central Bank governor. Guest speakers in the series have included EU president Mario Draghi, Professor Cormac Ó Gráda of UCD, Axel Weber, president of the Bundesbank, and Professor Harold James of Princeton University. In his inauguration speech, Jean-Claude Trichet, president of the European Central Bank (ECB), saluted Ken for 'the example you have shown to Central Bankers everywhere in your endurance and constant commitment to the public good':

> You, Dr Whitaker, deserve to take the satisfaction and pride of knowing that your contribution to the success of the Irish economy has not been bounded by Ireland's shores. Rather the process of transformation that you began over four decades ago has become a model for the millions of new citizens of the European Union. The new Member States of the EU have had to confront economic challenges whose magnitude and long-term importance are similar to those that faced Ireland when you began your work. Thanks to Ireland's economic success, to which you devoted your life, we can be confident that economic reform works.[109]

Perhaps M. Trichet might not have been so effusive in his praise if he had had Ken to contend with on the board of governors of the ECB in more recent times.

On 26 February 1976 Ken was invited to lunch with the president, Erskine Childers, at Áras an Uachtaráin. On the following day, after receiving presentations from the staff and management of the Bank, he made a final courtesy call on the minister for finance. In the conversation that ensued, the minister asked his opinion on the immediate economic prospects and, consistent to the last, 'I replied that, given the discipline of a pay pause and a medium-term widely agreed recovery programme, we still had a chance of being competitive when the rise in world demand began to be effective.'[110] The minister made no comment but, as Ken noted, 'we parted with mutual good wishes'. In a meeting with the Taoiseach, Liam Cosgrave, he had a more wide-ranging discussion on current economic and social issues. 'I congratulated him on his law and order stance and suggested that similar firmness was needed on the economic side. He thanked me for my public service contribution. The conversation was most cordial.'[111] Returning to his office to collect his personal belongings and with a final goodbye to his secretarial staff, Ken Whitaker departed from public office.

In an assessment of his role as governor of the Central Bank, Ken concluded, with his customary reticence: 'I think it can be claimed that a nationally useful relationship with the Government was maintained with a high measure of independence, but with due observance of the basic principles of democracy: in other words, the Bank respected the Government's final authority but faithfully discharged its critical advisory functions and was, in no sense, the "Government's creature".'[112]

Over time, the authority and status of the Central Bank would be gradually eroded by national and international developments. As an initiator and supporter of Ireland's entry to Europe, Ken Whitaker would undoubtedly have supported the establishment of the ECB and the centralization of European banking policy. That such 'blanket type' banking policy should have been adopted in Ireland, in respect of supervisory standards and credit control, especially in the light of the rampant consumerism of recent times, is another matter. It is difficult to imagine that as governor he would not have strongly resisted the politically motivated and, in hindsight, disastrous separation of the supervisory and regulatory functions from the Central Bank, and particularly their allocation to an authority under government influence. And while some of the diminution in the Central Bank's authority was the result of EU policy decisions, the Bank retained sufficient authority nationally to enable it, had it chosen to do so, to curb the doubling of house prices, the tripling of credit to the building industry and the sanctioning of loans up to

and beyond 100 per cent by banking institutions under its supervision that occurred in the space of seven years. Ken Whitaker
would have taken a lot of convincing that, as the Central Bank
asserted in November 2007, the fundamental position of the Irish
property market was sound, or that its prediction of a 'soft landing' for the economy was anything other than delusional. It is
also difficult to accept that he would have agreed to a
philosophy of light-touch banking regulation or tolerated
inadequate or incompetent supervision, especially if it was found
to be politically motivated or market-driven.

Ken Whitaker is the first to acknowledge the immense changes
that have revolutionized the banking sector since the 1970s. The
globalization of the industry, the mind-boggling impact of technological innovation, the blurring of demarcation between
financial institutions, the dazzling array of investments and credit
instruments on offer, the onset of the borderless world of finance:
all these have changed the sector utterly. But in view of the
calamitous, even corrupt, policies that have in recent times driven
not merely Ireland's financial institutions but those of far more
powerful countries, from reckless lending practices to the rigging
of key bank interest rates, along with the detachment of economics from any sense of societal responsibility or accountability
and the entitlement, greed and bonus-ridden mentality of the
world's banking elite, financial opinion worldwide might one day
be forced to revert to the more morally principled approach that
underpinned Ken Whitaker's role as governor of Ireland's
Central Bank. In his view, those involved in the operation of the
world's financial markets must take responsibility for the impact
their policies have on the lives of ordinary citizens and taxpayers.
In a world controlled and driven by an imperialistic market
economy, now more than ever the realization that there are
multiple choices available in pursuing the development of
individual economies, rather than the blanket formula imposed
by international financial institutions, is essential. Perhaps some

of Ken Whitaker's own words might help to inspire such a change: 'There are values, moral and intellectual, which are higher than just mere economics. But it makes for a happier and more contented society if everybody has some basic share in wealth and well-being.'

The greatest tribute the Central Bank of Ireland could confer on its illustrious former governor, and the one he would undoubtedly most appreciate, is that it rededicate itself to its prime responsibility, as set out in the Central Bank Act of 1942: 'that in what pertains to the control of credit, the constant and predominant aim should be the welfare of the people as a whole'.

9

Hands Across the Border
1963–67

The viewpoint presented here is that of a peaceful and patient Irishman,
born in the North, but for long resident in the South, who hopes that the
people of Northern Ireland will one day freely decide to join the people of
the Republic in a new Irish constitutional framework and who meanwhile
wishes the door to be kept open to such an eventuality.
T. K. Whitaker[1]

ONE OF THE PRINCIPAL motivations in Ken Whitaker's public life
is the desire for a peaceful solution to the vexed question of
Northern Ireland. This stems from the deep-rooted personal relationship he continues to have with the province of his birth, his
avowed aversion to violence and, as, he simply states, the fact that
'because I was born in the undivided Ireland of 1916, I took a
special interest in the possibility of reunification'.[2] As in his economic undertakings on behalf of the Republic of Ireland, so this
'special interest' was not expressed merely through armchair
rhetoric or emotive hand-wringing, but impelled him through
rational and constructive thought into a proactive, low-key
crusade sustained over half a century to bring about, by constitutional and cooperative means, peace in Northern Ireland.
The extent of his personal involvement in this process, the role he
played as adviser, mediator and policy-maker, on a voluntary

basis and mostly behind the scenes, is perhaps not fully known to or appreciated by the general public. As Maurice Hayes, former Northern Ireland Community Relations Commissioner and Ombudsman, attested: 'When everybody in the administration, ministers, soldiers, civil servants, diplomats, were running around like headless chickens Ken Whitaker stood out as a man for all seasons – a reference, it may be noted, to that other prototypical civil servant of history, Sir Thomas More.'[3]

Ken's interest in, and contacts within, Northern Ireland were established long before events in the province hit the international headlines in the late 1960s. In addition to being a native Ulsterman, in his capacity as secretary of the Department of Finance, at various international and cross-border meetings, he formed many personal contacts within the public service in Northern Ireland. His Ulster background, his work in the economic development of the Republic and his standing with international bodies such as the IMF, the World Bank and the UK Treasury, contributed to the development of a positive relationship with his counterparts in the Northern Ireland public service. This was further developed by the tentative, subtle but significant change in the Republic's official policy towards Northern Ireland that had quietly taken place by the early 1960s.

Even before 1960, Seán Lemass was talking about social, economic and cultural cooperation, including the establishment of a free trade area, as a means of developing a more harmonious relationship with the North. The term 'Six Counties', loathed by the Unionist majority in Northern Ireland, came to be used less in official contexts in the Republic. Preparatory work regarding potential cooperation between North and South in matters of common interest, such as transport, tourism, electricity supply and the Erne waterway, was quietly in train, spearheaded by civil servants such as Ken Whitaker and Thekla Beere, the first female head of a government department in the Republic. 'In contemplation of the Anglo-Irish Free Trade Agreement and eventual entry into the EEC, we had been trying to find ways of favouring Northern Ireland industry where it wasn't too competitive with our own', Ken recalls. Lemass's accession as Taoiseach in 1959 gave further impetus to these developments. While holding fast to the traditional Fianna Fáil 'ideal' of Irish unity, and at times – for example, on his visit to America in October 1963 – endorsing it in public, Lemass was gingerly moving away from the rigidity of hard-line Republican ideology to a more nuanced acknowledgement of practical economic reality. 'Quite apart from any views one may hold about the reunification of Ireland, is it not common sense that the two existing communities in our small island should seek every opportunity of working together in practical matters for their mutual and common good?' he asked; and he sought to achieve this by the creation 'of a climate of opinion . . . in which the realisation of that national aim will be achieved in harmony and agreement.'[4] There were, however, some flies in the soothing ointment being applied to North–South wounds, one being the obdurate, long-serving prime minister of Northern Ireland, Sir Basil Brooke, who tended to dismiss Lemass's overtures as emanating from 'purely political reasons'.[5] Few changes of significance towards harmonizing relations between the two parts of Ireland seemed likely to emerge under such leadership.

As an Ulsterman, Ken viewed Lemass's tentative efforts towards rapprochement with the North, based as they were on practical common sense, as a timely and welcome departure from the emotive and hitherto unyielding Fianna Fáil policy. He shared Lemass's hopes that one day the people of the North would freely join the people of the Republic in a new constitutional framework; but he realized also that a union of hearts and minds would have to occur long before that eventuality. The border campaign sustained by the Irish Republican Army from 1956 until its abandonment in 1962 merely served to rub salt into the still raw wounds of partition. The IRA's policy of enforced unity Ken considered futile, merely accentuating, rather than diluting, the differences and divisions that already existed – as well as being, in any case, impossible to achieve by arms alone. The Northern problem, as he viewed it, stemmed from the existence of a double minority on the island of Ireland, based on a conflict of nationality and compounded by differences of religion and tradition. Consequently, the only option open to the Republic in pursuit of any form of unity was to seek a form of agreement with the North; this, as he warned in 1968, by its very nature would have to be 'a long-term policy, requiring patience, understanding and forbearance and resolute resistance to emotionalism and opportunism', but, he considered, was 'nonetheless patriotic for that'.[6]

The appointment of Captain Terence O'Neill to succeed Brooke as Northern Ireland premier in 1963 signalled a more positive direction in North–South relations, just as de Valera's replacement by Lemass had done in 1959. Ken had first met Terence O'Neill in Paris in 1959 when, as secretary of the Department of Finance and minister for finance, respectively, they attended the formal opening of the European office of the World Bank. They were introduced by Tyrone-born Sir William (Bill) Iliff, vice-president of the World Bank, whom Ken knew through his attendance at Bank meetings. Iliff arranged that they were seated beside one another at the subsequent celebratory dinner in the Bois de Boulogne, and the two men hit it off from the start, as Ken recalls: 'Terence was a man of great personal charm, with a lively sense of humour and an infectious high-pitched laugh.' For his part, O'Neill's positive opinion of the Southerner developed into a lasting personal friendship that survived long after his own resignation. 'In some way I think I was a revelation to him, not being some violent Republican wanting to tear everything down!' Ken muses. Their initial friendship deepened over several journeys by sea to Washington for meetings of the IMF and World Bank, O'Neill having, as Ken remembers, inveigled himself into the UK delegation. The leisurely mode of transport allowed for much informal discussion and the development of camaraderie. Initially Ken found O'Neill to be more interested in the background and formation of the *Programme for Economic Expansion*, if somewhat envious of the recognition and status achieved by the Republic on the international stage; so, as he recalls, 'I went easy on the political side of things!' In 1968 Ken and his wife Nora were invited by the O'Neills to Belfast, where they visited local historical sites, in which O'Neill had a special interest, and in 1970 O'Neill and his wife, Jean, paid a return visit to them in Dublin. 'It was so nice seeing you "en famille",' O'Neill subsequently wrote to his host, 'and I was most impressed at seeing a copy of *Le Monde* lying by the fireside!'[7]

Terence O'Neill's pedigree reflected the complexity and the contradictions inherent in Irish Unionism. Incorporating descent from the ancient O'Neills, Gaelic rulers of Ulster, and from the seventeenth-century English Chichester family, he was proudly conscious of his dual background of Gael and Gall. As prime minister he invariably wore the Red Hand insignia of the O'Neills as a tiepin, and later on Ken helped him in researching one of his ancestors, the sixteenth-century Gaelic chieftain Turlough O'Neill. O'Neill's maternal grandfather, Baron Houghton, later the marquess of Crewe, was appointed lord lieutenant (viceroy) of Ireland by Gladstone in 1892. A liberal, he proved unpopular with the Protestant minority, who flung mud at his carriage as he drove through the streets of Dublin. In a later visit to Áras an Uachtaráin, O'Neill recalled how his mother as a child had played in what was then the Viceregal Lodge. Born in England and educated at Eton, serving in the Irish Guards in the Second World War, Terence O'Neill was, as Ken testified, 'a patrician, reared and educated at a distance from the tribal loyalties, antagonism, prejudices and fears of the Ulster heartland ... his vision was a generous one, transcending religious and political differences'.[8] This background created a barrier, both socially and politically, between him and some of his government colleagues. He married Jean Whitaker (no relation), a noted garden designer and expert on rare plants, and the couple had a son and a daughter. In 1946 Terence O'Neill was returned to the Stormont parliament as MP for Bannside, County Antrim, and served under the premiership of Sir Basil Brooke in various capacities before becoming finance minister in 1956. Early in his political career he had crossed swords with Brooke over the controversial appointment of a Catholic teacher to a Protestant school in Ballymena. 'The extremists, like the poor, are always with us,' he wrote. 'But it cannot be in our interests to drive the ordinary citizens into their camp.'[9]

O'Neill's appointment as prime minister of Northern Ireland in March 1963 was a defining if divisive moment in Ulster's troubled history. Carrying little tribal baggage, he was determined to bring political and social change to the province. Just how fundamental was the change he contemplated, nobody, North or South – with the possible exception of Ken Whitaker – could have guessed. One of O'Neill's first changes, initiating a new code of conduct to force his cabinet colleagues away from their traditional role as part-time ministers to a full-time commitment to the job, was, he remembered, 'less than welcome'.[10] His public message of condolence to Cardinal Conway on the death of the charismatic Pope John XXIII, his recognition of the Dublin-based Irish Congress of Trade Unions, his visits to Catholic communities, churches, hospitals and schools – all these visible signs of a radical departure from the old sectarian mindset were watched with amazement and wariness by both Unionist and Nationalist communities.

O'Neill's ambition – to heal the ancient divisions between Catholics and Protestants – was based on the practical assumption that such divisions weakened the community and wasted economic potential. It was a perception he shared with his friend Ken Whitaker. Reform, reconciliation and equality, under the umbrella of the United Kingdom, were the only way forward if Northern Ireland was to develop into a modern-day state. Its nearest neighbour had commenced its own journey towards modernity and economic viability, largely spearheaded by Ken Whitaker. For O'Neill, it was simple logic that closer cooperation between the two Irelands was both necessary and desirable. A UK Labour Party motion that triangular cooperation between Westminster, Belfast and Dublin on economic matters might 'provide new solutions for old problems',[11] as well as the potential impact on the Northern Irish economy of trade talks between the Republic and Britain, were added incentives. With what might be considered either guileless confidence or political naivety, O'Neill set about achieving his aim in the most spectacular and controversial way imaginable, by breaking the 43-year wall of silence between the leaders of the two parts of Ireland. For O'Neill, it was simply, as he later recorded, 'the right thing to do'.[12]

Ken credits O'Neill with setting up the now famous meeting with Seán Lemass that took place on 14 January 1965. 'He [O'Neill] must be given full credit for the initiative. I was a help to him because he knew that I was so placed that I could explore the possibility without embarrassment to him' – particularly important given that, as O'Neill later admitted, 'we did not even know if Mr Lemass would accept the invitation'.[13] O'Neill's private secretary, the Tyrone-born Squadron Leader James (Jim) Malley, a wartime hero of the RAF whose family originated in County Mayo, was sent to Dublin a few days beforehand to sound out 'the man to make the contact' with Lemass. Ken was already acquainted with Jim Malley before he appeared in his office in Upper Merrion Street and asked the question: 'If Captain O'Neill invited Mr Lemass to Stormont, would he go?' As Ken remembers, 'Jim supposed that I was surprised but I was in fact more delighted than surprised as I had been hoping for such a move for quite a time.'[14] He despatched his visitor to the nearby National Gallery while he hurried over to the Taoiseach's office. 'I was uncertain whether he [Lemass] would tear me apart for having compromised him even that far.' Instead, in his usual decisive manner, Lemass agreed immediately to the proposal. 'Indeed he was so quick to welcome the invitation that I ventured to remind him of the desirability of consulting his Government colleagues.'[15] There and then Lemass phoned Frank Aiken, minister for external affairs, who, while surprised, readily supported his decision. Ken then brought Jim Malley to the Taoiseach to extend the invitation in person.

The lengths to which both sides went to keep the historic meeting secret were, as Ken remembers, 'of a James Bond kind', but, at the time, were considered necessary. There were many on both sides of the border who would have wished to disrupt the meeting before it could have taken place, and many within both administrations who would seek to oppose it. 'We did not want to give time for people who might be against it to stir up trouble on both sides.'

O'Neill withheld news of the visit until the Taoiseach had safely arrived at Stormont. Since neither leader had ever met the other, a personal as much as a historical gulf had to be breached, and so the presence of Ken Whitaker was essential to smooth the path. 'So far as I was concerned,' Ken recalled, 'I decided that the best way to keep a secret was to tell no one . . . I said nothing at home as I had six children, some at school, some at university and I was afraid one of them might blurt it out . . . I told my wife the evening before.'[16] A Garda car, sent to bring him to the Taoiseach's house, was scheduled to arrive at 9.15 a.m., by which time he expected his children to have left the house for school. 'You can imagine my dismay when there was a knock on the hall door at about a quarter to nine and one of my sons came in breathless to say that there was "a Garda car at the door and they were looking for Daddy"!' He told the driver to park around the corner; 'I forget what explanation I gave the children, but they seemed relieved that I wasn't being arrested!'[17]

Ken found Lemass seemingly unperturbed by the significance of the occasion: 'Belfast, Henry,' was his terse direction to his

Above: Ken with his mother Jane in 1976, on becoming the first Irishman to be invested with the Order of Commandeur de la Légion d'Honneur.

Above: Ken and Nora at home in the early days of his busy retirement.

Left: Being presented to King Juan Carlos and Queen Sofia of Spain.

Above: Ken, as Chancellor of the National University of Ireland, presenting President Mary Robinson with an honorary doctorate of laws in 1991.

Below: Handing over to incoming Chancellor of the NUI (and former Taoiseach) Dr Garret FitzGerald, December 1996.

Above: With poet Thomas Kinsella, co-editor with Seán Ó Tuama of the groundbreaking *An Duanaire: Poems of the Dispossessed*.

Below: Three men in a boat. On the River Moy with former Taoiseach Jack Lynch and President Patrick Hillery.

Above: 'An irresistible temptation'.

Below: Tír Álainn, Bangor Erris, County Mayo (pen and ink by Billy Moore).

Above: Wedding bells: Ken and Mary, June 2005.

Below: Ken and Mary.

Above: Presenting a copy of *Retrospect* to President Mary McAleese at Áras an Uachtaráin, December 2006.

Below: Full circle: Turning the sod at St Joseph's CBS, Drogheda, 28 January 2014.

Top and middle: Making music, 'a civilizing part of life that has been one of my joys'.

Right: Ken with author Anne Chambers.

Sláinte!

surprised driver, who immediately informed his boss that he had only enough petrol to get as far as Dundalk. To forestall discovery of their destination, they decided to stop for fuel at the Garda station in Dundalk; and without further ado, formality or escort, the Taoiseach's car sped off on its historic journey north. During the long drive, as Ken remembers, he and Lemass did not 'talk about the historic significance of the visit and what might ensue, but neither did we talk about frivolous matters either. Lemass was not given to small-talk. I do recall, however, a short discussion about the American system of government about which he had lately been reading.'[18] At Dundalk Garda station there was a flurry at the unexpected arrival of the Taoiseach; Ken suspects that someone made a connection with crossing the border and later tipped off the press. Refuelling completed, the Taoiseach's car sped on its journey, crossing the border at Killeen customs post at around 11.30 that morning.

On the opposite side of the border, O'Neill too had taken few into his confidence: his wife Jean, close advisers such as Sir Cecil Bateman, secretary of the Northern Ireland cabinet, under-secretary Ken Bloomfield and Jim Malley, and the governor of Northern Ireland, Lord Erskine. Jim Malley was sent in the prime minister's Mercedes to bring the visitors from the border to Stormont. On arriving at the customs hut Malley discovered that a storm during the night had damaged the telephone lines and the customs officers had not received their instructions to allow the Taoiseach's car unhindered passage. After a short delay the car was waved on. Transferring to the Mercedes, Lemass agreed to pose for a photograph with his RUC escort. Driving on through the countryside, at 12.55 p.m. the small cavalcade approached Stormont. By then, as Ken recalls, a silence had fallen on the car's occupants, broken by Malley pointing out the statue of Edward Carson as the car slowly made its way towards Stormont House, the prime minister's private residence. As Terence O'Neill awaited his special guest, 'the thought occurred to me', he later recorded, 'that a wrong word would wreck the meeting before it started. It could even be that the future of Northern Ireland and of Southern Ireland might depend on mutual cordiality. "Welcome to Ulster" would rub salt into the wound. "Welcome to Northern Ireland" would be better, but might be a little "troublemaking". Finally, just as the car was arriving I hit on the right idea.'[19] O'Neill opened the car door and with a broad smile, extended his hand to Lemass and said 'Welcome to the North'.

Lemass, noted in any case for his reticence and lack of bonhomie, seemed suddenly to be engulfed by the enormity of what he had agreed to undertake and rendered speechless. Every tenet of his Republican background was about to be breached by a symbolic handshake with the head of what official Republicanism still regarded as a colonist regime with no legitimacy. And in the North, as Ken noted, 'there had been a rigid policy of no meetings before recognition'. Lemass's agreement to come to Stormont would be interpreted in some quarters as a kind of recognition, even to some a betrayal of the Northern nationalist community. At this point Ken stepped forward to rescue what was a somewhat awkward moment, warmly greeting his Northern acquaintances; this, as O'Neill notes, 'helped to mollify me'.[20] After the introductions were completed, in the privacy of the Stormont House bathroom Lemass voiced his dilemma to his host.

'I shall get into terrible trouble for this.'

'No, Mr Lemass,' O'Neill fatefully replied, 'it is I who will get into terrible trouble for this'.[21]

O'Neill then conducted his guest to the drawing-room and introduced him to his wife Jean, Sir Cecil Bateman and Ken Bloomfield who, together with Jim Malley and Ken, made up the party. Lemass gradually relaxed and 'became a very pleasant and amusing guest'.[22] Ken Bloomfield recalled him as having 'a face slightly wolfish, without being cruel, as if he were a kind of

Godfather figure turned into a modern businessman . . . his voice husky and throaty, redolent of Dublin and smoke-filled Fianna Fáil rooms and long, stuffy evenings in the Dáil'.[23] 'Our hosts', Ken recalls, 'thought the occasion worthy of champagne,' and over lunch of smoked salmon, chicken, leeks in cheese sauce, creamed potatoes, trifle and coffee, 'I imagine Dr Paisley's worst fears would have been confirmed if I were to say that the red wine we drank was Châteauneuf-du-Pape.'

After lunch the party strolled across to the prime minister's office in Stormont Castle. 'As we emerged up the shrub-lined path a pandemonium of journalists came running towards us,' Ken Bloomfield recalled.[24] Journalists and photographers jostled to get the copy and the pictures they knew would make the pages of the world's press. 'Seán Lemass, who we had to be reminded was the Southern Premier, was in Stormont Castle! It was something we could scarcely credit,' one journalist recalled. 'They [Lemass and O'Neill] did have a sense of occasion once they saw the pressmen there. Both of them realised that this was really something out of the ordinary.'[25] Asked by one of the photographers to stand closer together, Lemass quipped with a smile: 'That's what we're here for!'[26] Then it was up the steps of the Castle, through the hall and into the prime minister's study, to sit before a blazing fire to discuss potential areas of future cooperation between the two states in tourism, education, health, agricultural research, trade, tariff reductions relating to Northern Ireland manufactures (as part of the Republic's continuing GATT negotiations), electricity and fisheries – all without, as Ken notes, 'prejudice to political principles'. Lemass's proposal that both parts of Ireland might try to attract industry to the island as one unit was not pursued, O'Neill explaining that Northern Ireland received UK grants to this end, and the Treasury in London would not agree to a venture that would entail part of that funding going to a country outside the Commonwealth.

A return visit to Dublin by O'Neill was agreed. Lemass's

suggestion that it might be postponed until the weather improved was firmly rejected by O'Neill, who felt that 'unless I came right away pressure would be put on me to refuse to go'.[27] A carefully worded joint statement for the media was then prepared: 'We have discussed matters in which there may prove to be a degree of common interest, and have agreed to explore further what specific measures may be possible or desirable by way of consultation and co-operation.'[28] Then it was back to Stormont House for afternoon tea and to meet members of the Northern Ireland cabinet, including Brian Faulkner, William Craig and Jack Andrews, most of whom knew nothing of the visit until Lemass had arrived in the North. 'If they were surprised or dubious, their courtesy did not allow them show it,' Ken recalled.[29] One unexpected reaction to Lemass's presence at Stormont came from Brian Faulkner, who recalled:

> I said, 'How are you, Seán?' and he said, 'How are you, Brian?'
> He and I had met on many times previously and I don't think Captain O'Neill had met him until that day . . . The first thing Mr Lemass said to me was, 'I hear you had a great day with the Westmeaths [hunt] a few weeks ago.' I said, 'That's right – I didn't realize you knew.' 'Ah,' he said, 'the boys [Gardaí] told me!'[30]

In a convivial and friendly setting around the dining table in Stormont House, Lemass and Ken discussed matters, mainly of economic interest, with members of the Northern Ireland cabinet. 'Sean Lemass was in a particular good humour,' Brian Faulkner recalled, 'smoking his pipe pretty consistently. He was very alert . . . I don't think there was a single question raised . . . on which he wasn't very well briefed.'[31]

By now the visit had become public knowledge and a large crowd had gathered outside the gates of Stormont Castle. Uncertain as to their reaction, their hosts were anxious to see their Southern guests safely back across the border. Bidding farewell to the O'Neills, Lemass and Ken were sped through the evening traffic under police escort. RUC constables stood to attention to salute, some perhaps in the mistaken impression that the car contained the Northern premier rather than the Southern Taoiseach! At the border, taking their leave of Jim Malley, Lemass shook hands with every member of his police escort and, getting into the state car at Killeen, they drove back in a snowstorm to Dublin, arriving shortly after eight o'clock with, as Ken wrote, 'new hope in our hearts'.[32]

Reaction to the historic visit was instant and, for the most part, positive, in Ireland, North and South, and abroad. As Ken recalled, 'a palpable wave of goodwill and enthusiasm spread throughout Ireland in the immediate aftermath of the visit'.[33] In the North it was generally agreed that it had taken courage for O'Neill to issue the invitation and for Lemass to accept it. The Grand Master of the Orange Order, Sir George Clark, noting that there was no 'political issue' involved in the meeting, was of the opinion that, as 'one country lives beside the other', it was merely 'common sense that the two leaders meet to discuss ways of expanding their economies'.[34] It was 'the right thing to do', the Nationalist *Irish News* commented; 'it took place without a bite or a chip being taken out of the Government of Ireland Act.'[35] 'Most people of goodwill and common sense will welcome the news,' asserted Cardinal William Conway, head of the Roman Catholic Church in Ireland, 'and will pray that it may lead to the growth of mutual understanding.'[36] The *New York Times*, in a leading article headed 'The Crumbling Wall', wrote of the 'small note of hope' in a world of divided nations the visit represented,[37] and the British press too was broadly supportive.

All, however, was not sunshine and roses. The meeting brought to life many political ghosts. For diehard Republicans, the Taoiseach's very presence in Stormont Castle bespoke a form of recognition of the Northern Ireland administration and aroused accusations of betrayal. To constitutional Northern Nationalists such as Eddie McAteer, it was insensitive to Northern Ireland's minority, whose plight for the four decades since partition successive governments in Dublin had been more than willing to ignore. After the visit, however, Lemass persuaded McAteer to allow the Nationalist Party to become the official opposition at Stormont, a move considered to be a major political break-through at the time. Arriving at Stormont in a car bedecked with Union flags the day after the meeting, the Moderator of the Free Presbyterian Church, the Reverend Ian Paisley, delivered a letter of warning to O'Neill 'that Protestant Unionists are not prepared to sit idly by and have our heritage bartered by you or anyone else', and ominously threatened to 'act as the Ulster Volunteers acted to defend our rights'.[38]

Backing for O'Neill's historic gesture was confirmed by success at the polls in the October 1965 election. As the first prime minister to canvass in both Catholic and Protestant areas in Belfast, he recalled that the reception from the voters was 'equally warm' in both communities.[39] But, as he had predicted to his guest in the bathroom at Stormont House, from the moment Lemass left Stormont Castle on 14 January 1965, O'Neill's fight for his political survival began. Accompanied by his wife, Sir Cecil Bateman, Ken Bloomfield and Jim Malley, on 9 February he made his first official visit to Dublin, where he was welcomed by the Taoiseach, attended by various Irish government ministers and officials, including Ken and his wife Nora. This occasion, however, lacked the high drama and symbolism of the initial meeting; more a social event, it nonetheless served to normalize such meetings between North and South.

O'Neill's political problems were more sharply in focus by the time of Jack Lynch's visit to Stormont on 11 December 1967. By then, developments had begun to widen the sectarian divide. O'Neill's plan to develop Craigavon as a new model city to integrate Catholics and Protestants in one community was obdu-rately resisted by both sides. The recommendation of the

Lockwood Committee that a new university be sited in Coleraine, instead of, as had been expected, in the largely Catholic city of Derry, further provoked Nationalist ire as yet another example of discrimination and sectarianism. O'Neill's suggestion that a new bridge over the Lagan be named the 'Somme Bridge' to commemorate the fiftieth anniversary of the famous battle in which Northern Irishmen of both traditions had fought and died side by side, was rejected by the Loyalist-dominated Belfast City Council in favour of 'Carson Bridge', a name guaranteed to raise the hackles of their Catholic fellow citizens.

Across the border, the Republic's fiftieth anniversary commemorations of 1916, coinciding with a presidential election in which the aged de Valera won a second term of office, was laced with emotional Republican rhetoric regarding the unfinished business of the 'Six Counties'. In the North, Nationalist celebrations of the Rising, marches and demonstrations, and the widespread display of the Irish tricolour were met with determined opposition from Loyalist organizations and from within the ranks of O'Neill's party and cabinet. Even his liberal and progressive thoughts on segregated education and his questioning 'whether the maintenance of two distinct educational systems side by side is not wasteful of human and financial resources and a major barrier to any attempts at communal assimilation'[40] found short shrift from clergy of all denominations, including Cardinal Conway and the Catholic hierarchy. Every initiative to unite the two sides of his divided community seemed doomed to bring O'Neill into conflict with one side or another.

Accompanying the Taoiseach, Jack Lynch, and the government secretary, Nicholas Nolan, on his second official visit, Ken found Stormont blanketed in snow that December. As their car swung by Carson's statue, two black-garbed figures, Reverend Paisley and Reverend Beattie, pelted it with snowballs, 'poor shots both of them', as Ken remembers. Emerging from the car at the premier's residence, 'we could hear Paisley bellow in the crisp air,

"No Pope here!" – to which Jack Lynch turned to me and asked in his soft Cork voice, "Which of us does he think is the Pope?" '
A lunch, attended by Mrs O'Neill and the Northern Ireland cabinet, was followed by a meeting at Stormont Castle between the two prime ministers and their officials, attended also by Brian Faulkner, minister of commerce, and Major Chichester Clark, minister of agriculture. Issues of mutual interest were discussed, including concessions for the North's manufactures in the Republic and securing additional outlets in Northern Ireland for goods produced in the Republic. Progress was reviewed in tourism, transport, roads, electricity supply, the liberalization of cross-border traffic and the store cattle trade between North and South, and measures being undertaken on both sides of the border to prevent the spread of foot-and-mouth disease from Britain. On a personal basis, Jack Lynch asked for an end to the 'bidding war' between corresponding bodies in North and South in acquiring musicians for their respective symphony orchestras and Irish artefacts for their respective museums.

A follow-up visit to Dublin by Captain O'Neill, his wife and advisers took place on 8 January 1968. A formal lunch at Iveagh House was attended by various ministers and departmental secretaries. Again, progress in matters of mutual cooperation was reviewed; it was estimated that a recently signed agreement on electricity supply 'would save both Governments about a quarter of a million pounds'.[41] The 'possible use of Ballykelly Airport for civilian purposes', to facilitate access to Donegal, was raised by Erskine Childers, but was considered uneconomic by the Northern Ireland delegation in view of a planned new road system which would make 'Derry and the Donegal border only a 40-minute drive from Aldershot'. O'Neill raised the Republic's decision to adopt decimalization and its proposed introduction of breathalyser testing. A communiqué, drafted by Ken in English and Irish, was subsequently released to the media. As news of the meeting leaked out, threats that the prime minister's car would be targeted by dissident Republicans on the return journey to the North meant, as O'Neill later recorded, 'that we would have to return by a very circuitous road'.[42]

Such high-profile meetings and the ensuing discussions on practical issues of common interest were, to Ken Whitaker, a realistic road map out of the morass of the vacuous political rhetoric that had previously embittered North–South relations since partition. While in no way oblivious to the fact that those across the negotiating table were exclusively drawn from the dominant Unionist tradition, or that they represented a government that was, with good reason, viewed by the Nationalist minority as sectarian and undemocratic, to Ken Whitaker it was a smile, a handshake, a conversation, rather than flags, emblems or anthems, and most certainly not bricks or bullets, that offered the way to break down barriers and gradually build bridges, while cross-border cooperation on issues such as transport, industry and agriculture made a more immediate and practical contribution to everyday living than the emotionally charged but vague and divisive ideological arguments which merely served to deepen division and hatred. The friendships and contacts Ken Whitaker made in Northern Ireland, in both the political and administrative arenas, endured to become a vital channel of communication during the traumatic years that lay ahead. While Terence O'Neill's attempts at rapprochement with the South were to be violently derailed by subsequent events, the cross-border meetings he initiated through his friendship with Ken Whitaker succeeded in having, as O'Neill wittily wrote in 1972, 'cooperation between North and South publicly endorsed and today, when a militant Protestant housewife fries an egg she may well be doing it on Catholic power generated in the South and distributed in the North as a result of the first O'Neill–Lemass meeting'.[43] These first hands stretching tentatively across the border, however, were to be dramatically wrenched apart later in 1968 when North and South became convulsed in a quagmire of political and social upheaval that was to endure for thirty years at a cost of over 3700 lives.

Ken's friendship with Terence O'Neill continued after the latter's departure from Northern Ireland politics in January 1970. They corresponded on Northern issues, about which O'Neill regularly spoke in the House of Lords on being created a life peer as Lord O'Neill of the Maine. 'It seems that extremists on both sides are making all the running and this could lead to serious trouble and loss of life,'[44] he predicted to his friend shortly after his resignation as prime minister. Occasionally, through Ken's intervention, O'Neill briefed staff at the Irish Embassy in London on developments in Northern Ireland from a Unionist perspective, as well as on the machinations of his bitter political rival Brian Faulkner. To facilitate arrangements for a private holiday by Roy Jenkins, the British chancellor of the exchequer, in west Cork in spring 1970 – 'as soon as I heard Cork mentioned I knew Jack [Lynch] would want to know!'[45] – O'Neill wrote to Ken, who ensured that the necessary security arrangements for the visit were put in place. The two friends also met on O'Neill's many private visits to Dublin, O'Neill on one occasion enjoying 'a grand tea with Raymond [Ken's son]' during Ken's absence abroad on Central Bank business. And it was through Ken that the Irish government's invitation to Lord O'Neill to join the board of governors of the National Gallery of Ireland was extended and accepted.

On 21 April 1972, in a meeting redolent with both symbolism and sadness, Ken accompanied Terence O'Neill to Áras an Uachtaráin for a private and highly sensitive meeting, at the latter's request, with President de Valera. In a note he later wrote, Ken described the historic meeting: 'The President received us standing at his desk. He received Lord O'Neill warmly . . . and made a statement, which he repeated twice in the course of the interview – that one of his dearest dreams would be fulfilled if an O'Neill were to sit in his chair as a President of a united Ireland.'[46]

Over brandies, the three men sat down for a chat, their conversation ranging, as Ken recorded in his notes, from Lord O'Neill's grandfather's residence in what was then the Viceregal Lodge to more recent political events. In answer to O'Neill's query about 'the Government of Ireland Act 1920 and the beginning of Northern Ireland and the Irish Free State, President de Valera maintained that [Winston] Churchill had tricked Collins into acceptance of the position intended for Southern Ireland under that Act'. He had, the president told his visitor, been given to believe that no oath of allegiance to the king would be required. Dev also admitted that he had totally underestimated 'the depth of the religious antagonism of the Northern Protestants to Irish unity but that [Erskine] Childers had not'.[47] His opinion of Dublin-born Edward Carson – that he was no more than a political adventurer – was shared by his guest, who also judged that Carson was 'a disappointed opportunist', having been thwarted in his ambition of becoming Lord Chancellor of England. Carson, O'Neill also maintained, 'confirmed the fears and antipathies of the working-class Northern Protestants regarding Home Rule', and noted that such antipathies 'could still be played upon by present-day successors of Carson, the Paisleys, Craigs and Billy Halls'.

O'Neill was curious to know whether, if America had promised to persuade the British to accept a fully united Ireland, de Valera might have abandoned his policy of neutrality during the Second World War. On the contrary, the president insisted: 'it would not have deflected him from his policy . . . which he considered to be the only policy in the circumstances', a decision buttressed by his wish to save the Irish people from the suffering and death they had experienced in the First World War.

After posing for photographs, taken by Ken and de Valera's personal secretary Máire Ní Cheallaigh, in the president's study and on the steps of the south portico, Ken and Lord O'Neill took their leave. Before the publication of O'Neill's autobiography in 1972, Ken received permission from de Valera for O'Neill to make reference to the meeting in his book, with an accompanying photo, provided the details of their conversation remained confidential and that it would be made clear that the visit had taken place at O'Neill's request. An interesting postscript to the visit was de Valera's query afterwards to Ken: 'Cionnac a thárla gur thiontaigh duine de mhuintir Chichester in a Niallach?' (How come a Chichester turned into an O'Neill?) – in response to which Ken supplied the president with details of O'Neill's genealogical background.

Assessments of Terence O'Neill on his death in 1990 reflected the diversity of opinion his policies evoked during the course of his political life. While his adversary Ian Paisley accused him of putting 'the whole of our constitutional position in the melting pot', Jack Lynch noted: 'It is for the nobility and generosity of his ideals and his courage in changing old moulds that he particularly deserves to be remembered. History will, I believe, be kind to him.'[48]

The methods and policies O'Neill adopted to lead his fellow Unionists along the path of reform and reconciliation in the end fell foul of the wrath of extreme Loyalism and Republicanism alike, and his personal background and upbringing may have isolated him from the raw political realities on the ground in Northern Ireland. None the less, as Ken noted in his appreciation published on O'Neill's death, 'his aims for the people of Northern Ireland transcended religious and political differences'. As one who had intimate knowledge and understanding of O'Neill's hopes and ambitions for the North, as well as of the intransigence by which he was confronted, Ken Whitaker was well placed to offer his tribute: that Terence O'Neill was 'a decent, generous man who wanted to do good . . . He had to contend all along with the recalcitrance from within his own party and there were people on the green side who did not particularly want to see a benign unionist regime. They preferred a unionist front that they could hate.'[49]

10

A Good Marriage Settlement
1968–73

*I am not a politician. My working life has, however, been given . . . to
another form of public service and my greatest desire is to see the people of
this island happy and at peace, with work to do in Ireland which gives
personal satisfaction and provides good living standards and social conditions
for all. I make no distinction in these aspirations between North and South,
or between Catholic and Protestant.*

T. K. Whitaker[1]

THE TONE OF the late 1960s was set by international student
protests in Prague and Paris and by civil rights marches in the
United States, images of which became familiar to Irish television
viewers North and South. 'We shall overcome,' sang Martin
Luther King's supporters as they lay their burden of racial segre-
gation, discrimination and injustice at the foot of the statue of
Abraham Lincoln in Washington. Their aim was to achieve civil
rights by non-violent public demonstration. King's crusade and
his message struck a chord in Northern Ireland, releasing the
pent-up anger and frustration of the minority Nationalist
community. But while the demands of black marchers in America
focused on the issue of civil rights, some of their Nationalist
counterparts in Northern Ireland sought far more fundamental
change, calling into question the status of Northern Ireland itself.

On 5 October 1968 some three hundred marchers assembled

in Derry to protest against discrimination in the allocation of public housing and jobs. Indiscriminate police brutality and baton charges, captured by TV cameras and flashed around the world, inflamed further violent clashes which continued for two weeks, heralding the commencement of the three-decade-long 'Troubles'. Much to the annoyance, if not shame, of the British government, the civil rights demonstrations and the worldwide television coverage that ensued opened up, for the world to see, the 'can of worms' that had been allowed to exist for the previous forty years. Preoccupied with their own political and economic survival, successive governments south of the border had also ignored the welfare of Northern Nationalists.

As a member of the constitutional review committee established in 1967, Ken pursued his quest to improve North–South relations by persistent efforts to remove some of the more obvious constitutional obstacles. An exchange of correspondence with Charles Haughey in January 1968 was indicative, however, of the divergence of opinion that existed between them on the question of Northern Ireland. Article 3 of the Irish constitution which, as Ken noted, 'not merely lays claim to Irish unity [but] states in very blunt language the entitlement of the Oireachtas and Government in Dublin . . . to rule Northern Ireland', was, he told Haughey, unrealistic and 'a considerable irritant in our relations with Northern Ireland'.[2] He agreed with the committee's recommendation that it should be replaced by wording that proclaimed the firm will of the Irish people that its territory be reunited 'in harmony and brotherly affection' between Irishmen. 'It is quite obvious that having eschewed the use of force to bring about the reunification of the national territory, we must be content to wait for the agreement of Northern Ireland to reunification proposals.'[3] Haughey's reply, written in his own hand, that 'we would never abandon the moral right to use force. We have the right to use force to defend the national territory,'[4] was an emphatic harbinger of the difficulties to come. Nevertheless, unperturbed by the minister's obduracy, Ken's reply was equally unequivocal:

> I would not like to view this as a moral issue but purely as a practical matter . . . We have eschewed the use of force as a means of ending the partition of Ireland and we see the reunification of the Irish people as a matter for *Irishmen in Ireland*, to be achieved by agreement between them, the British being expected to display goodwill or, at least, indifference.[5]

To reinforce his point, he quoted de Valera's words to the Fianna Fáil Árd Fheis in 1957, regarding the use of force in relation to Northern Ireland: 'We would have left an abiding sore that would have ruined our national life for generations.'[6]

Constitutional debate, however, was abandoned as the situation in the North exploded into what amounted to civil war. Terence O'Neill's tentative steps towards reformation in the North and rapprochement with the South were frustrated from within his own party, by the all-powerful Orange Order, and by the vitriolic outbursts of public figures such as Ian Paisley. Political opportunism, as much as opposition to the reforms O'Neill attempted to implement, including the introduction of one person one vote, which many of his cabinet colleagues considered disastrous for Unionism, contributed to O'Neill's growing isolation. Even the British government's threat to withhold subsidies to Northern Ireland if reforms were not speedily introduced were considered to be merely a 'bluff' by some Northern ministers. Unionist suspicion that the civil rights movement was merely a front for the IRA further fuelled their antagonism and fears.

Ken Whitaker had a more realistic understanding of the social and political inequities that prevailed within Northern Ireland. On the one hand, as a Catholic and a Nationalist, he could identify with the frustrations and disappointments of his co-religionists, denied basic civil rights by a government which, by gerrymandering votes, redrawing council boundaries and exercising a policy of flagrant partisan patronage, especially in the areas of employment and housing, ensured that the Unionist political grip on the province remained strong and undiluted. Growing up in the South, he had heard the rhetoric voiced, mainly at election time, by successive Irish governments, regarding the 'imposition' of partition by the British, the 'inevitability' of reunification, and the 'invalidity' of the Northern government. As a public servant and economist, he was keenly aware of the impracticality and futility of such assertions. 'Emotion', he wrote, 'is a dangerous counsellor. It generates and exaggerates expectations and also strengthens fears and prejudices, in ways quite incompatible with the realities of life.'[7]

As disturbances continued in Northern Ireland Ken presented the Taoiseach, Jack Lynch, with a paper entitled 'A Note on North–South Relations'. Dated 11 November 1968, before even a single death had occurred, this thoughtful and concise evaluation laid bare the stark realities. Regarding partition, he wrote: 'It was much too naïve to believe that Britain simply imposed it on Ireland. For the Northern Unionists the main motive binding them to the United Kingdom is fear rather than loyalty – fear of loss of power, property, privilege and even religious independence, if they were subject to a Dublin Parliament.'[8] The use of force in any attempt to overcome Northern Unionists 'will get us nowhere', he warned. 'It will only strengthen fears, antagonism and divisions that keep North and South apart'; and from a military point of view, in any event, the attempt was doomed to failure. Donning his economist's hat, Ken reminded the Taoiseach that the annual subsidy payable by Westminster towards the upkeep of the Northern Ireland state was over £90 million. Consequently, reunification without, as he wrote, 'a good marriage settlement' would 'be imposing on ourselves a formidable burden which many of our own citizens, however strong their desire for Irish unity, may find intolerable'. Even the

Nationalist population in the north, despite their disadvantaged status, would find themselves worse off economically if partition were to be abolished immediately. He urged the Taoiseach and his cabinet to think in the long term, rather than the short term, and to continue the policy started by Lemass towards 'reaching agreement in Ireland between Irishmen' by demonstrating a 'good neighbour policy' and by encouraging the reform policies being pursued by Terence O'Neill. Besides being best for the welfare of Northern Ireland's Nationalist community, such reforms were also, he reasoned, 'most likely to loosen the roots of Partition and prepare the way for agreement between North and South on some form of re-unification'.[9] Unionist fears and mistrust, and Nationalist alienation, would be better addressed through more practical undertakings, such as ensuring the prosperity of both parts of Ireland, full employment and the satisfaction of housing needs. 'We can leave it mostly to public opinion and to pressure from the British Parliament and Government to prod the NI Government into more vigorous and effective reforms regarding social conditions and local franchise,' he advised. Referring to the Republic's claim of jurisdiction over the 'Six Counties', as enshrined in the 1937 constitution, as premature and dogmatic, he wrote: 'There is nothing we can do about this, in the present circumstances except to forget it!'[10] Copies of his note were forwarded to Hugh McCann, secretary of the Department of External Affairs, with whose minister, Frank Aiken, Ken had already discussed the details 'in a recent conversation in his rooms in Leinster House'.[11] The first of many policy discussion documents he was to write over the next thirty years, the 1968 paper was later hailed as 'a model of its kind – going so directly to the heart of the matter that it still has relevance today'.[12]

Ken's attitude to the emerging civil rights movement was one of caution. While initially the movement distanced itself from political issues, he was well aware that street movements such as this could easily be manipulated to foment violence, including police violence, by forces with a more sinister agenda. Barriers were beginning to come down in Northern Ireland and social reforms were being implemented, albeit, as he acknowledged, slowly, even reluctantly, by some of O'Neill's cabinet ministers, but even these initial steps, he felt, could easily be derailed by demonstrations of violence. As he stated in an interview in 1999, 'I tended to believe that it [the civil rights movement] was a loose cannon. Extremists were always willing to jump on any available bandwagon and the IRA certainly jumped on the civil rights bandwagon.'[13] In 1968 the situation, as he tried to impress upon the Dublin government, required patience, understanding and forbearance, and 'resolute resistance to emotionalism and opportunism'.[14] By 1969, however, patience and forbearance no longer suited the 'hawks' within the cabinets on either side of the border.

Against a background of worsening violence, nationalist protests and marches, increasing Loyalist paramilitary activity, the blowing up of Castlereagh power station in March and major riots in Derry in April, Ken sought to forestall one such 'hawk' in the government whom, together with some of his cabinet colleagues, he suspected of flexing his wings. Albeit no longer departmental secretary, Ken's terse seven-point statement to Charles Haughey left the minister under no illusion as to what he regarded as the only acceptable course of action:

> Do nothing to inflame the situation further . . . Avoid playing into
> the hands of extremists who are manipulating the Civil Rights
> movement . . . deplore . . . failures to protect peaceful protest and the
> recourse to disruption and violence . . . appeal for a period of
> restraint . . . from all form of protest on the streets . . . emphasise the
> desirability of the N.I. government to take early and positive steps to
> remedy the social and other grievances . . . convey to the UK
> government our anxiety that they should not add to an inflam-
> matory situation which might easily spread to the whole of this

partitioned island . . . and to use their influence to secure early and effective remedying . . . of the ultimate causes of the present crises.

He called for a full and authoritative statement by the Taoiseach of government policy on partition – which, as he spelled out to the minister, should be 'a peaceful solution based on agreement between North and South and British support and goodwill'.[15]

There is no evidence that Haughey replied. At a subsequent cabinet meeting it was decided that the Taoiseach would request an urgent meeting with the British prime minister, Harold Wilson, and that the minister for external affairs, Paddy Hillery, should seek a meeting with the secretary-general of the United Nations.

The internationalizing of the situation in Northern Ireland not only angered the British, who rebutted 'Éire's' right to interfere in an 'internal' UK matter, it also added to the mounting pressure on Terence O'Neill. His resignation as prime minister on 1 May 1969, after an election in which he almost lost his seat to the Reverend Ian Paisley, inexplicably with the assistance of Catholic votes, was deeply regretted by many – and by none more than by Ken Whitaker. Together they had started out on a road that, as both realized, was destined to be long and difficult, aiming first to normalize North–South relations and to introduce policy reforms north and south of the border, which they hoped might lead to a reunification of hearts and minds, before the more elusive ideal of political integration could be entertained. Through his friendship with O'Neill and his professional relationship with Lemass, Ken was ideally placed to act as a conduit between the two leaders.

On 12 August 1969, the slow-burning fuse in Northern Ireland, kept alight by rioting, intimidation and partisan police brutality, finally reached the powder keg of the annual Apprentice Boys' march. In the ensuing explosion, involving all the apparatus of civil strife – rioting, marches, Lambeg drums, barricades, tear gas, no-go areas, petrol bombs, water cannon: all the elements of what would become a familiar lexicon over the following thirty years – the North erupted into a frenzy of full-scale sectarian violence. The official response, by the Stormont government, now irrevocably split since the departure of Terence O'Neill, but also by the British and Irish governments, left a lot to be desired in respect of judgement, knowledge and direction alike. The situation required steady nerves and an ability to see above the smoke and fumes issuing from the streets of Derry, Belfast, Dungannon and Newry. And as governments North and South, as well as in Westminster, scrambled for a way through the morass, it was Ken Whitaker's words that brought some element of reason to the chaos.

Dramatic televised scenes of full-scale rioting, police and baton charges in Derry, Northern Ireland's most Nationalist city – what became known as 'the Battle of the Bogside' – unleashed emotive and alarmist reactions south of the border, including from members of the Irish government, hastily recalled from their summer holidays. Under pressure from Boland, Blaney and Haughey to send the Irish army to 'protect our people' in Derry and Newry, Jack Lynch tried desperately to steady the ship of state. 'He realized that he was caught in a situation in which he was not sure of his ground,' Ken recalls. As a compromise, Lynch agreed to make a tough and uncompromising statement in a live television broadcast on 13 August. In this speech, parts of which were drafted by Blaney and Haughey, Lynch uttered the often-misquoted phrase that 'the Irish Government can no longer stand by and see innocent people injured or worse'. The speech threatened involvement by the Irish army (reinforced by the construction of military field hospitals along the border), UN intervention and the establishment of a UN peacekeeping force within Northern Ireland, and asserted that 'the reunification of the national territory can provide the only permanent solution for the problem'.[16]

Following the broadcast, rumours that the Irish army was on the way to the North led to an intensification of rioting in Derry, the mobilization of the notorious B Specials and the start of weeks of bloody unrest, leading to many fatalities and the displacement from their burning homes by Loyalist mobs of some three thousand Catholics, many of whom fled across the border for sanctuary. The Lynch speech, which confirmed the worst fears of Unionists regarding the duplicity of the Dublin government, was deprecated by the Northern premier, Major James Chichester-Clark, as 'a clumsy and intolerable intrusion into our internal affairs'.[17] While dismissive of the Irish government's suggestion of UN intervention, the British government acknowledged the breakdown of law and order in the province and assumed direct control of security; and on 14 August 1969 the first contingent of British soldiers arrived. Under pressure, uncertain of the validity of the information he was receiving and hampered by disunity within his cabinet, resulting in the temporary resignation of Kevin Boland, minister for local government, Jack Lynch turned to the person whose advice he knew he could trust.

On his annual family holiday in a rented cottage in Carna, Connemara, Ken read with alarm of the unfolding events in the north, appalled at the 'horrifying degree of teenage hooliganism and anarchy . . . in part at least . . . organised by extremists on both sides in Northern Ireland'.[18] In the early morning of 15 August, a Garda car arrived at the cottage with a message that he was to contact the Taoiseach urgently. 'I phoned the Taoiseach', Ken recalled, 'about 10 a.m. from the Garda Barracks and gave him advice which I afterwards summarised in a manuscript letter, driving to Galway that same afternoon to ensure that it made the post that day.'[19] At the Taoiseach's request, Ken also gave him the names of contacts in the Northern Ireland administration who, he knew, were *au fait* with Unionist thinking. Over the years ahead, as he developed relationships and liaised with public servants and politicians in the British and Northern Ireland administrations, he remained ever the dutiful public servant, insisting that 'there was no tangential deviation or secret meetings without Government approval. I had a code of conduct to follow in that regard.'

Conscious of the enormous pressure being exerted on the Taoiseach, which could result in his being 'guided by either emotion or good sense', Ken Whitaker warned him that no government could benefit from appearing to support extremists on either side: 'There is a terrible temptation to be opportunist – to cash in on political emotionalism – at a time like this; but it should never be forgotten that a genuinely united Ireland must be based on a free union of *those living in Ireland*, on mutual tolerance and on belief that the ultimate governmental authority will be equitable and unprejudiced.'[20] He urged Lynch to avoid identifying solely with the Nationalist position, to reassure moderate Protestants, 'who otherwise may be driven to side with the extremists', and to avoid all appearances 'of being driven before the emotional winds fanned by utterly unrepresentative and irresponsible organisations such as Sinn Féin', which, as he stated, 'an outsider would be misled into thinking were the Government-party or at least its main opposition'.[21] The failure of the experiment of devolution in the North, he argued, was 'due *not just* to the unfairness and discrimination of the regime and its inability to maintain law and order without forfeiting the respect of a large body of its citizens, *but also* to the fundamental weakness of its constitutional position' and its repudiation by a majority in each of the counties of 'its artificial composition'. The key question, now, as he bluntly stated, was: 'Where do we go from here?' Taking over the burden of Britain's financial contribution was not a viable option for the Republic, nor was the terrifying task of keeping sectarian and anarchical mobs in order. Better, he advised, 'to confine ourselves to preventing groups from here intervening by strict control of the border' – a recommendation that was to become more relevant in light of the covert activities of some members of Lynch's own administration. Above all, he concluded, there could only be a 'slow-phased movement towards some form of unification' and there should be 'no rigid clinging to preconceived formulae' regarding what shape that unity should take.[22]

The deployment of the British army, initially welcomed by the besieged Nationalist community, and the visit to the North on 27 August of the British home secretary, James Callaghan, brought a temporary calm as both sides drew breath after weeks of rioting and lethal violence. In Dublin, a Government Information Bureau was hastily established to promote worldwide coverage for the Irish government's Northern Ireland policy; however, using means that at times proved counterproductive in both tone and content, this merely served, as Ken predicted, to raise tension and antagonism among Unionists. 'None of these chaps has a clue – or could have', Ken told Jack Lynch, 'about the kind of complicated constitutional mechanism we may have to accept as a first step towards reunification; and by barging in now with diverse and half-baked ideas they are liable to spoil everything.' Better, he advised, that they 'be sent back for the time being to their ordinary jobs';[23] and, eventually, they were. A new inter-departmental unit to advise on Northern Ireland policy, Ken noted, was open to 'too much ad-hocing . . . too much reliance on any one man's personal contacts or judgements, particularly if they arise from "us" rather than "them" sources. For years and years E.A. [External Affairs] did nothing whatever of a thoughtful or constructive nature about N.I. Studies on economic and constitutional aspects were initiated and completed entirely in Finance.'[24]

To further 'internationalize' the situation, the Dublin government decided to place a motion before the United Nations Security Council, requesting a UN peacekeeping force to contain the situation in the North. Despite British opposition, the minister for external affairs, Paddy Hillery, was subsequently permitted to address the Security Council, while the British ambassador to the UN countered that Northern Ireland was an internal matter for the British government and outlined details of the government's proposed reforms. This ploy by the Irish government, while it might serve in the short term as an outlet for pent-up antagonisms in the Republic, Ken considered not only ineffective but counterproductive. By virtue of the Government of Ireland Act 1920, Northern Ireland was de facto and de jure part of the United Kingdom, and no United Nations intervention, even if any were forthcoming, could alter that fact. Later in September, while attending a meeting of the IMF in Washington, Ken hurried to New York to make amendments to a speech, scheduled to be delivered by Paddy Hillery to the UN Assembly, the tone of which he considered to be too abrasive and which he had received permission from the Taoiseach to alter. Ken tracked Hillery to a club off Fifth Avenue, where he was taking a swim before delivering his speech, in time to make the necessary amendments.

As Ken had feared, the Northern Ireland civil rights movement was being pushed aside by a rejuvenated IRA, whose units, despite being ill-armed and poorly equipped, were reported to be active in Nationalist areas. The IRA leadership publicly demanded that the Dublin government 'support the victimised people of the North and . . . justify its claim to sovereignty over the whole of the national territory'.[25] The plight of the Nationalist community had already heightened emotions in the South and the IRA's demands found receptive listeners, including some within Jack Lynch's cabinet. The suffering of Northern Nationalists at the hands of Loyalist mobs and partisan security forces stirred up latent resentment among the generation born after the Easter Rising and the War of Independence, and fed on the rhetoric of a united Ireland, the illegitimacy of partition and the inequality of the Northern Ireland 'regime'. Whispers of meetings and exchanges between senior government ministers and the IRA were beginning to filter through. Under pressure from both within and outside his cabinet, Jack Lynch again turned to Ken Whitaker.

Following the arrival of the British army on the streets of the North, a period of calm had ensued. The British government promised reforms and James Callaghan had been well received behind the barricades in Nationalist areas. On 12 September the Cameron Commission Report laid responsibility for many of the grievances of the Nationalist population at the door of Stormont, and blamed the police for much of the disorder. Against this background, following a private meeting, Jack Lynch asked Ken to draft him a policy speech to deliver at a forthcoming function in Tralee. This speech, in publicly committing the Irish government to the policy of unification by the principle of consent, has come to be regarded, as one historian noted, as the 'most significant intervention in redirecting the course of the Irish Government's Northern Ireland policy'.[26] Modifying the more strident notes of Lynch's August broadcast, in 'clear and simple' terms Ken laid out the basis of the new policy, conscious of the occasion (a dinner to honour the retirement of Thomas McEllistrim TD, a former member of the old IRA) at which it was to be delivered. Reminding the Taoiseach's audience that even the authors of the 1920 Government of Ireland Act had envisaged partition coming to an end, the present government, he wrote, 'had no intention of using force to realise this desire . . . The unity we seek is not something forced but a free and genuine union of those living in Ireland based on mutual respect and tolerance.'[27] By its very nature, then, such unity could be achieved only in the long term, to allow time to win the respect and confidence of those now opposed to it, and its achievement would require 'goodwill, patience, understanding and, at times, forbearance'. Referring to 'the terrible events' of the previous few months, he said that change would have to come in Northern Ireland, so that 'the grievances of so many of our fellow Irishmen be quickly remedied and their fears set to rest'. In this the Irish government's views were entitled to be heard. To assuage the fears of the Unionist majority of 'domination' by Dublin, the Irish government was open, he wrote, to explore all possibilities regarding what form unity might take, whether along federal or other lines. While denouncing the achievement of unity by violent means, he asserted that it was unreasonable for any Unionist government to expect the government in the South, as well as those living in Northern Ireland possessing a similar hope, to renounce that aim.

The final draft of the speech omitted some of Ken's recommendations regarding the position of Northern Nationalists. One passage not included was:

> Those within the area of the Stormont Government who desire the reunification of Ireland would, I am sure, find it easier, meanwhile, to accept its authority and play their due part in public life, if the regime were fair and just and protected their right to work democratically for a change of regime or a different political relationship with Britain and ourselves.[28]

Also omitted was a reference to the 'early release to civilian life', of Irish army reservists who had been called up, a move that had roused particular fear and anger among Unionists.

'I shall be at the Bank every day next week (except Wednesday),' Ken told the Taoiseach in a covering letter, 'and will be on call if you need me.'[29]

With the exception of the two omissions noted above, what became known as the Taoiseach's 'Tralee Speech' was otherwise, word for word, Ken Whitaker's draft.

Reaction to the speech was mainly positive, from constitutional Nationalists such as John Hume, and from the Northern Ireland prime minister, James Chichester-Clark, and from a relieved British government, which had viewed the Taoiseach's 13 August speech and its reference to 'no longer standing by' with some apprehension. However, dissenting voices in the cabinet, especially that of Neil Blaney, posed the question who really represented government policy on Northern Ireland, giving rise, as one media report stated, to 'a perilous and improper situation'.[30] The Taoiseach's invidious position within the cabinet was not lost on Ken Whitaker. 'If only public speaking on this extremely delicate matter could be reserved to yourself, and, subject to your approval, to the M/EA [minister for external affairs]',[31] he wrote to Lynch.

Ken immediately set about giving practical application to his recommendations, turning his attention to formulating the genesis of what he hoped would be a 'constitutional setting that might be acceptable to a majority in the North'.[32] As secretary of the Department of Finance, he had contributed to the work of the Constitutional Review Group, often crossing swords with the minister, Charles Haughey, in the process. While Haughey now spoke in theoretical terms of fast-tracking national reunification, Ken Whitaker, with deeper knowledge and more comprehensive understanding of the impediments involved, applied himself to more realistic considerations and issues. For example, when Jack Lynch proposed to establish a study group under the direction of the attorney general, he argued: 'One of the crucial elements in any possible solution is how to keep the British £100 million-a-year for the North and to work this requirement into a constitutional arrangement [which] demands some knowledge of Common Markets, Customs Unions etc – economic information not normally possessed by lawyers'.[33] Instead, he had arranged for the constitution review paper, already under preparation in Finance, to be revised to incorporate the bread-and-butter considerations relating to unity and, in particular, the need for retention of the £100 million British subsidy. 'On the possible solution of the re-unification problem', he wrote to the two Finance officers, Denis Maher and

Kevin Murphy, who, under his direction, were engaged in the compilation of the study:

> I have, as you know, emphasised in the past the need for a fresh and flexible approach. I wonder is there a possible basis for retention by N.I. of the financial and economic advantages of being in the UK in some form of common market/customs union or even economic union relationship between N.I. and GB which left sufficient political sovereignty with N.I. to enable it to participate in a confederation or federation with us?[34]

On 27 October 1969 he wrote to the Taoiseach 'to give you a rough and ready explanation of the proposition that is taking place in my mind and will be reflected in the Finance paper',[35] and requested that he make the letter available also to the ministers for finance and external affairs.

A month later, on 24 November 1969, Ken presented the four-part study, entitled *The Constitutional Position of Northern Ireland* – significantly, directly to the Taoiseach rather than to Minister for Finance Charles Haughey; as he wrote, 'Maher will be sending the paper up the line in Finance.'[36] Little did he know that by this point Charles Haughey was pursuing a course of action diametrically opposed to that which Ken advocated. Parts one to three of the report set out a historical and analytical overview of the reunification issue. Part four 'outline[d] our ideas on a possible constitutional setting for an acceptable form of re-unification'.[37] Detailed and meticulous, without sentiment or rancour, the study bore the hallmarks of Ken Whitaker's impartial, at times bluntly honest and, in some respects, prophetic appraisal of future relationships between the Republic, Northern Ireland and Britain. Perhaps for the explicit benefit of some of the Taoiseach's cabinet colleagues, the paper reiterated the official government policy eschewing the use of force as a means of unification, and accepting the long-term nature of such a process: 'We must for the foreseeable future relegate to the background our hopes for a united Ireland in the form of a thirty-two county Republic ... We must accept, therefore, that any institutional arrangements must start with modest beginnings.'[38]

The financial and economic practicalities of unity were starkly presented, the report noting:

> (a) that a majority of the population in Northern Ireland would not agree to any reunification proposals entailing a loss of material advantages. This would be a stumbling block for Catholics as well as Protestants.
> (b) that the people of the Republic do not desire unity strongly enough to undertake the subsidisation of Northern standards now financed by Britain (about £100 million).[39]

The constitutional framework suggested in the study comprised two states, one of twenty-six counties and one of six counties, linked by a 'federal authority' which 'would constitute the apex or roof' in unifying both parts of Ireland, with each component state retaining a degree of sovereignty – including, for the North, the power of fiscal autonomy and the power to legislate. Britain would not be 'let off the hook' by gaining financially from 'a permanent solution to the Irish question' and would not be totally relieved of its financial liability towards the North. The report emphasized that the British government would not be asked to contravene its commitment not to end partition without the consent of the Northern Ireland government, and that any campaign, either national or international, to force its hand was futile. British goodwill towards the achievement of an eventual agreed settlement between the two parts of Ireland was as much as could be hoped for in the present climate. Many of Ken's suggestions were far-seeing; some remain relevant today, especially in relation to the formation of future 'all-Ireland' political structures. The financial and economic implications of

Irish unity became the focus of further studies which he subsequently undertook in collaboration with the Department of Finance and the Economic and Social Research Institute.

By mid-October the opposition was pressing for a debate on the situation in Northern Ireland in the Dáil, which Ken considered 'unfortunate' timing. The Stormont government had its hands full with dissidents, both inside and outside the cabinet, and any untoward comments emanating from the Dáil, he felt, would merely strengthen the hands of Loyalist extremists. He advised Jack Lynch to proceed with caution. 'The Unionists are naturally finding it difficult to swallow everything at once and [William] Craig must have a good deal of support from those who think the RUC and B Specials have got a hard and sudden knock. It would be tragic if anything we said or did just now built up new tensions and strengthened the Protestant extremists.'[40] Not being, as he put it, 'a Stormont-abolitionist',[41] it was better, he advised the Taoiseach, 'to have a representative Parliament there – the political opinion of which we and Northern moderates may hope to see altered in time – and a regime reformed in its policy towards Catholics, than to have no organs of public representation or government in the area and to be confronted with British administration'.[42] He urged Lynch to hold off the Dáil debate for as long as he could.

The debate finally took place on 22 October. The first since the outbreak of violence in Northern Ireland in August, it was of particular significance both inside and outside the country. The Taoiseach sent Ken a copy of the speech he proposed to make; word by word, sentence by sentence, Ken carefully perused it, making suggestions in both content and tone, changing expressions he considered provocative, favouring 'a mild tribute to Callaghan' for a speech he had made at Brighton that had included 'cryptic' references to lifting relations between the Republic and the British government to 'a new plane' and the 'inevitability' of Irish unity. 'I would go lightly on references to the Stormont Government', he advised, suggesting that the Taoiseach 'make clear that we are prepared to explore all possibilities . . . [that] our aim is a scrupulously fair deal for all, that we have no interest in extending the domination of Dublin; that we want to see religious freedom and civil liberties and rights protected for all Irishmen.'[43]

While it was received positively in most quarters, the speech did little to curb the militant and anti-democratic elements simmering within the cabinet. Neil Blaney made no secret of his contempt for Jack Lynch and covertly worked to undermine and reverse the policy to which he had committed the government. Recently released British and Irish state papers from the period reveal the extent of the subterfuge practised, which gave rise to much rumour and speculation as to the real motivations of those concerned. Both Blaney and Haughey were allegedly in direct contact with known IRA leaders in Dublin, and 'a deal was made that the IRA would be facilitated in the movement of arms to Northern Ireland and, in return, they would call off the burning and destruction of the property of foreign wealthy residents'.[44] At the same time, in October 1969, at his home in Kinsealy, Haughey held a meeting with the British ambassador, Sir Andrew Gilchrist, to offer NATO bases in Ireland in exchange for a commitment from the British government on Irish unity. Such machinations raised the question whether expressed concern for the plight of Northern Nationalists was merely a front for more personal and possibly sinister political motivations, as well as a means of diverting social and political agitation by the IRA from the Republic to the streets of Belfast and Derry. But it was a committee established by the government at the height of the Northern Troubles in August 1969 to 'provide aid for the victims of the current unrest in the Six Counties',[45] subsequently 'hijacked' by Haughey and Blaney allegedly to purchase arms for the Provisional IRA, that was to cause a seismic political upheaval in the South.

Much has been written about the events that led to the sacking of two senior government ministers, Charles Haughey and Neil Blaney, on 6 May 1970 and their subsequent trial and acquittal that October on the charge of smuggling arms for the IRA, and about the possible involvement of other members of the government, public servants and security personnel in the Machiavellian web which enveloped the events. As a public servant, Ken might well have been expected to steer clear of the political turmoil that engulfed the government and the country during 1970 as these dramatic revelations unfolded. But Ken Whitaker was no ordinary public servant. As the initiator of the change in official government policy towards Northern Ireland, he was 'totally opposed' to military intervention; and as a supporter of democracy, he viewed the insubordination of cabinet ministers as bordering on anarchy and betrayal. His support for and belief in the integrity of Jack Lynch as he tried to hold the government together, under the most difficult and unprecedented circumstances, was unwavering. In retrospect, as Ken recalls, 'the country and his party were fortunate that he [Jack Lynch] was Taoiseach at the time of the arms crisis. The decisive action then taken and the widespread loyalty he enjoyed avoided a real risk of internal division and even of civil disorder.' To this it should be added that the country and its people were fortunate to have Ken Whitaker to advise the Taoiseach during these traumatic times. On the dismissal of Haughey and Blaney from the government, Ken's verdict is unequivocal: 'He [Jack Lynch] had to take them out if democracy was to be preserved.'

Ken's work at the Central Bank, complicated by a lengthy bank strike during 1970 and 'my *deep* anxiety about the economic situation and the need for comprehensive and sustained Government initiatives to bring it under control',[46] occupied him during most of that year. But Northern Ireland remained an ever-present concern. In a postscript to one of his memos on the economy to the Taoiseach, he offered: 'If ever I can be of use in making discreet soundings on possible N.I. solutions, I hope you will call on me.'[47]

And the Taoiseach was more than anxious that the governor should continue to pursue such contacts, especially among his Unionist acquaintances. These included Terence O'Neill, with whom Ken continued to correspond during 1970 and 1971, sharing with the Taoiseach the former prime minister's views on developments within Northern Ireland.

There was much to consider. By mid-1970, better armed and growing in strength, the Provisional IRA had become a major force on the streets of the North. Throughout its decades-long campaign of killing and car-bombing, it would be matched in violence and intimidation by its Loyalist counterparts, the Ulster Volunteer Force (UVF) and the Ulster Defence Association (UDA). By September 1970 some hundred bombs had exploded throughout the North. Not all the developments were negative: new political parties came into being, notably in August 1970 a new Nationalist party, the Social, Democratic and Labour Party (SDLP), and the Alliance Party, which sought to attract members from both sides of the political divide. However, proceeding cautiously with a series of reforms forced upon it by the British, the Unionist government felt the full force of a Loyalist backlash led by Ian Paisley, whose election to Stormont in 1970 triggered a Prevention of Incitement to Hatred Act and forced moderate Unionism to become more hard-line. In March 1971 James Chichester-Clark, who had succeeded Terence O'Neill as prime minister, resigned and was succeeded by Brian Faulkner. In Britain, meanwhile, the June 1970 general election saw the Labour government of Harold Wilson unexpectedly defeated by the Conservatives under Edward Heath. In the Republic, after the revelations of the arms trial, Jack Lynch appeared to regain control of his party, and a political coup was averted. Lynch's control over Fianna Fáil was further copper-fastened amid turbulent scenes at the 1971 party's Ard Fheis, when the extreme policies on Northern Ireland propounded by the maverick element in the party were publicly repudiated.

In June 1971, through the chairman of Allied Irish Banks Group, E. M. R. (Mon) O'Driscoll, Ken was invited to a private meeting with the governor of Northern Ireland, the New Zealand-born Lord Grey. Ever scrupulous and mindful of his status as a public servant, Ken informed the Taoiseach that Lord Grey 'would like to meet some reasonable, non-political character from the South . . . I hope it won't be considered treasonable of me to go. I think it could be useful . . . I would not wish to go, however, if you thought such a private meeting could do harm in any way.'[48] Contacts at official level between Irish and British civil servants were in abeyance at the time, owing mainly to the creation of ex-'B Special' gun clubs and the issue and legalizing of thousands of gun licences by the Stormont government. Contact at 'unofficial' level thus became vital in maintaining a line of communication between North and South, and Lynch readily agreed to the proposal. Before the meeting, Ken discussed various policy options with the Taoiseach, including 'the difficulties about a tri-partite approach [to Northern Ireland] with which', as Lynch noted, 'you are familiar and know that if a federal solution did emerge as a possibility we would hope that it would lead to the final solution'.[49]

Two days before the meeting, in a four-page memo to the Taoiseach entitled 'N.I. – A Possible Solution',[50] Ken set down on paper a compelling and balanced assessment of the prevailing situation in relation to Northern Ireland and a possible long-term solution. In the document Ken offered an alternative to the perceived notion 'that the only hope of political change appears to lie in violence. How can the minority', he asked, 'be brought to reject violence in favour of a constructive approach? Only by giving them hope that there is a prospect of substantial political change; that the light does shine at the end, however long that tunnel may be.'[51] Envisaging a timescale covering between fifty and seventy-five years, he outlined a step-by-step progress towards Irish reunification. The first step was an immediate declaration by Dublin, Belfast and London 'of willingness to foresee and facilitate the complete re-unification of Ireland by the year 2025 (or 2050)'. He then presented a timetable for a phased transfer of political power from London and Dublin to a new all-Ireland federal authority, 'with the minimum disturbance of economic and financial links', to be completed within ten years. The federal authority would initially exercise powers transferred to it from Dublin and London, supplemented by additional powers following a joint-government review every ten years. It would consist of a dozen representatives from each of the parliaments of Northern Ireland and the Republic, have a unanimously elected Irish-born chairman, and be financed by the Irish and British governments. The final transfer of power would take place not later than 2025 (or 2050), at which point the federal authority would be renamed the 'State of Ireland'. Provision for regional authorities, corresponding to the two Irish former states, with a common commitment to non-discriminatory and socially progressive policies in both, was also proposed.

Over the following quarter-century the scheme became the template for future discussions and adaptations by governments, groups, interest groups, vested interests and individuals, eventually culminating in the Good Friday Agreement of 1998. Over forty years after he wrote it, one can only surmise how much death, destruction and distress Ireland, North and South, might have been saved had Ken Whitaker's 1971 proposal for peace been adopted.

Ken's meeting with the Northern Ireland governor was held on 8 July in Mon O'Driscoll's home in Belfast. Ken found Lord Grey 'urbane, dispassionate, a shrewd judge of people and their motives', noting that he was 'cautiously frank in his criticisms of various individuals', that he was convinced 'that the Orangemen were incorrigible' and that he believed present thinking on both sides was outmoded. 'Do we perhaps talk too much about

Ireland's woes?' the governor asked him. 'One ought not let talk be a substitute for action'[52] – a sentiment undoubtedly shared by his visitor. Ken presented his proposals, omitting, as he pointedly noted to Jack Lynch, those regarding the establishment of an all-Ireland federal authority. Grey agreed with him that 'the time seemed to have come for starting a quiet and confidential dialogue between the Governments on the political question'.[53] Impressed by his visitor's appreciation of and rational attitude to the complexities of the northern problem, Grey suggested a further meeting where Ken's ideas could be heard by a wider audience. By the time a second meeting was arranged, Ken had taken advantage of an IMF meeting in Washington to discuss his proposal document with the eminent economist, civil servant and banker Sir Eric Roll, who offered to bring them to the attention of the British prime minister, Edward Heath, and the home secretary, William Whitelaw.

By the time of Ken's second meeting with the governor, on 14 October, the situation in the North had deteriorated gravely. Following the shooting dead of two men in controversial circumstances in Derry by the British army in July, the SDLP withdrew from government and announced a campaign of civil disobedience, while Ian Paisley announced the establishment of a new Democratic Unionist Party (DUP). In August, provoked by the unrelenting IRA campaign of killing and bombing, the Stormont government introduced internment without trial. In dawn raids on Catholic enclaves more than three hundred men, almost exclusively Nationalists, were arrested, many later interned in Long Kesh prison. Many other Nationalists headed across the border; of those who remained, many became more radicalized, some joining the ranks of the Provisional IRA. Strenuously opposed by Jack Lynch, internment caused a major rift in Anglo-Irish relations, making the 'unofficial' contacts Ken Whitaker had established in the North and in Britain ever more vital.

The second meeting with the governor again took place in Belfast, hosted by Mon O'Driscoll. The meeting was also attended by James Callaghan, then shadow home secretary; Lieutenant-General Sir Harry Tuzo, the newly appointed general officer commanding in Northern Ireland; Bishop Philbin, Roman Catholic bishop of Clogher, accompanied by Monsignor Mullaly; the Reverend Eric Gallagher of the Methodist Church; Howard Smith, the UK government representative in Northern Ireland; and Maurice Hayes, the newly appointed Community Relations Commissioner in the North. Ken's notes provide an intriguing insight into the topics discussed and opinions expressed, especially by James Callaghan. In a private meeting before dinner with the shadow home secretary, Ken outlined his views regarding the North and what he called the 'artificial entity' that had been created there, whereby 'the Unionist Party could look forward to being in power for ever', and the necessity to make clear that the reunification of Ireland 'was a desideratum which Britain accepted and would support, as an ultimate objective to be reached by agreement in Ireland'.[54] Callaghan's idea for the establishment of a Council of Ireland, provided it had real powers from the outset, Ken considered a useful basis from which his proposal of a federal authority could evolve. Callaghan told him that he and many of his Labour Party colleagues 'saw a united Ireland as the only long-term solution', and ventured the opinion that even Conservative leaders such as Edward Heath and Reginald Maudling were not 'dyed-in-the-wool Unionists'. He also, as Ken recorded, stated that 'he would need to test out the ideas I had put forward, which were close to his own, on some representative Protestants'.[55] Discussions on various potential political formats then took place, including the possibility of the Republic rejoining the British Commonwealth. This latter proposal was one supported by some of Ken's contacts in the British administration, as giving 'greater impetus to an ultimate United Ireland . . . a gesture that would cost Dublin nothing but would be more effective than all the bombs ever thrown in terminating our sad love–hate relationship'.[56] However, as Ken told James Callaghan, 'any formal constitutional change, such as participation in a British Isles Federation or a return to the Commonwealth, would certainly be unacceptable to the Republic'.[57]

Over dinner, discussions continued, as Ken noted, 'with considerable frankness'.[58] When they turned to the question of internment and how to get the SDLP off the hook from refusing to talk until it was discontinued, he took little part, although, as he frankly noted, 'I privately shared the general view that no government which had introduced internment (whether wisely or not) could be expected to release known gunmen back on to the streets'.[59] The only way out of the internment stalemate, it was felt, was to release those presumed innocent and to ensure a clearly independent judicial process for the indicted. General Tuzo admitted that the security task on the ground would be made easier if a new political initiative were forthcoming. Lord Grey was of the opinion that 'Unionism was crumbling away' and looked to the EEC as one way of solving the Northern Ireland problem, while Bishop Philbin said that Catholic support for the IRA tended to ebb and flow and that there was a 'general weariness' among the Catholic population at the indiscriminate bombing and disruption of daily life. Mr Callaghan 'felt strongly that the British Government should take its courage in its hands and come forward with a political initiative', and urged Howard Smith to convey that view to the home secretary. He also, as Ken recorded, 'expressed his desire to maintain the personal contacts he had made under Mr O'Driscoll's roof'.[60]

In November 1972, when in the process of writing *A House Divided: The Dilemma of Northern Ireland*, James Callaghan requested permission to quote some of the ideas about the future of Northern Ireland which Ken had expressed at their meeting. 'As you are aware, imitation is the sincerest form of flattery,'

Callaghan told him. Welcoming the use of his proposals in the book, Ken refused any accreditation on the basis, as he informed Callaghan, that 'some day I may write my own memoirs'.[61]

By the time of this second meeting in October 1971, daily gun battles between the IRA and the British army on the streets were commonplace and public order had broken down. Twelve people had died on the first day of internment alone. The apparent level of toleration being shown by governments and public alike to the violence Ken found personally abhorrent and difficult to comprehend. In a letter written (in French) to Cardinal Conway from his holiday home in north Mayo, his revulsion and frustration are palpable.

> It is members of the IRA who lead the population and even the Southern Government by the nose. They think they will be looked on as 'the Resistance Heroes' and will hold a frightening power in the future. The SDLP have abandoned the Parliament and left it to the men of violence without attaining any satisfactory political option to put before the public.
>
> I am not against pacific resistance, but its aims must be precise. It is not enough to demand that Stormont be abolished without precisely stating what must replace it.[62]

In the wake of internment, Ken found it, as he wrote, 'monstrous that M and F (Maudling and Faulkner) could speak of "democracy" in Northern Ireland when, from the beginning, there was only one political party given over to a secret society'.[63]

His criticism stretched also to the apparent inaction of the Taoiseach, who, he maintained, seemed 'neither to have the will nor the government support to implement a rational policy'. Referring to his own proposal for the establishment of a representative parliament, government and administration, with social justice for all in Northern Ireland and financial support from both British and Irish governments, leading to the establishment of a federal entity or a Council of Ireland, 'someone else', he wrote, 'must perfect it'. The advantages emanating from such a proposal could be enormous: 'peace, prosperity, everything which would boost the economy and end social discrimination. However, should it be otherwise and violence wins, the situation will get worse and worse.'[64]

Such constitutional proposals, however logical and fair, seemed remote, even irrelevant, to the day-to-day hatred and fear that gripped the ordinary inhabitants of the dingy, terraced, working-class streets of the Falls, Shankill Road and Short Strand in Belfast and the high-rise Catholic enclaves of Derry. There Loyalist and Nationalist alike took refuge in the manic exhortations and violent acts of their militant self-professed 'protectors'. As the dustbin lids from the Catholic ghettos sounded their warning and the Lambeg drums their triumphalism, such calls for a political formula for reconciliation, justice and peace appeared to be lost in the din.

As far as Ken Whitaker was concerned, however, there could be no let-up in the search to find a way out of the terrible and terrifying impasse. The distinct lack of personal affinity between Edward Heath and Jack Lynch, reflected in their torrid public exchanges over internment, was barely modified by their meeting in London some weeks after the introduction of the policy, a meeting described by Sir John Peck, British ambassador to Ireland, as 'a dialogue of the deaf'.[65] Heath sought a security solution, Lynch a political one, and contacts at official government level remained strained. Against the background of an intensification of paramilitary violence and political paralysis, by November Ken was back on the trail of peace, this time armed with a strongly worded personal letter to the Taoiseach:

Should the Government not make a strong statement against the horror of the IRA campaign in the North – one dealing *exclusively* with their activities, which are inhuman as well as senseless? They are making Irish unity impossible, by alienating British public (and political) opinion and causing the deepest bitterness amongst the people of the North. I'm afraid that the Government are thought to be ambivalent, if not indulgent.[66]

Stung into action, Jack Lynch delivered a speech to the Fianna Fáil national executive which, as he informed Ken, 'covered the subject matter you suggested',[67] and received positive reaction in the British and Irish media. In a handwritten note to the Taoiseach, Ken urged 'that we be *seen* to be doing more to prevent the IRA using this state as a sanctuary', even suggesting that Irish troops should be recalled from United Nations duty in Cyprus to strengthen border patrols. There was, he told Lynch, 'still an impression out there that the Government is ineffective or ambivalent in relation to the IRA'.[68]

Behind the scenes he continued to exchange views and work on the development of constitutional remedies with his contacts in both the Northern Ireland and British administrations. Among them was Dr G. B. Newe, a respected Catholic community social worker who in September 1971 had been appointed the first Catholic minister in a Stormont government, and 'whose work and thinking had a profound influence on all aspects of social service work not only in Northern Ireland but also beyond its boundaries'.[69] While Dr Newe was criticized 'for swimming against the abstentionist Nationalist tide',[70] Ken found in the newly appointed minister 'a kindred spirit and an upright objective man, who shared the idea of a united Ireland, not in the political sense but unity in cooperation, and an urgent desire for the return of reason, order and peace to the region of our birth'.[71] Under no illusion as to the task before him, Newe confided to Ken, 'It is frightening that so many people expect me to work a miracle,' and urged him to continue his efforts in the South. 'You have the ear of the man who matters in the Republic and, somehow, we must find a way out of the present mess and the dangers that threaten all Ireland.'[72] In addition to Dr Newe, Ken continued to liaise with Ken Bloomfield, under-secretary at the Northern Ireland Office, Sir Cecil Bateman, former secretary of the Northern Ireland cabinet, Norman Dugdale, permanent secretary at the Ministry of Health, Paddy Shea, permanent secretary at the Ministry of Education, and Professor Norman Gibson of the University of Ulster. The Conservative MP David James (a relation of the Leslie family of Castle Leslie, County Monaghan) was instrumental in having Ken's united Ireland solution placed before the Conservative Party leader, while Sir Leslie O'Brien, governor of the Bank of England and a personal friend of Edward Heath, and Sir John Peck, British ambassador to Ireland – all, as Ken attested, 'men of the very highest integrity and quality'[73] – ensured that his views and proposals reached the centre of the British government.

Relationships formed with such trusted intermediaries did much to ensure that the information and advice reaching 'the top men' in London and in Dublin was reliable and unbiased. Unencumbered by party-political considerations, through their meetings and correspondence this group formed a sounding board for policy initiatives and reform proposals in the wider Anglo-Irish context. As the North became more and more deeply engulfed in sectarian conflict, and relationships between the two sovereign governments increasingly strained, such contacts were often the only form of communication. With cool, experienced and objective minds, these men searched for a reasonable and workable long-term alternative, as well as ways of dealing with more immediate issues such as internment and the containment of paramilitary influence. For Ken, such contacts were a continuation of the relationship he had started with Terence O'Neill, serving his determination to maintain lines of communication with Unionism through dialogue and friendship. In private discussions and correspondence he sounded out his British and Northern counterparts, enabling them to exchange views without any commitment or loss of face by either side on subjects whose discussion in public would have served only to raise the temperature even higher.

In addition to working through these ad hoc meetings, in 1972 Ken joined the British newspaper publisher David Astor, historian Robert Kee, Professor Lord Vaizey, Garret FitzGerald and author Thomas Pakenham, in becoming a founder member of the British–Irish Association (BIA). Established to promote greater understanding between the peoples of Britain and Ireland, this new body focused on conflict resolution and overcoming divisions in Northern Ireland. Drawing together government ministers, politicians, journalists, academics, trade unionists, business leaders, bankers, clergymen, writers, civil servants and economists, its annual conference provided an invaluable private venue where ideas could be freely exchanged and personal relationships developed across political divisions. The BIA evolved into a constructive forum that has helped to inform and drive policy in relation to North–South and Anglo-Irish relations to the present day, including through contributions from international leaders from Europe and North America, among them President Bill Clinton.

Few envisaged that 1972 would turn out to be the worst year of the Troubles, exacting a staggering death toll of five hundred men, women and children. Nor could it have been predicted that on Sunday, 30 January, thirteen marchers taking part in a civil rights protest in Derry would be shot dead, many as they fled, by British paratroopers. 'Bloody Sunday' and the resultant 'whitewashing' by the British government through the now disgraced Widgery Tribunal had, as one commentator recorded, 'a more damaging effect on Anglo-Irish relations than had the original Bloody Sunday of 1920'.[74] The terrible events added further urgency to Ken's behind-the-scenes search for a practical solution to the violence and chaos. 'The events of the weekend shocked us all,' G. B. Newe confided in a letter. 'Do what you can to keep party-political passions as calm as possible. It would help if your "boss-man" could somehow convey a message to our Opposition guys, to lay off me and others for a spell. I am doing all I can to influence my "boss-man" to speak quietly, moderately, even if firmly.'[75] Ken showed Newe's letter to Jack Lynch, who promised to 'see if I can discreetly do what he suggests'.[76]

Bloody Sunday shocked moderate Ireland. In Dublin on 2 February thousands of ordinary citizens spilled out from factories, offices, banks (including the Central Bank), building sites and homes to register their protest at the British Embassy on Merrion Square. After the marchers dispersed, the Embassy was burned to the ground by Provisional IRA infiltrators. Hoping, as he wrote, 'that reason would triumph over emotion', Ken extended his commiseration to the British ambassador, Sir John Peck. 'We have been rather busy emulating the Phoenix,' the ambassador stoically replied. Welcoming 'another chat', he assured Ken that he would not allow his 'spirit of reason . . . [to] be unduly clouded by emotion.'[77] Ken's own hope that the emotions aroused by Bloody Sunday would give way to a spirit of reason was the theme of a handwritten speech he prepared for delivery by the Taoiseach to the Fianna Fáil Ard Fheis in February. Once again it was Lynch's task to steady the ship of state, and yet again Ken Whitaker provided the words to help him: 'Emotion can too readily open the floodgates of bitterness, hate and violence, bringing more death, more estrangement and division and leaving wounds in the wind that may not heal within any timescale that matters to those alive today in these islands.'[78]

Reaffirming government policy on the North, as laid out in Tralee in September 1969 and approved at the 1970 Fianna Fáil Ard Fheis, the speech spelled out that 'we will have no part in bombing a million Protestants into a so-called "united" Ireland' but instead welcome 'a choice by Unionists to join us *now* in making and developing a new Ireland'.[79] Until that time comes, Ken wrote, the people of the Republic must show patience and be constructive in seeking 'to promote and facilitate our final union' and working towards suitable interim arrangements in the North 'set in the perspective of an ultimately reunited Ireland'.[80]

By the time this speech was delivered, British patience with Brian Faulkner's government was at breaking point. Stormont was seen as being as much part of the problem as any other element of the political situation: split and ineffective, stubbornly resistant to even minimum reforms, incapable of making political progress. The security situation was out of control, internment had failed to contain a rampant and emboldened IRA, Loyalists were more intransigent and dangerous than ever. Northern Ireland appeared to be on the threshold of anarchy. On 24 March Edward Heath announced the suspension of the Stormont parliament for one year (or until a more representative political entity could be devised), the imposition of direct rule from Westminster and the appointment of William Whitelaw, an engaging and consensus-driven high Tory, as secretary of state for Northern Ireland. The decision 'took us all by surprise', G. B. Newe confided to Ken; but it also provided them, as he wrote, with an incentive 'to get down to re-thinking attitudes and policies'.[81] For Ken, whose initial constitutional framework was based on the retention of a reformed Stormont, work towards achieving unity by consensus had now to accommodate a new political scenario. Already Heath had conceded one of the proposals he had advanced, the 'legitimate' right of Nationalists, North and South, to seek unification by peaceful and democratic means; and, more importantly, had stated that no British government would 'stand in the way' of the realization of that right. In a document entitled 'Draft Heads of Agreement' and dated June 1972, Ken presented a set of new proposals for both governments, which included the creation of a Northern Ireland Assembly – a precursor of developments to come.

The fall of Stormont fomented fear among Unionists of a 'sell-out' by the British government. Already talk in the North, as

G. B. Newe informed Ken, was 'that your man and the man in London are engaged in, or may become engaged in, some sort of "deal" involving unity. There is also an immense fear of the IRA.'[82] Ken accepted Newe's invitation to Belfast to meet a group of Catholics and Protestants who were anxious to air their fears in person 'to someone who could evaluate them and convey them to the "Boss Man"'.[83] Having cleared the trip with Jack Lynch, Ken travelled to Belfast to meet the group, which included Father Des Wilson, his brother Dr P. K. Wilson, the Reverend John Young, a Presbyterian minister, Terence Duncan, a Belfast businessman, and James Dickson, the husband of Anne Dickson MP. In his summary for the Taoiseach, Ken conveyed the fears expressed to him at the meeting: that London would do a deal with Dublin 'behind their backs'; that there was a tendency in the South to regard a united Ireland as an '*imminent*' possibility; that the IRA seemed to have freedom of movement and public speech in the Republic; that arms and explosives were being easily transferred across the border; and that the UDA was dangerous, well armed, organized and intent on causing serious trouble unless the IRA campaign was brought to an end. The newly established Special Criminal Court in the Republic, Ken informed the Taoiseach, was looked upon as a positive step towards meeting moderate Unionist concerns regarding security. The Taoiseach's subsequent article in the July issue of the influential American journal *Foreign Affairs*, in which he reiterated the government's policy of working for unity by consent and its intention of developing a positive relationship with Britain (especially in the context of an enlarged EEC), and referred to the possible replacement of the 1937 constitution by one guaranteeing explicit rights and liberties to all who lived in the 'new Ireland', reflected many of Ken's views and drew substantially on his advice.

The proroguing of Stormont and the imposition of direct rule heralded an attempt by the British, against the background of the worsening conflict, to engage with various factions and groups, both political and paramilitary. This extended to secret meetings between the new secretary of state and leading figures in both the IRA and the Loyalist paramilitary groups, held through a series of clandestine manoeuvres following a temporary ceasefire. This development, which had the approval of the British prime minister, was viewed askance in Ireland by the government, by most members of the opposition and by moderates on both sides of the divide, mainly for encouraging a belief that the British government was amenable to dealing with paramilitaries. The meetings, none the less, set a precedent which twenty-five years later would bring an end to the violent struggle in Northern Ireland, albeit at the expense of those who held the middle ground.

For Ken Whitaker, the secretary of state's action was the antithesis of his own approach of seeking a solution by consensual and constitutional means. As a public servant, however, he readily acknowledged that such decisions were the prerogative of governments and lay outside his domain. Before William Whitelaw's meeting with the IRA in London on 7 July 1972, Ken was invited to meet the secretary of state in Belfast. At their meeting Whitelaw discussed aspects of Ken's framework document on a united Ireland which had been given to him by David James MP. They met again in the Savoy Hotel in London at a dinner given in honour of the secretary of state by representatives of the City's banking and business community, hosted by Donal S. Carroll, chairman of Lloyds Bank, who also was a member of the board of directors of the Central Bank of Ireland. In the event Whitelaw's talks with IRA leaders proved unsuccessful and attention once again centred on constitutional dialogue between the two sovereign governments.

When the temporary ceasefire expired, the violence, both Republican and Loyalist, resumed with renewed and savage vigour, with tit-for-tat killings, mass parades by Loyalist paramilitaries and carnage resulting from IRA bombs, including

'Bloody Friday' on 21 July, when twenty-two devices exploded, killing eleven people in Belfast city centre, and an atrocity on 31 July in which six innocent victims lost their lives in the village of Claudy. Against this grim background, work towards formulating an alternative constitutional policy took on a new urgency. A flurry of correspondence and phone calls on the content and wording of various policy proposals took place between Ken and his Northern Ireland and UK contacts. On 18 July David James arranged for him to meet a number of key Conservative Party officials in the House of Commons, together with Frank Guckian, a prominent businessman from Derry, and David Wood from *The Times*. The Tory members expressed their dismay at the lack of contact between the Irish government and the Conservative Party generally, and at the refusal of the SDLP to enter talks, points that Ken brought to Jack Lynch's attention. He also pressed the Taoiseach to resist pressure to hold a referendum in the South, in conjunction with one proposed by William Whitelaw in the North, fearing that it would 'give a field day to extremists'. Better, he advised him, to have a special meeting of the Dáil and table a motion, supported by all parties, declaring their support for unity by agreement. To this end, he drafted notes for the Taoiseach's speech. Meanwhile, the British army's entry into 'no-go areas' of the Bogside and Creggan estates in Derry in 'Operation Motorman' in late July, and the dismantling of both Loyalist and Nationalist barricades in Derry and Belfast, for a time put the militants on the back foot and concentrated minds on political measures.

Attempts to persuade the SDLP to enter talks became a priority. G. B. Newe wrote to Gerry Fitt in July, urging him to 'find a formula to get to the conference table and really get stuck in' and warning that, in the light of the British government's willingness to engage with the IRA, if the party failed to respond, it risked 'becoming irrelevant'.[84] The SDLP's eventual agreement in August to take part in talks with the secretary of state and the other political parties was greeted with relief in both Irish and British political circles. A proposal Ken drafted for the establishment of a Council of Ireland, 'to which specific functions could gradually be transferred', and through which 'we could all creep up on a new and united Ireland',[85] were subsequently passed by Sir Leslie O'Brien to Edward Heath.

During August, from his holiday in Mayo, Ken continued to develop proposals leading towards a constitutional formula, from both a political and an economic perspective. The time was right, he told David James, 'to start with a cleaner sheet', and to construct 'a new treaty or agreement between the two sovereign states, governing the relationship of each to Northern Ireland and confirming whatever provisions are made for regional administration there, assuming these leave an opening for movement by agreement towards a united Ireland'.[86] Such an agreement, as he envisaged it, would be founded on conditions that enabled both traditions in Northern Ireland to work together for their mutual social and economic progress. All unofficial armies on the island of Ireland would be deemed to be illegal, and both countries would prevent any illegal organization from using their territory to carry out acts of violence or to prevent democratically agreed political change; there would be a withdrawal of all firearm licences and stringent regulations regarding the possession of firearms by individuals. Both sovereign governments, as well as elected representatives in the North, would agree to the formation of an acceptable police force. Security and law and order would remain the responsibility of the British government for at least ten years, as would the provision of capital to fund social welfare and other public services, including housing and unemployment relief. Unity by consent was to be a legitimate political aim, and the British government would not impede the establishment of a united Ireland once voted for by a majority. For the regional administration of Northern Ireland, Ken advocated an 'Assembly

... constituted in accordance with the system of proportional representation', for which elections would occur every five years. A number of commissions, each numbering not more than five people, drawn from the assembly and serving for a term of five years, would have responsibility for the daily administration of Northern Ireland, the chairmen of each commission meeting weekly as an executive council. An Irish Cooperation Council, comprising nominees of the Irish government and Northern Ireland executive council, with its own elected chairman, established by law in Britain and in the Republic, would coordinate economic and social policies for the island of Ireland.

David James offered to furnish the thoughts contained in Ken's document initially to William Whitelaw and Bill Deedes, an influential Tory backbencher. Ken, however, declined James's invitation to have his article published in *The Times* under his own name. Being, as he explained, a public servant, he could not publish anything of a political nature; 'better that I should go about things as unobtrusively as possible'.[87]

The document was subsequently forwarded to William Whitelaw, while Ken gave a copy to Jack Lynch. Emanating from a non-political source, it was of immense value to politicians, providing as it did a framework for a future constitutional solution. The document formed a basis for discussions held between Heath and Lynch at their subsequent meetings leading up to British and Irish entry into the EEC.

The Irish government's green paper, published that October, also encapsulated many of Ken's proposals, as did the document *The Future of Northern Ireland*, published by the secretary of state in November 1972. Building further on the proposals, the British government's white paper, *Northern Ireland Constitutional Proposals*, for the first time indicated a role in government for the Nationalist minority, the prospect of a Council of Ireland, the introduction of proportional representation and an 'Irish dimension' in the affairs of Northern Ireland. Ken welcomed it as 'a well-considered and well-balanced document, which, while satisfying no one fully, makes an irresistible appeal to reason . . . that every reasonable person must regard as balanced and progressive. I would expect that our Government should be able to respond to it positively.'[88]

While 'reasonable people' may well have welcomed such proposals, the IRA and extreme Unionists were less impressed, as evidenced by William Craig's subsequent outburst to his supporters declaring his readiness to 'shoot and kill' to retain Unionist majority rule. The proposals and attitudes enshrined in the white paper, however, were proof of how far along the road both sovereign governments had travelled in their realization that neither the old Republican ethos of Dublin nor London's colonial intransigence had a place in the future of Northern Ireland. While violence continued in the North, the feeling was that it had become more a question of law and order than an imminent civil war. This sea-change in attitude and understanding stemmed, in no small way, from the painstaking work conducted voluntarily and unobtrusively by Ken Whitaker.

11

Pathways to Peace
1973–98

For myself, I would be content with a degree of unity afforded by any political arrangement which resulted in Irishmen on their own sharing, in peace and harmony, in managing the affairs of the whole island within the EEC context. I would, on this basis, like to see Britain leave us all on this island to ourselves.

T. K. Whitaker[1]

AMID CONTINUED PARAMILITARY violence, Ulster Unionist Party dissension and division, and SDLP reticence, efforts by William Whitelaw to hammer out a political settlement pressed ahead. Despite his workload at the Central Bank in the lead-up to and following Ireland's accession to the EEC on 1 January 1973 and the continuing controversy over the construction of the Bank's Dame Street headquarters, Ken maintained his commitment to the North through correspondence and meetings with interested parties in Ireland and abroad. Yet somehow, as his family recall, life on the home front continued as normal. 'We had no idea, or any real understanding of what he was doing,' his son David recalls. 'We knew he was an adviser to Jack Lynch because we had often interruptions on our holidays, but it was never discussed at home. He was just Dad and as long as he fed you and bought you tennis balls and things . . . what did you care!' By the mid-1970s graduations, family weddings and the arrival of first grand-children were bringing not only additional demands on time, but also much joy and fulfilment into Ken's personal life.

In late February 1973 the Fianna Fáil government was surprisingly defeated in a general election by a coalition of Fine Gael and Labour. In relation to policy on Northern Ireland, the coalition was an unknown quantity. Differences towards the North existed not merely between the two coalition partners, but within Fine Gael itself. With the exception of Garret FitzGerald, appointed minister for foreign affairs, Ken had had little previous contact with members of the new government, especially in relation to the North. His contacts in the Northern Ireland administration expressed apprehension as to the line the new government was likely to pursue. Of special concern was the continuation of the relationship they had established, through Ken, with the previous Taoiseach. 'That I was able to communicate directly and indirectly with you, and in complete confidence, was of tremendous help and encouragement to me,'[2] G. B. Newe noted to Jack Lynch. Brian Walker of the New Ulster Movement in the North was not overly impressed with the men who would form the new front bench in Dublin, writing the previous autumn that he was 'appalled at their incredible ignorance of the Northern situation'.[3] To ease such apprehensions, Ken arranged for David James to meet Liam Cosgrave in March. James reported the new Taoiseach to be 'an excellent man with whom to discuss things'.[4]

Another significant change was the retirement of the British ambassador, Sir John Peck, with whom Ken had developed both a personal and a professional relationship, and his replacement by Sir Arthur Galsworthy. Neither the special relationship he enjoyed with the outgoing Taoiseach, Jack Lynch, nor the change in government, however, deterred Ken in his efforts to establish peace, and he simply resumed where he had left off with the previous administration.

The new government had barely assumed office when Garret FitzGerald received from Ken a summary of the 'ideas on desirable Northern Ireland arrangements' he had developed over the previous five years.[5] Aware of the opportunities, as well as the misgivings, especially among Unionists, raised by the British white paper, he was anxious that the change of government should not lead to any deterioration in an already fragile situation. In FitzGerald Ken had a like-minded and well-informed ally with whom he also shared a Northern Ireland background. They had collaborated in the past on economic matters, FitzGerald noting in his memoirs that Ken had 'become in a sense my mentor'.[6] Ken had initially tried to dissuade FitzGerald from entering politics, feeling that his forte lay in economic and political analysis, but, as FitzGerald wrote, 'he later admitted he was wrong on this issue!'[7] On his appointment as minister for foreign affairs, FitzGerald agreed that Ken would continue to pursue his unofficial contacts in Britain and Northern Ireland; or, as the latter puts it, 'he did not warn me off the pitch!' Ken's relationship with Conor Cruise O'Brien, the Labour Party's spokesman on the North, on the other hand, was, as he diplomatically notes, 'a more cautious one'.

As the North moved gradually and painfully towards the election of a new assembly, a process dominated by the thorny issues of power-sharing and the establishment of the proposed Council of Ireland, behind the scenes Ken continued his deliberations and scrutiny of various constitutional measures with his UK and Northern associates. At the behest of the British government and on the basis of a meeting with the Grand Master of the Orange Order, Willie Orr, David James sought Ken's views on the concept of a 'United Ireland united with the UK in the EEC' as a way 'to save Irish "face" and British "face"'.[8] As Ken duly informed the MP, however, the proposal being 'obviously intended to mean much more, it would, in my view, be quite unrealistic to expect any constitutional change in our relationship with Great Britain, other than, perhaps, a new treaty as outlined in my previous correspondence',[9] a reply which drew praise from Garret FitzGerald as having 'batted the ball neatly into his [David James's] court'.[10] On the issue of the Northern Ireland Emergency Powers Bill being debated at Westminster, while acknowledging that he might 'not be the best critic of the bill' because his 'personal bias is towards strict measures to uphold law and order against terrorist activities',[11] Ken registered his misgiving that the proposed powers of arrest it contained had no safeguard against the maltreatment of suspects in custody. He also expressed dismay that the UDA, which he deemed as 'patently paramilitary' as the IRA, had not been included in the list of proscribed organizations.

On 27 June elections to the new power-sharing assembly finally got under way. In an ominous repetition of the dilemma that had faced Terence O'Neill in 1969, Brian Faulkner entered the assembly leading a bitterly divided Ulster Unionist Party. The Nationalist vote was represented by the SDLP, while Republicans, mainly represented by Sinn Féin, chose to boycott the proceedings and their more extreme elements continued their campaign of violence. Despite the assembly's shortcomings, Ken remained hopeful that it would be able to operate, despite, as he wrote, the 'wrecking proclivities of the Loyalists'.[12] And, in spite of walkouts, assaults, rowdy conduct within and a campaign of violence and disorder by disaffected interests outside, the assembly managed to survive and achieve agreement on most issues. Ken extended his congratulations to William Whitelaw for having 'offset Lloyd George's mischief'; the secretary of state acknowledged in reply 'our talks and the encouragement you gave me'.[13] Whitelaw's tenure in Northern Ireland was, however, to be shortlived and, to Ken's dismay, in December 1973 he was unexpectedly replaced by Francis Pym.

On 6 December 1973 a milestone was reached in the protracted negotiations on the future of Northern Ireland. The

British and Irish governments, together with members of the new Northern Ireland Executive, met at Sunningdale in Berkshire to finalize agreement on the composition and functions of the proposed Council of Ireland, the constitutional status of Northern Ireland, and security cooperation between North and South. The Council of Ireland was to prove a divisive issue. Even a token involvement accorded to the Republic in the affairs of Northern Ireland was a step too far for extreme Unionists. Eventually agreement was reached on a formula not far removed from that originally suggested by Ken: a body with executive functions comprising seven Northern and seven Southern ministers, with a consultative body of thirty members drawn from the Irish parliament and thirty from the Northern assembly.

For Ken Whitaker the Sunningdale Agreement, as he wrote to Garret FitzGerald, 'was a great triumph for reason and fairness'.[14] His contribution behind the scenes leading towards the agreement was acknowledged by the Taoiseach, Liam Cosgrave, as having 'paved the way for the greater understanding that happily now exists between Northern politicians and ourselves',[15] after years of conflict and disillusionment. On 1 January 1974 a power-sharing executive comprising representatives of the Ulster Unionist, SDLP and Alliance parties, with Brian Faulkner as chief minister and Gerry Fitt, leader of the SDLP, as deputy chief minister, took office. But agreement at Sunningdale by the 'middle ground' on both sides of the sectarian divide did not translate into agreement on the ground in Northern Ireland. Despite the goodwill of the world, the brave efforts of the power-sharing parties in Stormont were no match for the intransigence and deep-seated hatred of their opponents and the violence that followed. The ensuing legal challenge mounted in Dublin over the constitutional status of Northern Ireland, as set out in the Sunningdale Agreement, confirmed Unionist suspicions and fears of the Republic's designs on the North. A general election in February saw the return of anti-Sunningdale candidates to

Westminster, and on 15 May a strike orchestrated by the Ulster Workers Council, involving roadblocks, carjacking and intimidation, brought Northern Ireland to a standstill. It was the final straw that broke the back of both the Sunningdale Agreement and the Northern Ireland power-sharing assembly. Bombs killing thirty-two people in Monaghan and Dublin further demonstrated the resolve of extreme Loyalism, aided on that occasion by elements in the British secret service, to oppose any diminution of their power. On 28 May 1974 Brian Faulkner resigned and the Northern Ireland Assembly was dissolved.

The fall of the assembly was a bitter setback for Ken and his collaborators. Five years of painstaking work to arrive at a formula whereby North and South could exist in a more harmonious relationship were wiped out. As his friend Ken Bloomfield wrote, however, 'there were lessons to be learned by all of us', and he urged his namesake to keep the channels of communication open, or else 'all will be deafened by the tramp of marching men'.[16] The lessons to be learned were clear. The territorial claim in the Irish constitution, upheld by the Supreme Court ruling, did not merely, as one Ulster commentator noted, 'put the tin hat on Sunningdale',[17] but guaranteed continued Loyalist opposition to the emergence of any North–South political entity for the foreseeable future. Meanwhile the IRA's campaign of violence, and the perception – albeit hardly justified, especially in view of the firm law and order stance adopted by the coalition government – that it was allowed the run of the country south of the border, contributed further to Loyalist intransigence. As the violence continued in the aftermath of Sunningdale and the Ulster Workers' Council strike, such sentiments also began to percolate into the more moderate Unionist mindset. It was a time to draw breath, take stock and start again.

During 1975 and 1976 Ken continued to hold talks and share ideas with many like-minded people in the North who were outside the official organs of government, but close enough to influence the policy-makers. 'It is useful at times to talk to someone who knows the vernacular of cabinet-making,' wrote Maurice Hayes, another of Ken's contacts, 'while remaining suitably distanced from both the trees and the wood!'[18] Ken's observations on the post-Sunningdale situation were also discussed within government circles in Ireland, North and South, and in Britain. 'We found your questions and your responses more realistic than those which we generally get. You gave us more ideas than perhaps you knew . . . and we are determined to follow them up,' Dr John Oliver, a Northern Ireland civil servant, acknowledged.[19] Outside the political arena, Ken facilitated contacts and meetings between officials from various government bodies in the South and their counterparts in the North, such as Paddy Shea, chairman of Enterprise Ulster, a statutory body founded in 1973 to promote job creation in environmental, amenity, cultural, community and social areas. Ken chaired the first meeting of Co-operation North, established in 1978, to stimulate better cross-border understanding and friendship among state-sponsored and private businesses, trade unions and voluntary bodies. He also chaired a confidential committee, composed of representatives from the departments of education in the Republic, Northern Ireland and the UK, charged with broadening the history curriculum in secondary schools in the three jurisdictions, to help alleviate bias and prejudice and to promote direct contact between pupils from different traditions.

In March 1976 James Callaghan succeeded Harold Wilson as Labour prime minister and appointed Roy Mason secretary of state for Northern Ireland. Mason introduced a tougher line on security and law and order, including the withdrawal of 'special category' status for IRA prisoners, which led to the 'dirty' protests and eventually to the hunger strikes. In June 1977 a general election in Ireland saw the return of a Fianna Fáil government, led by Jack Lynch, and the political rehabilitation of Charles Haughey, appointed minister for health and for social welfare.

While in opposition Fianna Fáil had reverted to the old-style Republican rhetoric promoted by Haughey and others in the party, as a platform from which to undermine Jack Lynch's authority. Continuing to voice this more aggressive approach in office, they now demanded Britain's withdrawal from the North. Contacts between the two prime ministers resumed but, given Labour's vulnerability in the Commons and the worsening economic situation in the Republic, there was little likelihood of any formal initiative either to resolve the political stalemate or to bring about an end to the violence.

Following his resignation from the Central Bank in 1976, despite his many other public voluntary commitments (see chapter 13) and his appointment to the Senate, Ken's commitment to the North continued. In view of the lack of progress on the official front, he sought a way out of the political vacuum which, to his personal dismay, continued to be filled by paramilitary atrocities. Between 1975 and 1976 almost six hundred lives were lost. In July 1976 the IRA's assassination of the newly appointed British ambassador to Ireland, Sir Christopher Ewart-Biggs, near his private residence in County Dublin gave the seemingly unending horror another dimension. At the request of Garret FitzGerald, and alongside the author Thomas Pakenham, Ken became a trustee of the Ewart-Biggs Trust, a writers' peace prize established as a memorial to the murdered ambassador. In 2001, however, he felt obliged to withdraw from the trusteeship on the basis, as he then indicated, 'that it was unwise and inequitable to be prepared to support a whole series of lectures on the sensitive issues relating to Northern Ireland by the able but eccentric Conor Cruise O'Brien',[20] whose opposition to the IRA had by then inexplicably extended to encompass the SDLP, a stance that Ken considered not conducive to the ethos of the Trust (O'Brien would later repudiate the peace process *tout court* in favour of extreme Unionism).

Following Brian Faulkner's sudden death in a riding accident in

February 1977, Unionism seemed to rest in the hands of extremists. At Westminster, Labour's slim majority in the House of Commons rendered the government's survival dependent on the Unionist members of parliament; and where the future of Northern Ireland was concerned, political expediency seemed destined to prevail. On the Nationalist side, with no political outlet or platform, the SDLP was in danger of becoming powerless and irrelevant. Its deputy leader, John Hume, sought to internationalize the Northern Ireland situation, with a particular effort in the United States to counter the support given to the IRA by the Irish American diaspora, and successfully engaged the committed help of a coterie of influential Irish American politicians.

Ken remonstrated at the lack of political movement at government level, and lamented the absence of a political forum in which democratically elected politicians in the North could express themselves. 'They need our encouragement to stay active in the search for a just and lasting peace. We must give them our backing or leave the field to savagery.'[21] Not content, as he told an audience at the newly established Centre for Peace and Reconciliation at Glencree in County Wicklow, 'to stay frozen in the old moulds', he was open to discussion of any possible way out of the stalemate. An independent Northern Ireland might well be, as he outlined in a 1977 paper entitled 'Northern Ireland: Some Financial Considerations', 'the best starting point towards building a genuinely united and co-operative all-Ireland community. In this age of "women's lib" we should have learnt by now that even cohabitation, not to mention marriage, if it is to be tolerable and stable, must be based on equality of status.'[22] His paper was subsequently published as a reference in a new study, *Beyond the Religious Divide*, devised by members of the UDA, spearheaded by Glenn Barr and John McMichael in what may have been a first inclination of paramilitary thinking towards a political alternative to violence.

In May 1979 Margaret Thatcher swept into power in Britain as Europe's first elected female prime minister. A staunch believer in and defender of the United Kingdom of Great Britain and Northern Ireland, she was intolerant of anything that undermined that principle. While open to initiatives to dilute the Unionist political monopoly in the North, she would not, as she categorically stated on a visit there, 'consider any plans for the political future of this part of the UK which could result in the weakening of the Union',[23] a statement which, in the context of the situation then prevailing, Ken criticized as one of 'uncaring opportunism'.[24] The murder of her closest adviser, Airey Neave, by a bomb planted by the Irish National Liberation Army in the car park of the House of Commons in March, followed in August by the murders of Lord Mountbatten and members of his family at Mullaghmore, County Sligo, and of eighteen British soldiers in Warrenpoint by the IRA, further conditioned Thatcher's outlook. Moreover, the Irish government's decision in March to abandon the link with sterling and join the European Monetary System (EMS), together with the continuing perception that the Republic continued to be a safe haven for IRA terrorists, its prime minister under attack from republican hawks within his own cabinet, all made 'Éire' appear an unstable and unfriendly state in Thatcher's eyes. Consequently, for her, Northern Ireland was a security rather than a political issue, and as such its position as part of the United Kingdom nonnegotiable. Irish civil servants attempting to convince their British counterparts of the urgent necessity for a new political initiative on the North, and to change the prevailing thinking in the new British administration, would face an uphill struggle.

Embattled within his own cabinet, under mounting pressure, Jack Lynch strove to fulfil his role as president of the EEC and oversee the historic visit of Pope John Paul II on 29 September. Uneasy at the 'apparent hardening' of Fianna Fáil statements on the North, Ken urged Lynch to reiterate in public the distinction between the aim of unity by agreement (a policy, as he reminded him, backed by the three major political parties in the Republic) and the aim of unity by compulsion, the objective of the Provisional IRA. He also urged him to curb those within his own party who were demanding a declaration of British intent to withdraw from the North – demands which, 'however carefully they are phrased are too close for comfort to the IRA's "Brits Out"'.[25] But Jack Lynch's days as Taoiseach were numbered, both by a clandestine campaign orchestrated from within his own party and by his own decision to retire, reached months previously before it became public knowledge in December 1979. From all political sides, genuine regret was expressed at his departure; as well as widespread anxiety as to the choice of his successor.

The election of Charles Haughey as leader of Fianna Fáil and Taoiseach had a marked impact on Ken in more ways than one. From a personal point of view, he had even less in common with the new leader than in his days in the Department of Finance and the Central Bank. By 1980, however, it was on the issue of Northern Ireland that their differences were most apparent. Fianna Fáil's departure in actuality from what remained its official policy stance on Northern Ireland was in his eyes more important than any antipathy that existed between himself and the new Taoiseach. That departure was sharply brought into focus by Síle de Valera's speech at a Republican commemoration ceremony, when the sentiments she expressed bore a disturbing similarity to extreme Republicanism. On 3 January Charles Haughey received Ken's detailed analysis of the current situation which, pointedly, reiterated Fianna Fáil's official policy on the North. In a terse reply Haughey promised to 'study it carefully'.[26] The Fianna Fáil Ard Fheis in February, however, which saw Haughey piped onto the stage to the strains of 'A Nation Once Again', to declare from the podium that Northern Ireland was 'a failed political entity', did not give Ken a sense that his document had made any impression. By then a member of Seanad Éireann (the Irish Senate), he expressed in a letter to his fellow senator Lady Valerie Goulding his anxiety at the tone and substance of government statements on the North. 'It would be most regrettable even to give the appearance of using violence in Northern Ireland as indicative of the unsatisfactory political situation there and particularly as a quasi-legitimate argument for new political structures oriented towards Irish unity.'[27] On political comments in the South that questioned the economic viability of Northern Ireland, he further cautioned that, 'being in a glasshouse ourselves, we are in no position to throw stones'.[28]

A summit meeting between Charles Haughey and Margaret Thatcher in May, aided by the Taoiseach's gift of the now famous silver teapot, brought a brief thaw in Anglo-Irish relations. A follow-up summit in Dublin Castle in December included some constructive discussion (albeit damaged by Haughey's later misinterpretation of the future constitutional position of Northern Ireland). In acknowledging that the economic, social and political interests of the two states in Ireland were inextricably linked, the summit communiqué is regarded as being an important step on the long road towards a political settlement. The main development in the North during 1980 was the adoption by Republican internees of the hunger strike in pursuit of the status of political prisoners – a tactic that was eventually to claim the lives of ten of their number, including the MP Bobby Sands. While evoking a huge emotional response in Ireland and widespread international condemnation, the hunger-strike fatalities received short shrift from Margaret Thatcher. Widespread street disturbances in the North were met head-on by the security forces and drove the death toll, which had been on the decrease, upwards once more.

Undeterred by the political setbacks, in his capacity as joint chairman of the Anglo-Irish Encounter, an organization established in 1980, and through the BIA, Ken continued his efforts to promote better understanding and relations between the

Republic, Northern Ireland and the UK. In March 1981, at a special meeting of the BIA in London, which included MPs, ambassadors, political commentators and members of the Anglo-Irish diaspora, such as the Earl of Longford and Lord Moyne, he presented a well-received paper entitled 'The Irish Question Today' (although, as he ruefully pointed out, given the speed at which events were then evolving in the North, it might have been more aptly entitled 'The Irish Question Yesterday'). On the invitation of Sir Jeremy Morse, chairman of Lloyds Bank, an acquaintance from his Central Bank days, he subsequently agreed to write an assessment 'on the current state of affairs between Dublin, Belfast and London' for the influential *Round Table*, a quarterly periodical dealing with Commonwealth and foreign affairs. 'Ireland: The Way Forward' thoughtfully and coherently set out the constitutional options for Northern Ireland. In it, Ken also argued for his beliefs that no solution was possible without the involvement of both the British and Irish governments – 'the sovereign motherlands' – and, as the Sunningdale settlement in 1973 had acknowledged, that the political and social interests of the Republic and Northern Ireland were interlinked. While direct rule, in the short term, was acceptable and less dangerous than either the restoration of Unionist supremacy or the absorption of the North into a unitary state within the United Kingdom, its retention in the long term, he wrote, 'would be a tragic reflection on statesmen and politicians in these islands and also on the ability of Ulster to raise fair and courageous leaders to open the way to a better future'.[29] In a statement which, in view of the years of death and destruction that still lay ahead, is imbued with a sense of prophetic tragedy, he further noted that it was only with the people of Northern Ireland 'that the final bargain must be struck, once Dublin and London have established conditions conducive to a settlement'. Sadly, as Ken noted, even before the article was published the North was again riven by the deaths of hunger strikers, deepening divisions and

322

sharpening antagonisms which, in turn, stimulated further fear and violence. On numerous visits to the North during this time, he was none the less impressed, as he wrote, 'by the air of normality that prevails there',[30] as, despite the violence and political inertia, people went about their daily lives.

In June 1981, in the first of an unprecedented series of five general elections in the Republic during the 1980s, the Fianna Fáil government, despite inflated election promises and the triumphalist campaign of its leader, was defeated. A second Fine Gael–Labour coalition took over a country immersed in economic crisis. Ken's reappointment to the Senate by the incoming Taoiseach, Garret FitzGerald, did not deter him from speaking his mind, whether on the perilous state of the economy, or the dangers posed by political instability, North and South, or the potential of the hunger strikes, as he wrote to the Taoiseach, to 'soften attitudes towards the Provos and sharpen antagonism to Britain'.[31] Differences between the policies of the militants and those of the Dublin government were, he felt, becoming blurred. Referring to FitzGerald's public statement on the death of one of the hunger strikers, while acknowledging that it might have been a 'necessary expression of regret', he urged the Taoiseach that 'those who respect the democratic process and institutions are, I believe, in desperate need of clear guidance from the Government'.[32] Public support for the hunger strikers by prominent figures such as Cardinal Ó Fiaich (who had succeeded Cardinal Conway) demonstrated, he wrote, 'a dangerous slide towards ambiguity, if not indeed alignment with Provo policy. It was appalling that emotional *men of the people* clergy can usurp political leadership and draw many into unthinking support of IRA propaganda.'[33] All the more reason, he argued, for the government to keep restating that it was completely opposed to violence and had no responsibility for the Provos' campaign, including their resort to hunger strike. Nevertheless, the hunger strikers' declaration that they sought reform for *all* prisoners offered an opportunity, he argued, for Mrs Thatcher to defuse the dangerous situation. 'She owes it to the neighbouring democratic Government to extend a helping hand when the stability of democracy and the rule of law and order are in such danger of erosion, not just on this island but in Britain itself.'[34]

Ken Whitaker's criticisms were directed not only at the Taoiseach and the government. In equally unequivocal terms he wrote 'in a mood of depression' to the British ambassador, Leonard Figg, deploring the state of Anglo-Irish relations 'which, to say the least, seem to have become signally uncooperative, in relation to the continuing crises, in relation to the hunger strikes'.[35] Regretting the lack of recognition by the British government 'of the difference between a quite justifiable stand on principle and the political need to defuse clever, emotive propaganda', he urged it to 'give urgent and sympathetic consideration to such proposals for further improvements of prison conditions as made by the International Red Cross and the European Commission for Human Rights'.[36] The ambassador duly forwarded copies of Ken's letter to the Foreign and Commonwealth Office. In the end it was the hunger strikers, through the intervention of their families and supporters, who called off the campaign, conceding victory, albeit pyrrhic, to Margaret Thatcher's intransigence, but at the same time, as Ken Whitaker in his letter to Leonard Figg had warned, handing victory in the propaganda war to the IRA.

As governments in the Republic rose and fell during the 1980s against a background of real and imagined heaves against Charles Haughey, public attention was distracted, even dominated, by expulsions and extraordinary incidents, such as the GUBU affair, the phone-tapping of journalists, and support for Argentina in the Falklands War. Meanwhile, in the background amidst this political turmoil, resolutely and quietly, Ken Whitaker continued his own campaign to help bring an end to the violence in the North. Publicly in the Senate and privately to politicians, clergymen, civil servants and political commentators, without fear or favour, debunking entrenched and ill-informed opinion whenever and wherever it appeared, he continued to debate the issues standing in the way of peace. The duration of the struggle was by now beginning to dull public sensibilities to the savagery of the atrocities still being perpetrated. Following the INLA bombing of a public house in Ballykelly, County Derry, in December 1982, in which seventeen people were murdered, Ken took to task an article by one writer, Desmond Fennell, for its 'appalling example of how words can be used to represent an atrocity . . . however immoral, as being in some sense a logical outcome of the Northern situation'.[37] Referring to the assertion made in the article that Britain imposed its rule by armed force on 600,000 Irish people in Northern Ireland, 'who or what', he asked, 'are the remaining 1,000,000 people in Northern Ireland? Are they obnoxious aliens to be excluded from "our country" and "our nation"?' By what means was the exclusion to be brought about: 'a new partition, banishment or worse?'[38] In response to a paper by the archbishop of New York, Cardinal Cook, he rejected what he considered the cardinal's 'simplistic view of Irish history', and of the causes of violence in Northern Ireland, and suggested that the prelate might look closer to his own church for cause and effect. 'Not being a prelate, I can be bold enough to say (as I have said many times to the late Cardinal Conway and various bishops) that a school system segregated on religious lines tends to perpetuate bigotry, misunderstanding and suspicion in an area where one would like to see better observance of the great Christian commandment "love thy neighbour".'[39] To Bishop Cathal Daly, on the other hand, he wrote of his 'admiration and total agreement' with his views and hopes for 'bridge-building' between Protestant and Catholic communities in the North – even though, as he noted, he had a 'strong prejudice against clergymen involving themselves in politics'.[40]

After the ending of the hunger strikes, with the emergence of Sinn Féin as a political force, official thinking and policy were slowly but purposefully moving away from the middle ground to embrace extremists on both sides. On numerous occasions over the previous years Ken had been critical of the abstention policy pursued by the SDLP. This he considered not merely a bad political tactic for the party, but, prophetically, a mistake in handing Sinn Féin the opportunity to replace the SDLP as the representative voice of Irish Nationalism, and not only in the North. The campaign being waged by the IRA to destabilize the North, in the course of which, with the assistance of the Libyan dictator Colonel Gaddafi, it had accumulated one of the largest illegal arsenals in the world, could also, he feared, engulf the Republic. In 1983 his concerns regarding the SDLP were discounted by Seán Donlon, secretary of the Department of Foreign Affairs, who maintained that Ken was 'being a little too harsh on the SDLP and also on those who have in different ways indirectly expressed support for their decision [to abstain from taking their seats on election].'[41] Ken's concerns, however, gradually came to be shared by Garret FitzGerald and by British politicians, such as the secretary of state for Northern Ireland, James Prior, who feared that the growing influence of Sinn Féin could turn the island of Ireland into, as he wrote, 'a Cuba off our western shore'.[42]

In 1983, prompted by John Hume, now leader of the SDLP, the Dublin government established the New Ireland Forum. Representing all shades of constitutional Nationalist opinion, it was a belated follow-through on a suggestion first mooted by Ken long previously: 'to have a blueprint of what we Nationalists were prepared to do and hoped to do in accommodating Unionists'.[43] Up to then, as he pointed out, official government policy in the Republic was based on the concept of Unionists accommodating Nationalist aspirations. In the run-up to the opening of the Forum, speculation abounded as to the choice of chairman.

The mention of Ken Whitaker, whose work and background, as one report stated, would ['lend] credibility to such a move',[44] and Ken's response that 'he would take seriously any such invitation', confirmed him as the front runner. But the long arm and even longer memory of Charles Haughey was to intervene to 'knock on the head', as Ken recalls, his nomination. A compromise candidate, Dr Colm Ó hEocha, president of University College Galway, was subsequently appointed. Showing a characteristic generosity of spirit and lack of pique, Ken sent his best wishes to his replacement, along with two policy documents on Northern Ireland. The papers were later somehow misplaced and consequently were not included in the Forum's report, published in 1984.

Derided by some Unionists as 'The Forum of Romance',[45] and by Conor Cruise O'Brien as 'Sancho Panza's New Ireland',[46] the Forum and its findings found little acceptance outside Nationalist circles. The three options put forward – joint sovereignty, a united Ireland and a federal Ireland – received short shrift from all shades of Unionism, and later, more forcefully and ungenerously, from Margaret Thatcher in her famous 'Out! Out! Out!' outburst after her meeting in Chequers with Garret FitzGerald in November 1984. Her negative attitude was understandable in the light of the IRA's attempt to kill her and members of her cabinet in the bombing of a Brighton hotel the previous month. But if nothing else, the report of the New Ireland Forum presented, for the first time, the stark reality of the staggering cost of the 'Troubles' to the Irish economy – £6.6 billion since 1969, in addition to a sum of £180 million expended on security. Together with the inestimable cost in human life, injury and suffering, this was among the more significant, if sobering, findings of the Forum.

The humiliation inflicted on both the Irish government and Northern Ireland Nationalists by Margaret Thatcher's pronouncement did not deter further attempts, at official level, to restore some balance in Anglo-Irish relations. This was regarded by both governments as essential if there were to be any way out of the political impasse; the alternative was to risk being overwhelmed by extremists on both sides. The Anglo-Irish Agreement, formally signed at Hillsborough in November 1985, was regarded as a positive step forward by most constitutional Nationalists, North and South; but by most Unionists, it was represented merely as a victory for Nationalism. For the first time a consultative role for the Republic in the affairs of the North was not merely acknowledged but put into practice by the establishment of an intergovernmental conference, manned by British and Irish civil servants and based at Maryfield, County Down. Moreover, the agreement provided for what from a Unionist perspective amounted to the unthinkable: that if in the future a majority within Northern Ireland voted for a united Ireland, Britain would not stand in its way. The agreement broke the monopoly of power enjoyed by Unionists since 1920 and sent a stern message from their erstwhile 'fairy godmother' that if they did not voluntarily agree to a system of true power-sharing with the Nationalist minority, they would be overruled by the British government.

The effect on Unionists was instant. Simultaneously incredulous and defiant, they resolved, as they had shown before, that it would take more than British threats to make them abandon their traditional ascendancy. Their opposition was manifest in making the North ungovernable, resulting in the prorogation of the Northern Ireland Assembly by the British government, and in public demonstrations, ending in serious rioting and violent confrontation with the security forces. Opposition to the agreement by Republican extremists, meanwhile, resulted in an intensification of the bombing campaign, targeting security forces in the North, in Britain and later on continental Europe. Nevertheless, while it had little or no perceptible impact in lessening the 'Troubles', in theory at least the agreement raised Anglo-Irish relations at government level above the quagmire of street politics and violence and provided a framework within which the two governments might work to resolve problems and develop structures for the future administration of Northern Ireland.

For Ken, the Anglo-Irish Agreement was no more than 'a purely interim agreement', albeit one which, he hoped, might lead to 'a widely acceptable political arrangement in Northern Ireland with a built-in potential for evolution'.[47] He saw little wisdom or equality in a forum from which the majority of Unionists were excluded, or had excluded themselves. He had warned the Irish government of the futility of establishing any symbolic (and, to him, provocative) presence in Northern Ireland, such as the Maryfield secretariat, since it merely served to accentuate Unionist perceptions of secret interference by the Republic in Northern Ireland affairs. The 'beleaguered staff' at Maryfield, he recommended, should be given 'a few months holidays and the non-scheduling of Council meetings for a time, provided the two Unionist parties, the SDLP and Alliance, agree to negotiate'[48] – a suggestion that was finally acted upon six years later in 1992, to facilitate the commencement of political talks at Stormont. While not suggesting 'abrogating the Agreement and yielding to Unionist bullying', he told the secretary of the Department of Foreign Affairs that the government's exclusive identification with the Nationalist community was not 'consistent in principle with our unity aspirations' and warned that it would only 'strengthen the fear that we are on a take-over course which would deny the Northern Ireland majority due influence in the management of their affairs'.[49]

Against the background of continuing paramilitary violence by both sides, including such atrocities as the bombing at Enniskillen in November 1987 and an intensification of the IRA bombing campaign in British cities during the late 1980s and early 1990s, peace seemed at times a lost cause, a reflection which left Ken, as he admits, 'profoundly depressed'. Even so, and notwithstanding an ever-increasing workload in retirement, even a health scare in

1989, in his late seventies, did not deter him from his pursuit of an acceptable formula for political resolution. Today he finds some difficulty in rationalizing what it was that propelled him on this quest over so long a period. 'It was not that I had some grandiose idea of myself as some wonderful operator. There was something subliminal about it, that you were engaged in a process that had a high motivation and that could bring peace, reconciliation, cooperation, social and economic advancement in the future.' His Northern birthright, he acknowledges, also contributed; while it may not have given him any practical advantage in his dealings with Northerners over the years, at the same time, as he admits, 'it is funny the way things like that can motivate and also instil a feeling in others that, as he is from these parts, he is one of us'. As the frenzy of bombing and killing continued, as the broken bodies were dragged from a fish shop on the Shankill Road and from a country village pub in Greysteel, for Ken Whitaker there simply could be no let-up in the search for peace.

Below the surface and above, on both the paramilitary and political fronts, change was afoot. By 1993 the talks that had begun in secret between John Hume and Sinn Féin's Gerry Adams in 1988 were public knowledge; and it also emerged that talks were taking place between the British government and Sinn Féin. The involvement of the IRA in such talks heralded, as Ken had predicted many years before, the sidelining of constitutional Nationalism. For someone whose dedicated work to achieve a just and peaceful outcome to the decades of murder and destruction had centred on the merging of the middle ground, in both the Unionist and Nationalist camps, and who viewed the extremists as 'an unrepresentative, fanatical and pitiless minority',[50] it was a difficult pill to swallow. 'I squirm at the extraordinary publicity (and respect) accorded to Adams while decent democrats are expected to wait patiently for him to deliver the decision of the IRA on whether murder and destruction are to continue,'[51] he confided to a friend in 1994. But as someone born in 1916, who had experienced the bloodied emergence of the Irish state and whose aversion to violence was moulded as a young boy by the sight from his bedroom window in Drogheda of 'a wild-eyed terrified man running into the street with a revolver in his hand pursued by Free State soldiers', this was, as he knew, merely history's implacable way of repeating itself. As a public servant in the 1930s, 1940s and 1950s, he had worked with politicians, government ministers and taoisigh who had, in the past, resorted to arms to achieve political aims, albeit with a popular mandate. While it is, as he admits, 'hard to find a rational response', and while he remains wary, he is nonetheless relieved at Sinn Féin's public repudiation of violence as a means of achieving political ends.

Like Sinn Féin, Ken Whitaker longed for a united Ireland; but his was a different interpretation of what unity meant and the process by which it was to be achieved. In 1993, while personal emotions and prejudice might draw him in one direction, the primary objective, to attain peace, remained paramount; and as a democrat and public servant, he accepted the political decision made by the Irish and British governments to engage with the extremists, no matter how personally painful, in the hope, as he expresses it, 'that the militants, confronted with the need to rationalize, would move from violence to constitutional means'. With hope, endurance and a stoicism that defied age, notwithstanding personal and family problems, he determined to continue to 'pursue my path within the new parameters'. Sending his paper 'Northern Ireland – The Way Forward' to Albert Reynolds, who had replaced Charles Haughey at the head of the government in 1992, as being 'the honestly held views of a concerned individual and nationalist who shares with many others an impatience at the slowness of professional politicians', he urged the new Taoiseach 'to get to grips effectively with the problem'.[52]

Ken Whitaker's final policy document, 'Northern Ireland – In

Search of a Solution', written in 1997, sets out his fresh thinking in the light of changed political circumstances.

> The climate has been transformed by the widespread acceptance of the principle of consent. Paradoxically consent may be more positively and firmly given when the choice is free and no surrender to pressure can be alleged. I would be content to see it take the form of agreement to Northern Ireland constituting, with the Republic, the twin entities of a Federal Ireland.[53]

The joint communiqué issued on 25 July 1997, following the historic meeting of Bertie Ahern, John Hume and Gerry Adams, publicly and unambiguously reinforced 'exclusively democratic and peaceful methods of resolving our political problems . . . with the participation and agreement of the Unionist people'. Followed in 1999 by the amendment of articles 2 and 3 of the Irish constitution and the abandonment of the Republic's claim to Northern Ireland, it seemed a vindication of what Ken Whitaker had striven over the previous decades to attain. Today, the need for realism and compromise, especially in the light of the attempts of dissident Republicans and others to derail the hard-won peace, remains as pressing as ever. In their absence, as he attests, 'unrealistic expectations may be entertained for too long, to be abruptly replaced by uncomprehending disappointment'. The eventual establishment of a stable Northern Ireland Executive in May 2007 and the ending of direct rule was a bittersweet culmination of his work and hopes. Political power, as he predicted, moved from the middle ground to rest in the hands of the DUP and Sinn Féin. His prophecy in 1971 that a United Ireland was as far away as 2025 or even 2050, a prediction subsequently echoed by Tony Blair in 1997, is one that in 2014 still seems likely to be fulfilled.

A framed copy in his study of the front page of the April 1998 (Good Friday) Belfast Agreement, personally signed by all the participating individuals, including Bill Clinton, Bertie Ahern and Tony Blair, is testimony to the contribution made by Ken Whitaker over the space of thirty years to the long and painful peace process. Many who lived through those dreadful years of carnage and destruction still find it difficult to forgive, let alone forget. For Ken Whitaker, who as early as 1968 had devised a peaceful formula to achieve what was eventually arrived at only after subsequent decades of violence and the loss of over 3700 lives, the solution came at a terrible price. 'I often look back to those mid-60s days of hope,' he wrote in 1997 to the widow of Sir Cecil Bateman, for many years a contact and friend in the Northern Ireland administration, 'blighted so soon, alas, by extremists, and I regret that sensible and sensitive public servants like Cecil and myself couldn't just settle between ourselves how things should be arranged.'[54]

Ever pragmatic and generous, now in his ninety-eighth year, Ken Whitaker views with some bemusement the sheer extent and scope of the work he undertook in the cause of peace – work encapsulated in the hundreds of documents, letters, notes, reports, memos, media articles and policy documents he composed, the countless meetings, debates, interviews and seminars he attended, all on a voluntary basis. 'For me there is still to this day a certain sense of wonder as to how I got so involved. It was so contrary to what would normally be expected of a public servant – to keep your mouth shut, eyes averted and just sing the "Soldier's Song"!'

12

Language Matters

Any Irish spoken in Ireland today is spoken out of love, will and
respect for the language rather than through compulsion.
T. K. Whitaker, 2014

THE SEA-CHANGE that occurred in the official attitude towards the
national language, from one of dour compulsion to one of
persuasion and encouragement, is in no small part due to Ken
Whitaker's lifelong commitment to the preservation and promotion of the Irish language in both his personal and his public
life. The words of Shakespeare scholar Ernest Dowson, 'I have
been faithful to thee, Cynara, in my fashion,' for Ken best
describe his relationship with the language, an attachment that
still burns with undimmed passion today. 'The heart', he insists,
'must play a large part in the attitude to the Irish language.' And,
as with his other great public undertakings – the economy and
Northern Ireland – his devotion manifested itself in a practical
approach and application towards achieving his goal, as well as in
constant support and encouragement of others.

His commitment to the preservation of the Irish language was
an integral part of his personal cultural formation and identity
long before it became a public duty: 'My interest in Irish and my
love for it go back to home and school influences – my mother's
recollection of prayers and nursery rhymes in Irish from her
County Clare childhood, an inspiring lay teacher of the language

at secondary school and the first of many visits to the Donegal Gaeltacht on a scholarship in 1931.'[1] That interest, in both the oral and the written tradition, inculcated in him during his youth, he in turn transmitted to his own family. His wife Nora shared his interest in Irish and it became the language of choice at home. As a newly married couple, in 1942 they undertook a cycling tour of the Donegal Gaeltacht as an enjoyable way of brushing up their Irish. In the remote Fanad Peninsula, as Ken remembers with amusement, his enthusiasm received an unexpected rebuff along the way. In what he thought to be his best *blas*, he sought directions from a local farmer they encountered driving a horse and cart on the road:

'Bhfuil muid ar an bhealach ceart go Portsalon?' [Are we on the right road to Portsalon?]

The farmer, reining in the horse, replied: 'What's that?'

I repeated what I said, this time with less assurance.

'Carry on down the road till you come to the crossroads and turn left,' the farmer replied in English.

'Go raibh maith agat,' [Thank you] I said, somewhat miffed.

'Tá tú ag foghlaim na Gaeilge?' [Are you learning Irish?], the farmer said, softening, as I thought.

'Tá' [Yes], I replied.

'Bhuel, bygor, níl mórán dí agat go fóill.' [Well, begor, you haven't much of it yet.]

And with that he whipped up the horse and, with a sardonic chuckle, was gone. What was worse, my wife also had a smile on her face!

The couple's attachment to the language was deepened in 1972 by their purchase of an abandoned schoolhouse in Glencullen, midway between Glenamoy and Bangor Erris in north County Mayo – a remote and enduring place, surrounded by a treeless expanse of mountainous blanket bog. It was Nora and their daughter Catherine, while visiting local archaeological sites in the area, who happened to see the 'For Sale' sign on the two-roomed schoolhouse, which Nora purchased as a family holiday home. Over the years they gradually renovated the property, and though, as Ken recalls, 'it was years before we had the comfort of electric light and running water', there were other compensations. 'In the early years we could hear the grouse calling at evening in the hill above us and a cuckoo came without fail to Glenturk.' The lure of salmon fishing in the nearby lake and rivers was an added incentive. That the property was located in one of the lesser-known Gaeltacht areas was also a statement of Ken's support for the language and for the distinctive dialect spoken in Erris, 'a halfway house between Ulster and Connemara Irish'.

Ken's first introduction to the north Mayo area was through the eminent folklorist and international scholar James (Séamus) Hamilton Delargy. A fellow Northerner and director of the Irish Folklore Commission, Delargy set out from Cushendall with a group of associates in 1935 on a mission to harvest Ireland's singular oral tradition of stories, rhymes, history, mythology and music from villages and communities throughout the country. Their efforts culminated in the assemblage of one of the largest collections of folklore in the world. During the war years Delargy took his precious collection for safe keeping to Altnabrockey, in the shadow of the Nephin Mountains, an area where he had personally collected some of the material. Following the war, while in the Department of Finance, Ken helped arrange for the transfer of the collection to the new Department of Irish Folklore at University College Dublin. Later, while on holiday in Carna, he received a telegram from his friend in Erris with the words 'tá tuile san abhainn, gaibh í leith' (there's a flood in the river, come) which resulted in a fishing trip that produced a bountiful harvest of salmon and sea trout. 'I was hooked! I spent happy days fishing with him in Erris and accompanied him on a sentimental journey along the course of the river Inny, as he revisited house after house of his friends of those war years.' Of Delargy, Ken attests: 'It was he who had the vision, the training, the warm humanity, the unflagging zeal and the organizational capacity to collect and safeguard this dying heritage before it was too late.' In his subsequent capacity as chairman of Comhairle Bhéaloideas Éireann (the Irish Folklore Commission), for fifteen years Ken kept a watching brief on Delargy's unique legacy.

Retaining some of the more visible marks of its previous incarnation – a blackboard and a school desk, as well as the original foundation stone, dated 1887 – Ken and Nora did little to change the character of the old schoolhouse. Tír Álainn became a home away from home, where, especially after Ken's 'official' retirement in 1976, they spent much of their spare time, joined by an ever-growing family circle. On the long road to Mayo, punctuated, as his grandson Matthew remembers, by a stop 'for a delightful (though potentially fatal) fry-up along the N4, we hit the open road with Ken at the helm of the mighty old navy Corolla. After a while I would notice Mum glancing down at the gear-stick . . . We must have covered twenty miles in third gear, Radio 1 blaring and Ken blissfully unaware that the car was reaching notes rarely heard from Formula I cars . . . to the unspoken amusement of his passengers.' Every morning it was up at the crack of dawn, with the wafting aroma of Ken's full Irish breakfast or less appetizing 'Mayo Weetabix' as he referred to porridge, to get them on their way. Days were spent on the lakes and river banks, obeying – to varying degrees – his strict orders to remain quiet and stationary, while he concentrated on catching the elusive salmon, and, as his granddaughter Nicola recalls, 'being held responsible for the ones that got away!' The ability he instilled in his grandchildren to stand motionless for many hours at a time was taken to a new level by two of his granddaughters, Nicola and Yseult, who took to dressing up in similar clothes and standing motionless on the schoolhouse gateposts, to the consternation of the occasional passer-by. 'Illegal' midnight feasts with food purloined behind their grandparents' backs; drinking Ken's special brew – TK red lemonade; playing rings, cards and board games to pass the time in wet weather: 'Every day was a new adventure – even those that rained,' his granddaughter Karen recalls. 'We explored, had picnics, fished on the lake, picked mussels and mushrooms, planted flowers in the garden and hoped that the sheep did not eat them during the winter.'

On crossing the threshold of the old schoolhouse, visitors who had made the long journey across the lonely expanse of moorland to Glencullen were assured of the warmest of welcomes, a slice of Nora's apple tart straight from the oven or Ken's smoked salmon atop home-baked brown bread, a view over Carrowmore lake from the vantage point that was once the schoolhouse cloakroom, memorable conversation – and a *deoch an dorais* [one for the road] before leaving. Some of their near neighbours, including Tom and Bill Finlay (a chief justice and governor of the Bank of Ireland respectively), who owned fishing rights on the nearby Owenmore river, they knew from Dublin; others were soon equally welcome. An initial housewarming party at the former schoolhouse let his neighbours know that 'I was interested in the area and in the language and that they were welcome to come and talk. In return we received great consideration, help and support locally.'

Quietly and unobtrusively they settled into the surrounding community. Like the many who voted him their 'man of the century', locals found their 'famous' neighbour approachable, friendly and helpful, a man they could trust to be objective and honest in his appraisal of any contentious issue that affected them and the district in which they lived. It was through his quiet diplomacy, as his neighbour and friend John Cosgrove recalls, that the angling rights of the Glenamoy river were transferred from private ownership to the Inland Fisheries Board, which in turn leased the rights to the local Bangor Angling Club. Ken's interest and intervention in the controversial Corrib gas project dispute, at nearby Bellanaboy, secured the company's sponsorship of a number of third-level scholarships for students in the Erris area. His acceptance as 'a part-time Mayoman' was confirmed when his appointment to Seanad Éireann in 1977 was hailed in the area as an additional seat for north Mayo! When a bay on Carrowmore lake was named in his honour after a particularly successful day's angling, culminating in a haul of three fine salmon, declining the invitation to have it named 'Whitaker Bay', he chose instead 'Paradise Bay' in memory of his old home in Drogheda – the name by which it is known today. In August 2006 Ken and his second wife, Mary, hosted a Mass and open-house day in the old schoolhouse for a reunion of over three hundred surviving past pupils and their families.

Ken sought to pass on to his children the 'joy and fulfilment' he personally derived from the Irish language, literature and music – but always, as they recall, through persuasion rather than by dint of parental enforcement. Gaeltacht areas such as Rannafast, Ballinskelligs, Muskery, Carna and later Erris were the destinations of choice for family summer holidays, usually incorporating attendance at local Irish-speaking summer schools. 'It was never about compulsion; merely a matter of choice,' his son Ken recalls. 'We normally spoke Irish at home. Summer holidays were spent in Gaeltacht areas where learning to speak Irish was combined with the usual holiday fun and invariably also with fishing,' an interest he shares with his father. Not all his children were won over, however. When his daughter Catherine fell ill at Coláiste na Leanbh, in Rinn, County Waterford, on the eve of the school holidays, and she was forced to remain on at the school, on her much delayed return home, to her father's amusement, she threw her schoolbag onto the floor, declaring: 'That is the last word of Irish I'll ever speak!'

That policy of gentle persuasion, by which he encouraged his own family's interest in the national language, was also in evidence in the way he set about extending the use of Irish in the public service. As an officer in the Department of Finance, he was involved in arrangements for the transfer of the last islanders from the Irish-speaking Blasket Islands in County Kerry to the mainland. In 1947 he was sent as part of a delegation to visit each of the Gaeltacht areas to investigate how best they might be developed. Leading by example, in departmental memos and reports, official meetings and conversations, and in 1957 two published articles, whenever the opportunity arose he communicated through the medium of Irish. As governor of the Central Bank, Ken instituted a series of articles in Irish in the Bank's bulletins and annual reports, commencing in August 1969 with his own contribution, 'An t-Ór' [Gold]. His intention 'to promote interest in the Irish language amongst bankers and business people' was vindicated on at least one occasion when his article 'An Ceangal le Sterling – Ar Cheart é a Bhriseadh?' [The link with sterling – should it be broken?] attracted the interest of the governor of the Bank of England, who ordered its immediate translation! As governor of the Central Bank, he also attended a week-long immersion in *caint na ndaoine* (the local dialect) in Rannafast, staying in the house of the host family of his youth. Noreen Duffy, the daughter of the house, recalls introducing her special guest to her young nephew as 'the money man'. To prove her point, Ken presented the youngster with a five-pound note which, as governor of the Central Bank, bore his signature. A more recent visit, made in 2005 accompanied by his second wife Mary, also a past pupil of Rannafast, was, as he recalls, 'an emotional return' to a place that has remained, throughout his life, close to his heart. He also regularly attended the annual Merriman Summer School in County Clare.

Ken Whitaker's most significant contribution towards the Irish language, however, was made as secretary of the Department of Finance, when he personally redefined official government policy. In 1964, on the publication of a report by *An Coimisiún um Athbheochan na Gaeilge*, a commission established to make recommendations for the revival of the Irish language, he found himself at odds with some of its findings. Chaired by Cardinal Tomás Ó Fiaich, with whom, as Ken diplomatically noted, he had some 'lively' discussions, the commission founded its recommendations on a particular definition of the word 'revival' (*athbheochan*), by which it meant the replacement of English by Irish as the everyday medium of communication in Ireland. This Ken judged to be, in the prevailing circumstances, unrealistic. As he explained, it served only to 'sharpen the antagonism of those who see no point in preserving Irish, alienate the sympathy of those who cherish Irish but value the possession of English and discourage even idealists who recognise such an extreme aim to be unattainable'.[2] Revival, he recommended, should be encouraged, not in order to replace English, but rather 'to preserve and cherish Irish as the national language; to strengthen the Gaeltacht and extend the use of Irish as a living language, oral and written; and to give everyone growing up in Ireland, through knowledge of the language and its literature, wider access to our cultural heritage'.[3] His advice was subsequently adopted by Seán Lemass, who in June 1965 dismissed compulsion as a means of saving the language and urged instead 'the building up of enthusiasm for its wider use, and reliance in the main on patriotism and voluntary effort',[4] as the way forward.

As a consequence of Ken's intervention, responsibility for drafting the government's white paper on the preservation of the language was transferred, under his direction, to the Department of Finance. 'I undertook this as a personal responsibility, ably assisted by Séamus Ó Ciosáin. I suspected that our drafts of the White Paper were sent quietly to the Park to test their acceptability to President de Valera. No member of the Government he had led for so long was quite as notable a supporter of the Irish language.'[5] Ken's assertion of the futility of any attempt to replace English as the country's 'working' language, given that some 98 per cent of the population spoke English as their mother tongue and the remainder spoke it as a second language, and of bilingualism as the only reasonable way to keep the Irish language alive, subsequently became official government policy.

The philosophy guiding the proposed policy of bilingualism he subsequently found difficult, in an Irish context, to define. Since bilingualism was a choice usually prompted by economic or cultural necessity, in a national context it could become, he reasoned, a divisive rather than a unifying force, giving rise to the establishment of language monoliths unable to communicate with or understand one another. Given the predominance of English among the population, the case for bilingualism in Ireland did not rest on any practical or economic necessity. Instead, Ken proposed that a policy of bilingualism should be based, as he eloquently wrote,

> on a recognition that the Irish language is a most precious heritage, the thing that most signifies and maintains our continuity as a distinctive people, the key to a treasure-trove of poetry and prose epics, folklore and song, which has expressed the imagination and feeling, the wisdom and humour, all the varied responses of generations of Irish people to life and its vicissitudes from the early centuries down, indeed, to our own day.[6]

He recommended, therefore, a practical and positive bilingualism, one that would accept English as the general vernacular, while according to Irish what he termed 'primacy of respect' as the national language; a wider knowledge of Irish to be incorporated into the educational system; the encouragement of the voluntary use of the language within families and groups outside the Gaeltacht areas; and a greater awareness of and pride in Irish culture.

Such a policy would, however, as he warned, 'be doomed to sterility if the living source of the language, the Gaeltacht, were to contract further and continue to weaken'.[7] In his lifetime he had witnessed a contraction of some 60 per cent in the *fíor* [true] Gaeltacht areas. As a young student in the 1920s he had personally conversed with the last native Irish speaker in the Gaeltacht of Omeath in County Louth. In the 1970s, in the Gaeltacht in north Mayo, he observed how the language was spoken mainly by the older generation and that fewer families were being brought up through the medium of Irish. 'What a tragedy it would be to see presented on our television screens the last native Irish speaker from Carna or Rannafast.'[8] The survival of the remaining Gaeltacht areas he considered vital to the survival of the language itself. Another aspect of the debate, in view of the intensification of the 'Troubles' in Northern Ireland, and one of particular and personal concern to him, was the hijacking of the Irish language by zealots as 'a badge of extreme nationalism in Northern Ireland',[9] an appropriation which served, he maintained, to exclude those Protestant Gaelic enthusiasts who, in the past, had been to the forefront in preserving the language from extinction. Just as he had advised regarding the usurpation of 'republicanism' by the IRA, now he urged the government to show 'more overt evidence of support . . . and not allow extremists [to] capture the Irish language'.[10]

Ken Whitaker's involvement in the revival of Irish was further deepened in February 1974 when, as governor of the Central Bank, he was asked by the minister for the Gaeltacht, Tom O'Donnell, to become chairman of Bord na Gaeilge, a new body established by the government to replace the former Comhairle na Gaeilge, of which he had been a member for the previous fourteen years. The Bord's aim – to promote the well-being of Irish and extend its use as a living language – was, as Ken well realized, a difficult and long-term undertaking, given the language's systematic decline and negative profile. Initially the Bord was an ad hoc body, with limited powers and subject to the vagaries of departmental bureaucracy; but, as the minister indicated, legislation to endow it with formal statutory powers was in train. Ken was at first reluctant to accept the position – 'I did not think I had either the qualifications or the time' – but when the minister persisted, he agreed to accept the post on a voluntary basis until the new legislation was enacted. 'I had no idea that it would take three years before the Bill was passed and the Bord was placed on a statutory footing.' Nor did he anticipate the difficulties and tardiness he would face from the Civil Service Commission in acquiring adequate staff; or, later, 'that so much delay would befall the implementation of the recommendations of the Bord'.

The Bord members were selected from a wide range of backgrounds and interests, drawing on public, private and state-sponsored institutions, churches, universities and other third-level institutions, with Seán de Fréine, an officer in the Department of the Public Service, as chief executive. The task facing them was stark: to prevent the loss of Irish as a living, spoken language. The mother tongue of merely 2 per cent of the population by the mid-1970s, it had to engage the interest and commitment of the other 98 per cent of the population to have any hope of achieving a resurgence. The Bord's stated policy was accordingly to win 'the free and willing cooperation of the Irish public in furthering Irish as a living language . . . [and] to promote a deeper understanding and wider acceptance of the value of the language both to the individual and to the whole community'.[11] One of Ken's priorities as chairman was to widen involvement and interest in the language among people outside the exclusive confines of Irish-speaking areas and Irish language groups, as he made clear in his public statement 'Sé pobal na hÉireann ar fad, agus ní pobal na Gaeilge amháin, pobal Bhórd na Gaeilge' [the general Irish public and not just Irish-speakers are Bord na Gaeilge's public].[12] Under his chairmanship, Bord na Gaeilge was to be not just another Irish-language organization, but one that involved and related to the majority English-speaking population, without ousting or belittling their use of

English, a policy at the time not always appreciated by Irish-language purists.

In anticipation of the promised legislation, and despite its limited powers, in the initial months of its existence the Bord set itself some practical objectives. To rescue the language from its perceived elitist status, it sought to bring it to the people, to encourage its use in the workplace, in schools and in the home. This it envisaged doing through the provision of effective educational opportunities, leisure, music, literary and entertainment facilities, better media coverage (with particular emphasis on television programming in Irish), and the improvement of publications in Irish, and by modernizing and standardizing the language itself. As with his other public undertakings, Ken ensured that the policy recommendations of the Bord were based on solidly researched foundations, including the most up-to-date scientific work in linguistics, sociolinguistics and psycholinguistics. Much of the scientific background for the initial work of the Bord was provided by the 1976 report of the Committee on Language Attitudes, a scientific and statistical study analysing the causes and consequences of the decline in Irish, covering such issues as attitudes, image, verbal competence and teaching methods. This more academic aspect of the Bord's work was complemented by outreach to seek proposals from communities and groups throughout the country for specific ideas to extend the use of the language in everyday life.

From a practical point of view, Ken felt there was little to be gained by promoting a wider use of Irish in the community if the quality and availability of books and magazines in the Irish language, as well as school textbooks, were substandard. As he informed the minister, Tom O'Donnell, in December 1975: 'One of the most essential requirements is for financial support for the creation of a culture of reading in Irish.'[13] This, he believed, could be achieved only if sufficient funding were made available by the Departments of Education and of the Gaeltacht to companies publishing books in the Irish language, including An Gúm, the state publisher. To provide a greater variety of books in Irish, the Bord commissioned biographies of popular Irish writers and musicians such as Seán Ó Riada, Pádraig Ó Conaire and Douglas Hyde. To extend knowledge and appreciation of the nature and quality of the Irish poetical heritage, on his own initiative Ken persuaded Seán Ó Tuama and the poet Thomas Kinsella, who had worked with him in the Department of Finance, to collaborate on a compilation of a new anthology of poems in the Irish language, with accompanying English translations. Published in 1981 and spanning the years from the fall of the old Gaelic culture in the early seventeenth century to the emergence of English as the dominant vernacular in the nineteenth century, *An Duanaire: Poems of the Dispossessed* was acknowledged by the late Seamus Heaney as 'a book of great worth and importance, one that could mark an epoch.'[14] Dedicated to Ken Whitaker, *An Duanaire* remains an enduring example of the ethos that guided his efforts to make Irish language and culture accessible to Irish-speakers and non-Irish speakers alike.

From the outset, Bord na Gaeilge encountered difficulties which, in the initial years, constrained its effectiveness. The government's reluctance to grant it statutory recognition created difficulties in its relationship with other government departments, especially the Department of Education and the Department of the Public Service. Pending legislation, the Bord had little or no discretionary power in relation to the hiring, pay and conditions of service of its staff or the funding of its activities. 'The Government must have trust in the initiative, enthusiasm and experience of the Bord members to perform their duties,' Ken advised the minister. 'If the Bord fails to do their duty in a reasonable length of time, then the Government is within its rights to dismiss them.'[15] Once established, the Bord was left much to its own devices in initiating policy towards the preservation of the language, with little support from the government – including the Departments of Education and of the Gaeltacht, which, as Ken reminded the minister, had prime responsibility for the language. The Bord also became the target of criticism and negative comment from the more zealous and vocal Irish-language groups, some of which, as Ken recalls, 'God himself could not satisfy', and some of whose members regarded the Bord, with a degree of justification, as 'little more than a smokescreen which was being used by the Government to hide their neglect of the Irish language'.[16] Critical of the Bord for 'underspending' its budget, they argued that the funding should be allocated instead to Irish-language groups, failing to understand, as Ken notes, 'that Bord na Gaeilge was there to serve all of the Irish people and not just Irish-speakers'.

By the end of 1977 the Bord found itself caught, as Ken wrote, *idir an dá thine Bhealtaine* (between the two fires of May). He arranged a meeting between the minister for the Gaeltacht and members of the Bord, significantly in Gweedore in the Donegal Gaeltacht. Privately he informed the new minister, Denis Gallagher, of his intention to resign. Coupled with the resignation at the beginning of 1978 of the chief executive, Seán de Fréine, his threat had the desired effect, and the long-overdue legislation to endow the Bord with statutory powers was speedily moved by the government. At the personal request of the minister, Ken agreed to remain at the helm until the new legislation had been formally enacted.

In February 1978, in his last year as chairman, Ken presented the fruits of the Bord's analyses and planning, achieved from a budget of just £300,000. Six pilot language growth locations, outside the Gaeltacht areas, were selected for support and funding. A travelling theatre company to showcase plays in Irish by local writers was announced, which, as well as providing work for actors, helped to expand the pool of acting and writing talent in Irish available for television, radio and the professional theatre.

To boost the use of the language in the media, a scholarship scheme to the Gaeltacht for journalists was established, and Irish-language groups in secondary and third-level educational institutions were encouraged and supported. The Bord's commitment was extended to providing a wider range of Irish-language books and magazines, as well as to developing skills and courses in Irish for teachers. The findings of a research scheme on the attitudes of Gaeltacht summer students to the language was submitted to the Departments of Education and of the Gaeltacht, while a study of all-Irish schools in the Dublin area was initiated, to assess their significance as focal points for the dissemination of Irish, and also as potential centres for social networking and education through the medium of Irish. All these schemes bore the imprimatur of Ken's philosophy to promote the language in contexts in which it was acceptable that it could become the spoken or written language of choice; or, in more modern-day parlance, to make Irish 'cool'.

Bord na Gaeilge was finally created as a statutory body on 1 November 1978. The TV presenter Liam Ó Murchú became its new chairman. In December 1999, as part of the Good Friday Agreement, the Bord was subsumed into a new North–South language body, Foras na Gaeilge, charged with the promotion of both Irish and Ulster Scots on the island of Ireland.

Ken's dedication to the Irish language did not end with his chairmanship of Bord na Gaeilge. In subsequent years, in conversations, interviews, speeches and articles, and as chairman of Comhairle Bhéaloideas Éireann, he maintained the commitment fostered in his schooldays in Drogheda and Rannafast. The establishment of Raidió na Gaeltacha and TG4, the introduction of the Official Languages Act in 2003, providing for more services through Irish in the public sector, the growth in all-Irish schools outside the Gaeltacht areas, improvements in the quality and content of publications in Irish, the popularity of Irish music and dance – all these more recent positive developments have contributed to preserving the native language. Meanwhile, Ken's aversion to any form of exclusivity in the promotion of the language remains steadfast, as does his pragmatic approach to its use. While fully supportive of the campaign which achieved official language status for Irish in the EU in 2007, he nevertheless judges it, as he noted, 'a waste of human ability and of money to require the translation into Irish of EU documents other than those of constitutional importance or of major significance to the general public'.[17] Similarly, he finds the prescription of Irish-only forms of local place-names a deterrent in promoting the use of the language. Far better, he advises, to find more effective ways of advancing an acceptable bilingualism, 'neither embarrassed nor embarrassing but founded on love and respect for Irish and a resolve to keep it alive'.

As Gaeltachta such as Rannafast and Erris struggle to compete for survival in the world of globalization, rampant technological innovation, social networking, multiculturalism and the changes in ideology and national identity that such developments bring, it is that self-same love and respect that may yet provide the means to preserve this fragile but priceless legacy. But it will also need the vision of another Ken Whitaker, to keep the momentum going. For, as he warned in 1978:

> if as a result of indifference, the Irish language were allowed to die, the loss would be irreparable. We would have lost one of the most important elements of our identity. We would have cut ourselves off from an invaluable heritage and made ourselves even more vulnerable than we are already to absorption in an amorphous Anglo-American culture.[18]

13

Man for All Seasons

An unpaid job is the hardest to resign from!
T. K. Whitaker

'TO MAYO': the two words written, with a flourish, in Ken's diary on 1 March 1976, the first day of his 'official' retirement, evoke a sense of both release from the responsibilities of public office and anticipation of the pleasures awaiting him in the west of Ireland. While the latter was, over succeeding decades, amply fulfilled, release from the duties of public office was destined to evade him for another thirty years. Not yet turned sixty and in good health, it seemed unlikely that someone of his ability, generosity, status and sense of civic responsibility would simply 'rest on his laurels' or on his pension in some long-drawn-out retirement – or, indeed, that he would be permitted to do so. 'Whitaker has much more to give and Ireland will hear much more from him in retirement,' an article in the *Irish Times* at the time accurately predicted.[1]

Following a brief stay in Mayo, he took off with Nora on a long-anticipated tour of archaeological sites in Greece and Italy. Thereafter, retirement gave him time to enjoy his ever-growing family circle and indulge his relationships with the next genera-tions. Five of his six children, now adults, were settled nearby, his third son, Raymond, the only family member to make his career abroad. Through their teenage and young adult years he shared in their development, from school examinations and graduations, careers, marriages and the births and baptisms of his grand-children. Eventually, and inevitably, there came also the pain and sadness of separation and loss.

In 1976, then in her ninety-seventh year, Ken's mother Jane was still hale and hearty. She lived with his sister Peggie in nearby Mount Merrion and continued to be a central part of family life. As Ken and Nora's grandchildren grew, the house on Stillorgan Road became the centre for family celebrations, after-school piano and violin practice, and school work, as Ken and Nora, now with more time to devote to them, entertained, minded and guided the next generation, with varying degrees of success. 'One thing I never got the hang of was the timekeeping and the "aul economics",' their granddaughter Nicola recalls of her many after-school evenings and of Ken's noted adherence to the former and expertise in the latter. Odd jobs around their grandparents' house were part of their training, including observance of the exacting standards demanded of those entrusted with mowing the lawn. 'I would often turn at the end of the garden to see Ken . . . casting an eye over my work,' his grandson Matthew remembers. Supportive and generous with both his time and his advice, in good times and bad, Ken became counsellor and confidant to his grandchildren, encouraging their varying talents and ambitions, but never, as his granddaughter Jane recalls, putting them under any pressure 'to achieve any more than we have'. His 'amazing ability to make everyone feel special' was augmented by his advice to them in the form of a principle which perhaps best epitomizes his own life: 'Never let other people's expectations determine what you do or who you are.'

Every year Ken and Nora hosted a Christmas Day morning get-together, the centrepiece of which was a smoked salmon, caught during the preceding summer. 'Christmas at 148 [Stillorgan Road] was always such a warm occasion. As a child, I thought the love and generosity of Ken and Nora almost filled the house,' their grandson Ross recalls. 'The rest of the space was taken up with smoked salmon!' – and also with presents selected personally by Ken and Nora (as on birthdays) for each family member: an ever more demanding task as the number of grand-children continued to increase to the latest count of twenty-seven, plus five great-grandchildren. The traditional Christmas Day visitation continues today. As one now grown-up grandchild, Peter, recalls of a more recent occasion, on being the first family member to turn up, he was greeted at the door by his grandfather with the words: 'Thank God. I was beginning to think it was Christmas Eve!'

It was their grandfather's passion for salmon fishing, however, that evokes the most powerful childhood memories. Ken's interest in the 'lordly' salmon, fuelled in his boyhood days in Drogheda, took many years to develop. Reflecting a hesitancy notably at variance with his downright approach to tackling complex national undertakings, his reluctance to engage in the sport was uncharacteristic but, to fellow anglers, perhaps understandable. There is something epic, mysterious, even magical about engaging with the king of fish that demands an initiation period of due reflection and preparation. But there is also a psycho-logical dimension to the process that can prevent the novice from indulging until he finds himself in the right frame of mind. Consequently, it was not until 1963 that Ken felt confident enough to try his luck.

Kitting himself out with an expensive rod and tackle, abandoning the notion of purchasing a new fishing jacket in the hope of earning credit with Nora for his economy, only to have her observe of his outlay that 'she could buy a dozen salmon for what it cost',[2] and armed with an end-of-season permit, he took off with the family to Carrick in County Donegal. As every salmon angler can confirm, catching your first salmon leaves an indelible memory. When the first he hooked and played for what seemed like hours escaped, partly through his impatience but also by virtue of a previously damaged hook, he found the experience devastating. 'I became cold, sad and tired all at once. Is there any sport in which failure can be so poignantly disappointing? In other sports there is a chance for recovery but a salmon lost is gone for ever.' Undaunted, his perseverance was finally rewarded when, with the help of his son Raymond, he successfully hooked, played, netted and landed his first catch. 'That moment was sweet. So also was the moment when the cooked fish was set before me to serve the family and, by common consent, I awarded myself the *curadh-mhír* or hero's portion.'[3]

From then Ken was himself hooked. 'So interested was I in fishing that I ignored rain and wind and could not bring myself to read or write . . . To be away from the river was a deprivation.'[4] Such intense dedication can shorten the usual long fuse of tolerance extended to one's nearest and dearest, including grandchildren, should they come between the angler and his catch. Idle chatter or any unnecessary movement on the river bank were summarily forbidden. Ripples thought to be made by a big salmon lurking beneath the water, but which turned out instead to be the result of stone-throwing, evoked, as Andrew, the guilty party, testifies, 'a silence in the old schoolhouse that was deafening' and the question: 'Andrew, can you tell me why I spent the whole bloody day out on the river and caught nothing?' An inadvertent and untimely lift of a net by another grandson, Greg, spilling a feisty salmon that had given Ken a good run for his efforts, was greeted by the fisherman with a look of horror, a punishment walk back to the car, and silence. On the occasion of catching his own first salmon, Steve learned the rules of the sport the hard way when, on measuring his catch, his grandfather found it was half an inch short of the minimum length allowed and promptly released it back into the river. 'I was upset at the time,' Steve recalls, 'but in the end it's the example set that day that stuck with me through the years – rules are to be respected.' Flycasting occasionally resulted in hooking something other than fish, as Allen recalls to his discomfiture: for during one fishing expedition with his grandfather on the Shannon, two hooks of Ken's treble became embedded in the back of his head. On another occasion, Ken's latent medical skills were brought to bear during one holiday in Mayo, when he skilfully removed a deeply lodged salmon bone from Barry's throat.

His enthusiasm for the sport has never waned. In September 2011, at the age of ninety-five, in north Mayo with his son Ken and grandson Allen for 'the last fling' before the fishing season closed, he enjoyed another notable success with the rod. 'We were in a nice pool on the Owenmore [river]. I was waiting to be allowed to try, with hopes dwindling as I saw they had no action whatsoever. When I started I had only made a few casts when there was a fish on the hook. With instructions from all quarters I landed the fish. Quite a good one, about eight pounds, which put up a good fight. I continued and almost immediately hooked a six-pounder. It gave me a wry pleasure that the son and grandson had tried for much longer but had caught nothing, while, almost casually, I had caught two!' As well as enabling him to indulge in the 'irresistible temptation' not only in the lakes and rivers of Mayo but on the Shannon and Slaney, Loughs Corrib and Sheelin, and farther afield in Scotland and Iceland, retirement also gave Ken and Nora the opportunity to travel to France each year to explore new areas of the country he regards as 'ma deuxième patrie'.

In 1976, in media interviews prior to his retirement, Ken outlined his future plans as involving further study, some useful activity and indulging in his favourite pastimes, notably fishing. That 'useful activity' already covered an extraordinary spread of voluntary work, undertaken as chairman or board member of numerous bodies, most of which he had helped to establish. These included the ESRI, the NESC, the School of Celtic Studies, the Folklore Commission, Bord na Gaeilge, the Royal Victoria Eye and Ear Hospital, Dublin (on whose board he served as chairman from 1976 to 2001), the Dublin Institute for

Advanced Studies and the Statistical and Social Inquiry Society of Ireland. He also continued to serve as chairman of the Agency for Personal Service Overseas (APSO), a national voluntary organization which he had co-founded with the aim of assisting and coordinating service overseas by people with technical and educational skills, in order to promote economic and social development in the Third World. His expertise, experience and reputation as an independent voice now resulted in invitations to address societies and organizations the length and breadth of the country and also in Britain, as well as to compose articles on a range of topics for the media. The time and care devoted to each composition over so wide a range of subjects in these talks, speeches and articles,* all on a voluntary basis, was enough in itself to fill whatever free time came with 'retirement'. His mediation skills were also brought to bear in a dispute between the National Union of Journalists and Independent Newspapers, as an independent assessor in a pay dispute between the board of the Abbey Theatre and Irish Actors Equity, and later as an arbitrator between Actors Equity and RTÉ.

Also with 'retirement' came a slew of honorary degrees from academic institutions, North and South. The citation conferring upon him an honorary degree of Doctor of Laws by the New University of Ulster in 1980 proclaimed him 'a democrat and liberally-minded man who suffers, it appears, from only one character defect – the stubborn inclination to disclaim expertise in so many areas where his prowess is unmatched and where, for once, the rest of us do know better'.[5] His lifelong interest in French language and culture was recognized in his appointment as president of the Alliance Française in Dublin in 1976. A few months after his retirement from the Central Bank, he became the first Irishman to be invested with the Order of Commandeur de la Légion d'Honneur by the French government. 'When asked

* See Appendix 3, p. 396.

355

why I should have received such an honour,' he mischievously remarks, 'I sometimes pretend it was for fighting alongside de Gaulle in North Africa!' His interest in Franco-Irish cultural relations, on both a personal and a public basis, was further demonstrated by his support for the restoration of the Collège des Irlandais in Paris, for which he was instrumental in negotiating tax relief status. After leaving the Central Bank, he rebutted media reports that he was to become adviser to Fianna Fáil. 'This was a piece of journalistic invention . . . I have not been asked and do not intend to advise any particular party.'[6] By then, a far more satisfying opening had presented itself that further deferred any prospect of a quiet retirement.

In late 1975, 'out of the blue', he was approached by the three presidents of the constituent colleges to allow his name to go forward for election to the office of chancellor of the National University of Ireland in succession to Éamon de Valera, who had worn the gold-threaded black gown for the previous fifty-four years. Though not a graduate of the NUI himself, having received his degrees as an external student of London University (albeit 'nationalized' in 1962 by the award of an honorary doctorate in Economic Science from the NUI), he was assured that his nomination would receive strong support and eventually agreed to stand. Declining an invitation to present his policies publicly because, as he pointed out, 'the only policy I could properly have was to promote the best interests of the University as decided from time to time by the Senate',[7] he none the less won by a substantial majority of votes. 'Never having attended a university', he muses, 'it was nice to enter at the top!'

At his installation on 19 May 1976, as he informed members of the NUI Senate, he did not intend to be a 'figurehead chancellor'. His experience as an administrator and policy-maker made him want to gain a thorough understanding of the issues affecting third-level education and, over the coming months, he visited each of the colleges to meet representatives of its authorities, staff and students. Appointed for life (or until resignation), the chancellor was the head of the governing body of the university, known as the Senate. One of the few practical perks of the job, as he recalls with amusement, was a free space in a car park in Earlsfort Terrace. Shortly after his election, he presented himself at the manned barrier to be told by the conscientious attendant that he had to have a permit to park there. Informed that the hopeful driver was the new chancellor, the attendant merely shrugged, telling him that 'a hell of a lot of chancers try to park here!' Next time Ken was careful to come armed with the appropriate permit.

The appointment came at a time of great debate and controversy regarding the status of third-level institutions in Ireland. In 1976 the NUI comprised the three constituent colleges of University College Dublin (UCD), University College Cork (UCC) and University College Galway (UCG), St Patrick's College, Maynooth (a recognized college within the NUI since 1910), the Royal College of Surgeons and various other colleges of education. Proposals and counter-proposals regarding the future of the NUI emanated from a variety of sources, most notably successive ministers for education, the Commission of Higher Education and the Higher Education Authority. In 1974 the minister for education, Richard Burke, indicated his intention to make UCD an independent university, leaving UCG, UCC and the other colleges under the aegis of the NUI. In 1976, shortly after Ken's election as chancellor, the minister changed tack, proposing instead five independent universities, TCD, UCD, UCC, UCG and St Patrick's College, Maynooth, but these plans, in the event, did not materialize.

Internally, too, there were problems in the structure and administration of the NUI. The Senate Ken Whitaker inherited was 'unbelievably disorderly', with no adherence to an agenda and little constructive discussion, yet with meetings that 'went on for hours', with the registrar announcing decisions 'that brooked no dissent'.[8] Quietly but determinedly, Ken brought order to proceedings. Meetings began and ended on time – with, as he humorously recalls, the new registrar's 'appetising snacks as a magnetic *terminus ad quem*!' His policy of 'ensuring a judicial process – the hearing of both sides' led to more productive debates on issues such as matriculation, appointments and procedures, and the future role and status of the NUI. Of personal concern was a commitment to excellence as an overriding priority in third-level education, the adequacy of degree standards, and the suitability of appointees to posts as lecturers and professors. He insisted that staff appointments, hitherto dependent on a lobbying system as competitive and intense as any obtaining in the political arena, should be made on merit only, with no canvassing or favouritism, and that degrees and diplomas awarded should be of a high international standard.

In choosing Ken Whitaker, the NUI had placed at its helm a person with the proven ability and standing to steer it through decades of change and uncertainty. He oversaw the at times contentious and drawn-out debate about redefining the role and composition of the NUI, and also contributed his views on the relevant legislation in the Senate. The growth in university education in the 1970s, mainly as a result of the introduction of free secondary education in the 1960s, gave rise to a rapid expansion in the structure, extent and variety of courses and degrees available. From the start of his period of office, he supported efforts to secure constituent university status (granted in 1997) for St Patrick's College, Maynooth, anxious, as he indicated, 'to see a secular university develop at Maynooth to take over from the declining seminary',[9] and during the transitional period was instrumental in developing structures for examinations for the college in conjunction with UCD. He was sympathetic to the situation forced upon the National Institute of Higher Education (NIHE) Limerick, which found itself bound by academic requirements laid down by the NUI that had little relevance to the Institute's vocational ethos. 'We have been joined together,' he told graduates at the historic first conferring at the institute in July 1977, at which he chose to present the degrees personally, 'the young and vigorous institution with the venerable and condemned university – by a form of shotgun wedding with the Government holding the gun.'[10] In his joint capacity as chancellor and as a member of Seanad Éireann, he publicly led the protest against the government's treatment of the NIHE Limerick as some 'state corporation rather than a pioneering third-level educational institution, needing special freedom and flexibility if it is to succeed in the urgent national objective of promoting technological studies and skills in a country still too biased in favour of the purely academic'.[11] His views were eventually vindicated by the conferring of university status on the former NIHE, now the University of Limerick.

Away from the more contentious issues, the office brought with it more pleasant ceremonial duties. At the official unveiling of a statue of James Joyce, the university's most famous graduate, on the new UCD campus in 1982, given the writer's less than distinguished academic achievements, Ken wondered whether the monument should serve as an example or a warning to the current crop of students. 'It might be better', he advised his young audience, 'to dodge the moral issue and simply declare that no Irish student of this century has displayed so creative an imagination or achieved such eminence as a writer of English and no Pass BA better deserves permanent recognition and commemoration in today's spacious groves of academe!'[12] While the presentation of degrees brought him into welcome contact with the staff and students of the constituent colleges, the conferral of honorary degrees on national and international 'celebrities' could, at times, give rise to public controversy, as in the case of US President Ronald Reagan.

In 1995, to celebrate the 150th anniversary of the founding of the former 'Queen's Colleges' at Cork, Galway and Belfast, Ken was invited to St James's Palace for a commemoration ceremony in the presence of Queen Elizabeth II and President Mary Robinson, together with his friend, Sir David Orr (Chancellor of Queen's University Belfast). After David Orr was presented, the Queen turned expectantly to Ken. Understanding that one must not speak until spoken to, he remained silent, and there was an embarrassing pause, which he decided to break by jocosely informing Her Majesty that as chancellor of the National University of Ireland, he could be considered the 'foster-father of twins' – Cork and Galway universities. The humour being lost on Her Majesty, she quickly passed on. 'I entertain a vision of her reporting wearily that evening to Prince Philip that her afternoon was spoiled by a mad Irish academic, claiming to be the foster-father of twins!'

By the time of Ken Whitaker's retirement as chancellor in December 1996 (to be succeeded by Garret FitzGerald), and mainly through his efforts, a new phase in the history of the NUI had opened. This culminated in the passing of the Irish Universities Act 1997, the first major enactment in the sector since 1908. Under the new law, the three original constituent colleges, and St Patrick's College, Maynooth, became autonomous universities of the NUI within the historical federal fabric. In bringing this about, Ken Whitaker's skill as a mediator, his logical interpretation of key issues, the order and sense of purpose he brought to proceedings, matched by his innate courtesy, good humour and forbearance, were recognized and appreciated. 'If only the same combination of wisdom, effectiveness and courtesy could be shown by others across the whole spectrum of Irish life, who knows what we couldn't achieve,'[13] Professor Joe Lee of UCC acknowledged. During his chancellorship the universities underwent the most fundamental transformation in their history.

Up to 1976, Ken's working life had been focused on public service, and this remained his primary focus thereafter.

Retirement also, however, afforded him the opportunity to dip his toes into the waters of the commercial world. He did so with customary care and forethought. From the many offers of directorships he received from private companies on his retirement from the Central Bank, he agreed to accept just two: those of Guinness (on whose board he sat from 1976 to 1984) and the Bank of Ireland (1976–85). 'I took the Guinness one to see how industry works and the Bank of Ireland was a natural extension of my banking career.' Ken was on holiday in Mayo in 1976 when Lord Iveagh, an acquaintance through the British–Irish Association, phoned to invite him to become a director of the International and Irish boards of Guinness. 'There was great amusement in the family as he had never had a pint of Guinness in his life,' his son Ken remembers. 'There and then we brought him to a little pub in Glencullen where he ceremoniously drank his first ever pint' of what is now his tipple of choice. Ken recalls with amusement his first introduction to the other board members at Guinness UK headquarters in Park Royal, London. On being asked his preference for a pre-lunch drink, he requested a gin and tonic; as he took his place at the dining table, this suddenly seemed a bad choice, when he observed that the rest of the board, 'including the ladies', each had a trademark pint of the 'black stuff' before them. 'Perhaps it gave notice that the "new boy" was of a more independent mind!' he likes to think. During his tenure on the Guinness boards he witnessed the company's transition from a family-run brewery to an international conglomerate. 'I had quit, on age grounds', he recalls, 'on the eve of the exciting events associated with the name of the managing director "Deadly" Ernest Saunders, but I was, of course, personally acquainted with all the *dramatis personae*.'

In retirement he retained his commitment to the three issues that had driven his working life as a public servant: the economy, Northern Ireland and the Irish language. By 1976 he viewed the government's policy of liberal foreign borrowing to finance day-to-day spending, in order to counteract the deflationary effects of high oil prices and global recession, as 'perverse'. In media interviews, he warned that 'what is unsustainable and ruinous, the bubble that must burst, is the high inflationary pay and cost trend . . . and the steep plunge into foreign indebtedness'.[14] Worse was to come in what he terms the 'crowning folly' of the 1977 Fianna Fáil election manifesto, which 'could not be described as an economic programme but rather a national disaster which . . . nearly smothered the economy in foreign debt'.[15] But extravagant promises, especially in relation to employment, the abolition of rates and other sweeteners, as well as the undoubted charisma of Jack Lynch, persuaded the electorate to return a Fianna Fáil government with a twenty-seat majority.

Following the election, Ken got an opportunity to voice his views in the political arena when he was selected as one of the Taoiseach's nominees to Seanad Éireann. 'I still recall my surprise, but also my sense of pride, when Jack Lynch asked me to serve in the Senate in 1977.' As the first public servant to be appointed, he felt it 'an honour not just for myself but for the public service I felt I was representing'. He accepted the nomination with one important proviso, as he told Lynch: that he would sit as an independent member and be 'free to speak my mind'. It was not long before the Taoiseach realized he had appointed not only a senator intent on speaking his mind but one who was an outspoken critic of the economic programme being pursued by his administration.

The government's decision to establish a new Department of Economic Planning and Development brought the first salvo from the newly appointed 'independent' senator, who declared with characteristic forthrightness that he considered it his duty 'to speak here according to my judgement and experience'.[16] As a 'Finance Man' through and through, he viewed with suspicion any weakening of the powers of the department over which he had once presided. Planning for the national economy, as he had shown in the 1950s, was well within the capabilities of the Department of Finance; and even though, as he conceded, in more recent years it had 'for one reason or another . . . tended to let slip its planning function',[17] that function should now be strengthened rather than diminished. Whatever policy emerged from the proposed new department, it would, he pointed out, still have to be executed by Finance; consequently, it would merely have an advisory function and so, in essence, would be a waste of taxpayers' money. Division of responsibilities had, moreover, proved a disaster in other countries. In the event the new department was short-lived, being abolished in 1979 by Charles Haughey, who transferred its functions, significantly, not to the Department of Finance but to the Department of the Taoiseach.

The extravagant projections in the government's 1981 budget, heralded in its white paper, *National Development 1977–1980*, were nothing more, Ken contended, than 'a mirror image' of Fianna Fáil's pre-election manifesto, full of 'irrational optimism',[18] totally out of line with the stark economic reality and opening up a chasm between budgetary projections and future results. The national debt, he said, was on a relentless upward curve, and he produced the devastating evidence to prove it: a rise from £4.2 million in 1977 to £10.2 million in 1981, figures at odds with the government's promises to 'greatly reduce the current deficit.' The drive for employment in the private sector to boost tax revenue backfired when the promised jobs turned out to be in the already inflated public sector. The harsh reality, as he pointed out, was that the national debt, which had taken fifty years to rise above £1,000 million, by the end of 1981 would approach £10,000 million, and 'no one can say that over the past decade there has been a matching increase in productive assets'.[19] For all his plain speaking, his 'biting the hand that fed me' stance in the Senate did not affect his relationship, on either a professional or a personal level, with Jack Lynch. On meeting the Taoiseach outside the Senate Chamber after delivering one of his broadsides, as Ken recalls, Lynch told him: 'That's what I put you there for.' His intention was not, as he told Lynch, to score points but 'to be constructive by helping to keep plans within attainable limits and by emphasising the real priorities'.[20]

The brakes, however, were not applied to the high-risk strategy being pursued by what even the partisan journalist John Healy described as 'a gambler's government',[21] driven by the demands of militant trade unionism. A second oil crisis in 1979, followed by inflated wage demands, unappeased by previous wage increases and cuts in personal taxation, resulted in a period of industrial chaos. Unofficial strikes, work-to-rule and absenteeism were the order of the day as rubbish piled up on city streets and scenes of violent confrontation between striking post office workers and gardaí were aggravated by petrol rationing.

At a conference on industrial relations in Cork in May 1979, Ken presented a thoughtful, analytical and constructive address entitled 'Industrial Relations: Is There a Better Way?' Describing himself as 'a concerned observer of a troubled scene', in a world 'where the seven deadly sins are powerful motivators, [and] it would be unwise to be too starry-eyed',[22] Ken addressed the factors that affected the relationship between workers and employers. In comments that prefigured the concept of social partnership initiated some years later, he regretted that the workplace was regarded solely as a centre of power. 'Is it not also a centre of production,' he asked, 'requiring a cooperative and efficiently functioning assembly of management, financial, personnel and other skills in order to achieve maximum added-value for the benefit of worker and society?' Active participation in decision-making from the shop floor upwards, more consultation and profit-sharing schemes for workers, the 'honourable observance of negotiated agreements and, where disputes arose, a firm acceptance by both sides of Labour Court recommendations', was the preferable way. Critical of the lack of leadership being shown in industrial relations, Ken made a passing comment about the actions of unions and employers, doctors who provided medical certificates for fake illnesses, and strikers who resorted to strong-arm tactics to promote sectional interests without due regard to the economic ability of the country to pay. At the conference he also questioned the 'professed concern' of sectional groups for the welfare of their lower-paid colleagues. 'The community cannot allow itself to be forced to its knees by any group which finds itself in control of essential supplies or services and callously and selfishly uses this power to enforce outrageous demands.'[23] He suggested that in such cases the security forces might need to be trained to man vital national services and protect the wider community in times, as he wrote, of 'extreme contingencies'.

To his dismay sensationalist headlines – 'Scorching for the Chaos Makers'; 'Call in the Army . . . Suggests Senator'; 'Train Army to Beat Strikes says Whitaker'[24] – and inaccurate reports of his speech appeared in the national newspapers. While his comments found much support from the general public, by then at the end of their tether, there was also some negative reaction, especially from more militant elements in the trade union movement, who interpreted his comments as a challenge to their right to strike. A month later, when his wife Nora was alone in the family home, on answering a knock at the door she was confronted by three masked raiders, who forced their way into the house, bound and gagged her, and tied her to a chair, telling her that her husband 'should keep his mouth shut about bringing in troops to deal with public sector strikes'.[25] After searching through her husband's papers they departed empty-handed. On his return home, Ken found his wife still bound and in a distressed state. It was a terrifying ordeal which left Nora for a time, as her daughter-in-law recalls, 'extremely traumatized' and having lost 'a lot of her confidence'. While the intruders were never identified, the speculation endures that militant strikers – indeed, in view of Ken's involvement in the Northern Ireland issue at the time, perhaps militants with an additional terrorist agenda – were responsible.

Following a botched first attempt to join the European Monetary System, a poor showing in the European elections in June 1979 and the loss of a 'winnable' by-election in his home city of Cork, all against the background of a continuing deterioration in the national finances, Jack Lynch's tenure as Taoiseach and leader of Fianna Fáil drew to a close. By mid-1979 covert plans were afoot to have him replaced, with Charles Haughey as the main conspirator. Towards the conclusion of Ireland's presidency of the EEC, on 5 December 1979, Lynch formally announced his decision to resign. While Ken could be critical, both privately and publicly, of Lynch's tendency not to rock the boat, to be, at times, too hands-off in his role as leader, allowing too much freedom in speech and in action to his ministers, their friendship endured. In their respective capacities as politician and public servant they recognized that each had a specific role to play, and that these were not always compatible. It says a lot about the calibre of both men that in these circumstances, as Ken testified, 'our good relationship in the official context broadened into a lasting personal friendship'.[26] Appalled by the greed and corruption he saw enveloping public life, and particularly the party he once led, like a toxic mist, Jack Lynch was all the more appreciative of Ken Whitaker's dedication and contribution as a public servant, writing some months before his resignation: 'Now in my declining years . . . I all the more recognise the un-honoured and unsung public service of those who more profitably and with less contumely, could have given of their time in more personally profitable pursuits.'[27]

Of similar outlook and age, the two men also shared an interest in salmon fishing, as captured by the iconic photograph of them, with President Hillery, on the famous Ridge Pool on the river Moy. Ken's grandson Allen recalls another day's fishing on the Moy as a young boy, when he lost the 'flying condom' fly loaned him by Paddy Hillery and was consoled by 'Jack Lynch who opened the President's bag and handed me another, telling me, "Don't worry. He's rich. He can buy plenty more!"' Golf, too, occasionally brought Ken and Jack Lynch together in an environment in which they could relax and discuss political or economic problems away from the cauldron of public office. They shared a wry sense of humour. 'I recall a sweltering day in Baltray, when taking a break from the golf, we spied a rather obese bather in green swimming trunks entering the water. "I take it that is what you economists would call a Gross National Product," Jack observed.' Ken continued to draft speeches and articles for Lynch long after the latter's retirement from politics, urging him in 1992 'to give up speaking engagements and get down to writing a memoir of your period in Government'.[28] Both men were members of 'Murphy's', a private dining club 'dedicated to candour' and to monthly discussion, under 'Chatham House rules', on matters of common interest to representatives of both the private and the public sector. Founded in 1963 on the crest of the first *Programme for Economic Expansion*, over the decades the club attracted many of the country's principal movers and shakers. Ken was instrumental in bringing Jack Lynch into the club on his retirement from politics and, through his contacts in Northern Ireland, having people such as Cardinal Conway and Ken Bloomfield attend as guest speakers.

In their private lives, in stark contrast to the ostentation that was becoming the badge of success among the country's public figures, both men preferred quiet domesticity. 'You and Ken are wonderful hosts,' Máirín Lynch wrote to Nora. 'I can think of no better people to ensure the perfect climate and atmosphere for the complete relaxation and enjoyment of your guests.'[29] Occasionally the home cooking was supplemented by something special, as when, for one such supper, in Jack and Máirín's honour, Ken produced a bottle of Château Lynch Bages he had been given as a present. In his note of thanks, Jack jocosely remarked how the delicious home cuisine and the Lynch Bages 'brought me back to my early days in Chateau Ui Loinsigh Cois Laoi'![30] In his latter years, when the former Taoiseach was in failing health, Ken was a regular visitor to his house in Rathgar. In 1993 the two were sitting beside each other at an informal dinner when Lynch suffered an incapacitating stroke in which he virtually lost his sight. Visiting his friend in the Royal Hospital in Donnybrook, Ken helped maintain his spirits to the last, remembering with fondness Jack's rendition of 'The Banks' on his eighty-first birthday. Although he was out of the country when Jack Lynch passed away in October 1999, it was to Ken Whitaker that Máirín turned to write her husband's obituary and to design an appropriate tombstone. When Ken suggested that it should be made of Cork limestone and engraved with the words 'happy is the man who finds wisdom', Máirín simply acknowledged that the idea 'makes me happy'.[31] On Máirín's death in 2004, Ken recalled how, in the absence of children, all her devotion, wisdom and concern had centred on her husband. 'Having given him her best in life and, indeed, also in commemoration of his death, it seemed to her friends that, more recently, she was at ease, awaiting a loving reunion.'[32]

After a bruising and bitter internal party struggle dominated by accusations of intimidation and bribery, the election of Charles Haughey as Taoiseach on 11 December 1979 did little to alleviate the country's precarious economic situation – and nothing to deter Ken Whitaker in his determination to continue to do what he considered to be his duty. Haughey's words to the nation in his first broadcast as Taoiseach, that 'we are living way beyond our means', might well have brought a wry smile to Ken's lips, as well as a hope, albeit faint, that the new Taoiseach, whose ability was unquestionable, would come to grips with the dire economic situation. Haughey's first budget, however, failed to live up to his stated intention to curb government spending and bor-rowing, which in the event shot up even further, resulting in major tax hikes. Having suggested in a speech in Ennis that reflationary action might be an option, Haughey subsequently found himself in receipt of a letter, enclosing an article entitled 'How Much Room for Reflation?', from his former departmental secretary, whom he must surely have thought to have left far behind. 'With the current budget again coming apart and the pay proposals discouraging, the true and short answer to the query, "How Much Room for Reflation?" is "none",' Ken uncompromisingly informed him. 'The best hope lies in an early (by mid-1981) upturn in world trade and nothing done meanwhile should retard or reduce our capacity to benefit from it.'[33] Haughey's reply, promising to 'study your paper carefully',[34] was not matched by any worthwhile action.

In 1982 the two men had a more public difference of opinion. Haughey's advocacy during the February election campaign of increased borrowing for non-productive purposes, such as the provision of five thousand jobs in the public sector, cut no ice with more responsible commentators. In January 1982, during a talk to the United States Chamber of Commerce in Ireland, tracing the detrimental changes that had occurred in the country's balance of payments, Ken concluded: 'Against the background I have outlined today, anyone who would advocate a continuation of Government borrowing on its present scale must be seen to be disgracefully irresponsible.'[35] Widely covered in the media, his words were interpreted as a direct reprimand and reference to Haughey. In a subsequent radio interview, Haughey stated that he found it difficult to understand the stance now being taken by Senator Whitaker and suggested that the former Finance secretary had done 'an about turn' on foreign borrowing.

When he was in government and had responsibility for these matters, it was he, as much as anybody else, who set out a programme of borrowing and investment to build up the economy of this country ... His status in life has changed and that may be why his views on these matters have changed. But mine have not. They are the same as they were when, in agreement with him, we set about building up and developing the economy.[36]

Ken's public response was muted but to the point:

It was wrong of Deputy Haughey to say that my views about foreign borrowing have changed. There is no reason why they should. I have always been in favour of a reasonable and sustainable rate of foreign borrowing to boost productive investment at home and I have always been against an excessively high level of foreign borrowing, and in particular the misuse of foreign borrowing, to finance everyday expenses.[37]

Charles Haughey's known predilection for taking umbrage was to have personal repercussions for Ken Whitaker. Unique in having been appointed a senator by the leaders of both Fianna Fáil and Fine Gael, Ken found Haughey unwilling, on his election as Taoiseach in 1982, to follow the example of his predecessors.

To have served two terms in the Seanad Éireann, on the nomination of the two major political parties, is something Ken views with pride. During his tenure as senator, he contributed to debates on many issues, economic, constitutional, cultural and educational. He was chosen by the press correspondents as 'Political Speaker of the Year' in 1978 for his consistently constructive and independent approach and for the high degree of expertise and analysis he demonstrated in Senate debates. He has a profound regard for the Senate as a political entity: 'I came to appreciate the important political and constitutional role this democratic forum plays in our public life. In particular, I saw at first-hand the platform which the Seanad gives to independent voices and the important, though often unglamorous, work the second chamber does in scrutinizing, initiating and revising legislation' – views he reiterated in 2013 in support of the campaign to retain the second chamber.

Corrective national economic measures were impeded by the revolving-door nature of national politics between 1979 and 1987. With four general elections – two in 1982 alone – destabilizing heaves against Charles Haughey within Fianna Fáil, scandal and skulduggery in high places, as Ken starkly acknowledged, 'all we managed to do in the first half of the 1980s was to slow down the slide to national bankruptcy'.[38] Finally, a belated conversion to the path of fiscal rectitude by the Haughey-led Fianna Fáil minority government elected in 1987, with the support of the outgoing Taoiseach Garret FitzGerald, and reinforced by what became known as the 'Tallaght Strategy' of his successor, Alan Dukes, finally took the country's finances in hand. Through the benefits of EU membership, notably the availability of structural funding, more favourable exchange rates through membership of the European Monetary Union, improvements and developments in education, infrastructure and new technology, large-scale inward investment attracted by grants and low taxation – and, most significantly from Ken's perspective, the moderation in incomes negotiated through social partnership, the country slowly began to emerge from its long and destructive period of indebtedness and stagnation to embrace a new era of remarkable growth and development. 'No change in my lifetime has been more remarkable or less predicted,'[39] Ken recalled of the transformation. But history, particularly economic history, as he more than anyone else realized, had a devastating way of repeating itself.

Haughey's decision not to reappoint Ken to the Senate in 1982 was offset by appointments to numerous committees dealing with a diverse range of issues, many unglamorous. In 1984, following a serious riot in Mountjoy Jail and an accelerating crime rate, the Taoiseach, Garret FitzGerald, asked him to chair an inquiry into the penal system, the first official analysis of the Irish prison service undertaken since a royal commission of 1881. 'I was dumbfounded,' Ken recalls. 'Never having been in prison, my only qualification, as I told him, was ignorance, which he generously transformed into open-mindedness!' With a committee of eight, of whom he recalls, 'not since the golden period of preparing *Economic Development* ... I have experienced such friendly and eager cooperation',[40] he set out on a far-reaching investigation into Ireland's long-neglected underbelly. Visiting jails around the country, he and his committee interviewed inmates and staff – including the governor of Mountjoy, John Lonergan, whom he found one of the few 'thoughtful and engaged managers of a prison'. They also interviewed victims of crime, as well as visiting prisons and engaging with those in charge of penal systems in England, Scotland and Scandinavia. Their report, described by the chairman of the Prisoners' Rights Organization as 'a comprehensive, enlightened and caring document',[41] was presented to government within seventeen months.

Society must first deal with its economic and social problems, the report asserted, if it wanted to deal with crime. Because of its limited positive value, its possible harmful effects, and the exorbitant cost to the taxpayer of keeping one prisoner in jail – £29,000 per year in 1985 – imprisonment should be considered a last resort, reserved for the most grievous offences. The report dealt with every aspect of the penal system, from prison conditions and neglected infrastructure to the custodial care of young offenders, treatment facilities for drug and alcohol abusers, facilities for female prisoners (who, as the inquiry found, were mainly 'young and the victims of an array of personal problems which cried out for attention') and the needs of political prisoners, 'whose physical isolation from spouses and children has been a disgrace.'[42] The report's recommendations included the transfer of responsibility for the day-to-day running of the prison service from the Department of Justice to local prison management, improvements in industrial relations, the greater investigation and use of alternatives to imprisonment, and the establishment of an inspector of prisons. Anticipating the formation of the Criminal Assets Bureau (CAB) by over two decades, it also recommended the confiscation of 'ill-gotten gains' amassed through criminal activity, whether or not the offenders were in receipt of prison sentences.

While positively received by all sides as 'an overdue recognition of the need for radical reform of the present system',[43] the report was destined to languish on the sidelines, its recommendations ignored, for many years. Fifteen years after the inquiry was set up, two of those recommendations, a new remand centre and a women's prison, were given the green light, and also in 1999 the Irish Prisons Board took over the management of Irish prisons from the Department of Justice, albeit with limited powers. However, most of the inquiry's recommendations still await implementation. As Ken pointed out, the report fell foul not merely of political expediency, but also 'of indifferent and unenlightened public attitudes',[44] especially in relation to the reluctance of many citizens, particularly victims of crime, to accept non-custodial options such as probation, fines, confiscation, restitution and community service instead of prison for lesser crimes.

In 1989 Ken found himself 'back in prison again': this time as chairman of a Sentence Review Group, on which he served from 1989 to 1993. Revisiting prisons, he interviewed around a hundred inmates serving sentences for crimes ranging from murder to petty larceny. 'One of my strongest and most encouraging impressions is how indomitable the human spirit can be even in the grimmest of circumstances.' He was critical of the lack of thought and experiment being applied to major issues, such as alternatives to incarceration and ways of dealing with addiction: 'In neither of these areas does prison provide a promising remedial environment.' He viewed the Probation and

Welfare Service as being a crucial element towards achieving a more effective, economical and humane penal system. This was the core outcome of the two investigations he chaired.

While still, as he said, 'serving time' in 1985, he was elected president of the Royal Irish Academy for a term of two years. He presided over the bicentenary celebrations of the academy's foundation, which included events involving representatives from twenty European and American academies, a series of lectures by eminent Irish and international scientists and scholars, and a range of seminars, publications and conferences. His steward-ship was deemed by the academy to have been 'formidable'.[45] On 15 December 1986 Ken delivered his presidential address, entitled 'Ireland: Land of Change', a reflective and unflinching appraisal of the country's development from the 1920s to the mid-1980s.

On her election as president in 1991, his former fellow senator, Mary Robinson, appointed him to the Council of State, 'an hon-our' he modestly considers 'far beyond my deserts'. But many Irish citizens would agree that failure to entice Ken Whitaker himself through the portals of Áras an Uachtaráin as president was to the country's great loss.

In 1991 his chairmanship of the Common Fisheries Policy Review Group was an appointment that gave him both personal and professional satisfaction. As well as having a sporting interest in salmon, following a serious decline in stocks during the 1970s he had developed a scientific interest in the issue of salmon preservation, and in 1977, as a director of the board of Guinness, he had been appointed to the committee of management of the Salmon Research Trust established by the company in 1955. Situated at Furnace, Newport, County Mayo, jointly funded by Guinness and the Irish government, the trust conducted scientific and field research for the purpose of improving and extending salmon and sea trout fisheries in Ireland 'for the benefit of the people of Ireland and the community at large'.[46] Situated between two interconnected lakes, Furnace (saltwater) and Feeagh (freshwater), and connected to the famous Burrishoole river system, the trust was ideally placed to monitor upstream and downstream movements of fish. In 1980, as chairman of the trust, Ken facilitated the handover of the facility from Guinness to the state. Operating one of the longest-established monitoring sites and most significant index systems for salmon, sea trout and eel in the North Atlantic, the Salmon Research Agency, as it was renamed in 1981, developed into one of the world's greatest natural laboratories for the study of wild Atlantic salmon and a research base for salmon, sea trout and eel, providing invaluable scientific advice in the conservation and regeneration of fish stocks. In 1999 the agency was incorporated into the newly established Marine Institute, and in 2003, to Ken's great delight, its research and scientific facilities were further extended.

Following a virtual collapse in sea trout stocks, in 1993 he was asked by the minister for the marine to chair a Sea Trout Task Force, representative of all interested parties, including fishery boards and owners, fish farms and An Bord Iascaigh Mhara (the Irish Sea Fisheries Board). The ensuing report, delivered with characteristic promptness within the timespan allocated, was both comprehensive and unanimous. In fair and balanced terms, it found a correlation between sea farms and the demise of sea trout stock. To save the sea trout from possible extinction, it recommended the elimination of sea lice in the vicinity of sea farms, the combination of the commercial development of sea farming with the preservation of sea trout, and access to the wild sea trout population as a source of brood stock to augment future stocks. Within three years of the report's publication, the levels of sea lice on fish farms were greatly reduced and, with the replenishment of new stock, a slow but steady recovery in sea trout stocks had begun.

In 1995, as chairman of the Wild Salmon Support Group, a working group concerned with the management, conservation and strategies for the protection of salmon stocks, Ken wrote a series of five articles for the *Irish Times*. Impeccably researched, balanced, reasonable, clearly and concisely written, and showing a consummate knowledge and love of his subject, they laid out the stark realities that threatened the future existence of 'the king of fish' and proposed appropriate solutions, including the abolition of drift-netting, which was subsequently enforced.

As Ken entered his eightieth year, a further investigative crusade beckoned when in 1995 Garret FitzGerald sought his services as chairman of a Constitution Review Group to prepare a report for an all-party committee of the Oireachtas 'to establish those areas where constitutional change may be desirable or necessary'.[47] Given his experience as a member of the 1967 Constitution Committee and his carefully considered contributions to constitutional issues, both in Seanad Éireann and in the media – especially in relation to the removal of articles 2 and 3 on Northern Ireland, on various referenda relating to the EU, and on the issue of abortion in the light of the 'X' case of 1992 – he was clearly a most suitable choice. Nevertheless, it was a daunting undertaking. And yet, to judge by the erudition, comprehension and sagacity displayed in his personal notes and memos involving the complex range of issues investigated by the group, as well as those he expressed personally in additional articles, it must be acknowledged that in Ken Whitaker the legal profession lost out on the services of a skilled and talented potential practitioner. His trademark organizational and inspirational talents were brought to bear in the production of a 700-page report for the government within the stipulated twelve-month timetable.

His starting principle for the project was: 'If it ain't broke, don't fix it.' The 1937 constitution had, he maintained, stood the test of time, and any proposed adaptation to meet modern-day socio-political requirements should aim 'to keep it as clear and concise as possible so that its basic statement of powers, rights and responsibilities will be generally understood'.[48] The task of the review group was to set out, in a clear and orderly manner, aspects of the constitution that, under prevailing current circumstances, including those attributable to membership of the EU, required change by way of amendment, deletion or extension. From the preamble and article 1 through to article 50, each individual article and subsection of the constitution was examined and a recommendation of 'change' or 'no change' proposed. Significantly, given the extensive subject matter under review, few changes and deletions were recommended and even fewer additions, those notably in relation to the Ombudsman, local government, the environment and human rights. Many changes, as the report pointed out, were already in the power of the Oireachtas and of legislators, and did not require constitutional amendment through referendum.

The report formed the basis for the proceedings of the All-Party Oireachtas Committee, established in 1996. Ken agreed to appear before the committee to give his personal views on aspects of the constitution, which, as he reiterated to the committee, should be concerned only with perennial principles, leaving the treatment of particular social and other issues to the more effective and democratic (and also less expensive) process of legislation. Ranging over issues as varied as government structures, electoral reform, the fundamental rights of citizens, abortion and the position of the family, and, later, the various EU referenda held during the late 1990s and more recent issues, such as gay marriage, his contributions demonstrate a careful, comprehensive and balanced analysis of difficult, technical and, at times, emotionally charged issues that would do justice to the most eminent legal brain.

On delivery of the Constitution Review Report to the government, Ken circumspectly refused to give media or public interviews about the findings, 'on the basis that *res ipsa loquitur* and that it is no part of my function to defend comments or conclusions or adopt a crusader role'.[49] One particular aspect of the report, which he had personally drafted, came under fire from Archbishop Desmond Connell. This related to articles 41 and 42, concerning natural law and its relationship to man-made or positive law. In his submission to the All-Party Oireachtas Committee, the archbishop accused the review group of having an 'inadequate understanding' of, and of seeking to undermine, the theory of natural law, on the questions of the right to life of the unborn, abortion and the definition of what constituted a family, and by the elimination of religious language in the report. In a reasoned but candid reply, Ken rebuffed each of the archbishop's arguments and accusations, noting that 'one would expect that . . . anything published in the church's name would be expressed in temperate language and be scrupulously fair and free from attributions of ignorance or sinister intent, recognising, or at least charitably assuming, in those criticised, a parity of intelligence and integrity'.[50]

While many of the recommendations of the reports of the various commissions he chaired remain unfulfilled today, Ken is philosophical at the lack of action. 'You develop a hard hide as a civil servant. Reports, particularly those which recommend solutions that may be considered politically awkward, take time to be adopted. I realized that there were ancient and strong vested interests at work and that it would take time. I wasn't waiting breathlessly for things to be changed.' Indeed, with a pragmatism born of long experience he acknowledges that 'some reports are just done simply to take the matter off the agenda . . . postpone it for a couple of years, especially if it results in awkward recommendations . . . then everyone simply forgets about it.' None the less, he devoted time and diligence, on a voluntary basis, to every commission; and the reports themselves stand as testimony to his own ethos of public service: 'We were asked to do a job and we did it: it was up to those in political power to implement the recommendations.'

The huge contribution Ken Whitaker has made to Irish public life was celebrated with a publication launched on 8 December 1996, the occasion of his eightieth birthday. Organized by Fionán Ó Muircheartaigh, a former T. K. Whitaker Research Fellow of the ESRI, it was entitled *Ireland in the Coming Times* and, 'like the man it is designed to honour . . . looks to the future'.[51] In a series of nineteen essays, reflecting Ken's economic, social, political and cultural undertakings during the course of his public life, experts in each field examined the future challenges and implications facing Ireland. As a retrospective, however, it proved somewhat premature, as he gave notice on his eightieth birthday: 'I thank God for having had so far an interesting, fulfilling and happy life and I look forward to its continuing that way for a while longer.'[52]

14

Evening is the Best
Part of the Day

*We are all, it has been said, the slaves of some defunct economist. In
retrospect, the blind spots are only too visible. What, I wonder, will
turn out to be the blind spots of today?*
T. K. Whitaker

THE ULTIMATE TEST of human beings is not how they deal with
success but how they cope with adversity. No life, especially one
as long as that enjoyed by Ken Whitaker, can be expected to pass
without its share of personal loss and sadness. How he has dealt
with personal tragedies is as inspiring as the triumphs he has
achieved on the public stage. His interest and participation in so
many issues and projects of national importance, his personal
and continuing quest for knowledge, his openness to new ideas,
his generosity towards others, his outgoing nature and sense of
fun, the 'irresistible temptation' of fishing: all have served as anti-
dotes to the sadness generated by personal family tragedy and loss
which, if indulged, can often tend to overwhelm. 'He has suffered
such personal loss in his life that anyone else would be utterly
devastated,' his daughter-in-law Teresa attests. 'But he has an
extraordinary core of inner strength, an internal locus of self-
control, helped by being outgoing, helpful and optimistic.'

His first grandchild, Anne, born in 1970 with a rare and

incurable condition, died two months after her birth. It was a devastating time for her parents, Ken and Maeve, as well as for the wider family. As Maeve recalls, it was her father-in-law and her own father who took it in turns to sit by the bed of the tiny infant in Crumlin Children's Hospital every day for the duration of her short life. In 1979 there was the sad inevitability of Ken's mother's death in her hundredth year. Jane Whitaker lived her lifespan, mentally and physically, to the fullest extent, retaining her status as family matriarch throughout. 'She was part of the very fabric of Ken's life to the end,' his daughter-in-law Deirdre recalls. 'He thought the world of her and she of him, while taking his achievements in her stride.' Then in 1988 came the tragic and untimely death at thirty-three of Priscila, wife of Ken's son Brian, after a lengthy battle with cancer. Argentinian-born, educated in Ireland, positive and inspirational, Priscila battled bravely with her illness and many medical setbacks to the end. After her passing, Ken and Nora stepped into the breach to help her two young sons, seven-year-old Andrew and five-year-old Greg, cope with the enormity of their loss.

For someone active and energetic, who generally enjoyed robust good health, illness came to Nora as a bolt from the blue. In 1991, attending an exhibition in the National Gallery, she missed her step on descending a staircase. She was taken by ambulance to hospital but there seemed to be no repercussions. On the subsequent eve of their fiftieth wedding anniversary, which they planned to celebrate with a party for their family and friends, with invitations sent out and arrangements in place, Nora suffered a brain haemorrhage. Rushed to hospital, after a brief respite she suffered a second and more severe haemorrhage that left her in a deep coma lasting for many months. Sitting beside her bed every day, talking and joking to his comatose wife, Ken never lost hope, even when the medical team suggested that it might be time to consider withdrawing the intravenous treatment that was keeping her alive. After discussions with his family and close friends, he instructed the doctors to continue with the treatment. His perseverance was rewarded when one morning, on making his daily enquiry: 'Good morning, Nora. How are you today?' he received an unexpected reply: 'Very well, Ken, and how are you?' From then Nora started the journey back to some semblance of health, eventually becoming well enough to return home and enjoy a further two years of a relatively positive lifestyle. Readily adjusting to the position of carer, Ken was 'always positive', as his daughter-in-law Erika remembers, 'never letting it get him down, just accepting the circumstances', until Nora's death in May 1994.

Over the fifty-three years they had spent together, their union had been a happy and fulfilling one. 'Nora ruled the roost at home,' her daughter-in-law Maeve remembers. 'Ken went to work and she did everything else.' Confident, able and calm, Deirdre recalls, 'nothing fazed her . . . she was her own woman, always had a presence and was a great support for Ken in his varied public undertakings'. Rearing her family with a characteristic common-sense approach, sometimes unselfishly adjusting her personal life to her husband's many commitments, she nevertheless ensured that his public work was not carried out at the expense of family and friends and, efficiently and effortlessly, kept their lives in balance. Her passing left a huge gap in Ken's personal world. 'I don't know if she was ever conscious of how supportive a role she played,' he wonders. Not being the most domesticated of men, living on his own was a practical as well as an emotional challenge, and he rose to it: while his elderly housekeeper, Mrs Duggan, continued to maintain the day-to-day running of the house, Ken eventually found his métier in bread-making and in serving up, as he claims, 'the best fry in Dublin or Mayo'!

With Nora's passing, his only daughter, Catherine, took up the role of her father's main support. Helpful and generous of her time, Catherine became, as her extended family recall, the organizer of family get-togethers and a presence for everyone in times of bereavement and trouble. A short time after her mother's death, still in her early forties, she was diagnosed with breast cancer. A rock of support during her mother's lengthy illness, she may well, as her brothers suspect, have been somewhat neglectful of her own condition. Enduring the ensuing chemotherapy and radiotherapy with a quiet stoicism, as her father recorded, 'she never complains, never seems depressed and is a tonic for everyone who visits her'.[1] During one of Catherine's remission periods, in February 1997 he brought her on a holiday to Andalusia, to visit the Moorish capitals of Málaga, Seville, Córdoba and Granada and the 'pueblo blanco' mountain villages. It was both an opportunity to spend time together, knowing as they did that the prognosis was not hopeful, and his way of attempting to provide his only daughter with a temporary release from the anxiety and debilitating effects of her illness. Catherine's death in 1998, following so closely on that of his wife, was a severe blow, which he sought to alleviate by helping her four children – Barry, Nicola, Matthew and Peter – and her husband Oran cope with their loss. 'It was devastating . . . to all of us,' Catherine's brother Ken recalls. 'We had only the one sister, with whom we all got on so well.' For many years, on the anniversary of her death, her father hosted a 'little commemoration' at his home for Catherine's close friends, his way of keeping alive the memory of his beloved daughter.

When Ken's second son, Gerry, took early retirement from banking, with more time on his hands he frequently teamed up with his father to enjoy holiday breaks and the occasional pint together. In September 2002, while walking his dog on a beach near his home, Gerry suffered a brain haemorrhage. Lack of ambulance access to the beach meant a delay and his transfer to hospital by helicopter, where he subsequently died without regaining consciousness. Ken's care and concern for Gerry's family was and continues to be demonstrated, as Gerry's widow,

Deirdre, attests, 'in so many ways that you might not even be aware of . . . keeping an eye out for you, ensuring that you were included, keeping in contact with the children. It is as if he tries to put right everything that goes wrong.'

This series of losses – of his wife, grandchild, two children and daughter-in-law – according to his youngest son Brian 'took a heavy toll on him'. He did not really open up about it, preferring, as Brian's brother David maintains, to cope by 'stoically putting it away and pulling himself together, so that it is hard to know how he is really feeling'. Falling back on his inner reserves of strength and fortitude and, as he puts it, on the realization that, just as 'you have been fortunate in having had such relationships and warm feelings, [so] it is part of your make-up that you have upsurges of optimism that keep you going'. That ability to soldier on was, perhaps, a legacy too of the resilience imbued in him by his Northern background. 'Ken is of that generation that did not have the same sense of entitlement as the present generation,' his daughter-in-law Erika reflects. 'They simply accepted things as they were, were grateful for what they had and possessed that inherent capacity to move on.'

As the next generation of his family grew up, Ken was always supportive and available, never intrusive, always interested. He offered advice and practical assistance with homework and school projects, his editorial eagle eye bringing to their attention any misspelling or other inaccuracies. 'We had great chats after the news . . . when you kindly put me up – put up with me! – for a few months,' his granddaughter Yseult recalled. 'And helped with my upcoming history exam.' To one grandson, temporarily confused as to his career choice, came the invitation to 'please come and talk to me . . . to help you overcome your difficulties and realise your great potential'. For his granddaughter Karen, he 'stepped into the breach', in place of her father Gerry, to 'give me away on my wedding day'; he travelled to Seville to link up with another grandson, Paul; and when his granddaughter Julie from America chose to study in Dublin, he would 'bring me to and from the airport, take me out to dinner and bring me to movies and concerts'.

On Brian's marriage to Erika, a new generation of grandchildren began to appear in the 1990s. 'Ken is undoubtedly a new-born baby magnet,' Erika testifies. 'I never met a man, no matter what age, who enjoys new-born babies as much as Ken. He can sit contentedly with a baby in his arms for hours.' With nine children to their credit, they had reason to be grateful for Ken's baby-holding expertise.

The traffic is not, however, all one way. The younger generation visit their grandfather and accompany him to functions, lunches and musical events, as well as helping him cope with the complexities of computers, emails and the internet to which, in his nineties, he adapted. 'They care enough to want to do it,' Erika maintains. 'It is not an obligation. They enjoy his company and are delighted to share time with him.' They are proud, too, of his achievements and of the reputation and affection he enjoys among the Irish public. 'When people hear my surname, there's always a question in their eyes,' his granddaughter Jane recounts. 'At this point I cringe and hope they won't mention the whistling, singing Roger Whittaker, but more often than not they simply ask: "Are you related to the great man himself?"'

With the passage of time, it was inevitable that Ken Whitaker would lose many of his friends and colleagues. His obituaries and eulogies for Lord O'Neill, Seán Lemass, Con Cremin, Professor Tadhg Ó Ciardha, Thekla Beere, Seámus Delargy, Dr J. P. Beddy, Ben Dunne senior, Frank Aiken and Jack and Máirín Lynch are testament to his literary skill as well as to his empathy with each individual friend. In December 1987, 'with a great sense of privilege', he launched a volume of essays, initiated by the Law Society in memory of his friend and colleague Alexis Fitzgerald, whom, as he noted, he 'would be relieved to see seated as Special Adviser beside the Almighty on Judgement Day'.[2] Ken's generosity to many writers – checking drafts of their work with his trademark editorial diligence, delivering speeches at book launches – and his unfailing cultural energy (unveiling statues, opening exhibitions, attending concerts, even embarking on cello lessons at the age of eighty-eight) would have exhausted the forbearance and the stamina of many half his age.

Honours and accolades pursued him. One portrait was commissioned and hung in the National Gallery of Ireland, another in the headquarters of the ESRI. He became an honorary member of many and varied organizations and societies.* In 2001 RTÉ viewers named him 'Irishman of the Twentieth Century', and the following year he became the recipient of a special ESB/Rehab 'Greatest Living Irish Person' award – at which, he remarked, 'I feel like Rip Van Winkle emerging, confused, blinking, into unexpected and undeserved sunlight'.[3] Schools, libraries and landmarks have all been named in his honour. His love of travel has remained undimmed, trips in his eighties taking him to France, and to Lewis in the Outer Hebrides to fish and to brush up his Scottish Gaelic, and in his nineties to Barcelona for his granddaughter Nicola's marriage, to Düsseldorf and Cologne to renew acquaintance with family friends, and more recently to California, to visit his son Raymond and daughter-in-law Anne. He keeps alive, too, his connections with north Mayo, and with Rannafast in the Donegal Gaeltacht – where, as his diary for August 1996 records, he took part in a céilidh, dancing 'Fallaí Luimnigh le Nell McCafferty'.[4]

Behind all the activities, however, was the gnawing loneliness of widowerhood, of coming back to a silent home, of not having someone to share the moments and the interests, someone to care for. On the death of her husband in 1999, Ken took to visiting his widowed sister Peggie more regularly and, in the process, renewed acquaintanceship with a neighbour and family friend, Mary Moore, a nurse tutor. 'She was there all the time,' Ken

* For details, see Appendix 2, p. 395.

recalls, somewhat in amazement. Mary shared his love of music and it was, as he recalls, 'a delight to have her company to concerts and other functions'. The relationship developed into, as he simply notes, 'a friendship brightening life for both of us and making us happy'. To their families, and to all who knew them, Ken and Mary's devotion to each other was obvious from the start. Although Ken was many years Mary's senior, the age difference between them evaporated in love and in the aura of romance they radiated. 'Because of my age, I hesitated to ask her to marry me,' Ken recalls, 'until 2005 when, to my great delight, she accepted.' They were married that June in a quiet family ceremony in Piltown, County Kilkenny, with Mary's brother, Father Paschal Moore, officiating and with Ken's beloved Bach as the wedding music of choice. Their honeymoon took in visits to places from Ken's childhood, including his mother's home in Coolmeen and Rannafast.

In 2006 Ken celebrated his ninetieth birthday at a function in the Royal College of Surgeons, accompanied by Mary and surrounded by his extended family, friends and colleagues; it was a memorable occasion. An invitation to tea at Áras an Uachtaráin to mark the event renewed his acquaintance with President Mary McAleese, also a former resident of Rostrevor. This was followed by a return visit to the Áras in 2010 on the occasion of the fiftieth anniversary of the establishment of the ESRI.

Ken's expectation that, because of the age difference, he would be first to depart 'ar slí na fírinne', was destined, 'like hail in September', to be confounded when, after some months' illness, Mary died in 2008. Ken had become her carer and support during the spells of ill-health and hospitalization that had dogged their few years together. 'In some ways the loss of Mary was even greater than Nora,' his son Ken acknowledges. 'It happened at a stage when he was so happy to have the companionship . . . someone to look after.' Mary's death was followed in 2010 by that of his sister Peggie.

With a stoicism born of character and experience, despite the relentless passing of time and its inevitable physical constraints, Ken's determination to continue to live his lifespan to the fullest continues to inspire. Each day brings a new interest and a new challenge. The heartbeat of his family circle, his sense of hope, his generosity and good humour, all continue to burn brightly. To be in his company in public, as strangers come to greet him, thank him and shake his hand, makes one realize how much he is appreciated and the affection with which he is regarded by his fellow countrymen and women. It is as if his very presence connects them to a time and a society motivated by a caring and more ethical set of principles.

Regarding the three main motivations at the core of his life-time of public service, he is not without hope. On the Irish language, it is to him 'a marvel and delight that it is still alive as a medium of inspiration as well as communication'. As he acknowl-edges, however, government intervention alone is no longer enough to ensure its survival; also required is acknowledgement by the general public that the language is worth saving. In a world exposed to such powerful and ever-changing technological advances, and to the standardization and globalization of every aspect of life, including culture and language, it is, he feels, 'increasingly difficult to inspire admiration or devotion to such remote and individual causes as the preservation of Irish. But I am always hoping that some other influence will come along, something that will breathe new life into it.'

On the North–South question, while he is happy to have lived to see, after the decades of murder and mayhem, acceptance by all shades of political opinion on the island of the initial proposal he made in 1969 to outlaw violence as a means of achieving Irish unity, for Ken Whitaker there is still one missing link in the pro-gression towards a lasting peace. Despite the Good Friday Agreement and the peace process, or because of them, he still sees the need for the establishment of a representative political entity whereby North and South can participate in matters of common concern. 'I think that the potentiality still exists for a Council of Ireland, as originally intended in the early 1920s, to be part of the political relationship between North and South. Because it never actually came into existence and consequently never incurred any criticism . . . its potentiality is still green.'

On the state of the Irish economy, for Ken it is, perhaps, more a question of *plus ça change, plus c'est la même chose*. Ireland's recent economic woes, brought about by at worst the collusion and at best the incompetence of those in political power, in collaboration with the banking sector, were undoubtedly exacerbated by a lack of accountability and an ethos of self-interest and entitlement that has come to permeate the public service. The transformation of Irish society from one that was prudent, innovative and caring to one of crass materialism and narcissistic self-indulgence, where everyone seemed to know the cost of everything and the value of very little, is for Ken Whitaker an anathema. Irish society, in the main, happily bought into the economic philosophy of never-ending credit, the painful question of repayment being nonchalantly placed, by both lender and borrower, on some distant back burner. From the novice investor in properties in a distant and unknown retreat in Bulgaria to the cash-rich developer, with manor house, private helicopter and a repository for his residual loot in the Cayman Islands, to the ordinary householder, who, on the strength of grossly inflated property values and the misplaced largesse of his local bank, threw caution and personal credit to the winds, most of the Irish nation fell for the 'good life' on offer. Those who questioned the ethics or the prudence of such gross excesses were sidelined and silenced.

Today, in a world economy where democratically elected governments and the people they represent appear as mere pawns, driven and controlled by financial markets and rating agencies, the question posed by Ken Whitaker in the 1980s, when

Ireland was being torn apart by internal industrial strife, sectional greed and government excess, can be applied in a wider context:

> In Ireland, as in other democracies, the reality differs markedly from the ideal of government of the people by the people for the people. It differs so much indeed as to raise the question: who governs? Is it little more than a fiction that the Parliament and Government are sovereign? Does the State's power rest precariously on day-by-day tolerance of its authority by powerful sectional interests? ... Are Governments nowadays to be compared to the totally deaf Beethoven in his later years, just being allowed to go through the motions of conducting the orchestra while the real control is being exercised elsewhere?[5]

Despite the folly and greed of the 'Celtic Tiger' rampage in Ireland, Ken remains non-judgemental. 'It would be foolish to expect the sun to shine on us all the time.' From his long experience, he realizes that politicians on all sides are, after all, mere mortals, prisoners not merely of the ballot box but of the expectations and demands of the society from which they emanate, the Lemasses and Sweetmans being exceptions that come along but rarely. As for most countries, Ireland's economic graph shows a series of highs and lows, boom followed by bust, a cycle which, regardless of whether or not we are captains of our economic destiny, will undoubtedly be repeated in the future.

While the balance of payments, so often the marker by which Ken Whitaker measured and criticized government profligacy in the past, may no longer be relevant today in its more traditional guise, there still is the need, he maintains, 'for a reliable, automatic, objective, independent warning, such as used to be provided by persistent balance of payments deficit on the current account, not matched by increased productive domestic investment ... A red light should flash – impossible for public, politicians or authorities to ignore – when real economic growth is being pushed beyond reasonable sustainability.'[6] Aware, as he generously admits, 'of the difficulty and unpopularity of issuing warnings and imposing brakes when boom conditions, however precarious, prevail', he nevertheless could well repeat his words at an Irish Trade Union Congress summer school in July 1976, words that in current circumstances appear even more relevant: 'The problem and tensions of today are acute and serious and they are aggravated by the disruptive effect of selfish and basically irrational actions, inspired by pettiness, spite, envy and greed, rather than [by] any sense of social responsibility or national interest.'[7]

In 2012 the Whitaker Institute for Innovation and Societal Change was established in his honour at University College Galway. Drawing inspiration from Ken Whitaker's work in setting Ireland on the road to recovery in 1958, this new foundation, the largest multi-disciplinary research body in the country, aims to rebuild a sustainable and inclusive society in the wake of the challenges facing Ireland and the international community as a result of the most recent national downturn.

Remaining, as he wrote, ever 'a student', Ken has never stopped learning, his mind open to new ideas and to advances in modern science and technology. In his ninety-eighth year, turning the sod for the development of a new extension at his old school in Drogheda, he is an inspiring example of positive ageing. While his faith remains constant, 'gone for all of us', he admits, 'in these better-educated but more secularist times, is the fervent, unquestioning faith of our mothers and grandmothers. Our faith, if graphically represented, would be a hatched, undulating curve rather than a firm unbroken line.'[8] His own mortality and thoughts of an afterlife he approaches philosophically and with humour:

Can no one brush up on the image of Heaven? Who wants to have eternal rest? Who would hanker after 'a bed amongst the

saints'? Who would like to be tormented by eternal light shining
on him? One is unattractive to lively spirits, the other associated
with interrogational torture! . . . One of my regrets is that Limbo
was abolished in my lifetime. It was just the sort of place in which
I would have been content to spend the next life, renewing close
relationships and old friendships in pleasant surroundings![9]

In Ken Whitaker the Irish people are reminded of what is best
in all of us, both as a society and as individual citizens; it was for
this that they selected him as the ideal man of the century. For
him it was simply a case of performing his duty as well as he
could. He remains sanguine about reputation, jocosely noting
that 'if you live long enough you would either be canonized or
found out – the worst fate being to be found out after you were
canonized'. His words in 1969 best sum up the essence of the
motivation that has guided him in his many undertakings and
achievements on behalf of the Irish people and the state:

> Let us remember that we are not seeking economic progress for
> purely materialistic reasons but because it makes possible relief of
> hardship and want, the establishment of a better social order, the
> raising of human dignity, and, eventually, the participation of all
> who are born in Ireland in the benefits, moral and cultural, as well
> as material, of spending their lives and bringing up their families
> in Ireland.[10]

Such a motivation, as he pointed out, leads to individuality,
independence and humanity, the mark, he maintains, of 'a good
man and a good citizen' – a fitting description of Ken Whitaker
himself, as is the old Irish accolade:

Ní bheidh a leithéid arís ann.

Appendix 1

Positions and Memberships

Positions Held

1951–6	Director, Dollar Exports Organization
1951–6	Director, Córas Tráchtála (Irish Export Board)
1956–69	Secretary, Department of Finance
1958–69	Director, Central Bank of Ireland
1961–75	Member, Comhairle na Gaeilge
1963–71	Chairman, National Industrial Economic Council
1963–78	Founder and Chairman, Agency for Personal Service Overseas
1969–71	President, Statistical and Social Inquiry Society of Ireland
1969–76	Governor, Central Bank of Ireland
1971–4	Member, Broadcasting Review Committee
1971–87	President, Economic and Social Research Institute
1972	Chairman/Trustee, Action Aid
1972–	Founder member and patron, British–Irish Association
1972–96	Chairman, Comhairle Bhéaloideas Éireann (Irish Folklore Commission)
1973–82	Member, National Economic and Social Council
1974–8	Chairman, Bord na Gaeilge
1975–	Member, Royal Irish Academy
1976	Member, Trilateral Commission
1976–84	Director, Arthur Guinness
1976–85	Director, Bank of Ireland
1976–92	President, Alliance Française, Dublin
1976–95	Member, governing board of School of Celtic Studies

1976–96	Chancellor, National University of Ireland
1976–98	Member, Finance Committee of the Catholic Hierarchy
1976–2001	Chairman of the Governing Board, Royal Victoria Eye and Ear Hospital
1976–2001	Trustee, Ewart Biggs Memorial Fund
1977–82	Senator, Seanad Éireann
1981–94	Chairman, Salmon Research Agency
1981–95	Chairman, Dublin Institute for Advanced Studies
1983–5	Chairman, Committee of Inquiry into the Penal System
1983–90	Joint Chairman, Anglo-Irish Encounter
1985–7	President, Royal Irish Academy
1985–7	Member, Board of Governors, National Gallery of Ireland
1986–91	Chairman, European Studies (Ireland and Great Britain) Project
1989	Board member, Collège Irlandais, Paris
1990	Member, Dáil Constituency Commission
1990–2	Chairman, John Henry Whyte Trust Fund
1990–4	Chairman, Sentence Review Group
1991	Chairman, Common Fisheries Policy Review Group
1991–8	Member, Council of State
1992	Patron, Initiative 92 (Queen's University Belfast)
1993–4	Chairman, Sea Trout Task Force
1995	Chairman, Wild Salmon Support Group
1995–6	Chairman, Constitution Review Group
1998	Chairman, O'Reilly Foundation

Other Memberships

Elm Park Golf and Sports Club
Institute of European Affairs
Irish Hospice Foundation
Murphy's Club
National Concert Hall
National Library of Ireland Society
Old Drogheda Society
Project of Churches on Human Rights
Royal Dublin Society
Rush Golf Club

Appendix 2

Honours and Awards

1962	D.Econ.Sc., National University of Ireland
1976	*Business and Finance* 'Man of the Year'
1976	D.LLD, Trinity College Dublin
1976	Hon. Vice-President, Commerce and Economics Society, University College Dublin
1976	Order of Commander, Légion d'Honneur
1976	Hon. Fellow, Institute of Engineers of Ireland
1978	Political Speaker of the Year
1980	D.LLD, Queen's University Belfast
1982	Ireland–USA Council for Commerce and Industry Award
1982	Hon. Life Member, Royal Dublin Society
1984	D.Sc., New University of Ulster
1993	Honorary Fellowship, Royal College of Surgeons Ireland
1995	D. Phil., Dublin City University
1998	University College Dublin Charter Day Medal
2000	Freeman of Drogheda
2000	Irish Management Institute Millennium Gold Medal
2001	Irishman of the Twentieth Century
2002	Ireland's Greatest Living Irishman
2003	Honorary Patron of the Irish Psychiatric Association
2005	Honorary Fellowship of University College Dublin Literary and Historical Society
2008	KPMG Special Recognition Award
2009	Distinguished Contribution to Irish Management Practice Award (renamed the T. K. Whitaker Award)
2013	D.Sc. (Econ.) *honoris causa*, London University
2015	Honorary Fellowship of the Institute of Bankers in Ireland

Appendix 3

Publications, Speeches and Broadcasts

Articles, Speeches and Papers

'The Problem of Full Employment' (with Patrick Lynch), *Journal of the Statistical and Social Inquiry Society of Ireland*, 27 April 1945

TKW, 'The Balancing of International Payments', 1947

'Ireland's External Assets', *Journal of the Statistical and Social Inquiry Society of Ireland*, 29 April 1949

'Symposium on National and Social Accounts' (contributor), *Journal of the Statistical and Social Inquiry Society of Ireland*, 29 April 1949

'The Dollar Problem Reviewed', *Studies*, Summer 1954

'The Finance Attitude', speech to discussion group of Association of Higher Civil Servants, 28 October 1953, published in *Administration*, vol. 2, no. 3, Autumn 1954

'Why We Need to Export Overseas', *Administration*, vol. 3, no. 1, Spring 1955

'Industrial Development', *c.* 1955

'Capital Formation, Saving and Economic Progress', *Journal of the Statistical and Social Inquiry Society of Ireland*, 28 May 1956

'Forbairt na Tíre Feasta', speech to Coiste Gairm-Oideachas, Dublin, 4 November 1957, published in *Comhar*, Christmas 1957

Economic Development (with collaborators), November 1958

'Staid na Tíre, Léacht an Oireachtais', published in *Administration*, vol. 8, no. 3, Autumn 1960

'The Civil Service and Development', speech to Conference of

Higher Administrative Studies, Killarney, 3 May 1961,
published in *Administration*, vol. 9, no. 2, Summer 1961

'The Graduate in State Administration', *Administration*, vol. 10, no. 3,
Autumn 1962

'Merits and Problems of Planning', *Christus Rex Journal of Sociology*,
October–November 1964; *Administration*, vol. 26, no. 4, Winter 1964

'What the Layman Expects of the Priest in Modern Ireland', speech
at Dominican Abbey, Tallaght, 30 January 1966

'The New Ireland, its Progress, Problems and Aspirations', speech to
Institut Royal des Relations Internationales, Brussels, May 1966

'Economic Planning in Ireland', *Administration*, vol. 14, no. 4, Winter
1966

'Cultural Planning and Regional Initiative', speech to Management
Development course, University College Cork, 7 February 1969

'Demand Management', speech to Economics Society, University
College Dublin, 27 February 1969

'The New Role of the Central Bank', interview, *Business and Finance*,
7 March 1969

'Productivity and Full Employment', speech to College of Industrial
Relations, Dublin, 18 and 25 March 1969, published in
Administration, vol. 17, no. 1, Spring 1969

'The Third Programme – Its Implementation for Development and
Marketing in the Tourist Industry', 29 March 1969

'The Manager's Role in Economic and Social Development', speech
to Irish Management Institute Annual Conference, Killarney,
25 April 1969

Notes for 'Tralee Speech', by Taoiseach Jack Lynch TD, September
1969

'The Church in Ireland of the Seventies', speech to Hierarchy
Conference, Mulranny, County Mayo, September 1969

'An tÓr', Central Bank *Bulletin*, Autumn 1969

'The Ouzel Galley', speech to Corporation of Insurance Brokers of
Ireland, 18 October 1969

The Constitutional Position of Northern Ireland (co-author), November 1969

'Monetary Policy', speech to Institute of Bankers in Ireland,
12 November 1969, published in Central Bank *Bulletin*, Winter 1969

'Banking and Credit in Ireland Today', speech to Cork Chamber of
   Commerce, 28 November 1969, published in Central Bank *Bulletin*,
   Winter 1969

'Problems of Economic Development', speech to Federation of
   Builders, Contractors and Allied Employers of Ireland,
   16 December 1969

'National Economic Planning', contribution to seminar for senior
   management, Córas Iompair Éireann (Irish Transport Authority),
   December 1969

'The Role of the Central Bank', speech to Economics Society,
   University College Dublin, 5 February 1970, published in Central
   Bank *Bulletin*, Spring 1970

'The Finance of a Creative Society', speech to Tuairim: Intellectual
   Debate and Policy, 6 February 1970

'The Value of the Irish Pound', speech to Dublin Chamber of
   Commerce, 19 February 1970

'Developments in Irish Central Banking', speech to Association of
   Certified and Corporate Accountants, 23 February 1970

'The State of the Economy', speech to Forum Discussion Group,
   24 February 1970

'Monetary Developments at Home and Abroad', speech to Insurance
   Institute of Ireland, 18 March 1970, published in Central Bank
   Annual Report 1969/1970

'The State of the Irish Economy', speech, University College Galway,
   5 May 1970

'Irish–American Economic Relations', speech to US Chambers of
   Commerce in Ireland, 21 May 1970

'Inflation – Are We Doing Enough to Curb It?', speech to Dublin
   University Business and Economics Society, 24 November 1970,
   published in Central Bank *Bulletin*, Winter 1970

'The Central Bank and the Commercial Banking System',
   speech to Institute of Management Consultants, 26 November
   1970

'National Economic Management', speech to senior management,
   Aer Lingus, 28 January 1971

'World Poverty', speech to Theological Society, Trinity College

Dublin, 8 February 1971, published in *Administration*, vol. 19, no. 1, Spring 1971

'The Banking System in Ireland', speech to Dublin Business and Professional Woman's Club, 9 February 1971

'Productivity and Incomes', speech to Rotary Club, Dublin, 22 February 1971, published in Central Bank *Bulletin*, Spring 1971

'Todhchaí Eacnamaíoch agus Shóisialta na hÉireann', Central Bank *Bulletin*, Spring 1971

'Economic and Social Future in Ireland', speech to Economics Society, University College Dublin, 18 March 1971

'World Poverty', *Administration*, vol. 6, no. 1, Spring 1971

'The Management of the Economy', speech to Institute of Public Administration, 7 May 1971

'Aims of Economic Policy', speech to Rotary Club, Wexford, 24 May 1971

'The Central Bank and the Banking System', speech to Institute of Bankers, Cork, 10 November 1971, published in Central Bank *Bulletin*, Winter 1971

'The Changing Face of Irish Banking', speech to Manchester Statistical Society, 30 November 1971, published in Central Bank *Bulletin*, Spring 1972

'National Economic Management', speech to senior management, B&I and Irish Shipping Ltd, 14 January 1972

Opening address, Third Irish International Coin Fair, Royal Dublin Society, 14 January 1972

Opening address, Mategot Exhibition, Trinity College Dublin, 25 February 1972

'Ireland and Foreign Money', speech to Commerce and Economics Society, University College Galway, 3 March 1972, and Dublin Chamber of Commerce, 13 April 1972, published in Central Bank *Annual Report 1971/1972*

Formal opening address, Henry Guinness Building, Trinity Street, Dublin, 24 April 1972

'Ireland's Development Policy', speech to Central Bank of Iceland, Reykjavik, July 1972, published in Central Bank *Bulletin*, Autumn 1972

'Mergers and Takeovers', speech to *Irish Times* Conference,
4 October 1972, published in Central Bank *Bulletin*, Autumn 1972

Opening address, Sáirséal agus Díll, Silver Jubilee Exhibition, Trinity
College Dublin, 23 November 1972

'The Meaning of Inflation', speech to Irish Transport and Workers
Union, Dublin, 14 December 1972, published in Central Bank
Bulletin, Winter 1972

'The Money Supply and Economic Growth', speech to Dublin
Society of Chartered Accountants, 7 March 1973

'The Future Roles of Gold and SDRs in a Reformed International
Monetary System', Central Bank *Bulletin*, Spring 1973

'Monetary Integration: Reflection on Irish Experience', published in
Moorgate and Wall Street: Review, Autumn 1973, and Central Bank
Bulletin, Winter 1973

'From Protection to Free Trade – The Irish Experience', First Lemass
Memorial Lecture, Exeter, 17 January 1974, published in
Administration, vol. 21, no. 4, Winter 1973

'The Role of the Central Bank in the EEC', speech to Institute of
Bankers in Ireland, 29 January 1974

'Planning Ireland's Future', address to fourth annual ICTU summer
course, 20 July 1974

'Prosperity to Ireland', toast given at Institute of Bankers in Ireland
meeting, 16 November 1974

'The International Value of the Irish Pound', speech to Dublin
University Business and Economic Society, 26 November 1974

'Monetary Policy at Present', speech to Dublin Society of Chartered
Accountants, 5 February 1975, published in Central Bank *Annual
Report, 1975/1976*

'Irish Off-Shore Oil and Gas – From Discovery to Development',
speech to Institute of Engineers of Ireland, 20 March 1975

'Currency Realignments and European Monetary Integration',
contribution to Irish Council of the European Movement
symposium, 2 July 1975, published in Central Bank of Ireland
Bulletin, Summer 1975

'Financing Investment in Ireland', speech to Round Table
Conference, Dublin, October 1975

'Monetary Policy', speech to Commerce and Economics Society, University College Dublin, 5 November 1975, published in Central Bank *Bulletin*, Winter 1975

'The Irish Economy since the Treaty', speech to University College Galway, 3 January 1976, and at Nullamore University Residence, Dublin 13 February 1976, published in Central Bank *Annual Report, 1976/1977*

'An Ceangal le Sterling – Ar Cheart é a Bhriseadh?', speech to Ghaeleagras Na Seirbhíse Poiblí, 27 January 1976, published in Central Bank of Ireland *Annual Report, 1976/1977* and in *Administration*, vol. 24, no. 1, Spring 1976

'Living Beyond Our Means', interview, *Irish Farmers Journal*, 6 March 1976

'Can Ireland become Bilingual?', speech to Adult Education Congress, University College Cork, 21 March 1976

'Planning Irish Economic Development', speech to Fourth Annual Irish Congress and Trade Unions Summer Course, Wexford, 31 July 1976, published as 'Planning Irish Development' in *Administration*, vol. 25, no. 3, Autumn 1977

'National Development', speech to Seminar for Adult Participation in Social Studies, Maynooth College, 16 October 1976

'An Ghaeilge agus an Béarla Araon', speech in Sligo, 16 November 1976

Address to Irish Universities Club Banquet, London, 17 March 1977

'An tSeanchruach Fhéir: Scéal on Ioslainn', *An tUltach*, March 1977

'Cultural Links', John Snow Memorial Lecture, Royal College of Surgeons, Dublin, September 1977, published in *Administration*, vol. 26, no. 3, Autumn 1978

'How People Can Help the Government in Economic and Social Development', speech to Assembly of Comhlachas Daonscoil, Bellenter, Navan, Co. Meath, 16 October 1977

'Mise agus an Ghaeilge', *An tUltach*, February 1978

'Some Points on Policy', speech to Publicity Club of Ireland, 30 March 1978

'Employment Aims', speech to Fianna Fáil Comhairle Ceantair, Dublin South East, 19 September 1978

'Can Ireland Become Bilingual?', speech at Shannon Airport,
28 September 1978

'Cultural Links', *Administration*, Autumn 1978

Address to Institute of Structural Engineers, 18 November 1978

'The Republic of Ireland since Independence', speech at Queen's
University Belfast, 1 December 1978

'The Jobs Problem', speech to Irish Management Institute, Western
Region, Galway, 12 December 1978

'Senate Review', interview, *Irish Times*, 23 July 1979

'Industrial Relations – Is There a Better Way?', speech to Cork
Chamber of Commerce, May 1979, published in *Administration*, vol.
27, no. 3, Autumn 1979

'Energy Prospects', speech to Limerick Chamber of Commerce,
12 November 1979

'Ireland's External Reserves', speech to Institute of Bankers,
22 November 1979, published in *Journal of the Institute of Bankers in
Ireland*, January 1980

'Realignment', speech to Leinster Society of the Association of
Certified Accountants, 4 December 1979

'Economic Retrospect', *Irish Independent*, 8 January 1980

'The Financial Dilemma', *Sunday Press*, 27 January 1980

'Ireland's External Reserves', speech to Institute of Bankers, January
1980, published in *Journal of the Institute of Bankers in Ireland*, vol. 82

'Income and Taxation', speech to Institute of Taxation, 15 February
1980

'Inflation – An Endemic Problem of Modern Capitalism', speech to
Trinity College Dublin Philosophical Society, 15 May 1980

Address to Westport Chamber of Commerce, 10 October 1980

'Instruments of Financial Policy', speech to Marketing Society,
6 November 1980, published in *Management*, January 1981

'The Irish Pound – Echoes from the Past', *Irish Banking Review*,
December 1980

'Who Governs?', *Business and Finance*, December 1980

'A New Social Order', *Business and Finance*, 18 December 1980

'An Economic Retrospective', speech to Maynooth Community
Steering Group, 12 January 1981

'Budget Retrospect', speech to Institute of Chartered Secretaries and
   Administrators, Dublin, 20 February 1981

'Planning for Economic Recovery', speech to Institute of
   Management Consultants in Ireland, 26 February 1981

'The Economic Need to Adjust to Technological Change', *Science and
   Technology Journal*, February 1981

'Costs and Benefits to the Irish Republic of a United Ireland', speech
   to Dublin University Business and Economics Society, 3 March 1981

'Economic Progress and Security', speech to Curragh Military
   College, 10 March 1981

'Ireland in the New Europe', Inaugural Lecture, Irish College
   Louvain, 15 May 1981

'The Irish Question Today', speech to Round Table Conference,
   London, 18 May 1981

'Adaptation: Key to Progress', *Journal of the Irish Management Institute*,
   May–June 1981

'The Major Economic Issues', speech to Confederation of Irish
   Industry, 15 July 1981

'Ireland – The Way Forward', *The Round Table: Commonwealth Journal of
   International Affairs*, July 1981; also published in *Initiative 92* (1982)
   and *Interests* (1983)

'Éire agus an Eoraip Nua', *Comhar*, August 1981

Untitled talk to Drogheda Chamber of Commerce, 8 October 1981

'Future Possibilities', speech to Council for Social Welfare seminar,
   Kilkenny, 7 November 1981

'The Irish Economic Scene, North and South', speech to Church
   Committee, Church of Ireland, 17 November 1981

'Sixty Years On – Achievement and Disappointment', *Irish Times*,
   4 December 1981

Commemorative talk on J. H. Delargy, Glens of Antrim Historical
   Society, 1981, published in *Interests* (1983)

'Our Changing Balance of Payments', speech to United States
   Chamber of Commerce Ireland, 20 January 1982

'Aims of Economic Policy', speech to Rotary Club, Wexford, 24 May
   1982

'Ireland's Development Experience', speech to Annual Conference of the Development Studies Association, 28 September 1982

Ireland, the Way Forward: National Economic Plan, 1983–1987, 21 October 1982, published in *Interests* (1983)

'My Ireland', speech to Royal Dublin Society, 4 November 1982

'Cora an tSaoil', speech to University College Galway, 26 November 1982, published in *Comhar*, December 1982

'Le Developpement d'une région périphérique: l'Irlande', 1982

'Is There Life after Death?', speech to Irish Association of Pension Funds, 15 March 1983

Untitled address to Cobh and Harbour Chambers of Commerce, 20 May 1983

'Face-to-Face with Dr T. K. Whitaker', interview, Irish Management Institute, Mid-West Region, 24 November 1983

'The Bank of Ireland – Origins and Consolidation 1783–1826', in *Bicentenary Essays 1783–1826*, Bank of Ireland, May 1983

'Postscript 1983', in *Interests* (1983)

'Éire sa Chomhphobal – Ar Mealladh Sinn?', *Irish Press*, 1 March 1984

'Public Finances', talk to Confederation of Irish Industries, 14 March 1984

'Foreword' to Manning and McDowell, *Electricity Supply in Ireland: The History of the ESB* (Dublin, 1985)

'Economic Development 1958–1985', Thomas Davis Lecture, 10 November 1985

'Ireland: Land of Change', presidential address to Royal Irish Academy, December 1986, published in *Éire*, Spring 1987; also delivered to the Irish American Cultural Institute, Baltimore, Boston and St Paul, May 1986

'Exploitation of Salmon – Ireland' speech to Third International Atlantic Salmon Symposium, Biarritz, 21 October 1986

'Conditions for Recovery', *Irish Times*, 23 February 1987

Address to Roscrea Chamber of Commerce, February 1987

'The Cost-Cutting Road to New Jobs', *Irish Times*, 13 October 1988

'Changes in the Ireland of Our Time', Probus Club, Drogheda, October 1988

'Arthur Guinness', speech at Nullamore University Residence, Dublin, 30 November 1988

'Ireland: Land of Change', speech to senior officers' course, The Curragh, County Kildare, 11 April 1989

'Ireland and the New Europe', speech to The Ireland Funds, Kilkenny, 23 June 1990

'Éire mo Linne', speech to Institiúd Diagachta agus Féalsúnachta, Baile na Mhuilinn, 13 March 1991

'EC Common Defence Policy', *Irish Times*, 12 August 1992

'When Civil and Moral Law May Have to Part Company', *Irish Times*, 27 August 1992

'European Community Membership and Implications for Irish Sovereignty and EU Neutrality', response to address by Jack Lynch, Institute of European Affairs, 25 February 1993

'Gains and Goals: Reflections of a 1916 Man', speech to Tinakilly Senate, September 1993

'The Role of the University in Society', opening remarks to National University of Ireland conference, May 1994

'An Ghaeilge agus Lucht Ollscoile', March 1995 (private papers)

'Wild Salmon – A Dwindling Resource', *Irish Times*, 15 April 1995

'Wild Salmon – Commercial or Recreational Exploitation?', *Irish Times*, 22 April 1995

'Wild Salmon – Conservation Initiative', *Irish Times*, 29 April 1995

'Wild Salmon – Terms for Ending Netting', *Irish Times*, May 6 1995

'Some Thoughts on Policy, Politics and Taxation', Foundation for Fiscal Studies, n.d.

'Reminiscences' speech to Murphy's Club, 28 April 1997

'Alternatives to Custody', speech to Conference on Crime, Probation and Welfare Officers, 7 April 1999

'The Ireland of My Time', speech to Murphy's Club, 27 March 2000

'This Changing Ireland', speech to St Joseph's Past Pupils' Union, Drogheda, 17 October 2001

Talk to Elm Park Golf Club, 29 January 2002

'Religion and Politics in Ireland', speech at launch of book *Religion and Politics in Ireland*, Dublin, 8 September 2003

Address to North–South Round Table Group, Dublin 24 November 2003

Talk to students, Kildare Place School, Rathmines, 4 December 2003

Address at launch of Whitaker School of Management, Institute of
Public Administration, 12 July 2004

'Opening up to the International Economy: Ireland in the 1950s',
speech in occasional seminar series, Trinity College Dublin,
19 January 2005

Opening address to 'Keeping the Books' exhibition, Chester Beatty
Library, 7 February 2005

Address to Greater Louisville (Kentucky) Chamber of Commerce,
Dublin Castle, 10 September 2007

Address to students, Gonzaga College, Dublin, 2008

'Looking Back to 1958', published in Michael Mulreany (ed.), *Economic
Development 50 Years On, 1958–2008* (Dublin, 2009)

Books

Financing by Credit Creation (Dublin, 1947)

Interests (Dublin, 1983)

Protection or Free Trade: The Final Battle (Dublin, 2006)

Retrospect 2006–1916 (Dublin, 2006)

Broadcasts (radio)

O'Neill Meets Lemass, BBC NI, December 1975

Thomas Davis Lecture Series, RTE, November 1985

History Makers series, RTE, February 1992

Gains and Goals, speech to Tinakilly Senate, RTE, November 1993

Seven Ages – The Story of the Irish State, RTE, 2000

Broadcasts (television)

Nation Builders, RTE1, 2003 (interview)

Taoiseach series, TV3, 2009 (interview)

Seirbhíseach an Stait (Servant of the State), TG4, 2010 (documentary)

Notes

Quotations throughout the text not allocated note numbers are from the author's interviews with Dr T. K. Whitaker and his family over a period between 2012 and 2014.

Some of Dr Whitaker's papers are deposited in the University College Dublin Archives (UCDA). References to these papers are based on the provisional catalogue available during the period 2012–13. The remainder (private papers) remain in his possession.

Chapter 1: Paradise Cottage 1916–34

1   The Queen's Nursing Institute, 'The History of the QNI': see http://www.qni.org.uk/about_qni/our_history.
2   Teresa (Teesie) Whitaker to TKW, 1979 (private papers).
3   Talk to students, Clongowes College, undated, c. 1980s (UCDA, box 12, no. 12).
4   TKW to Captain of Elm Park Golf Club, 15 May 1998 (private papers).
5   Ibid.
6   Speech by TKW at launch of book *Religion and Politics in Ireland*, 8 September 2003 (private papers).
7   *Drogheda Independent*, centenary edn, May 1984.
8   *Drogheda Independent*, 3 November 1978.
9   Address by TKW to Labasheeda Reunion, County Clare, 9 July 2003 (private papers).
10 *Drogheda Independent*, 3 November 1978.
11 Tribute by TKW for Brother James Marcellus Burke, CBS, Drogheda, 1993 (private papers).
12 Appreciation by TKW for Peadar McCann, 1958 (private papers).
13 *Prospectus 1931*, The Children's College, Rannafast, County Donegal, Áislann Rann na Feirste.
14 Miss E. C. Kenny to TKW, March 1976 (private papers).
15 Anthony Cronin, *No Laughing Matter* (Dublin, 1989), p. 160.

Chapter 2: *Nostri Plena Laboris* 1934–38

1 TKW, *Interests* (Dublin, 1983), p. 162.
2 D/F 2/109/42/38 (NAI).
3 TKW, 'Foreword', *Electricity Supply in Ireland: The History of the ESB* (Dublin, 1984).
4 'The Lead-up to Joining the European Community', notes by TKW to Jack Lynch, 28 November 1992, P175/61 (UCDA).
5 TKW, *Interests*, p. 5.
6 TKW, 'The Republic of Ireland since Independence', speech at Queen's University, Belfast, 1 December 1978 (private papers).
7 Quoted in TKW, *Interests*, p. 59.
8 TKW, 'Some Comments on Korten – the Post Corporate World', 2000 (private papers).
9 Ronan Fanning, *The Irish Department of Finance 1922–1958* (Dublin, 1978), p. 9.
10 Noel Browne, *Against the Tide* (Dublin, 1986), p. 113.
11 *Léargas*, March 1969.
12 TKW, *Interests*, p. 163.
13 TKW, 'The Civil Service and Development', *Administration*, vol. 9, no. 2, Summer 1961.
14 Ibid.
15 McGilligan papers, P35a (UCDA).
16 Ibid., P35c/3.
17 TKW, *Interests*, p. 167.
18 TKW to E. Fitzgerald, 26 March 2007 (private papers).
19 F. S. L. Lyons, *Ireland since the Famine* (London, 1973), p. 480.
20 Quoted in Fanning, *The Irish Department of Finance*, p. 64.
21 TKW, *Interests*, p. 277.
22 Quoted in Fanning, *The Irish Department of Finance*, p. 586.
23 D/F E.5677.
24 George Shackle, *Expectations in Economics* (Cambridge, 1949), p. 37.

Chapter 3: A Finance Man 1938–44

1 TKW, *Interests* (Dublin, 1983), p. 161.
2 TKW, address to discussion group of the Association of Higher Civil Servants, 28 October 1953 (private papers).
3 TKW, *Interests*, p. 161.
4 TKW, 'The Finance Attitude', *Administration*, vol. 2, no. 3, Autumn 1954.
5 Ronan Fanning, *The Irish Department of Finance 1922–1958* (Dublin, 1978),

p. 306.

6 Ibid., p. 631.

7 TKW, 'From Protection to Free Trade – The Irish Experience', First Lemass Memorial Lecture, Exeter University, 17 January 1974, published in *Interests*, p. 76.

8 Bryce Evans, *Seán Lemass: Democratic Dictator* (Cork, 2011), p. 72.

9 Quoted in Fanning, *The Irish Department of Finance*, p. 306.

10 TKW, *Interests*, p. 166.

11 D/F, no. E/S677.

12 TKW, *Interests*, p. 288.

13 Ibid., p. 162.

14 Ibid.

15 D/F, no. E/S677.

16 D/F E 1/22.

17 TKW, *Interests*, p. 162.

18 Bulmer Hobson, *Ireland Yesterday and Tomorrow* (Dublin, 1968), p. 112.

19 D/F 9/23/38.

20 Ibid.

21 D/F, no. E/S677.

22 TKW, *Retrospect 2006–1916* (Dublin, 2006).

23 TKW, 'The Finance Attitude', address to discussion group of the Association of Higher Civil Servants, 28 October 1953, P175/48 (UCDA), published in *Administration*, vol. 2, no. 3, Autumn 1954.

24 Ibid.

25 Mary E. Daly, *Industrial Development and Irish National Identity* (New York, 1992), p. 114.

26 D/F, no. E/S677.

27 Tim Pat Coogan, *Ireland in the Twentieth Century* (London, 2003) p. 343.

28 S/12/117/6.

29 D/F, no. E/S677.

30 TKW, 'Is There Life After Death?', speech to Irish Association of Pension Funds, 15 March 1983 (private papers).

31 TKW, *Interests*, p. 164.

32 Correspondence with Professor James Meenan (UCD), Dr M. D. McCarthy (UCC) and Dr B. Menton (UCDA, box 18, no. 8, P/175).

33 Ibid.

34 TKW, address at launch of Whitaker School of Management, Institute of Public Administration, 12 July 2004.

35 D/F, no. E/S677.

36   TKW (private papers).

37   Ibid.

38   TKW, *Interests*, p. 82.

Chapter 4: Public Servant 1945–56

1   TKW to G. P. S. Hogan, internal memo, 7 February 1949, P175/43 (UCDA).

2   *Journal of the Statistical and Social Inquiry Society of Ireland*, vol. 17, no. 3, 1945/6, p. 447.

3   Quoted in Ronan Fanning, *The Irish Department of Finance 1922–1958* (Dublin, 1978), p. 393.

4   *Irish Independent*, 5 November 1987.

5   Aiken papers, 18 November 1947, P4140.

6   *Irish Independent*, 27 September 1947.

7   TKW, *Financing by Credit Creation* (Dublin, 1947), p. 66.

8   TKW, 'The Balancing of International Payments' (private papers).

9   TKW, *Interests* (Dublin, 1983), p. 65.

10   Ibid., p. 67.

11   John F. McCarthy (ed.), *Planning Ireland's Future: The Legacy of T. K. Whitaker* (Dublin, 1990), p. 83.

12   Tim Pat Coogan, *Ireland in the Twentieth Century* (London, 2003), p. 345.

13   Michael Mulreany (ed.), *Economic Development: 50 Years On, 1958–2008* (Dublin, 2009), p. 29.

14   Dáil Debates, 9 May 1950.

15   McGilligan papers, P35c/60 (UCDA).

16   Ibid.

17   Ibid., P35c/57.

18   Ibid., P35c/60.

19   Anthony J. Jordan, *John A. Costello: Compromise Taoiseach, 1891–1976* (Dublin, 2007), p. 68.

20   McGilligan papers, P35a/39.

21   Ibid., P35c/4.

22   Ibid.

23   Ibid., P35c/4.

24   Ibid.

25   Fanning, *The Irish Department of Finance*, p. 449.

26   D/F, no. E/S677 (NAI).

27   Ibid.

28   TKW (private papers).

29 Ibid.

30 Fanning, *The Irish Department of Finance*, p. 553.

31 D/F E1/22.

32 Ibid.

33 Author interview with Seán Cromien, March 2013.

34 TKW (private papers).

35 TKW, 'The Finance Attitude', address to the Association of Higher Civil Servants, 28 October 1953, P175/48 (UCDA), published in *Administration*, vol. 2, no. 3, Autumn 1954.

36 TKW, *Interests*, p. 84.

37 Ibid., p. 83.

38 Ibid., p. 85.

39 D/F 17/P52.

40 TKW, *Interests*, p. 175.

41 John Horgan, *Seán Lemass: The Enigmatic Patriot* (Dublin, 1997), p. 175.

42 TKW, *Interests*, p. 175.

43 TKW to Seán MacEntee, 2 June 1954, MacEntee papers, P67/227 (UCDA).

44 TKW, *Interests*, p. 87.

45 Author interview with Seán Cromien, March 2013.

46 TKW, 'The Finance Attitude'.

47 *Irish Times*, 12 June 1980.

48 TKW, 'The Finance Attitude'.

49 TKW, 'Future Possibilities', speech to Council for Social Welfare seminar, Kilkenny, 7 November 1981, P175/58 (UCDA).

50 *Sunday Independent*, 10 March 2013.

51 *Irish Times*, 26 January 1974.

52 Quoted in Fanning, *The Irish Department of Finance*, p. 494.

53 Ibid., p. 502.

54 TKW, 'Capital Formation, Saving and Economic Progress', speech to Statistical and Social Inquiry Society of Ireland, 25 May 1956, box 13, no. 3, P175, published in *Administration*, vol. 4, no. 2, Summer 1956.

55 Ibid.

56 *Connacht Tribune*, 9 June 1956.

57 *Irish Times*, 27 September 1956.

58 Box 13, no. 3(i), P175.

59 *The Statist*, 29 June 1957.

60 P175/48.

61 TKW to Professor Carter, 6 June 1957, P175/49.

62 TKW, memo, 15 August 1957, D/F E/S677.

63 McGilligan papers, 10 October 1957, P35/117.

64 Ibid., 14 September 1956, P35c/117.

65 Ibid., 10 October 1956, P35a/117 (emphasis in original).

66 TKW, *Protection or Free Trade: The Final Battle* (Dublin, 2006), p. 421.

67 Seán Cromien, notes (private papers).

68 Author interview, T. Ó Cofaigh, July 2013.

Chapter 5: Fortune Teller 1957–58

1 Central Bank of Ireland, *Annual Report, 2002*.

2 Tim Pat Coogan, *De Valera: Long Fellow, Long Shadow* (London, 1993), p. 693.

3 De Valera papers, P150/3069 (UCDA).

4 TKW (private papers).

5 Quoted in Liam Skinner, *Seán Lemass: Nation Builder*, unpublished biography (UCDA, P161, 1961), p. 7.

6 Martin Mansergh, *The Spirit of the Nation: The Speeches and Statements of Charles J. Haughey* (Cork, 1986), p. 2.

7 *Irish Times*, 3 May 1973.

8 TKW to Desmond Fennell, 16 March 1982, box 12, no. 3 (UCDA).

9 TKW, 'Memo for Information of the Government', 16 December 1957, P175/68 (UCDA).

10 TKW, 'Planning Irish Economic Development', speech to Fourth Annual Irish Congress and Trade Unions Summer Course, Wexford, 31 July 1976, published as 'Planning Irish Development' in *Administration*, vol. 25, no. 3, Autumn 1977.

11 TKW, address to Clongowes Leadership Course, 1968 (private papers).

12 TKW, 'The Irish Economy', March 1957, P175/48 (UCDA).

13 Ibid.

14 TKW, 'Has Ireland a Future?', December 1957, box 13, no. 1 (UCDA).

15 TKW, *Protection or Free Trade: The Final Battle* (Dublin, 2006), p. 314.

16 D/F memo, 24 May 1957, Ó Cofaigh private papers (emphasis in original).

17 Ibid.

18 'Some Points on Policy', speech to Publicity Club of Ireland, 30 March 1978, P175/11 (UCDA).

19 TKW, 'Memo for Information of the Government', 16 December 1957, P175/68 (UCDA).

20 *Dublin Opinion*, September 1957.

21 *Business and Finance*, 7 March 1969.

22 TKW, 'Has Ireland a Future?'

23 Ibid.

24 TKW, 'Introduction', *Economic Development* (Dublin, 1958), p. 5.

25 D/T S16734B, TKW to J. C. Nagle, 27 October 1960 (NAI).

26 Author interview with Tomás Ó Cofaigh, July 2013.

27 Ibid.

28 TKW, 'Memo for Information of the Government', 16 December 1957.

29 Ibid.

30 Quoted in Ronan Fanning, *The Irish Department of Finance 1922–1958* (Dublin, 1978), p. 515.

31 Ibid., p. 516.

32 'Comments on Draft Economic Development', P175/50 (UCDA).

33 D/T S16066(3).

34 *Economic Development*, p. 9.

35 D/2001/3/7.

36 D/2001/3/8.

37 TKW to Donal Nevin, 30 March 1999 (private papers).

38 TKW, 'Notes on Lead-Up to Joining the EEC', notes by TKW for Jack Lynch's address to the Institute of European Affairs, 25 February 1993, P175/61.

39 John Horgan, *Seán Lemass: The Enigmatic Patriot* (Dublin, 1997), p. 178.

40 TKW, 'Looking Back to 1958', published in Michael Mulreany (ed.), *Economic Development: 50 Years On, 1958–2008* (Dublin, 2009).

41 F. S. L. Lyons, *Ireland since the Famine* (London, 1973), p. 628.

42 *Drogheda Independent*, 3 November 1978.

43 *Irish Times*, 28 November 1958.

44 *Financial Times*, 29 November 1958.

45 TKW to Desmond Fennell, 16 March 1982, box 12, no. 3 (UCDA).

46 Raymond Crotty, *Ireland in Crisis: A Study in Capitalist Colonial Under-Development* (Dingle, 1986), p. 80.

47 Raymond Crotty to Louden Ryan, 24 March 1989, box 12, no. 6 (UCDA).

48 TKW to Louden Ryan, 31 March 1989, ibid.

49 Paul Bew and Henry Patterson, *Seán Lemass and the Making of Modern Ireland* (Dublin, 1982), dustjacket.

50 TKW (private papers).

51 TKW, *Interests* (Dublin, 1983), p. 13.

52 Author interview with Tomás Ó Cofaigh, April 2013.

53 Ronan Fanning, 'The European Community: The Political Context', in Mulreany, *Economic Development: 50 Years On*, p. 25.

54   John Flanagan (ed.), *Belling the Cats: The Selected Speeches of John Kelly* (Dublin, 1992), p. 42.

Chapter 6: The Promised Land 1959–62

1   *Economic Development* (Dublin, 1958), p. 9.
2   TKW, 'Planning Irish Economic Development', speech to Fourth Annual Irish Congress and Trade Unions Summer Course, Wexford, 31 July 1976, published as 'Planning Irish Development' in *Administration*, vol. 25, no. 3, Autumn 1977.
3   Ibid.
4   Ibid.
5   S 16474 (NAI).
6   TKW, 'The Civil Service and Development', *Administration*, vol. 9, no. 2, Summer 1961.
7   TKW, address on Golden Jubilee of ESRI (private papers).
8   Ibid.
9   TKW, 'From Protection to Free Trade – The Irish Experience', *Interests* (Dublin, 1983), p. 76.
10   Ibid.
11   TKW, 'Foreword', *Economic Development*.
12   TKW, *Protection or Free Trade: The Final Battle* (Dublin, 2006), p. 10.
13   Ibid.
14   D. J. Maher, *The Tortuous Path: The Course of Ireland's Entry into the EEC 1948–1973* (Dublin, 1986), p. 97.
15   TKW, *Protection or Free Trade*, p. 68.
16   Ibid.
17   Ibid.
18   J. J. McElligott to TKW, 19 November 1959, P175/51 (UCDA).
19   TKW to J. J. McElligott, 24 November 1959, ibid.
20   TKW to Seán Lemass, 5 January 1962, P175/62.
21   *Irish Times*, 12 August 1992.
22   Gary Murphy, *In Search of the Promised Land: The Politics of Post-War Ireland* (Cork, 2010), p. 278.
23   *Evening Press*, 18 January 1962.
24   *The Times*, 11 January 1994.

Chapter 7: The Golden Age 1963–68

1   TKW, 'The Republic of Ireland since Independence', speech at Queen's University Belfast, 1 December 1978 (private papers).

2 D/F 43/5/64, pt 1 (NAI).

3 TKW, *Interests* (Dublin, 1983), p. 77.

4 D/F E/S677.

5 John Horgan, *Seán Lemass: The Enigmatic Patriot* (Dublin, 1997), p. 191.

6 TKW, *Protection or Free Trade: The Final Battle* (Dublin, 2006).

7 'Lemass: A Profile', *Nusight*, December 1969.

8 Quoted in Bryce Evans, *Seán Lemass: Democratic Dictator* (Cork, 2011), p. 263.

9 TKW, 'Planning Irish Economic Development', speech to Fourth Annual Irish Congress and Trade Unions Summer Course, Wexford, 31 July 1976, published as 'Planning Irish Development' in *Administration*, vol. 25, no. 3, Autumn 1977.

10 D/T C/65.

11 TKW, 'Some Thoughts on Planning and Taxation', draft notes, February 1997 (private papers).

12 Tim Pat Coogan, *Ireland in the Twentieth Century* (London, 2003), p. 438.

13 D/T S17405 C/63.

14 Ibid.

15 Ibid.

16 Dermot Keogh, *Jack Lynch: A Biography* (Dublin, 2008), p. 113.

17 TKW, *Interests*, p. 96.

18 TKW to Charles Haughey, 30 January 1969, box 15, no. 6 (UCDA).

19 TKW to Maurice Moynihan, 9 August 1968, P175/56 (UCDA).

20 Ibid.

21 *Sunday Independent*, 18 March 1975.

22 *Sunday Tribune*, 1 March 1998.

23 Ibid.

24 Quoted in D. J. Maher, *The Tortuous Path: The Course of Ireland's Entry into the EEC 1948–1973* (Dublin, 1986), p. 230.

25 TKW, memo to J. Carroll, September 1989, P175/61.

26 J. Carroll, 'General de Gaulle and Ireland's EEC Application', ibid.

27 Quoted in Maher, *The Tortuous Path*, p. 232.

28 'Ireland's New Integration Strategy and the Beginning of European Integration', interview with TKW, 24 March 2007 (private papers).

29 Quoted in T. Ryle Dwyer, *Nice Fellow: A Biography of Jack Lynch* (Cork, 2001), p. 174.

30 Interview with TKW, *Business and Finance*, 7 March 1969.

31 TKW, 'The EEC: Ten Years After', 21 November 1983 (private papers).

32 TKW, memo (private papers).

33 TKW, 'The EEC: Ten Years After'.

34 *Business and Finance*, 7 March 1969.

35 Interview with TKW, *Léargas*, March 1969.

36 TKW to Minister for Finance, 30 January 1969, box 15, no. 6 P/175.

37 *Studies*, vol. 87, Autumn 1998, p. 298.

38 *Irish Times*, 16 November 1984.

39 TKW to Patrick Hillery, 14 January 1969, Hillery papers, P205/28 (UCDA).

Chapter 8: The Ivory Tower 1969–76

1 *Business and Finance*, 7 March 1969.

2 *Irish Times*, 19 December 1968.

3 TKW to J. J. McElligott, 15 March 1971, Central Bank file 438 pt 1.

4 *Business and Finance*, 21 September 1972.

5 Maurice Moynihan, *Currency and Central Banking in Ireland 1922–60* (Dublin, 1975), p. 2.

6 TKW, 'The Role of the Central Bank', speech to Economics Society, University College Dublin, 5 February 1970, published in Central Bank *Bulletin*, Spring 1970.

7 *Business and Finance*, 7 March 1979.

8 TKW to Minister for Finance, 12 February 1969 (private papers).

9 Ibid.

10 Ibid.

11 Moynihan, *Currency and Central Banking in Ireland*, p. 23.

12 TKW, 'Central Bank and Government 1969–1976' (private papers).

13 Moynihan, *Currency and Central Banking in Ireland*, p. 421.

14 TKW, 'Ireland's External Reserves', *Journal of the Institute of Bankers in Ireland*, January 1980.

15 TKW, *Retrospect 2006–1916* (Dublin, 2006).

16 TKW, 'Central Bank and Government, 1969–1976', p. 168.

17 TKW to Declan Costello, August 1956, P175/45 (UCDA).

18 TKW, 'Central Bank and Government, 1969–1976', p. 90.

19 TKW to Maura Mullane, March 1976 (private papers).

20 *Irish Times*, 28 November 1973.

21 Central Bank file 71/72, pt 20.

22 *Hibernia*, February 1975.

23 Seanad debates, 3 December 1980.

24 TKW to John Bruton, 1 August 1985 (private papers).

25 Quoted in TKW, 'Central Bank and Government, 1969–1976', p. 7.

26 TKW to Jack Lynch, 5 May 1969, box 16, no. 1.

27 TKW, 'Central Bank and Government, 1969–1976', p. 11.

28 Ibid., p. 27.

29 TKW to Minister for Finance, 25 August 1969 (private papers).

30 TKW, 'Central Bank and Government, 1969–1976', p. 28.

31 TKW to Charlie Murray, 27 October 1969, box 19, no. 6(a).

32 TKW, note, 12 December 1969, box 7.

33 TKW to Jack Lynch, 16 December 1969, box 19, no. 7.

34 TKW, 'Central Bank and Government 1969–1976', p. 34.

35 Ibid., p. 35.

36 Ibid., p. 35.

37 Ibid., p. 35.

38 Ibid., p. 37.

39 Ibid., p. 43.

40 TKW, *Interests* (Dublin, 1983), p. 98.

41 TKW, 'Central Bank and Government, 1969–1976', p. 44.

42 Ibid., p. 46.

43 Ibid., p. 52.

44 TKW, *Interests*, p. 99.

45 TKW, 'Central Bank and Government, 1969–1976', p. 75.

46 TKW, 'Financial Turning Point', *Interests*, p. 103.

47 TKW, 'Central Bank and Government, 1969–1976', p. 88.

48 TKW to George Colley, January 1973, box 18, no. 4b.

49 TKW to Professor Louden Ryan, 6 February 1973, box 20, no. 2.

50 TKW to Professor Louden Ryan, 6 February 1973, box 18, no. 5.

51 Ibid.

52 TKW to Richie Ryan, 6 October 1973, box 20, no. 2.

53 TKW to Charlie Murray, 19 October 1973 (private papers), quoted in 'Central Bank and Government, 1969–1976', p. 114.

54 TKW, *Interests*, p. 105.

55 TKW to Minister for Finance, 24 January 1974 (private papers).

56 TKW to Charlie Murray, 27 February 1974 (private papers).

57 *Business and Finance*, 13 June 1974.

58 TKW, 'Central Bank and Government, 1969–1976', p. 118.

59 TKW, *Interests*, p. 106.

60 *Irish Business*, February 1979.

61 M. Moynihan, memo, CBI file 186/72, 8 December 1967.

62 *Irish Business*, February 1979.

63 *Hibernia*, 4 January 1974.

64 *Irish Business*, February 1979.

65 *Irish Times*, 15 November 1973.

66 TKW to Sam Stephenson, 15 November 1973, Central Bank file 25/67, pt 2.

67 *Irish Times*, 8 January 1974; *The Times*, 17 December 1973; *Sunday Independent*, 16 December 1973.

68 *Irish Independent*, 19 April 1974.

69 TKW to Minister for Finance, 2 January 1974, Central Bank file 186/72, pt 40.

70 *Irish Times*, 8 January 1974.

71 TKW to Minister for Finance, 31 July 1974, Central Bank file 186/72, pt 42.

72 *Irish Independent*, 9 August 1974.

73 *Irish Times*, 5 February 1975.

74 *Irish Times*, 24 July 1974.

75 TKW, 'Central Bank and Government, 1969–1976', p. 119.

76 Ibid., p. 120.

77 Ibid., p. 123.

78 Ibid., p. 123.

79 Ibid., p. 124.

80 Ibid., p. 128.

81 Ibid., p. 128.

82 Ibid., p. 129.

83 Ibid., p. 137.

84 Ibid., p. 134.

85 TKW, *Interests*, p. 156.

86 TKW, notes for *Radio Senate*, RTE Radio, 1 September 1993 (private papers).

87 TKW, *Interests*, p. 125.

88 TKW, 'Central Bank and Government, 1969–1976', p. 97.

89 Ibid., p. 99.

90 TKW to Tomás Ó Cofaigh, 14 March 1975 (private papers).

91 TKW, 'Central Bank and Government, 1969–1976, p. 102.

92 Ibid., p. 142.

93 Ibid., p. 167.

94 Ibid., p. 167.

95 Ibid., p. 167.

96 TKW, *Interests*, p. 182.

97 Ibid., p. 141.

98 Ibid., p. 142.

99 Ibid., p. 148.

100 *Irish Independent,* 17 October 1975.

101 *Irish Press,* 17 October 1975.

102 Richie Ryan to TKW, 27 February 1976 (private papers).

103 *Business and Finance,* 23 October 1975.

104 Ian Morrison to TKW, 24 February 1976 (private papers).

105 *Business and Finance,* 23 October 1975.

106 TKW (private papers).

107 TKW (private papers).

108 TKW (private papers).

109 Central Bank Whitaker Lecture, 31 May 2004.

110 TKW, 'Central Bank and Government, 1969–1976', p. 149.

111 Ibid., p. 150.

112 Ibid., p. 169.

Chapter 9: Hands Across the Border 1963–67

1 TKW, *Interests* (Dublin, 1983), p. 202.

2 Ibid., p. 19.

3 *Irish Independent,* 5 January 2001.

4 Quoted in John Horgan, *Seán Lemass: The Enigmatic Patriot* (Dublin, 1997), p. 258.

5 *Belfast and Irish News,* 21 December 1960.

6 TKW, 'A Note on North–South Relations', 11 November 1968 (private papers).

7 Terence O'Neill to TKW, 21 October 1970, P175/3 (UCDA).

8 TKW to Jack Lynch, 1979, P175/42 (UCDA).

9 Terence O'Neill to Sir Basil Brooke, 13 October 1948, CAB/9/D/4, Public Record Office, Northern Ireland (PRONI).

10 Terence O'Neill, *The Autobiography of Terence O'Neill: Prime Minister of Northern Ireland 1963–1969* (London, 1972), p. 50.

11 *Irish Times,* 15 January 1965.

12 O'Neill, *The Autobiography of Terence O'Neill,* p. 68.

13 Ibid.

14 TKW, 'The First Visit to Stormont 14 January 1965', notes supplied to BBC NI for radio documentary, October 1975 (private papers).

15 Ibid.

16 Ibid.

17 Ibid.

18 TKW, note, 4 November 1983 (private papers).
19 O'Neill, *The Autobiography of Terence O'Neill*, p. 72.
20 Ibid.
21 Ibid.
22 Ibid.
23 Transcript of BBC NI radio documentary, *O'Neill Meets Lemass*, 4 December 1975, P175/42 (UCDA).
24 Ibid.
25 Ibid.
26 Ibid.
27 O'Neill, *The Autobiography of Terence O'Neill*, p. 73.
28 Transcript of BBC NI radio documentary.
29 Ibid.
30 Ibid.
31 Ibid.
32 P174/42 (UCDA).
33 Ibid.
34 *Irish Times*, 15 January 1965.
35 *Irish News*, 15 January 1965.
36 Ibid.
37 P175/1 (UCDA).
38 Ibid.
39 O'Neill, *The Autobiography of Terence O'Neill*, p. 75.
40 Ibid., p. 79.
41 TKW, notes on meeting between Terence O'Neill and Jack Lynch, 8 January 1968, P175/1 (UCDA).
42 O'Neill, *The Autobiography of Terence O'Neill*, p. 74.
43 Ibid., p. 75.
44 Terence O'Neill to TKW, 11 March 1970, P175/3 (UCDA).
45 Ibid.
46 TKW, note, P175/4 (UCDA).
47 TKW, note re visit by Lord O'Neill of the Maine to President de Valera, 21 April 1972, P174/4 (UCDA).
48 TKW, note to Jack Lynch re appreciation Lord O'Neill, June 1990 (private papers).
49 *Irish Times*, 14 June 1990.

Chapter 10: A Good Marriage Settlement 1968–73

1   TKW to G. B. Newe, 28 January 1972, P175/4 (UCDA).
2   TKW, memo to Minister for Finance, Charles Haughey, 5 January 1968, 175/28.
3   Ibid.
4   Minister for Finance to TKW, 5 January 1968, 175/28.
5   TKW to Minister for Finance, 8 February 1968, ibid.
6   Ibid.
7   TKW, memo for Jack Lynch, 15 February 1972 (private papers).
8   TKW, 'A Note on North–South Relations', 11 November 1968 (private papers).
9   Ibid.
10 Ibid.
11 P175/1.
12 *Irish Independent*, 5 January 2001.
13 *Drogheda Independent*, 8 January 1999.
14 Ibid.
15 TKW to Minister for Finance, 21 April 1969, P175/1.
16 TKW, notes for public statement by Taoiseach, 13 August 1969, P175/1.
17 *Irish Times*, 14 August 1979.
18 TKW, Summary of notes sent to Jack Lynch, 15 August 1969, P175/1.
19 Ibid.
20 Ibid.
21 Ibid.
22 Ibid.
23 TKW to Jack Lynch, 18 October 1969, P175/2.
24 TKW to Jack Lynch, July 1970, P175/2.
25 *Irish Times*, 19 August 1969.
26 *Sunday Independent*, 16 January 2000.
27 TKW to Jack Lynch, 13 September 1969, P175/1.
28 Ibid.
29 Ibid.
30 *Irish Independent*, 21 September 1969.
31 TKW to Jack Lynch, 22 September 1969, P175/1.
32 Ibid.
33 TKW to Jack Lynch, 22 September 1969 (private papers).
34 TKW to D. J. Maher, assistant secretary, Department of Finance, 15 September 1969, P175/1.
35 TKW to Jack Lynch, 27 October 1979, P175/2.

36   TKW to Jack Lynch, 24 November 1969, P175/2.

37   Ibid.

38   'The Constitutional Position of Northern Ireland', part 4, p. 22, P175/2.

39   Ibid.

40   TKW to Jack Lynch, 15 October 1969, P175/2.

41   TKW to David James MP, 15 February 1972, P175/3.

42   TKW to Jack Lynch, 18 October 1969, P175/2.

43   Ibid., 15 October 1969.

44   *Irish Times*, 1 January 2001.

45   D/F 2000/5/12, 16 August 1969 (NAI).

46   TKW to Jack Lynch, 23 July 1970, P175/3.

47   Ibid.

48   TKW to Jack Lynch, 10 June 1971, P175/3.

49   Jack Lynch to TKW, 12 June 1971, P175/3.

50   TKW to Jack Lynch, 6 July 1971, P175/3.

51   Ibid.

52   TKW to Jack Lynch, 12 July 1971, P175/3.

53   Ibid.

54   TKW, note, 16 October 1971, P175/3.

55   Ibid.

56   David James MP to TKW, June 17 1972, P175/4.

57   TKW, note, 16 October 1971, P175/3.

58   Ibid.

59   Ibid.

60   Ibid.

61   James Callaghan to TKW, 24 and 29 November 1972, P175/4.

62   TKW to Cardinal W. Conway, 17 August 1971 (private papers).

63   Ibid.

64   Ibid.

65   Quoted in David McKittrick and David McVea, *Making Sense of the Troubles: A History of the Northern Ireland Conflict* (London, 2012), p. 84.

66   TKW to Jack Lynch, 3 November 1971, P175/3.

67   Jack Lynch to TKW, 11 November 1971, P175/3.

68   TKW to Jack Lynch, 14 December 1971, P175/3.

69   *The Northern Ireland Council of Social Services Report, 1971–72* (Belfast, 1972).

70   McKittrick and McVea, *Making Sense of the Troubles*, p. 86.

71   TKW to G. B. Newe, 28 January 1972, P175/4.

72   G. B. Newe to TKW, 29 November 1971, P175/3.

73   TKW to G. B. Newe, 7 December 1971, P175/3.

74 Tim Pat Coogan, *Ireland in the Twentieth Century* (London, 2003), p. 559.
75 G. B. Newe to TKW, 4 February 1972, P175/4.
76 Jack Lynch to TKW, 4 February 1972, P175/4.
77 Sir John Peck to TKW, 15 February 1972, P175/4.
78 TKW to Jack Lynch, 15 February 1972, P175/4.
79 Ibid.
80 Ibid.
81 G. B. Newe to TKW, 5 May 1972, P175/4.
82 Ibid.
83 Ibid.
84 G. B. Newe to Gerry Fitt, 19 July 1972, P175/4.
85 TKW to Sir Leslie O'Brien, 14 March 1972, P175/4.
86 TKW to David James MP, 10 August 1972, P175/4.
87 TKW to David James MP, 28 August 1972, P175/4.
88 TKW to David James MP, 4 April 1973, P175/4.

Chapter 11: Pathways to Peace 1973–98

1 TKW, note, 5 September 1979, P175/13 (UCDA).
2 G. B. Newe to Jack Lynch, 5 March 1973, P175/5.
3 Brian Walker to Garret FitzGerald, 6 October 1972, FitzGerald papers, P215/4.
4 David James to TKW, 17 March 1973, P175/7.
5 TKW to Garret FitzGerald, 6 March 1973, P175/5.
6 Quoted in Garret FitzGerald, *Just Garret* (Dublin, 2011), p. 93.
7 Ibid.
8 David James to TKW, 4 April 1973, FitzGerald papers, P214/756.
9 TKW to David James, 13 April 1973, P175/5.
10 FitzGerald papers, 16 April 1973, P215/746.
11 TKW to David James, 13 April 1973, P175/5.
12 TKW to David James, 27 November 1973, P175/5.
13 TKW to W. Whitelaw, 24 November 1973, P175/5 UCDA; W. Whitelaw to TKW, 30 November 1973, private papers, P175/5 (UCDA).
14 TKW to Garret FitzGerald, 30 April 1973, P215/746.
15 Liam Cosgrave to TKW, 12 December 1973, P175/6.
16 Ken Bloomfield to TKW, 3 June 1974, P175/6.
17 Brian McK McGuigan to TKW, 3 June 1974, P175/5.
18 Maurice Hayes to TKW, 25 November 1975, P175/8.
19 Dr John Oliver to TKW, 3 December 1975, P175/8.
20 TKW, note, January 2001 (private papers).

21 TKW, 'Some Points on Policy', speech to Publicity Club of Ireland, 30 March 1978, P175/8.

22 TKW, 'Northern Ireland: Some Financial Considerations', 11 February 1977, P175/10.

23 Quoted in *Irish Times*, 20 June 1978.

24 TKW to Douglas Gageby, 20 June 1978, P175/12.

25 TKW to Jack Lynch, 5 September 1979, P175/13.

26 Charles Haughey to TKW, 4 January 1980, 175/12.

27 TKW to Lady Goulding, 23 July 1980, P175/14.

28 Ibid.

29 TKW, 'Ireland: The Way Forward', July 1981, P175/15.

30 Ibid.

31 TKW to Garret FitzGerald, 3 August 1981, P175/17.

32 Ibid.

33 Ibid.

34 Ibid.

35 TKW to Leonard Figg, 13 August 1981, P175/17.

36 Ibid.

37 TKW to Desmond Fennell, 13 December 1982, box 12, no. 3 (UCDA).

38 Ibid.

39 TKW to Monsignor Murray, 14 March 1983, P175/21.

40 TKW to Bishop Cathal Daly, 18 May 1983, ibid.

41 Seán Donlon to TKW, 16 June 1983, P175/21.

42 Quoted in David McKittrick and David McVea, *Making Sense of the Troubles: A History of the Northern Ireland Conflict* (London, 2012), p. 185.

43 *Evening Herald*, 22 April 1983.

44 Ibid.

45 *Unionist Review*, no. 1, Autumn 1983.

46 *Irish Times*, 27 September 1983.

47 *History Makers* series, RTE, February 1992.

48 TKW to Seán Donlon, 23 September 1986, P175/24.

49 Ibid.

50 TKW to Michael McDowell, 15 January 1994 (private papers).

51 Ibid.

52 TKW to Albert Reynolds, 11 February 1992 (private papers).

53 TKW, 'Northern Ireland – In Search of a Solution', August 1997 (private papers).

54 TKW to Doris Bateman, 30 September 1997 (private papers).

Chapter 12: Language Matters

1 TKW, 'An Ghaeilge agus Lucht Ollscoile', March 1995, p. 1 (private papers).
2 TKW, *Interests* (Dublin, 1983), p. 228.
3 Ibid., p. 231.
4 Seán Lemass, speech, Dun Laoghaire, 26 June 1965, P175/28.
5 TKW, *Retrospect 2006–1916* (Dublin, 2006), p. 16.
6 TKW, *Interests*, p. 239.
7 Ibid., p. 240.
8 Seanad Debates, 14 June 1978.
9 TKW, 'Ireland: Land of Change', speech to senior officers' course, The Curragh, County Kildare, 11 April 1989 (private papers).
10 TKW, note, *c.* 1976 (private papers).
11 Statement, Bord na Gaeilge, 1975 (private papers).
12 Seanad Debates, 14 June 1978.
13 TKW to Minister for the Gaeltacht, 19 December 1975 (private papers).
14 Seán Ó Tuama and Thomas Kinsella, *An Duanaire 1600–1900: Poems of the Dispossessed* (Mountrath, County Laois, 1981), dustjacket notes.
15 TKW to Minister for the Gaeltacht, 15 April 1977 (private papers).
16 *Irish Times*, 28 March 1978.
17 TKW, note, January 2006 (private papers).
18 TKW, *Interests*, p. 239.

Chapter 13: Man for All Seasons

1 *Irish Times*, 8 March 1976.
2 TKW, *Interests* (Dublin, 1983), p. 305.
3 Ibid, p. 307.
4 Ibid.
5 Citation, New University of Ulster, Dean of Faculty of Law, 9 July 1980 (private papers).
6 *Sunday Press*, 21 March 1976.
7 TKW, farewell address, NUI, 23 November 1997 (private papers).
8 Ibid.
9 TKW to Dr S. Smith, president, Maynooth College, 22 June 2004 (private papers).
10 *Irish Times*, 19 July 1977.
11 Seanad Debates, 2 July 1980.
12 TKW, speech, UCD, 18 July 1982 (private papers).
13 Professor J. J. Lee to TKW, 20 January 1997 (private papers).
14 *Irish Press*, 28 April 1976.

15   TKW, 'Some Thoughts on Planning, Politics and Taxation', February
     1997 (private papers).

16   Seanad Debates, 23 November 1977.

17   Ibid.

18   *Irish Times*, 4 December 1981.

19   Ibid.

20   TKW to Jack Lynch, July 1978, P175/38 (UCDA).

21   *Irish Times*, 14 January 1978.

22   TKW, 'Industrial Relations: Is There a Better Way?', speech to Cork
     Chamber of Commerce, May 1979, P175/63 (UCDA).

23   *Irish Press*, 4 May 1979.

24   *Evening Press*, 3 May 1979; *Evening Herald*, 3 May 1979; *Irish Press*,
     4 May 1979.

25   *Evening Press*, 13 June 1979.

26   TKW, 'Jack Lynch: An Appreciation', 1999 (private papers).

27   Jack Lynch to TKW, 6 July 1979 (private papers).

28   TKW to Jack Lynch, October 1979 (private papers).

29   Máirín Lynch to Nora Whitaker, 24 November 1972 (private papers).

30   Jack Lynch to TKW, 6 July 1979 (private papers).

31   Máirín Lynch to TKW, 5 August 2001 (private papers).

32   TKW, 'Máirín Lynch: An Appreciation', 17 June 2004 (private
     papers).

33   TKW to Charles Haughey, 4 September 1980 (private papers).

34   Charles Haughey to TKW, 8 September 1980 (private papers).

35   TKW, 'Our Changing Balance of Payments', speech to United States
     Chamber of Commerce Ireland, 20 January 1982 (private papers).

36   *Irish Press*, 23 January 1982.

37   *Irish Times*, 23 January 1982.

38   TKW, 'The Ireland of My Time', speech to Murphy's Club, 27 March
     2000 (private papers).

39   TKW, 'This Changing Ireland', speech to St Joseph's Past Pupils' Union,
     Drogheda, 17 October 2001 (private papers).

40   P175/68.

41   Ibid.

42   Ibid.

43   *Sunday Tribune*, 11 August 1985.

44   TKW, address, 18 May 1994 (private papers).

45   Author's correspondence with Siobhan Fitzpatrick, librarian, Royal Irish
     Academy, 2 January 2014.

46 TKW, address to Salmon Research Centre, Furnace, 16 May 2003 (private papers).

47 *Report of the Constitution Review Group* (Dublin, 1996), p. x.

48 TKW, address to All-Party Oireachtas Committee on the Constitution, March 2003 (private papers).

49 TKW to T. Murphy, Department of Law, UCC, 9 October 1998 (private papers).

50 TKW to Archbishop Desmond Connell, 18 November 1996 (private papers).

51 Fionán Ó Muircheartaigh (ed.), *Ireland in the Coming Times* (Dublin, 1996), jacket notes.

52 TKW, address to the IPA, 8 December 1996 (private papers).

Chapter 14: Evening is the Best Part of the Day

1 TKW, note, 3 December 1997 (private papers).

2 TKW, 3 December 1987 (private papers).

3 TKW, at 'Greatest Living Irish Person' award, 16 November 2002 (private papers).

4 TKW, 'The Ireland of My Time', speech to Murphy's Club, 27 March 2000 (private papers).

5 TKW, 'A New Social Order', *Business and Finance*, 18 December 1980.

6 TKW to Professor Frances Ruane, 20 June 2010 (private papers).

7 TKW, 'Planning Irish Development, 20 July 1976 (private papers).

8 Note dated December 2004 (private papers).

9 Ibid.

10 TKW, 'Productivity and Full Employment', speech to College of Industrial Relations, Dublin, 18 and 25 March 1969; published in *Administration*, Vol. 17, No. 1, Spring 1969 (private papers).

Bibliography

For publications and speeches by T. K. Whitaker, see Appendix 3.

Primary Sources

Interviews

Dr T. K.Whitaker

Whitaker family

Tomás Ó Cofaigh

Seán Cromien

Archives and private papers

Áislann Rann na Feirste

Central Bank of Ireland

National Archives of Ireland (NAI)

    Department of Finance

    Department of Foreign Affairs

    Department of the Taoiseach

    National Library of Ireland

University College Dublin Archives (UCDA)

    Whitaker papers (P175/1–P175/73 and boxes 12–20)

    Aiken papers (P104)

    Costello papers

    De Valera papers (P150)

    FitzGerald papers (P215)

    Hillery papers (P205)

    MacEntee papers (P67)

    McGilligan papers (P35)

    Ryan papers (P88)

    Skinner papers (P161)

Tomás Ó Cofaigh private papers
T. K. Whitaker: private papers (uncatalogued)

Secondary Sources
Parliamentary debates
Dáil Éireann
Seanad Éireann

Periodicals / papers
Administration (various issues)
Belfast Magazine, no. 34
Central Bank of Ireland, *Bulletins* and *Annual Reports* (various issues)
Central Bank of Ireland, T. K. Whitaker Lectures
Economic and Social Review (various issues)
Economic History Review, new series, vol. 37, no. 3, August 1984
History of the Central Bank: A Chronology of Main Developments 1943–2013
Irish Business, February 1979
Journal of the Institute of Bankers in Ireland (various issues)
Journal of the Institute of Public Administration (various issues)
Journal of the Statistical and Social Inquiry Society of Ireland (various issues)
Léargas
Lemass International Forum papers
Northern Ireland Council of Social Services Report, 1971–72
Nusight, December 1969
Public Affairs, July–August 1969
The Statist (various issues)
Studies (various issues)
Ulster Unionist Information, no. 8, Summer 1991
Unionist Review, Autumn 1983

Newspapers and magazines
Belfast and Irish News
Business and Finance
Connacht Tribune
Drogheda Independent
Dublin Opinion

BIBLIOGRAPHY

Evening Herald
Evening Press
Financial Times
Hibernia
Irish Independent
Irish Press
Irish Times
Sunday Business Post
Sunday Independent
Sunday Press
Sunday Tribune
The Times (London)

Published books

Paul Bew and Henry Patterson, *Seán Lemass and the Making of Modern Ireland* (Dublin, 1982)

Noel Browne, *Against the Tide* (Dublin, 1986)

P. J. Browne, *Unfulfilled Promise: Memories of Donogh O'Malley* (Kildare, 2008)

Anna Bryson, *No Coward Soul: A Biography of Thekla Beere* (Dublin, 2009)

Stephen Collins, *The Power Game: Fianna Fáil since Lemass* (Dublin, 2000)

Tim Pat Coogan, *De Valera: Long Fellow, Long Shadow* (London, 1993)

Tim Pat Coogan, *Ireland in the Twentieth Century* (London, 2003)

Matt Cooper, *How Ireland Really Went Bust* (Dublin, 2011)

Anthony Cronin, *No Laughing Matter* (Dublin, 1989)

Raymond Crotty, *Ireland in Crisis: A Study in Capitalist Colonial Under-Development* (Dingle, 1986)

Mary E. Daly, *Industrial Development and Irish National Identity* (New York, 1992)

Terry de Valera, *A Memoir* (Dublin, 2004)

T. Ryle Dwyer, *Nice Fellow: A Biography of Jack Lynch* (Cork, 2001)

Bryce Evans, *Seán Lemass: Democratic Dictator* (Cork, 2011)

Ronan Fanning, *The Irish Department of Finance 1922–1958* (Dublin, 1978)

Brian Farrell, *Seán Lemass* (Dublin, 1983)

Garret FitzGerald, *Garret FitzGerald: An Autobiography* (Dublin, 1991)

Garret FitzGerald, *Just Garret* (Dublin, 2011)

John Flanagan (ed.), *Belling the Cats: The Selected Speeches of John Kelly* (Dublin, 1992)

R. F. Foster, *Modern Ireland 1660–1972* (London, 1988)

Brian Girvan and Gary Murphy (eds), *Politics and Society in the Ireland of Seán Lemass* (Dublin, 2005)

P. Hannon and J. Gallagher, *Taking the Long View: 70 Years of Fianna Fáil* (Dublin, 1996)

Bulmer Hobson, *Ireland Yesterday and Tomorrow* (Dublin, 1968)

John Horgan, *Seán Lemass: The Enigmatic Patriot* (Dublin, 1997)

John Hume, *Personal Views* (Dublin, 1996)

Gemma Hussey, *Ireland Today: Anatomy of a Changing State* (Dublin, 1993)

Anthony J. Jordan, *John A. Costello: Compromise Taoiseach, 1891–1976* (Dublin, 2007)

Dermot Keogh, *Jack Lynch: A Biography* (Dublin, 2008)

John Lonergan, *The Governor* (Dublin, 2010)

F. S. L. Lyons, *Ireland since the Famine* (London, 1973)

John F. McCarthy (ed.), *Planning Ireland's Future: The Legacy of T. K. Whitaker* (Dublin, 1990)

Justine McCarthy, *Mary McAleese* (Dublin, 2006)

David McCullough, *John A. Costello: The Reluctant Taoiseach* (Dublin, 2010)

David McCullough, *A Makeshift Majority: The First Inter-Party Government, 1948–51* (Dublin, 1998)

Padraig McGowan, *Money and Banking in Ireland* (Dublin, 1990)

David McKittrick and David McVea, *Making Sense of the Troubles: A History of the Northern Ireland Conflict* (London, 2012)

D. J. Maher, *The Tortuous Path: The Course of Ireland's Entry into the EEC 1948–1973* (Dublin, 1986)

Maurice Manning, *James Dillon: A Biography* (Dublin, 1999)

Maurice Manning and Moore McDowell, *Electricity Supply in Ireland: The History of the ESB* (Dublin, 1985)

Martin Mansergh, *The Spirit of the Nation: The Speeches and Statements of Charles J. Haughey* (Cork, 1986)

Maurice Moynihan, *The Central Bank of Ireland* (Dublin, 1969)

Maurice Moynihan, *Currency and Central Banking in Ireland 1922–60* (Dublin, 1975)

Michael Mulreany (ed.), *Economic Development: 50 Years On, 1958–2008* (Dublin, 2009)

David Murphy and Martina Devlin, *Banksters* (Dublin, 2009)

Gary Murphy, *In Search of the Promised Land: The Politics of Post-War Ireland* (Cork, 2010)

Cormac Ó Grada, *Ireland: A New Economic History 1780–1939* (Oxford, 1994)

Fionán Ó Muircheartaigh (ed.), *Ireland in the Coming Times* (Dublin, 1997)

Terence O'Neill, *The Autobiography of Terence O'Neill: Prime Minister of Northern Ireland 1963–1969* (London, 1972)

Seán Ó Tuama and Thomas Kinsella, *An Duanaire 1600–1900: Poems of the Dispossessed* (Mountrath, County Laois, 1981)

Albert Reynolds, *My Autobiography* (Dublin, 2009)

George Shackle, *Expectations in Economics* (Cambridge, 1949)

Liam Skinner, *Seán Lemass: Nation Builder*, unpublished biography (UCDA, P161, 1961)

Picture Acknowledgements

All photographs not credited below were kindly supplied from the private collections of T. K. Whitaker and the Whitaker family. The publishers have made every effort to contact copyright holders where known. Copyright holders who have not been credited are invited to get in touch with the publishers.

First section:
p. 5: On a mission to EEC capitals © Jack McManus/*Irish Times*
p. 7: Terence O'Neill at Áras an Uachtaráin © T. K. Whitaker Papers, UCD Archives

Second section:
p. 1: Ken with his mother © Eddie Kelly/*Irish Times*
p. 3 (top): With Thomas Kinsella, courtesy of Institute of Public Administration
p. 3 (bottom): Three men on a boat © Hillery Papers, UCD Archives, P205/191
p. 6 (bottom): At Drogheda CBS © Andy Spearman
p. 7 (right): Ken with author Anne Chambers, courtesy of Anne Chambers

Index

Anne Chambers is a biographer, novelist, short-story and screenplay writer. Her books include the bestselling biography *Granuaile: Grace O'Malley – Ireland's Pirate Queen*; *Eleanor Countess of Desmond*; *La Sheridan: Adorable Diva*; *Ranji: Maharajah of Connemara* and *At Arm's Length: Aristocrats in the Republic of Ireland*. Many of her books have been translated and published abroad and have been the subject of international television and radio documentaries.